Preface

The Journals of Lewis H. Morgan's western field trips, here published for the first time, were kept by him while he was in the field, as the dates indicate. They were bequeathed by Morgan, along with other manuscripts, letters, and his library, to the University of Rochester, and are now housed in that university's library. The authenticity of the Journals and their authorship are established by the record of the bequest, by internal evidence, by Morgan's handwriting, and his signature.

I have for many years been gathering material for a biography of Morgan. During this time I have studied the large amount of unpublished manuscript material in the Morgan archives and have published *Extracts from the European Travel Journal of Lewis H. Morgan* (Rochester Historical Society Publications, Vol. XVI, 1937), the letters of Adolph F. Bandelier to Morgan (*Pioneers in American Anthropology: The Bandelier-Morgan Letters, 1873-83*, 2 vols.; Albuquerque: University of New Mexico Press, 1940), and "Lewis H. Morgan's Journal of a Trip to Southwestern Colorado and New Mexico, 1878" (*American Antiquity*, Vol. 8, 1942, 1-26). Also I have

published a number of articles on Morgan, some of which are cited at the end of Chapter I. When I discovered the journals of the western field trips I was much impressed with their value, and in due time had them transcribed for publication. The work of editing was interrupted by World War II. In the fall of 1949, I read a paper, "Lewis H. Morgan's Western Field Trips," at the twenty-ninth International Congress of Americanists in New York; it was subsequently published in the *American Anthropologist,* Vol. 53 (1951): 11-18. This paper acquainted several scholars who were working on problems of Plains Indian cultures with Morgan's travels and investigations, and thus made the early publication of the Journals themselves highly desirable. Other tasks and obligations have, however, prevented the competion of the laborious task of editing until now.

I am greatly indebted, and wish to express my gratitude, to many persons and organizations for assistance in the preparation of these Journals for publication: to Mr. John R. Russell, Librarian, University of Rochester Library, for permission to publish the Journals and for many favors;

to Miss Margaret Butterfield, Assistant Librarian in Charge of Special Collections, University of Rochester Library, for her most generous co-operation and much assistance; to Betty Ann Wilder and Grace L. Wood, who as research assistants helped to ferret out and to identify many of the persons mentioned in the Journals; and to many other persons too numerous to mention by name. The Historical Society of Montana has kindly supplied me with microfilms of three journals of men who ascended the Missouri River on the *Spread Eagle* in 1862, and has permitted me to cite them. Mrs. Anne McDonnell of that Society has assisted greatly with the Journal of 1862.

The Horace H. Rackham School of Graduate Studies and the Wenner-Gren Foundation for Anthropological Research have assisted me from time to time with the researches upon Morgan's life and work.

My greatest debt, however, is to my wife, Mary, who has performed the prodigious labor of proofreading the transcriptions and preparing the final manuscript for publication.

LESLIE A. WHITE

THE INDIAN JOURNALS, 1859-62

Edited, and with an introduction, by Leslie A. White

Illustrations selected and edited by Clyde Walton

LEWIS HENRY MORGAN

THE INDIAN JOURNALS

1859-62

Ann Arbor: The University of Michigan Press

To the memory of my wife, Mary

DESIGNED BY GEORGE LENOX

COPYRIGHT © BY THE UNIVERSITY OF MICHIGAN 1959   LIBRARY OF CONGRESS CATALOG CARD NO. 58-10122

PUBLISHED IN THE UNITED STATES OF AMERICA BY THE UNIVERSITY OF MICHIGAN PRESS AND SIMULTANEOUSLY IN TORONTO, CANADA, BY AMBASSADOR BOOKS, LTD.

MANUFACTURED IN THE UNITED STATES OF AMERICA

Contents

COLOR PLATES

Illustrations

About the Illustrations

The illustrations in this book depict the places and the people—missionaries, traders, adventurers, government agents, and above all the Indians—Lewis Henry Morgan saw and wrote about.

It is entirely proper to emphasize here—as did the late Bernard De Voto—how very little we know about those who pictured the West, both painters and photographers. In general, the study of photography in our country has been limited to those who first practiced the technique—to Mathew Brady and his assistants and to certain of our own contemporaries. The lives and the works of a few of the artists who pictured the West have been studied, but by and large we know little or nothing about most of them. In our libraries, museums, and historical societies there are thousands of art works that describe the West. But there are few satisfactory lists of these paintings and sketches—here, indeed, there is a real need for the sure touch of the bibliographer. Of course, it should be said that there are exceptions to these generalizations. Charles Russell, Frederic Remington, and other "cowboy" artists are now much in vogue. And everyone interested in American photography and in western portraiture is greatly indebted to the work of the late Dr. Robert Taft.

The sixteen color plates which illustrate the text are taken from four very early (and now very rare) books. "The Bear Dance" and "Archery of the Mandans" are taken from Catlin's *North American Indian Portfolio* published in 1844 by the artist George Catlin. He had been admitted to the bar, but abandoned the law to paint "without teacher or adviser." Greatly impressed by a delegation of Indians visiting Philadelphia, he decided to make a permanent record of American Indian life, because "…the history and customs of such a people, preserved by pictorial illustrations, are themes worthy the lifetime of one man, and nothing short of the loss of my life shall prevent me from visiting their country and becoming their historian." Catlin did go West to paint Indians, and the details of the career he built around these paintings are too well known to elaborate on here. While it was once fashionable to be very critical of Catlin's work, no one denies that he made a lasting contribution to our knowledge of Indian life.

Karl Bodmer's paintings are often compared with Catlin's, since they both painted Indians on the upper Missouri, Catlin in 1832 and Bodmer in 1833-34. Bodmer, a gifted, imaginative painter with a fine technique, had been trained in Paris and hired by Prince Maximilian of Wied to accompany him to America to record for scientific purposes the habits and customs of the Indians. Prince Maximilian was an accomplished scientist, who, accompanied by Bodmer and a servant with the improbable name of Dreidoppel, traveled up the Missouri in the cause of scientific investigation. Bodmer's magnificent and detailed work was published with the prince's *Reise in das Innere Nord-Amerika in den Jahren 1832 bis 1834* (Coblentz, 1839-41), and it constitutes a detailed and accurate addition to our national history. We reproduce in color "Funeral Scaffold of a Sioux Chief," "Buffalo Dance of the Mandan," "Mato-Topé," "The Interior of the Hut of a Mandan Chief," "A Mandan Village,"

"Noapeh, an Assiniboin Indian; Psihdja-Sahpa, a Yanktonai Indian," and an interesting "Fac Similie of an Indian Painting."

James Otto Lewis, best known for his *Aboriginal Portfolio* (Philadelphia, 1835), traveled with General Lewis Cass to the tribal assemblies to sign treaties at Prairie du Chien, Fond du Lac, Mississinewa, Fort Wayne, and Green Bay. At these treaty councils he was able to record Indians in all the vivid color of their native costumes and paint. Knowledge of the impending publication of McKenney and Hall's volumes on the American Indian prompted Lewis to rush his work through the press, and it was placed before the public in 1835, a year before McKenney and Hall and six years before Catlin's *Portfolio*. Little is known of his life. But his paintings are valuable as a record of the Indians of the Old Northwest at the time they were being removed from their tribal lands. We reproduce in color "Interior of a Sioux Lodge," "Pe-che-co, a Pottawattomie Chief," "Me-no-quet," and "Tens-qua-ta-wa."

The final three color plates are from *The Indian Tribes of North America* (Philadelphia, 1836-41) by Thomas L. McKenney and James Hall. Colonel Thomas L. McKenney, famous as an honest superintendent of Indian trade, and as head of the Bureau of Indian Affairs, was with General Cass (and J. O. Lewis) at a number of treaty signings. He was instrumental in establishing the Indian Gallery, an extensive collection of Indian paintings, in Washington. Many of these portraits were painted from life, although some of them were copies of paintings by J. O. Lewis, S. M. Charles, G. Cooke, and Joshua Shaw. McKenney desired to make a permanent record of the features of prominent Indians, and to accomplish this endeavor took as a collaborator the Ohio Valley literary figure James Hall. Hall's best-known work is probably *Letters from the West* (London, 1828), although his *Legends of the West* (Philadelphia, 1832) and *Sketches of History, Life and Manners in the West* (Cincinnati, 1834) are also important. He was state's attorney and a circuit judge in Illinois, and editor of the first literary magazine published in that state. Their three volumes reached a receptive audience and have been published in many editions.

We reproduce "Tah-ro-hon, an Iowa Warrior," "Le Soldat du Chene, an Osage Chief," and "No-way-ke-sug-ga, an Otto," all painted by Charles Bird King, an artist of reputation who had studied abroad.

Many individuals and institutions have assisted in locating the 100 black and white illustrations. I am particularly indebted to Mr. Nyle H. Miller, secretary of the Kansas State Historical Society; Dr. William D. Aeschbacher, director of the Nebraska State Historical Society, and Miss Myrtle D. Berry of that institution; Mrs. Alys Freeze of the Denver Public Library Western Collection; Mr. Michael Kennedy, director of the Historical Society of Montana, and Miss Virginia Walton of that institution; Mr. James Anderson, historian, Native Sons of Kansas City; Dr. Frank H. H. Roberts, Jr., director of the Bureau of American Ethnology, Smithsonian Institution; Mr. Eugene D. Becker, curator of pictures, Minnesota Historical Society; the Illinois State Historical Library; the Library, Hudson's Bay Co., Winnipeg; Professor Leslie A. White; Major Jack C. Vaughan, Grand Prairie, Texas.

CLYDE C. WALTON

THE INDIAN JOURNALS, 1859-62

From picture mounted inside front cover
of Morgan's family Bible.

Lewis Henry Morgan:
His Life and His Researches

Chapter I

On the morning of May 17, 1859, in Rochester, New York, an energetic attorney in his early forties bade his wife and children goodbye and set out for Kansas and Nebraska territories—Indian country. The purpose of the trip was to ascertain how Indians of various tribes designated their relatives. The man was Lewis Henry Morgan.

Morgan had made a rather thorough study of the culture of the Iroquoian tribes of New York state, and had published a book on the subject, *The League of the Ho-de-no-sau-nee, or Iroquois* (Rochester, N.Y., 1851). In the course of his investigations he discovered that the customs of designating relatives among the Iroquois differed radically from those in vogue in our society. He found, for example, that they called father's brother ''father,'' and mother's sister ''mother.'' In harmony with this usage, the children of father's brother and mother's sister were called ''brother'' and ''sister.'' A man called his brother's children ''son'' and ''daughter,'' but a woman called her brother's children ''nephew'' and ''niece.'' And there were other usages, too, that differed from our own.

Morgan did not think much about the significance of these facts at the time; they were curious customs of Indians, and that

was that. Years later, however, as his interests turned more and more toward science, he began to realize that these ''curious customs''—calling your mother's sister's son ''brother''—might have great significance. But the customs of one tribe, or a group of closely related tribes such as the Iroquois, were not enough for scientific purposes; one must have knowledge of more, many more. It was to obtain information on other tribes that Morgan undertook the field trips described in the journals that follow. But we are getting ahead of our story.

In a farmhouse on the shores of Lake Cayuga, a few miles south of Aurora, New York, Lewis Morgan was born on November 21, 1818. His father moved the family to Aurora while Lewis was still a child. After attending the Cayuga Academy in Aurora, Lewis went to Union College for his junior and senior years, graduating in 1840. He then returned to Aurora where he ''read law'' to prepare himself for the legal profession. He also continued his studies of the classics of ancient Greece and Rome, in which he was much interested. But he did something else, too, that proved to be enormously significant: he became a member of *The Gordian Knot*, a young men's

literary and social club. Before long, however, the society decided to reorganize itself and construct a new organization, using as their model the famed *League of the Iroquois*. This they did, and they called their new society the *Grand Order of the Iroquois*. Their constitution was written by Morgan; the preamble began: ''To encourage a kinder feeling towards the Indian, founded upon a truer knowledge of his civil and domestic institutions, and of his capabilities for future elevation. . .''[1] Several chapters of the *Order* were established in western New York and eastward as far as Utica. Another member besides Morgan was to become a prominent student of Indian cultures also: Henry Rowe Schoolcraft (1793–1864), pioneer American ethnologist, married an Ojibwa Indian; author of *The American Indians* (1857), and other works. The chapters used to hold meetings at which times ceremonies were performed and addresses delivered. Everyone—or at least the more prominent members—had an Indian name; Morgan's was Skenandoah, a prominent Iroquois chief of former times.

During the 1840's a group of land speculators organized as the Ogden Land Company were aggressively trying to deprive the Senecas of their lands. They "pursued and hunted . . . [the Senecas] with a degree of wickedness hardly to be parfalleled in the history of human avarice," wrote Morgan; "Not only have every principle of honesty, every dictate of humanity, every christian precept been violated by this company, in their eager artifices to despoil the Senecas; but the darkest frauds, the basest bribery, and the most execrable intrigues which soulless avarice could suggest, have been practised, in open day, upon this defenceless and much-injured people."[2]

The *Grand Order of the Iroquois* fought the Ogden Land Company with every means at their command. They circulated petitions, aroused citizens and urged them to appeal to their Congressmen. Morgan went to Washington to carry the fight to Congress itself. Some gains were won, and in recognition of his services on their behalf, the Seneca tribe adopted Morgan in 1847. He was made a member of the Hawk clan, and given the name Tayadaowuhkuh, or "One Lying Across," or "Bridging the Gap," "referring to him as a bridge over the differences . . . between the Indian and the white man."[3]

If the new society, the *Grand Order of the Iroquois*, were to be constructed in the image of the great Iroquoian confederacy, it would be necessary to know, in some detail as well as in general, how this intertribal organization was constructed and how it functioned. As Morgan remarked years later, "the real structure and principles of the league eluded . . . [the] inquiries" of "Jesuit missionaries, and both French and English travellers [who] had written volumes upon . . . [the] civil and domestic affairs [of the Iroquois] . . . [The] general features [of the league] were well known, but were so incumbered by errors

that the knowledge was of little value."[4] Consequently Morgan and other members of the *Order*, but especially Morgan, set about ascertaining the facts and discarding the erroneous beliefs that had become traditional. "Whatever interest I have since taken in Indian studies," Morgan wrote in 1859, "was awakened through my connection with this Indian fraternity."[5]

The "institutions of our Indian races are obscure and complicated," Morgan observed, "and can only be worked out by careful and patient research, carried down to minute particulars."[6] He had a fine sense of scientific inquiry, as his unpublished field notes and journals demonstrate. He was an acute and a resourceful observer and a faithful reporter; he distinguished meticulously between direct observation and verbal reports from others.[7]

Morgan made many visits to the reservations of the Iroquois, to Onondaga and Tonawanda especially, but also to the Grand River and Alleghany reserves. He observed their games and ceremonies. He studied their social organization and political structure and recorded their legends and mythology. The Regents of the University of the State of New York commissioned him to collect specimens of Iroquoian culture for the state museum in Albany. This he did, accompanying the specimens with rather full information concerning their use and significance.[8] Morgan's essays on the material culture of the Iroquois were well illustrated, not only with line drawings in the text but also by beautiful colored plates, which are still bright and distinct after more than a hundred years (see the *Third Report of the Regents*, 1850, especially).

Fairly early in his studies among the Iroquois, Morgan met a young Seneca Indian who was destined to play a prominent role,

not only in Morgan's ethnological inquiries but in the affairs of the nation as well. This young man was Ely Samuel Parker (1828–95). He was an intelligent and eager youth who wanted to make a career for himself in the white man's world, but who was determined also not to sever his ties with his home and his tribe. He succeeded to the office of one of the Seneca sachemships of the Iroquoian confederacy. In 1857, Parker met Captain Ulysses S. Grant in Galena, Illinois. During the Civil War Parker served on General Grant's staff; it was he who penned the articles of surrender of Lee at Appomattox. He eventually rose to the rank of Brigadier-General.[9]

But it is as an Indian and as a friend and co-worker of Morgan that Parker interests us most here. The two men became fast friends. Ely and members of his family rendered Morgan generous and priceless assist-

Ely S. Parker, the prominent Seneca Indian, who encouraged and helped Morgan in his early ethnological studies.

ance in his ethnological inquiries, both as informants and interpreters. It was to Parker that Morgan dedicated *The League of the Iroquois*, "the fruit of our joint researches."

Thanks to Parker's friendship and assistance, to Morgan's spirited defense of the Senecas against the rapacities of the Ogden Land Company and to his subsequent adoption into the Seneca tribe, Morgan obtained an entrée into Iroquoian society that proved to be tremendously fruitful. He soon became an authority on the Iroquois. He read papers at meetings of the *Grand Order*. In 1846 he read a paper on "Constitutional Government of the Six Nations" before the New York Historical Society. In the following year he published fourteen "Letters on the Iroquois, by Skenandoah, addressed to Albert Gallatin, LL.D., President of the New York Historical Society," in the *American Review; a Whig Journal of Politics, Literature, Art and Science* (Vols. v and vi).

In 1851, Morgan published *The League of the Ho-de-no-sau-nee, or Iroquois*. It was made up in rather large part of the previously published "Letters on the Iroquois" and of material from his reports on collections of specimens for the museum in Albany, revised, arranged and supplemented for this purpose. Major John Wesley Powell, Chief of the Bureau of American Ethnology, called *The League* the "first scientific account of an Indian tribe ever given to the world."[10] And as recently as 1922, Alexander Goldenweiser, who had himself done field work among the Iroquois, remarked that "the best general treatise on the Iroquois still remains Lewis H. Morgan's *The League of the Iroquois*."[11]

In the same year that *The League* was published, Morgan married his cousin, Mary Elizabeth Steele, of Albany, New York. They moved into a house on South Fitzhugh Street in Rochester,[12] and Morgan devoted himself wholly to his professional and domestic life; "from the close of 1850 until the summer of 1857, Indian affairs were laid entirely aside."[13]

But matters were not to remain thus. "In the year 1856," writes Morgan, "having attended the Albany meeting of the [American] Association for the Advancement of Science, my interest in Ethnology was quickened to such a degree that I resolved to resume the study as soon as the state of my business would permit."[14] In the following year, "as a preparation for the Montreal meeting of the Association, I took up anew the Laws of descent and Consanguinity of the Iroquois," he wrote, "and gave to it a more particular examination than ever before."[15] The result was a paper, "Laws of Descent of the Iroquois," which he presented at the meeting and which was published in the *Proceedings* of the Association.[16]

In the summer of 1858 Morgan set out for Marquette, in Michigan's upper peninsula, where he had business interests. He was, among other things, attorney for and director of the Bay de Noquet and Marquette Railroad Company. "On the train from Suspension Bridge," Morgan wrote in his journal,[17] "was a delegation of 28 Sioux, on their return from Washington, where they had been for the last three months on business with the government. The most of them were fine looking Indians, with deeply marked and intelligent faces. . ." Morgan talked to them and tried to obtain information on their kinship system and social organization. But the language barrier was considerable, even with an interpreter, and, as Morgan records, "they seemed unwilling to give much information . . ." However, Morgan felt, on the basis of their conversa-

tion, that the Sioux reckoned descent "in some manner as the Iroquois did," although "none of their statements could be taken as true" at that time.

Later, in the summer of 1858, Morgan met some Ojibwa Indians at Marquette and had ample opportunity to obtain information from them, and to check and recheck his data.[18] "To my surprise," he wrote later, "and not a little to my delight, I found their system was substantially the same as that of the Iroquois."[19] This discovery may, perhaps, have marked a turning point in Morgan's life and career. Years earlier he had been an assiduous student of the Iroquois—not of the American Indians or of primitive peoples generally, but of the Iroquois, and especially of the Senecas, his neighbors, his friends, and even his relatives by adoption. But he had "laid Indian matters aside" at the time of his marriage. Years later his interest was revived as we have already seen, and he again took up the question of Iroquoian kinship. But had he not discovered the Iroquoian type of kinship nomenclature among the Ojibwa in Marquette in 1858, he might have continued to live as a successful attorney, with ethnology as merely an interesting diversion. But after the summer of 1858, ethnology came to absorb more and more of his life. He eventually gave up his legal practice, and except for urgent business matters, devoted almost his entire time to his researches. For ten years he gave himself with unremitting zeal and passion to his ethnological labors, to which he himself erected a fitting monument: *Systems of Consanguinity and Affinity of the Human Family*.

After Morgan had discovered that many tribes and peoples had kinship systems like that of the Iroquois he named this kind of system "classificatory" as distinguished from our own system which he termed "descriptive." One of the principal features of classificatory systems is the terminological merging of collateral and lineal kin at certain points: e.g., calling father's sister's son "father," mother's sister's son "brother," etc. Morgan was not the first person to discover a classificatory system of kinship and to recognize it as a definite system, functioning naturally in a social system as ours does in our society. Joseph-Francois Lafitau, a Jesuit missionary, published a clear and concise account of the Iroquoian system in Paris in 1724 in his notable work *Moeurs des Sauvages Americains*, etc. Morgan never knew about this work, however, at least not until after he had published *Systems of Consanguinity*.[20]

Morgan published a brief account of Iroquoian kinship nomenclature in February, 1847, in the third of his "Letters on the Iroquois"; it was reprinted four years later in *The League* (pp. 85–87). He noted that it differed from "the civil or canon law; but was yet a clear and definite system," something that was intelligible in terms of Iroquoian social organization. This was more than many of Morgan's contemporaries were able to appreciate. Dr. Chester Dewey, a friend of Morgan and a member of "The Club" before which Morgan read many of his scientific papers, "could see nothing in it [i.e., the Iroquoian system] but the total depravity and perversity of the Indian mind —that it could ever have thought of such utterly absurd ways of characterizing relationships..."[21]

When Morgan discovered the classificatory system of relationship among the Senecas, he "did not as much as surmise that it extended beyond this Indian family [tribe], and much less that it might have important

ethnological uses."[22] Subsequent reflection, however, upon ethnological matters brought him to two conclusions: (1) that the social and political institutions of the Iroquois were organizations of kinship relations: "in fact their celebrated league was but an elaboration of these relationships into a complex, and even a stupendous system of civil polity";[23] and (2) that all American Indian cultures belong to one and the same class: "Now the institutions of all the aboriginal races of this continent have a family cast. They bear internal evidence of a common paternity, and point to a common origin, but remote, both as to time and place."[24]

The first of these conclusions was matured in Morgan's mind and eventually found expression in 1877 in *Ancient Society* (p. 6) as one of the most basic and significant generalizations of ethnology, namely, that primitive society is organized upon the basis of kinship relations, whereas modern civil society is based upon property relations. The second conclusion, a recognition that all American Indian cultures belonged to a single class, may seem commonplace today, but it was far from being so a hundred years ago.

The next question logically to be considered was: where did the American Indians come from? It is not easy for us to appreciate the significance of this question today; it is taken for granted, and it seems so obvious, that they came to America from Asia. But a hundred years ago the question was wide open to all kinds of speculation. Some believed that the American Indians were descended from the Lost Tribes of Israel. Others derived them—or some tribes at least—from Wales, Greece, or Phoenicia. On the other hand there were men like Samuel G. Morton, M.D. (1799–1850), Pro-

fessor of Anatomy in Pennsylvania Medical College, the "Father of American Physical Anthropology," who maintained that the Indians were indigenous in America. George Gibbs (1815–73), an American ethnologist, wrote to Morgan in 1859: "To tell the truth, I am not a believer in the Asiatic origin of the American Indians. I think . . . [they are], like the buffalo and the grizzly bear, indigenous . . ." In the 1890's, Daniel Garrison Brinton (1837–99), Professor of American Linguistics and Archeology at the University of Pennsylvania and probably the most distinguished American anthropologist of that decade, held that the Indians had come to America from western Europe.[25] And as recently as 1911 the question was still being debated: a joint session of the American Anthropological Association and Section H (Anthropology) of the American Association for the Advancement of Science considered "The Problems of Unity or Plurality and Probable Place of Origin of the American Aborigines" at length from biological, geological, paleontological, archeological, linguistic, cultural —and even astronomical—points of view.[26]

Now it occurred to Morgan, rather early in his ethnological reflections, that in the distribution of kinship systems one might find decisive proof of the Asiatic origin of the American Indians. In the summer of 1857, when he read "Laws of Descent of the Iroquois" before the American Association for the Advancement of Science, he "did not know that the [classificatory] system extended beyond the Iroquois, although . . . [he] surmised its probability."[27] A year later he had found it among the Ojibwa in Michigan's upper peninsula. Upon his return to Rochester in late summer 1858 he "found some of the features of the same system among the Dakotas in Riggs'

Reverend Stephen Return Riggs, who furnished kinship information to Morgan, had an extensive knowledge of the Dakota Sioux in Minnesota, among whom he labored as a missionary for many years.

Lexicon[28] of that language, and also some trace of it among the Creeks."[29]

By this time Morgan's theory was well worked out in his mind: if the classificatory system of relationship—so different from that of western Europe—were generally possessed by American Indian tribes, and, further, if it could be traced to, and found in, Asia, the Asiatic origin of the American Indian could be definitely established. His reasoning ran something like this: If two peoples living in noncontiguous areas speak languages related to each other, then one may reasonably conclude that the peoples, too, are genetically and historically related. There are some instances in which a people abandons its own language and adopts that of a neighbor just as they might

in the case of tools or ceremonies; some of the pygmy groups for example speak only the language of their respective neighbors. But, for the most part, language and people go together: individuals acquire their language from their parents in infancy, and pass it on in turn to their children. Discovery of linguistic relationships has often been a means of establishing ethnic and cultural relationships. When it was learned, for example, that the Chiricauhua Apache of northern Mexico, the Hupa of California, and the Kutchin of Alaska spoke related languages, a firm basis for historical reconstruction had been laid.

But there is a limit to historical reconstruction based on linguistic similarities. Related languages may change and diverge so greatly that their common origin can no longer be established. No one so far has been able to establish a genetic connection between the Zuñi language, spoken in Zuñi Pueblo in western New Mexico, and any other language, yet it seems highly unlikely that it is unrelated to any other language in the world.

The situation with regard to kinship systems differs, Morgan argued, from that of languages: "Language changes its vocabulary, not only, but also modifies its grammatical structure in the progress of ages: thus eluding the [historical] inquiries which the philologists have pressed it to answer; but a system of relationship once matured and brought into operation is, in the nature of things, more unchangeable than language; not in the names employed as a vocabulary of relationships, for these are mutable; but in the ideas which underlie the system itself."[30] He pointed out that the Indo-European system of relationship contains "a number of permanent and unchangeable ideas which have survived and

will continue to survive all changes in vocabulary as well as all subdivisions and migrations of the parent stock."[31] It was Morgan himself who discovered that the same ideas, the same principles, underlay the Iroquoian and Ojibwa systems of relationship despite the fact that their languages were quite unrelated so far as anyone could determine. "There is, perhaps," Morgan reasoned, "nothing in the whole range of man's absolute necessities so little liable to mutation as his system of relationship."[32] He felt, therefore, that he had discovered a "new instrument" of ethnological investigation, and one that could yield significant results.

Already in 1857, Morgan felt that evidence pointed to an Asiatic origin of clan organization and the custom of reckoning descent unilineally found among many American Indian tribes. These traits, he wrote, found "among American races, whose languages are radically different, and without any traditional knowledge among them of its origin, indicates a very ancient introduction; and would seem to point to Asia as the birth-place of the system."[33] After discovering the classificatory system among the Ojibwa, and evidence of it among the Dakotas and Creeks in 1858, Morgan determined to push his inquiries farther and with dispatch.

Accordingly he worked out a questionnaire which he proposed to send to missionaries and to government agents on Indian reservations. The questionnaire asked such questions as "How do the Indians among whom you reside designate their father's brother, mother's brother's son, father's sister's daughter?", and so on through all of the relationships that might be significant in the social life of a primitive community. A letter, explaining the purpose of the inquiry, accompanied the questionnaire; it stated that its goal was the solution of the problem of the Asiatic origin of the American Indian. The letter also included an essay, "Laws of Consanguinity and Descent of the Iroquois"— which was substantially an abbreviated version of his previously published paper, "Laws of Descent of the Iroquois"—which described the structure and the working of the Iroquoian system.

The results of this inquiry by mail were somewhat disappointing, although not a failure by any means. The first questionnaire to be returned had been filled out by the Reverend Stephen Return Riggs in "the most complete and scholarly manner." Many were not returned, however, or were filled out imperfectly. Morgan supplemented his inquiry by mail by personal solicitation of delegations of western Indians on trips to Washington. He even obtained an Eskimo kinship system from natives brought to New York by an arctic explorer.[34] But all of these sources of information proved to be inadequate, so Morgan determined to go to the Indian country himself and collect his data at first hand. Accordingly he went to Kansas and Nebraska territories in May 1859, and thus began the series of four field trips in the summers of 1859–62, which are described in the journals presented here.

After returning to Rochester from his first trip to Kansas and Nebraska, Morgan set to work on a paper, "System of Consanguinity of the Red Race in Its Relations to Ethnology," which he read at the thirteenth meeting of the American Association for the Advancement of Science at Springfield, Massachusetts, in August 1859.[35]

Morgan did not have long to wait for data to arrive. Shortly after returning from the Springfield meeting he received the kinship system of the Tamils of southern India from a missionary to whom a questionnaire had been sent.

Morgan had predicted, on the basis of reason and evidence, that the classificatory system of relationship would be found in Asia in much the same way that, thirteen years earlier, astronomers and mathematicians predicted that the planet Neptune would be found in a certain sector of the heavens. (A brief account of this remarkable discovery was set forth in the *Third Annual Report* of the Smithsonian Institution for the year 1849. Morgan had these *Reports* in his library.) During the early stages of his investigations Morgan "lived and worked in a state of great mental excitement," according to his friend, the Reverend J. H. McIlvaine,[36] and "the answers he received [to his questionnaires], as they came in, sometimes nearly overpowered him. I well remember one occasion when he came into my study, saying, 'I shall find it, I shall find it among the Tamil people and Dravidian tribes of Southern India.' At this time I had no expectation of any such result; and I said to him, 'My friend, you have enough to do in working out your discovery in connection with the tribes of the American continent—let the old world go.' He replied, 'I cannot do it— I can not do it—I must go on, for I am sure I shall find it all there.' Some months afterward, he came in again, his face all aglow with excitement, the Tamil schedule in his hands, the answers to his questions just what he had predicted, and, throwing it on my table, he exclaimed, 'There! What did I tell you?' I was indeed amazed and confounded; and still more as his predicted re-

sults poured in upon him from a great multitude of independent sources."[37]

Morgan describes the occasion of the discovery of the Tamil system as follows: "My astonishment was greater than I can well express to learn that the Tamil system and the American Indian system were substantially identical; and that, too, in the most special and intricate features which characterize the two systems."[38]

The Tamil and Telugu systems of relationship provided Morgan with what he considered to be "decisive evidence of the Asiatic origin of the American Indian race,"[39] but he was not content to stop here. On the contrary, "it now became doubly desirable to extend the field of inquiry, not only so as [to] include the whole of India, but also Mongolia, Tibetan, Siberia, China, Siam, Japan, Australia, the Islands of the Pacific, Africa and South America, as well as to finish the inquiry among the North American Indians."[40]

At the meeting of the American Association for the Advancement of Science in August 1859, even before the Tamil system had been received, Morgan arranged with Joseph Henry,[41] Secretary of the Smithsonian Institution, to send out his questionnaires under the auspices of the Institution. Together they requested permission of General Lewis Cass, then Secretary of State, to send questionnaires abroad "in the governmental mailbags under the franc of the Secretary of State."[42] This permission was granted. A "Circular in Reference to the Degrees of Relationship Among Different Nations" was drawn up for wide distribution.[43] It consisted first of a letter from Joseph Henry, commending Morgan and his investigation to the addressee. Next was a letter from Lewis Cass, giving the project the official sanction of the Department of

State. Then came a long letter from Morgan, explaining the investigation in some detail and soliciting aid. In addition to the questionnaire dealing with kinship terms, a page of questions on various aspects of social organization was included. The circulars were ready for distribution in January 1860, and were then sent "to the principal diplomatic and consular officers of the United States in foreign countries, to the United States army officers at the several military posts, and also to the principal missionaries of the English and American Boards . . . [in] Asia, Africa, Islands of the Pacific, Mexico, and South America . . ." ("Circular," p. 12).

The process of obtaining data by mail was slow. It took two and sometimes three years to send out a questionnaire and get it back again; one sent to New Zealand in 1859 was returned to Morgan in 1866 (Morgan to Henry, June 14, 1866). But it was not only places on the other side of the earth that resisted investigation; regions much closer to hand could be difficult also. In 1866, Morgan wrote Henry that he had "tried for six years unsuccessfully to reach these [Pueblo] Indians [in New Mexico], and have thus far obtained but one schedule, and that very imperfect." And when the questionnaires were returned they were often imperfectly or incompletely filled out. Sometimes the one who filled out the questionnaire merely translated the questions but left them unanswered: e.g., in reply to the question with what kinship term is mother's sister's daughter's son designated, the answer would be "mother's sister's daughter's son." "I have been continually disappointed by the commission of this blunder," Morgan wrote to Baird on May 17, 1860, "although it is fully explained in the printed letter, or

at least as fully as I thought necessary."

There were other and even more frustrating replies. For example, Morgan sent a questionnaire to a missionary on a lonely island in the Pacific. Some two years later he received a letter from the missionary which said, in substance: "My dear sir, I received your request for information concerning the system of consanguinity of the natives of this island, and I set out to comply with your request. But upon inquiring into the matter I found that the natives here, who are very benighted, have no *system* of consanguinity at all. In fact, so far removed from civilization are they that they do not know how properly to address their kin. For example, an old man told me that he calls his father's sister's son 'son.' I therefore decided not to waste your time and mine in such an investigation."

Morgan devoted all of the time that he could possibly spare from his law practice and his business interests—and this amount of time was very considerable—to his researches. He sent out his questionnaires and tabulated the results as they came in. Each summer, from 1859 to 1862, inclusive, he went out into the field to gather data personally. And all this time he was pondering the problems posed by his material and working his way towards solutions of them. The Smithsonian Institution had, as we have seen, endorsed Morgan's researches, and now they expressed[44] a willingness to publish the results, providing they could meet the Institution's high standards.

By the end of 1864, Morgan had his monograph virtually completed, and he planned to deliver it to the Smithsonian by the first of January, 1865. It was fortunate that he did not, however, for a disastrous fire destroyed part of the Smithsonian building

on January 24.[45] "It was a marvellous escape," Morgan wrote to Baird[46] on January 26, referring to his manuscript, "as it would be next to impossible to replace it." The manuscript of *Systems* was eventually sent off in March 1865, but many years were to elapse before publication was achieved.

During the years when Morgan was conducting his investigations and writing and rewriting his monograph, he read a number of papers on kinship before the Club,[47] an organization of Rochester men who were interested in scientific and literary matters:

1. "The Indo-European System of Consanguinity and Relationship," January 17, 1860.
2. "The System of Consanguinity and Affinity of the Semitic Nations," March 31, 1863.
3. "The Growth of Nomenclature and Relationship," March 31, 1863.
4. "Iroquois System of Consanguinity and Affinity," January 4, 1864.
5. "Comparison of the System of Relationship of the Several Families of Mankind," January 12, 1865 and January 24, 1865.
6. "A Conjectural Solution of the Origin of the Classificatory System of Relationship," September 29, 1868.

As we have seen earlier, Morgan knew that other men were working along somewhat the same lines of investigation as himself and that—especially in view of the slowness of publication of his monograph—they might precede him in publication. Consequently he delivered a paper, "A Conjectural Solution of the Classificatory System of Relationship," in which he set forth the principal results of his researches and reflections, before a meeting of the American Academy of Arts and Sciences on February 11, 1868. This paper was published, after obtaining clearance from Joseph Henry, in the Academy's *Proceedings* (VII, 436–77).

Almost six years elapsed between the time that Morgan sent his monograph to the Smithsonian and its eventual publication. First, it had to be sent to a commission of scholars to be evaluated. Then there was revision and rewriting of some parts and a second evaluation by another commission. Difficulties were encountered in stereotyping the plates.[48] But, finally, early in 1871, *Systems of Consanguinity and Affinity of the Human Family* was published as Volume XVII of the *Smithsonian Contributions to Knowledge*.

Systems is a huge volume: 13 inches long, 10 inches wide, 2 inches thick, and weighs about 7 pounds. It contains 600 pages, of which almost 200 are tables of relationship terms from tribes and nations of North America, Europe, Asia, Oceania, and Africa. It cost the Smithsonian Institution almost $8,000 to publish; it was the largest and costliest monograph that had appeared in the *Contributions to Knowledge* up to that time. The cost to Morgan was considerable also: "eight years of hard labor . . . and about $25,000 . . ." (*Extracts from the European Travel Journal*, p. 370; letter to Lorimer Fison, June 30, 1879). Morgan got his first glimpse of *Systems* in London in the summer of 1871 while he was on his European tour; in his Journal he records his emotions and reflections upon seeing it (*Extracts*, p. 370).

It is interesting to ponder the significance of *Systems* and its contributions.[49] The investigations, of which *Systems* was the result, were undertaken in order to demonstrate the Asiatic origin of the American Indian. Attempts to explain the various kinds of kinship systems and to render their curious features intelligible led Mor-

gan to formulate a theory of social evolution: human society began in a condition of promiscuity, without marriage or the family, and subsequently evolved through a series of stages to the monogamous family of today.

But Morgan's supposed demonstration of the Asiatic origin of the American Indian was unsound: the similarity, or virtual identity—as in the case of the Tamil and Seneca—of kinship nomenclatures does not necessarily mean genetic relationship; such similarities or identities are more properly explained in another way: as functions of like social systems. And his theory of the evolution of the family, which he regarded as "the most remarkable result by far of the investigation," has been obsolete for decades.

Yet, *Systems* was, and remains today, a great work, one that may properly be called "monumental," as the British anthropologist, A. C. Haddon, has termed it. Professor Lowie has called it "a towering monument," a "colossal achievement." And Radcliffe-Brown refers to *Systems* as "a monument of scholarly, patient research."[50]

In the first place, Morgan's achievement in *Systems* is almost unique in the history of science: it had virtually no precedent. Almost every eminent figure in the history of science has been preceded by other great figures in his field—Newton, Darwin, Einstein, *et al*. But Morgan had virtually no predecessors in the field: he literally created the science of kinship. "Morgan's unique distinction," says Lowie, "lies in literally creating the study of kinship systems as a branch of comparative sociology."[51] Murdock has asserted that "the scientific significance of kinship systems was first appreciated by Morgan . . ."[52] And the considered judgment of a distinguished British

anthropologist, W. H. R. Rivers (1864–1922), on this point is as follows:[53]

"I do not know of any discovery in the whole range of science which can be more certainly put to the credit of one man than that of the classificatory system of relationship by Lewis Morgan. By this I mean, not merely that he was the first to point out clearly the existence of this mode of denoting relationship, but that it was he who collected the vast mass of material by which the essential characters of the system were demonstrated, and it was he who was the first to recognize the great theoretical importance of his new discovery."

Secondly, the mass of new scientific data presented in *Systems* was enormous and is still unequalled: in this respect, says Lowie, "it is incomparably fuller than anything yet brought together by any of his successors."[54] In the preface to his monograph, "The Distribution of Kinship Systems in North America," Leslie Spier remarks that "the data are drawn largely from Morgan's tables."[55]

Thirdly, Morgan formulated a bold and original theory to explain the various kinds of kinship systems that he had discovered. It was, says Murdock, "perhaps the most original and brilliant single achievement in the history of anthropology."[56] This theory was all-embracing, too; it encompassed the length and breadth of cultural history, from the origin of man to the present day.

Fourthly, Morgan worked out a classification of kinship systems that is at least as good as any that we have today, and better than many. It is better, for example, than classifications that do not recognize and appreciate the fundamental difference between "classificatory" systems, i.e., in which lineal and collateral kin are merged terminologically at certain points, and "descriptive" systems—such as our own. Even the terms, "classificatory" and "descriptive," by which he designated these two great types, have not been improved upon, in the opinion of Radcliffe-Brown,[57] one of the foremost students of kinship since Morgan, although they have been much criticized.

And, finally, Morgan provided the theoretical basis for a valid explanation of kinship nomenclatures: they express forms of social organization. Although Morgan erred, as we now believe after much testing of his conclusions, in believing that an Hawaiian type of terminology—in which the brothers and sisters of both mother and father are called "mother" and "father"—indicated that at one time brothers and sisters intermarried with one another in a group, his basic premise that kin terms express social relations is still sound.

After he had read the last of the printer's proofs of *Systems*, Morgan sailed for Europe with his wife and son on July 25, 1870; they returned to New York on August 13, 1871. Before long he was at work again. On March 4, 1873, he wrote to Joseph Henry that he was at work on a book. In May, two years later, he finished the last chapter of *Ancient Society, or Researches in the Lines of Human Progress from Savagery through Barbarism to Civilization*. It was published by Henry Holt and Company in 1877.

Ancient Society became Morgan's best known and most influential work. Due chiefly to the fact that it was recognized as a fundamental and significant work by Karl Marx,[58] and, as a consequence, became a classic in socialist literature, *Ancient Society* has been widely translated: twice into Russian—Czarist and Soviet—German, Bulgarian, Spanish (two translations), Chinese,

and Japanese (at least four translations). But, judged from the standpoint of scientific achievement rather than of influence upon society, *Systems* may be regarded as Morgan's greatest work, for reasons already cited; *Ancient Society* was, to a great extent, an extension and an amplification of theories worked out in *Systems*. But *Ancient Society* had a "message." It presented society and culture as an unfolding, developing process: what is today will not be tomorrow. He had much to say about the role of property in western civilization of the nineteenth century:[59]

"Since the advent of civilization, the outgrowth of property has been so immense, its form so diversified, its uses so expanding and its management so intelligent in the interests of its owners, that it has become, on the part of the people, an unmanageable power. The human mind stands bewildered in the presence of its own creation. The time will come, nevertheless, when human intelligence will rise to the mastery over property, and define the relations of the state to the property it protects, as well as the obligations and the limits of the rights of its owners. The interests of society are paramount to individual interests, and the two must be brought into just and harmonious relations. A mere property career is not the final destiny of mankind, if progress is to be the law of the future as it has been of the past. The time which has passed away since civilization began is but a fragment of the past duration of man's existence; and but a fragment of the ages yet to come. The dissolution of society bids fair to become the termination of a career of which property is the end and aim; because such a career contains the elements of self-destruction. Democracy in government, brotherhood in society, equality in rights and

privileges, and universal education, foreshadow the next higher plane of society to which experience, intelligence and knowledge are steadily tending. It will be a revival, in a higher form, of the liberty, equality and fraternity of the ancient gentes."

Ancient Society was revolutionary in import as well as evolutionary.

Ancient Society was last printed by Henry Holt and Company, the original publisher, in 1907, thirty years after its first appearance. Since then it has been published for decades by the Charles H. Kerr Company of Chicago. And, since 1950, a publishing house in India, the Bharati Library in Calcutta, has been issuing it.

Morgan published relatively little after *Ancient Society*: a few articles and his last book, *Houses and House-Life of the American Aborigines*. But some of the articles had been written years earlier, and *Houses and House-Life* was an expansion of Part IV of *Ancient Society* as that work was originally planned: it was entitled "The Growth of the Idea of House Architecture" (Morgan to Henry, March 3, 1875).

Morgan made one more field trip, however, after the publication of *Ancient Society*.

In 1878, in company with two sons of his nephew, David P. Morgan, and two other young men, all students in Columbia College, he explored a portion of the archeologically rich region in southwestern Colorado, barely missing the discovery of the now famous remains in Mesa Verde: Cliff Palace and Sprucetree House. On the return journey they dipped south into New Mexico and visited the great pueblo ruins at Aztec, and the inhabited pueblo of Taos. Morgan made a thorough observational study of Aztec which he published under the title "On the Ruins of a Stone Pueblo on the Animas River in New Mexico; with a Ground Plan," in the *Twelfth Annual Report* of the Peabody Museum of American Archaeology and Ethnology, 1880. His journal, which I edited, was published as "Lewis H. Morgan's Journal of a Trip to Southwestern Colorado and New Mexico, June 21 to August 7, 1878," in *American Antiquity*, 8 (1942): 1–26. The diary kept by William Fellowes Morgan, one of his great-nephews, was published by Professor Temple R. Hollcroft in *Scientific Monthly*, LXXVII (1953): No. 3, 119–28.

No sketch of Morgan's life and work, no matter how brief, should fail to mention his study of the beaver. In 1855, Morgan made the first of many trips to Michigan's upper peninsula in connection with his business interests there. He became much intrigued with the numerous beaver colonies in the region around Marquette. Before long he found himself engaged in a serious and intensive study of this rodent. He pursued his investigations whenever and wherever the opportunity arose. Thus, we find him making inquiries about the beaver on his trip to the Red River Settlement in 1861, and making exhaustive inquiries and as much observation as was possible on his trip up the Missouri River in 1862. His researches were published in 1868 in *The American Beaver and His Works*. This work was cited by Darwin in *The Descent of Man* (Chapter 3).

Little more need be said here about Morgan's life.[60] His career as a scientist was spent entirely as a private citizen. He acquired a modest fortune from business ventures—in railroads, mines, and iron furnaces—in Michigan's upper peninsula which enabled him to give up law practice and to devote himself in his later years almost wholly to ethnology. He never sought or accepted a position on the faculty of a college or university, although Andrew D. White, President of Cornell University, urged him to accept a chair at that institution. Nor was he ever a member of the staff of a museum or other scientific institution. But he was well acquainted with or corresponded with many of the foremost scientists and scholars of his day in the United States: Henry Adams, the historian; Charles Eliot Norton, professor of the history of art at Harvard University, co-editor of the *North American Review*, and founder and first president of the Archaeological Institute of America; Francis Parkman, historian; Henry Wadsworth Longfellow; William Cullen Bryant; Oliver Wendell Holmes, Jr.; Eben Norton Horsford, chemist and inventor; Asa Gray, a distinguished botanist at Harvard; Jeffries Wyman, a zoologist and archeologist at Harvard; Wendell Phillips Garrison, editor of *The Nation*, *et al*. He knew all of the leading anthropologists of his day— Horatio Hale; Major J. W. Powell, first director of the Bureau of American Ethnology; F. W. Putnam, curator of the Peabody Museum at Harvard University; O. T. Mason of the U. S. National Museum; A. S. Gatschet of the Bureau of American Ethnology; Adolph F. Bandelier—and many others who have long since been forgotten. Many of them sought his counsel and advice on anthropological matters. The Archaeological Institute of America, at its inception in 1879, requested him to prepare for them a program of research for the Americas, which he did: "A Study of the Houses of the American Aborigines, with Suggestions for the Exploration of the Ruins in New Mexico, Arizona, the Valley of the San Juan, and in Yucatán and Central America," published in the *First Annual Report* of the Executive Committee of the Archaeological Institute of America (Cambridge, Mass., 1880), pp. 28–80. And he corresponded with a number of scholars and scientists in Europe: Charles Darwin, Herbert Spencer, Sir Henry Maine, J. J. Bachofen, *et al*.

Morgan was elected to membership in the American Association for the Advancement of Science in 1856 and eventually became active in their affairs. He was elected president of the Association in 1879, and thus presided at the annual meeting in Boston in 1880. In 1875 he was elected to membership in the National Academy of Sciences. These are the two highest honors that American science can bestow upon any American anthropologist.

Death came to Morgan on December 17, 1881. He was buried in the tomb in Mount Hope Cemetery, Rochester, that he had built for his family in 1863, a few months after the death of his two little daughters.

Kansas and Nebraska in 1859

Chapter II

The great prairies of Kansas and Nebraska were undisturbed by white men until 1541, when Coronado and his band of sturdy adventurers sought the "province of Quivira" in their quest of gold and treasure. Few Europeans came after them for about a hundred and fifty years. During the eighteenth century, however, the French and Spanish were there, competing with each other for the trade of the region. In 1762, the French ceded to Spain their claims to land west of the Mississippi. Thirty-eight years later it was returned by treaty to France, and in 1803, the United States bought from France a huge tract—the Louisiana Purchase—including Kansas, Nebraska, and much more.

First there were exploring parties, then the establishment of forts, missions, and settlements. Lewis and Clark ascended the Missouri River in the summer of 1804. Zebulon M. Pike explored parts of Kansas and Nebraska two years later. A scientific expedition under Major Stephen H. Long came up the Missouri, in the first steamboat to enter the country, in 1819. Lieutenant John C. Frémont explored the Kansas and Platte rivers in 1842. Fort Atkinson was established near Council Bluffs in 1820, Ft. Leavenworth, Kansas, in 1827, Ft. Scott in 1842, Ft. Kearney in 1847. George Catlin, the famous artist and painter of Indians, journeyed up the Missouri by boat to the Mandan villages in 1832. In the following year, Prince Maximilian, accompanied by the artist, Carl Bodmer, made the same trip in the same steamboat, the *Yellowstone*, but went even farther than Catlin.

Two Presbyterian missions were established among the Osage Indians in Kansas in 1820: one on the Neosho River, the other on the Marais des Cygnes. The first Methodist mission was located among the Shawnee in 1829. In Nebraska, Moses Merrill established a Baptist mission among the Otoes in 1833. The Ottawa (Kansas) Baptist Mission, now Ottawa University, was founded by the Reverend Jotham Meeker in 1837. It was Meeker who brought the first printing press to Kansas in 1833; two years later he issued the *Shawnee Sun*, the first newspaper published in Kansas.

Bellevue was one of the earliest settlements in the Kansas-Nebraska area; fur traders' records mention it as early as 1823. It was located on the Missouri River in Nebraska. The first white child to be born in the region was born in Kansas in 1828. Settlements did not become extensive or numerous, however, until after Kansas and Nebraska had been organized as territories in 1854. The towns of Leavenworth, Atchison, and Lawrence were laid out, and Topeka was founded in that year. In 1855 the white population of Nebraska was 4,494. The Kansas State Library was founded in 1858; the Scientific and Historical Society of Kansas was chartered a year later. Baker University was established at Palmyra (Baldwin) in 1858; two years later the Baptists organized Ottawa University. Nebraska was sufficiently advanced by 1857 to suffer widespread bank failures.

Kansas-Nebraska Territory played a prominent and important role in trade and transportation with the West in the 1840's and 1850's. In addition to the river traffic, which was considerable, there was a voluminous trade with Mexico over the Santa Fe Trail. Long trains of Conestoga wagons, laden with cottons and woolens, silks, velvets, and hardware would set out from Independence, Missouri, pass through Westport, and head southwest for Santa Fe. They would return with furs, blankets, and heavy bags of Spanish gold and silver. By 1843, the annual monetary value of the trade was about $450,000.[1]

Migration over the Oregon Trail began in 1832; the "Great Migration" got under

Bellevue, Nebraska Territory, as sketched in 1854 by George Simons. Bellevue, an important early Missouri River settlement, was the location of the Peter A. Sarpy Trading Post and a Presbyterian mission, visited by Morgan in 1860.

way in 1843. The Trail began at Independence, Missouri, crossed the Kansas River near Topeka, and headed northwest into Nebraska where it followed the Platte River westward.

The Mormon Trail followed the Platte River, also, crossing Nebraska from the Missouri River to Ft. Laramie and thence on west. In 1846 and 1847 great numbers of Mormons traversed this route on their way to Utah. The discovery of gold in California in 1848 and in Colorado, near Denver, a decade later, increased migration westward to enormous proportions; it is estimated that 90,000 people went west over these trails in 1849–50. In 1850 the first monthly overland stage service between St. Joseph, Missouri, Salt Lake, and California was inaugurated; by 1861 there was daily coach service each way. In 1860 the famous Pony Express mail service between St. Joseph, Missouri, and Sacramento, California, was instituted. There were 190 relay stations along the 2,000 mile route; two trips each way were made per week. The journey required nine or ten days, fifteen in winter. The fastest trip was made in seven days and seven hours. The Express was abandoned in 1861 when a transcontinental telegraph line was completed. The first steam loco-

motive was brought to Kansas in 1860; railroad service in Nebraska began six years later.

Indians in Kansas and Nebraska. The situation with regard to Indian tribes in the Mississippi and Missouri river valleys during the 1840's and 1850's was simple: the Indians were occupying the region; the whites wished to remove them from it and to possess their lands themselves. And the whites were not to be denied; they would find ways, of one kind or another, to dispossess the Red man and move in.

When Morgan entered Kansas and Nebraska territories in 1859 he found some tribes who were native to the land, i.e., they had been living there for a considerable period of time. But, in addition to these, there were many tribes that had only recently been removed from the East and settled upon reservations in Kansas-Nebraska Territory. In Kansas the native tribes were the Kansa, Osage, and Pawnee. The Delawares were settled in Kansas in 1829; reservations were established for the Kickapoo, Potawatomi, Kaskaskias, Peorias, Weas, and Piankashaws in 1832; Sauks, Foxes, and Iowas came to Kansas in 1836; the Miamis were moved there in 1840, the Wy-

andottes three years later. In Nebraska were the Oto, Omaha, Pawnee, Ponca, Iowa, and Siouan tribes.

In the 1820's a Baptist missionary named Isaac McCoy[2] led a movement to remove the Indians living east of the Mississippi to lands west of that river where he envisaged the organization of an Indian state. Kansas-Nebraska Territory was generally favored as the most suitable place for the new home of the displaced tribes. Major Long had labelled this area "Great Desert" on his map, and characterized it as "almost wholly unfit for cultivation, and, of course, uninhabitable for people depending upon agriculture for their subsistence."[3] Daniel Webster called Kansas and Nebraska a "vast and worthless area . . . [a] region of savages and wild beasts, of deserts . . . cactus and prairie dogs," and asked "to what use could we ever hope to put these great deserts . . . ?"[4] Kansas and Nebraska were thought to be of no use to white men: let the Indians have it.

Most of the tribes removed from states east of the Mississippi and settled in Kansas and Nebraska "were removed . . . under assurances that it would be their permanent home, while, to some, specific pledges were given that they should never be disturbed in their new possessions, nor be included within the limits, or brought under the jurisdiction, of any future Territory or State. The country was set apart and dedicated to their special and exclusive use." Thus wrote the Commissioner of Indian Affairs in his report to the Secretary of the Interior for 1859 (p. 15).

These assurances proved to be of no avail however. It was soon discovered that there was much arable land in Kansas and Nebraska, and there were hundreds of thousands of land-hungry white men. Over two and one-half million immigrants entered the United States between 1851 and 1860. A report of the Massachusetts Emigrant Aid Company, organized in 1854, observed: "It is to be remembered that all accounts agree that the region of Kansas is the most desirable part of America now open to the

Reverend Isaac McCoy, visionary Baptist missionary, wanted to move the eastern Indians west of the Mississippi River, and then create an Indian state.

immigrant . . . Its crops are very bountiful . . . its mineral resources . . . [in certain parts] are inexhaustible."[5] Why should Indians, who stubbornly refused to settle down, till the soil, embrace Christianity, and become civilized, be allowed to hold lands against the needs of white civilized Christians? "It appears to me," wrote the U. S. Indian Agent for the Potawatomi Agency in Kansas Territory in his report for 1859, "that the idea of the Pottawatomies being able to hold in common . . . their beautiful, rich, and fertile reservation, in the center of Kansas, is preposterous . . ."[6]

"It was hoped," said the Commissioner of Indian Affairs in 1859, that when eastern Indian tribes were settled in Kansas and Nebraska "they could be shielded from the vices attendant upon civilization, until they could gradually be taught its advantages and blessings, and so be prepared to meet successfully the uncertain contingencies of the future." But, he added, "various causes operated to render such hopes futile. Amongst the most mischievous and fatal of which were *their possession of too great an extent of country, held in common,* and the right to large money annuities; the one giving them ample scope for indulgence in their unsettled and vagrant habits, and preventing their *acquiring a knowledge of individuality in property,* and the advantage of settled homes; the other fostering idleness and want of thrift, and giving them means of gratifying their depraved tastes and appetites."[7] We have supplied the italics in the preceding quotation to call attention to a cardinal point in the white man's policy toward the Indian. We shall return to it later.

The Indian agent for the Sac and Fox tribes in 1859 reported that they held 435,-200 acres, "embracing the choice lands of

Central Kansas." This would amount, he calculated, to 352 acres per capita, whereas "40 acres, put in proper cultivation, would yield them ample sustenance."[8] He also reported that the Indians themselves wanted to dispose of some of their land, believing that "their interests would be better subserved by a concentration of their people on a small reservation of land, where all the inducements would be thrown around them, *provoking* to industry, and an assimilation into the manners and customs of the whites . . ."[9] The Commissioner of Indian Affairs obligingly relieved them of 300,000 acres by a treaty negotiated in 1859.[10]

The Indians had "too much land," not only from the point of view of white settlers, but in the opinion of the Commissioner of Indian Affairs and Indian agents. They possessed, in the words of the Commissioner, "large quantities of land which they could not occupy, and were of no use to them, [and] it was impossible to prevent settlements [by whites] being made thereon."[11] Of the streams of immigrants to Kansas there was "a large class of persons having but little regard for the obligations of law, and none whatever for the rights and welfare of the Indians . . . . As many as two hundred and fifty persons had settled within the limits of the Kansas reservation" by 1859.[12]

The policy of the United States government towards Indians in 1859, as expressed by the Bureau of Indian Affairs, was simple: make them live like white men. There was little understanding of Indian culture and meager appreciation of the difficulties involved in bringing about a profound change in a people's way of life. Why *couldn't* the Indians simply give up their roaming, shiftless, pagan mode of life and adopt the example of sedentary agriculture, thrift, and

Christianity held out to them by white settlers? They were expected to settle down on homesteads held individually; private property was to replace communal, or tribal, tenure. And the obligations of kinship and clan membership were to give way to individualism and a monetary economy. Only a wilfull stubbornness, dissolute habits, a wild untamable nature, or downright cussedness could keep the Indians from giving up their old ways and adopting American civilization. So ran the prevailing attitude amongst the whites.

From the Secretary of the Interior and the Commissioner of Indian Affairs down to the lonely Indian agent on an isolated reservation, everyone was firmly of the opinion that the Indians should not be permitted to roam about freely on vast tracts of land; they should be settled on small homesteads held in severalty.[13] The "system of allotting almost boundless reservations to the tribes, which can be of no earthly value to them, tend . . . to induce feelings of utter dependency, and . . . dissoluteness of both habits and life," wrote the agent for the Sac and Fox tribes in his report for 1859. "Let them understand that forty or eighty acres of land is allotted to each to build them up a home upon, to rear their children . . . that gov't is willing to assist them in their struggle to throw off their old shackles of idleness and dependency [*sic*]"; the government would help them build homes, mills,

schools, and furnish them with agricultural implements. The result of all this, he continued, would be that "the industrious would seek reform. The idle and dissolute would be prompted doubly to engage in the work also: first from example; second from necessity. Those who would labor willingly, could not long be induced to support the lazy" (p. 153)—regardless of the obligations of kin and clan!

"Private property in the soil and its products stimulates industry . . ." wrote the Secretary of the Interior in 1860 in that portion of his report dealing with Indians. A few Indians who had settled down to farming were pointed out as examples of industry and thrift that others could follow.

As a consequence of the philosophy of "how to civilize the Red man," tribes were persuaded to cede vast tracts of land to the government. This was done in "their best interests, if not their very existence," according to the commissioner.[14] Between

1853 and 1859, tribes in Kansas and Nebraska had been induced to give up 25.5 million acres of land which were then thrown open to white settlers.[15] And while Commissioner Greenwood was in Kansas in 1859 he "succeeded in negotiating treaties with the Kansas . . . tribe . . . and the Sacs and Foxes" as a consequence of which they ceded 200,000 and 300,000 acres of land, respectively, to the government "to be disposed of for their benefit."[16]

Great pressure was put upon the Indians to surrender their lands: "Scarcely has a tribe alienated the greater portion of its land [as a consequence of allotments in severalty], and begun a settlement upon a smaller portion retained for a new and more permanent home," observed an Indian agent, "when the Indians are again urged to 'sell out' and assailed with all the appliances which those speculators who are unscrupulous enough know so well how to use . . . intimations are sometimes made to

The War Dance of the Winnebagoes by the Swiss artist Peter Rindisbacher, from McKenney and Hall, HISTORY OF THE INDIAN TRIBES OF NORTH AMERICA, volume I. The dancers are warriors and as they dance they pantomime the exciting and dramatic incidents, the heroic deeds of Indian warfare.

chiefs, head men, and interpreters that they shall be well paid for their aid in effecting this object."[17]

But when Indians were settled on homesteads held in severalty they were frequently exposed to deleterious influence from white settlers. Commissioner Greenwood spoke of the "lawless conduct of the whites toward the Indians" in 1859,[18] and the Secretary of the Interior observed that Indians on homesteads "scattered among the white settlements . . . [were] exposed to all the evils resulting from unrestrained intercourse with the whites."[19] As a consequence, he reported, the Indians were "not only making no progress, but are rapidly deteriorating." He therefore recommended that they be removed to Oklahoma Terri-

tory. This would "offer the double advantage of removing the Indians from influences that are surely working for their destruction, and relieving the future State of Kansas from the burden of a large pauper Indian population." And "besides," he added, "it will open to settlement some of the richest and most productive lands in Kansas."[20] It is remarkable to note how frequently the welfare of the Indians was to be served by transferring their rich lands to the whites.

Relations between Indians and whites in the United States in general, and in Kansas and Nebraska in particular, in 1859, were, on the whole, peaceful, according to the Secretary of the Interior. There were occasional outbreaks and depredations, but these

were the work of outlaws and renegades; "in no case has a whole nation avowed the purpose of making open and deliberate war upon our settlements."[21] On the other hand, we have already noted the "lawless conduct of the whites towards the Indians" in Kansas. In 1860, the agent for the Ottawas reported that "many of their horses and ponies . . . [had] been stolen by lawless and unprincipled whites," and that he had been unable either to prevent it or to apprehend the thieves."[22] A heinous massacre of immigrants in Utah in 1859, the "Mountain Meadow Massacre," was widely attributed to Indians at the time, but the Secretary of the Interior reported that his office had "sufficient evidence" that it had been "committed by white men wearing the disguises of Indians."[23]

During the Civil War relations between Indians and whites deteriorated greatly and there was considerable bloodshed. In 1863, a detachment of Confederate troops was wiped out by the Osages in Kansas.[24] In the following year, frontier settlements in Kansas were attacked by Indians; the raids were continued for several months. In the fall of 1864 a Cheyenne chief, Black Kettle, surrendered to Major Wynkoop of the U. S. Army in Colorado, who promised him protection. But a regiment of Colorado state militia surprised Black Kettle and some five hundred men, women, and children asleep in their camp, slaughtered almost all of them, and mutilated their bodies;[25] Black Kettle and a few others escaped.

With the close of the Civil War, more Federal troops became available for the pacification of the Indian tribes, who, in their turn, were being driven to desperation by the invading stream of settlers and by a militia which showed them no mercy. In 1866, the Sioux ambushed and killed Captain W. J. Fetterman and his entire party of eighty-two soldiers in the Big Horn country.[26] In the following year, American troops destroyed an Indian village of 300 lodges on Pawnee Fork. In 1868, Chief Black Kettle and a band of Cheyenne and Arapaho warriors were surprised and defeated by a military force under the command of Colonel Custer; Black Kettle and 103 of his men were killed.[27] And so it went. The dramatic climax of this struggle was reached, perhaps, in June 1876, in the Battle of the Little Big Horn, in which Colonel Custer and his entire force were wiped out. This disaster greatly excited the white Americans and incited them to vengeful retaliation against the Indians. It was this that moved Morgan to cry out in defense of the Red Americans in two articles in *The Nation*: "Hue and Cry Against the Indians" [23, 1876, 40–41] and "Factory System for Indian Reservations" [23, 1876, 58–59].

Slavery, Statehood, and Civil War. The Missouri Compromise of 1820 provided that Missouri be admitted to the Union as a slave state, but that thereafter any state created from territory north of 36° and 30′ should be admitted as a free state. The Kansas-Nebraska Act of 1854, which organized Kansas and Nebraska as territories, nullified the Compromise of 1820, and decreed that the question of slavery *vs.* freedom was to be decided by the settlers themselves. This position was reaffirmed by the Dred Scott decision of 1857, and by a sec-

CITIZENS OF LAWRENCE!

☞ L. Arms, a Deputy U. S. Marshal, has come into your midst for the avowed purpose of NEGRO HUNTING, and is watching your houses, by his piratical minions, night and day, and will enter and search them for victims. KNOW YOUR RIGHTS, and STAND TO THEM. He has no right thus to INVADE your CASTLES. Do we live on the Guinea Coast, or in FREE America?

The Eldridge House is the head-quarters of the gang.—Mark them well.

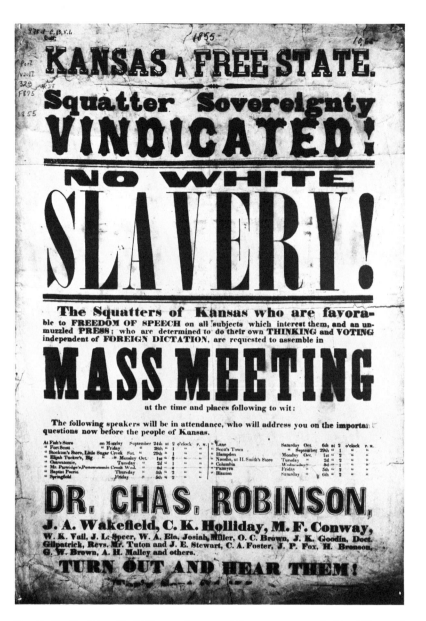

Top Left: On May 19, 1858, proslavery settlers, accompanied by Missouri ruffians, rode into the Free State village of Blooming Grove, Kansas, herded 11 antislavery citizens into a ravine near the Marais des Cygnes River, and opened fire upon them. This act of premeditated murder, called the Marais des Cygnes massacre, is but one example of the violence that ranged throughout "Bloody Kansas," for Kansas Territory was the early major test for both factions in the slavery extension controversy.

Bottom Left: A Free Soil broadside from the storm center of Lawrence, urging all citizens to resist the efforts of a United States marshal attempting to track down fugitive slaves.

Center: Another example of the campaign carried on by the antislavery organization in Congress. Printed in 1855, this broadside announces times, dates, and locations of Free State mass meetings.

Top Right: This call for a state antislavery convention to be held at Big Springs, Kansas, notes, "The pro-slavery party are fully and effectually organized. No jars or minor issues divide them. And to contend against them successfully, we also must be united. Without prudence and harmony of action we are certain to fail."

Bottom Right: John Brown, the fanatic abolitionist, whose murderous activities in Kansas were a prelude to his ill-conceived raid on Harper's Ferry, was a martyr to some, a traitor to others.

ond ruling of the Supreme Court in 1859 which upheld the fugitive slave law.

The Act of 1854 precipitated a struggle between the slavery and the antislavery forces for the possession of the new territories, but especially of Kansas. The New England Emigrant Aid Company was formed in 1854 with the announced determination to send 20,000 Free Soilers to Kansas each year. The proslavery forces countered with "Sons of the South," the "Blue Lodge," and other organizations. In this struggle no holds were barred: stuffing ballot boxes was the least of offenses committed; ambush and murder were the ultimate. "Massacres" were common; outrage and retaliation succeeded each other repeatedly. "Border Ruffians," "Beecher's Bibles" (Sharp's rifles), "bogus legislature," "Black Laws," Quantrill's raids, "Wakarusa War," etc., dot the pages of the history of these times. After the "Potawatomi Massacre," staged by John Brown in 1856, "bands of 'Border Ruffians' or northern bushwhackers roamed the territory, burning, pillaging, and murdering, until the sky over the war-torn region was alight from flaming dwellings. Some $2,-000,000 worth of property and two hundred lives were lost as 'Bleeding Kansas' earned its name."[28]

To be sure, as Billington points out, all of the fraud and violence was not the result of struggle over the slavery issue; some of it, without doubt, was a normal accompaniment of frontier life and settlement. But the burning question of freedom or slavery dominated the scene during the late 1850's.

The struggle for statehood in Kansas was long and bitter, and we shall not even summarize the story here. Constitutions were drawn up and capitols were established.

Eventually, in the summer of 1859, a constitution was drawn up in a convention at Wyandotte;[29] it provided for freedom. It was ratified by the electorate in October, approved by Congress in January 1861, and Kansas was admitted at once as a free state.

It is interesting to note that some distinguished persons visited Kansas in 1859, the year of Morgan's first visit. Horace Greeley went there in May to attend a Republican party convention in Osawatomie. Abraham Lincoln arrived in Kansas in December for speeches at Elwood, Troy, Doniphan, Atchison, and Leavenworth.[30] "Four years later, John Wilkes Booth appeared in Leavenworth in Richard III."[31]

On April 15, 1861, President Lincoln issued a call for 75,000 volunteers. Kansas responded at once with 650 men. Before the war was over Kansas supplied more than 20,000 troops, over 3,000 above her quota. Of the eighteen regiments from Kansas, three were composed of Indians, two of Negroes.[32] Nebraska, with a population of only 30,000 in 1861, provided 3,300 men for the Union armies.

Most of the fighting in Kansas from 1861 to 1865 was of the nature of guerilla warfare, the most notable episode of which, perhaps, was the capture of Lawrence by Quantrill in the summer of 1863, and the slaughter of 150 of its inhabitants. Kansas troops took part in a battle at Wilson's Creek, south of Springfield, Missouri, in August 1861. The Eighth Kansas Volunteer Infantry became a part of the Army of the Cumberland, fought at Chickamauga, and marched with Sherman to the sea. In 1864, a Confederate force under General Sterling Price invaded Kansas, but was soon expelled.

Such was the country that Morgan entered in the late spring of 1859, and again in 1860 and 1862. We find almost no allusion to the Civil War in his journals, but there is much reporting on the local scene—its climate, flora, fauna, and topography. Indian agents, missionaries, emigrants, traders, and settlers, as well as, of course, the Indians—tribes and individuals—are the characters that move about on this half-wild frontier stage. But back of all this, and providing the core of the journals, is the account of how he obtained his data on kinship systems and other aspects of Indian culture.

FAC SIMILIE OF AN INDIAN PAINTING

BY KARL BODMER

This picture of Indian combat is a detail from a buffalo robe painted by Mato-topé. Prince Maximilian acquired the robe and Bodmer copied it. In this scene Mato-topé is fighting a Cheyenne chief. They have both fired, missed, and dropped their guns. Mato-topé has his tomahawk, the Cheyenne a knife. Mato-topé has seized his opponent's naked blade, and although his hand is cut, will pull it from the Cheyenne's grasp and stab him. Note the guns on the ground and the footprints of the combatants. The otter skin on the Cheyenne's head marks him as a distinguished man.

About the Journals

Chapter III

The principal purpose of Morgan's field trips was to gather data on kinship systems, but he sought and recorded much information on other subjects as well: social organization, the office of chieftainship, dances and ceremonies, mortuary customs, and many other topics. In view of the fact that he virtually ignored religion in his published writings (see his comment on this point in *Ancient Society*, pp. 5–6), it is interesting to note how much he concerned himself with this subject in the field.

We find much concern in the journals with the distribution of natural resources in North America and with the mode of subsistence of tribes in various regions. These matters had a direct bearing upon the question of migrations of Indian tribes and the peopling of the New World, a subject of prime concern to Morgan. But they also formed the basis of a theory of cultural interpretation which Morgan, more than any other anthropologist up to that time, developed, namely, a materialist, ecological interpretation of cultures and their development. According to Friedrich Engels, "Morgan had, in a manner, discovered anew the materialistic conception of history, originated by Marx . . ." (Preface to the first edition of *The Origin of the Family*,

Private Property and the State, 1884). We have never found any mention of Karl Marx or of any of his works in Morgan's published works, unpublished manuscripts, or correspondence. But he did not need to read Marx to espouse a materialistic conception of culture and history. Morgan was a naturalist as well as an ethnologist: witness his book, *The American Beaver and His Works*. He studied the Seneca Indians *in situ*. He saw groups of wretched Indians, sunk in poverty, on the banks of the Missouri. He observed the Great Plains, with its vast herds of bison, with his own eyes. He witnessed the great and crucial experiment in the sixties and seventies of trying to persuade the roving, hunting, and fighting tribes of the Plains to settle down and raise corn and hay. The myriad of lakes of Minnesota, teeming with fish, was at once related by Morgan to Indian occupation and cultural development. The materialist conception of history—i.e., an appreciation of the role of habitat, especially the subsistence factor, and of the technological means of exploiting natural resources upon settlement, migration, cultural development, the accumulation of property, customs of inheritance, forms of the family, the origin of the state, etc.—emerged, naturally and

logically, from Morgan's own observations and reflections.

One custom which interested Morgan greatly was that of "sleeping nude." Whenever he visited a tribe, or interrogated an informant, he almost always asked about this. This seems rather quaint and curious to us today because we do not attach any particular significance to it. But Morgan was trying to find ways to demonstrate the Asiatic origin of the American Indian. It occurred to him that three customs—saluting relatives by kinship terms, wearing the breechcloth, and sleeping nude—might yield significant evidence upon this point. Each of these was a "domestic custom," i.e., practiced within the family or kinship group, and as such was passed down from one generation to another. Consequently, if one found two peoples living in widely separated areas that practiced these customs, it might reasonably be inferred that they were descended from a common ancestry. Few anthropologists, if any, today would accept Morgan's reasoning; but a century ago his hypothesis was certainly a reasonable one and deserved to be tested.

In the late 1850's and early 1860's, reliable knowledge about Indian tribes west of the Mississippi was both meager and spotty.

Even the languages spoken by them and the relationships of these languages, one to another, were but little known. J. W. Powell's linguistic classification of North American languages was not worked out until 1891. Consequently we find Morgan making inquiries regarding linguistic affiliations of various tribes—and frequently getting erroneous information or even none at all—and compiling vocabularies (which we have omitted in our transcription).

Morgan noted, and accurately described, the sororate among many of the tribes he visited. He also gathered data on clan organization. He was inclined to believe that clans—or tribes as he then called them—were universal among the North American Indians. Sometimes, when he could find no evidence of clans, he was disposed to conclude that they had lost them as a consequence of an enforced change in mode of life rather than to admit that there were tribes without clans. It is interesting to note that the *Handbook of American Indians* cites Morgan as authority for the presence of clans among about half of the tribes he visited, namely, the Oto, Missouri, Ottawa, Ponca, Potawatomi, Crow, Delaware, Mandan, Miami, Wyandotte, and Chippewa. "Nothing definite was known of the clans of the Hurons until the publication of Morgan's *Ancient Society* in 1877 . . ." says J. N. B. Hewitt in the *Handbook*. And Lowie remarks that Morgan "discovered the matrilineal clan organization of the Crow, an observation once doubted but wholly confirmed by later research."[1]

A subject that interested Morgan very much, and which finds a prominent place in the journals, was the status of the Indian in American society. What fate or destiny awaited him? What was the duty of the American government with regard to him

and how was it being discharged? What was the effect of trader, trapper, and emigrant settler upon the mode of life of the various tribes? And what of the nature and results of missionary influence? These questions Morgan faced and tried to answer repeatedly. The government's agency system was a failure in his opinion, the trader was part thief, and even the missionary was not always above profiting at the Indian's expense. But let the journals tell their own story on these points. Suffice it to say that Morgan tried to carry his message to the American people in three articles in *The Nation*: "Hue and Cry Against the Indians," Vol. 23 (1876); "Factory System for Indian Reservations," *ibid.*; "Indian Question in 1878," Vol. 27 (1878); and in other ways.

Finally, I might mention considerable data on the American beaver in the journals of 1861 and 1862, especially the latter. I have omitted most of this material in order to economize on space. I have likewise omitted, or cut short, some of his descriptions of scenery. But in every instance of omission I have told the reader, in brackets, what has been omitted so that he may have full knowledge of the original journals' contents.

In some instances we have related the journals to modern ethnographic studies or to archeologic research. But for the most part we have left this for the reader with specialized interests. To have annotated the journals fully, ethnologically and archeologically, would have been a task impossible for me to execute to everyone's satisfaction, to say nothing of my own. Let those with specialized interests make such use of Morgan's memoir as they can.

Morgan wrote in his journal when and as he could; on one occasion, as he tells us,

he was sitting on the river bank, writing on his knee, as he waited for a steamboat. In some instances I have not been sure of the accuracy of our transcriptions. When this has occurred, I have put a question mark in brackets—[?]—immediately after the doubtful transcription. When a word has been completely undecipherable, I have indicated this by substituting ellipses—. . .— for the unreadable word, and have added in brackets "word undecipherable." I have inserted words in brackets when I have been sure that Morgan intended them. All other material in brackets has been inserted by me.

There was little uniformity of spelling the names of Indian tribes in 1860; Cheyenne, for example, was spelled Shiyan, Sheyenne, etc. And Morgan himself was not consistent; sometimes he used one spelling, sometimes another. In these instances I have left his orthography unchanged.

I have rearranged his ethnographic data somewhat. That is, I have, in some instances where chronological sequence was not significant, gathered together a number of entries on a given tribe instead of leaving them scattered discretely through many pages.

On the whole, however, the journal is here presented essentially as Morgan wrote it; the changes that I have made are everywhere trivial, and nowhere, I believe, has the meaning been changed in the slightest.

Morgan illustrated his journals, especially those of 1862, with sketches—of costumes, dwellings, graves, topographic features, etc. These sketches were no doubt informative and useful to Morgan, but they were hastily and crudely executed.

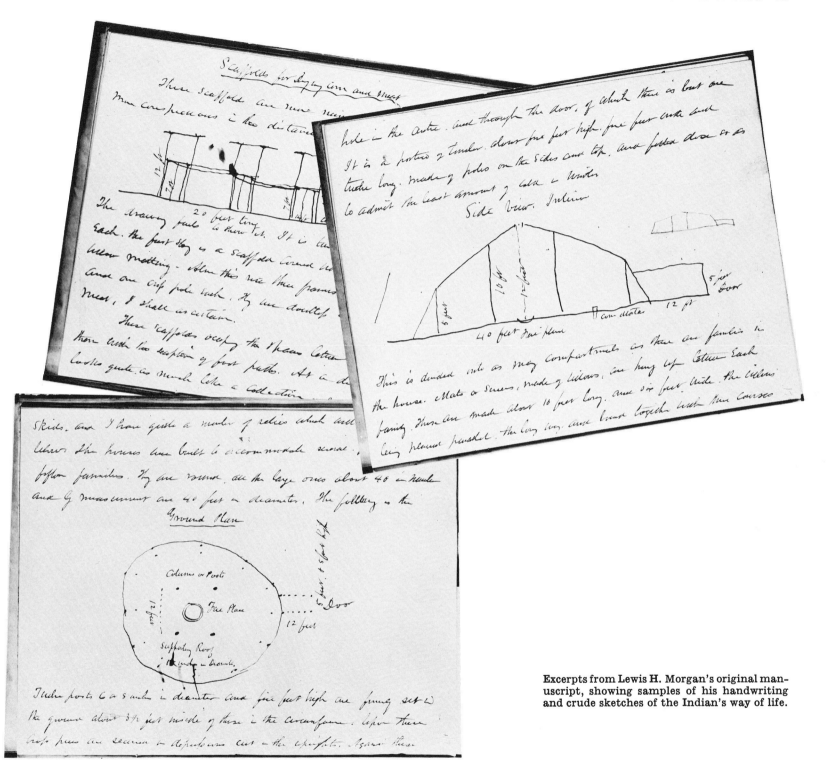

Journal of a Visit to Kansas and Nebraska in May and June, 1859

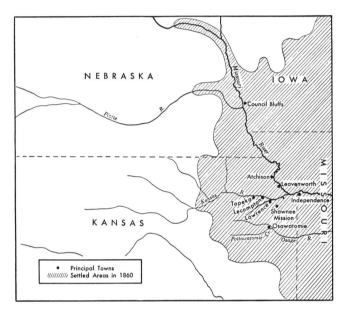

The settlement of Kansas and Nebraska, 1854-60, showing the principal towns and settled areas in 1860.

Chapter IV PART I

Left home Tuesday morning May 18 [it was the 17th], 1859 for Kansas and Nebraska, and came *via* Cleveland, Toledo, Lafayette, Springfield, St. Louis, Jefferson City by Railroad, and from thence to Kansas City on the west side of the River, and on the Missouri side of the boundary line by the ordinary Missouri steamers, and reached this place (Kansas City) at 2 P.M. Tuesday, May 24. The city of St. Louis is not as large a place[1] as I expected to see, but yet it has all the indications of a prosperous place. The Railroad which has taken the name of the "Pacific"[2] shows the agricultural advantages of the State to some advantage. Yet but a small portion of the part the Road passes through is under cultivation.

From Jefferson City, 125 miles from St. Louis, along the Missouri the country for the whole distance is wild and unsettled, as far as this place [Kansas City], with here and there a small village or landing place, and an occasional clearing for a wood station for boats. The river is bordered with noble forest most of the way to Kansas City. The cottonwood tree borders the river along the low bottom lands, but the elm is conspicuous at intervals along the entire route. The river banks are low and the back country on either side seldom rises one hundred feet. Occasionally lime stone rocks rise in naked and massive walls upon one side of the river to the height of one hundred feet in the form of perpendicular cliffs

which assume fantastic forms, and remind one at a glance that in olden times they would have made splendid sites for castles and fortresses if this country had passed through a Norman period.

The river itself is the principal marvel. It is half a mile to a mile in width, until you are quite near Kansas City, 400 miles above St. Louis, where it falls to about one fourth of a mile in its narrowest places, but it varies. The banks are low and of loose sand, which is constantly tumbling in during the period of high water, when the current impinges on the banks. They are therefore constantly shifting by wearing into the bank on one side and then forming a bar or widening on the opposite. The farmer who

St. Louis, Missouri about 1856, from the famous work of Henry Lewis, DAS ILLUS-TRIRTE MISSISSIPPITHAL.

culated for the business of this river where there are no docks but a levee or sloping planed bank so that the loads come up to the landing on an inclined plane, and find it always the same no matter what the level of the water in the river. They can also lay them up to the sand banks of the river to the wood yards which are usually where the channel is near the shore. Our Boat, the *J. D. Perry,*[3] which was as large as any I saw, drew but four and a half feet, as I saw the mark myself. In crossing the river from one side to the other, which was frequently done, soundings were taken as we went and 5½ and 6 feet were often called out and no change made in the course of the boat. At 12 and 13 ft. the lead was taken in, that depth being satisfactory. In low water the stream is much narrower than now. It is now full from bank to bank, but in the dry season is not so and besides the river is full of sand bars which then come above the water. Our rate of speed up the river against the current was about an average of five miles per hour, about one or one and a half miles faster than a boat on the Erie Canal. They run down at great speed, that is about 150 miles per day, laying by at night which the underwriters require.

buys bottom lands has no certainty how long he will keep his farm. A farmer on board told me that he purchased some years ago 300 acres of which 200 were uplands and 100 bottom, at $26 per acre, and that with three years he lost 20 acres of the latter by the shifting of the river banks. The river is bordered with timber only. Above Jefferson City I am told that 15 miles back of the river the forest ceases and prairie begins, and there the farms are principally settled. The water of this river is extremely muddy. Everybody has heard of the turbid Missouri, but no one can form any idea of it without seeing it for miles together and washing his face in it. It is the color which a peck of sand would make a pail of water

take on and about as thick. That is, it holds in suspension just as much as it can carry, and it looks thick as it runs in a swift current down the channel. The current of this river is remarkably swift, they say seven miles per hour, but this is very high. The river is now subsiding from a high flood and the channel is yet full, and the current strong.

The number of boats on the river is very great. We met about three per day on our way up, which would be one for about each 20 miles. They are all alike, of good size and tolerably strong. All open on the lower deck, the cabin being set up on stilts and the wood work of the wheel house alone coming down entire. They are exactly cal-

Kansas City, Missouri, about the way Morgan saw it in 1859. Incorporated nine years earlier the city was still "a picturesque site" to Morgan, although it was even then a major western city.

I asked an Irishman who lived in Missouri how long it took this water to settle. He said he had never heard of its settling, and he thought it never did.

Kansas City is in Missouri, although on the west side of the river, the boundary line between the state and territory of Kansas being along the western margin of the place. Wyandotte 2 miles up is in Kansas and wishes to be a mail place, but I fear [they] will not make it one. This place [Kansas City] claims to have 5000 inhabitants,[4] and Wyandotte 2000. This place is upon a bluff which is broken into ravines, giving to the place quite a picturesque site. They have undertaken the immense labor of removing the bluff by a grade to the water's edge. This involves taking off a bank of sand about 50 feet high at the highest point and having a base line of at least

⅛ of a mile. The streets only are cut through, [there] being many houses high up on the hill and above the streets. It shows the town has some spunk.

The climate of Missouri and Kansas at this season at least is splendid. A bright sky, a soft air, and a glowing vegetation delight the senses and the eyes, but it is growing warm, nearly as warm as our July but without its oppressive character.

The first thing I noticed on landing was a company of Mexicans from Taos and Mora [?] in New Mexico. My first efforts were made to get at them. They claim to be Castillians,[5] that is pure Mexicans as distinguished from the native Indians. This was quite amusing. It is true they have a little Spanish blood which gives them a beard, but they have Indian black hair, high cheek bones and eyes. They speak

Spanish altogether, and have lost their native language. I have ascertained that there are two or three Peons among them, that is what they call pure native Indians who still speak the old Indian language, wear the long hair, etc. They call them Pueblo Indians. They are here with traders after goods, and are loading up their wagon trains preparatory to a start over the plains to New Mexico. I am to see these Peons tomorrow. Not much will come of it, but I shall ask a good many questions, and if I can make an arrangement with them I will stay over and attempt to make out a schedule. They all talk Spanish and I have engaged a Spanish interpreter. In making up their wagon trains they put about 4 to 5000 pounds in each wagon and then cover it with two or three thicknesses of canvas to keep out the rain. To these heavy wagons thus covered they attach several yokes of oxen and make the journey in large trains from ten to fifty wagons in about 2 months. The mail stage goes the same journey in twenty days.

Friday May 27. We left Kansas City May 25 on the little steamer *Colona*[6] for Topeka, 65 miles west of Kansas City by stage and about 80 or 90 by the Kansas or Kaw river. The steamer was new and made slow work of it.[7] We were two entire days in reaching Lawrence, 40 miles west of Kansas City and about 50 or 60 by river, but we lay aside by night. The river is lined with a narrow margin of timber the whole distance but yet is sufficiently dense to prevent us from seeing the prairie. At Lawrence where the bank is cleared, we [?] see the prairie within a hundred rods of the river, but it [is] what is called the rolling prairie, and therefore we could not see far back into the country. The river is about one fourth of a mile wide and is now full of water, said to be six feet above its ordinary summer level. Two or three small steamers drawing when loaded about 2½ feet have just commenced running from Kansas City to Lecompton and occasionally as far as Fort Riley, 120 miles by land. The river is not deep, such soundings as the boat has taken in going from bank to bank in crossing showing 9, 12 and 14 feet. It is believed that these steamers will be able to run through the season, even in July and August when the channel is well known. There is a daily line of stages out from Kansas west as far as Topeka and I believe to Fort Riley.

As to the climate of Kansas, so far it is perfectly delightful, the air pure and cool, the sky bright, and the river banks or the trees upon them a bright green. An elderly clergyman on board who came into the country four years ago and spent four years in it, and who has traveled over the whole territory as far as inhabited, says the climate is a fine one and not hotter than in his native state of Maine, that the prevailing winds on the prairie make it cool in summer, and that there are no fogs, but much clear weather. In the spring and fall the winds he says are tremendous and blow for days together. They are usually from the south, but these south winds, however long they blow, do not bring rain. The rain comes usually with thunder and lightning, like a sudden thunderstorm which passed over us yesterday morning about daybreak, in which we had clap after clap, close by or immediately over us. He says the summers are not oppressively warm, the heat being relieved by the breezes or winds which prevail so constantly.

The great want of the country is wood, one want we can but little appreciate in the east, where the forest is ever near us, and well filled with hard timber. Here the forest is rarer and is principally confined to the margins of the rivers and creeks. The timber also is of poor quality, soft and light. The beach and maple, pine and hemlock are all wanting I believe throughout the state and also throughout Missouri. We saw neither pine nor hemlock on the Missouri, neither have we on the Kansas. The cottonwood borders the rivers, of which there are several species, a large one and a small one readily distinguished. The small grows thick in the low and bottom lands and another kind quite large where the banks are a few feet in height. It is a light and spongy wood used for fire wood by the steam boats but not very good even for that. The elm however is frequently seen along the shore and is by far the most beautiful tree on the Missouri and the Kansas. It does not grow as large as in New York where [it] is often seen when alone in a field to attain a great height and spread, but it is a very graceful and splendid tree whether large or small.

To compensate for the want of wood, there is an abundance of coal throughout the state.[8] It is generally found, that is the seams come out to sight, on the banks of the rivers and creeks. We stopped yesterday and took on some yesterday from a coal seam just opened. It is the variety known as cannel coal, a slaty and poor coal, but yet of great value to the country. Whether most of the coal is of this kind or not I am not able to say.

This is the morning of the third day on the Kansas river and we shall not reach Topeka until night. Notwithstanding our slow motion I am enjoying Kansas decidedly. The weather is so cool, with a bright sunshine and I am so much in the open air that I feel not only the benefit but the pleasure of it.

The clergyman before mentioned has visited all the Indian Missions in the state, and through him I have made my information more special in relation to several of the tribes, and have made out my plan of work or visitation.

Yesterday for the first time I saw a flock of turkey buzzards [*Cathartes aura*] or rather several flocks at different points. They are of a dark brown color, sail in the air precisely like a hawk, and appear to have a body a little larger than a crow with a greater breadth of wing. They are a carrion bird and are of use to any country as scavengers. But they are shy, and after they are hunted they leave the country. We frequently saw them in a flock sitting on the drift wood at the head of the little islands in the river, and also sitting up on the tall trees on the shore. Several were fired at, but without killing any.

Lawrence I did not see well as [we] were there in the night. I went up to the famous Lawrence Hotel, where Sheriff Jones[9] pointed his cannon etc. It is now a spacious and very comfortable looking hotel, but I shall stop at Lawrence on my way down and will then know more about it.

I did not succeed at Kansas City in seeing the Mexican Peons. Those I did see call themselves Mexicans of Castillian origin. They have lost their Indian language and speak the Spanish. But I heard of two Peons who are Pueblo Indians and who speak their native language. They are to be there several days and as I could not find them I hope to see them on my return. I left a schedule with Joseph Traverse, a Mexican, who resides at Kansas City, and is the interpreter of Chick and Co., and another with a New Mexican trader, an American, who is about to go to Santa Fe and who offered to take one along and see if he could work it out for me.[10] Up to the present time I have gained nothing but preparatory information. About next week I hope to begin to see results. My first stopping place will be at the Baptist Mission to the Pottawatomies, five miles beyond Topeka on the river, under the care of Rev. John Jackson. I sent him a schedule which will at least prepare him to aid me, if he has received it.

Along the Kansas River are the Indian Reservations. First we have at the mouth on the north side the Wyandottes, a branch of the Iroquois family. Next west of them are the Delawares, and above them are the Pottawatomies; on the south side are the Shawnees, whose lands extend from Kansas City to near Lawrence. There are short breaks between the reservations between which the white settlers have got in, but the settlers are excluded from nearly the whole of the splendid land along this river. They have continued to lease some of it and to marry Indian wives and get adopted into the tribes and thus some few have gained farms, or the possession at least of valuable land. The whites of course are anxious for the further removal of these Indians, and their wiser men will see the necessity of their removal if they would save them from extermination by the usual process.

I understand the Shawnees have by treaty with the government[11] divided up their lands as to give to each man, woman and child 200 acres of land, to be owned in fee by each but without the power of sale for eight years, after which each may sell. The balance of these lands they have sold to the government for 60 cents per acre. Upon these last lands the settlers have entered. The Delawares have also made a new treaty, by which after reserving a portion of their splendid reserve, they have agreed that the Government may sell the remainder for their benefit at public sale by auction, and that after deducting the expenses of the survey and sale, they are to have the remainder.[12] If the Indians located in this territory manage their property rights well, they will become well off, every individual, from the proceeds of their lands. They have possessed themselves of the finest part of Kansas under the treaties which provided for their removal.

We saw Wyandottes at Wyandotte, Delawares at the Delaware Crossing 10 miles above, Shawnees at the Shawnee Crossing 14 miles above, and at other points along the river. Their principal inquiry as usual is for whiskey, their bane and curse. We saw a Delaware girl about 16 years of age with her face covered about the nose, mouth and eyes with red, fiery red, spots or sores. It looked to me like some eruptic difficulty at the height of its irritation, but I was told to my astonishment by some one that it was *syphilis.* If this is so, then it must have been through her own vices, and not by inheritance. What a monstrous shame that a simple and ignorant Indian child, for she was nothing more although nearly grown, should be so used by any white man! They never doctor themselves and besides know no remedies for this difficulty, I presume, and the result will be a miserable death.

P.M. At Lecompton we went ashore to see the famous place where the proslavery constitution of Kansas was adopted [in 1857]. It is a small place of perhaps 1000 inhabitants situated like Lawrence and To-

The governor's mansion at Lecompton, Kansas, as seen by a HARPER'S WEEKLY artist in 1857. Morgan stopped to see this building two years later.

peka on the south side of the river. The house of the Governor was pointed out to us. It was a long log house one story and a half high, and not as good as many other houses in the place. Here Walker and the several governors of Kansas have resided, and I believe still reside, although it is not yet settled where the Capitol of the state will be located. I saw there an immensely large heron, as it seemed to me. They called it a crane. He was tied to a stake by a man's house and partly tamed. I should think it was the great White Heron, the "Ardea Candidissima" from which the Heron tribe[13] of the Iroquois is named. He was 2½ feet high, or at least two feet, and perfectly white except a little black about the head.[14] This place does not appear as well as Lawrence, although it is well situated. There is a ferry over the river.

Just below Lecompton we came upon a prairie visible from the river. The trees were wanting on the bank, and we had a sight of a splendid prairie. Several thousand acres were in sight, and along the other edge it rose suddenly into a small hill which shut out the view beyond. Near the summit of the hill, a rock of some kind, probably limestone, cropped out, and I am told it is so all over the Kansas prairie. Where they rose up into a hill the stone comes out, and thus they have what is wanting in Illinois, an abundance of stone for building and fencing purposes. We landed and went out on the prairie. The grass, flowers and weeds are mingled together. At this time they are up about a foot. In mid-summer they will be up as high as a man's head. I am told by the old clergyman that he has ridden through Kansas prairies when the grass came up to his shoulders, when on his horse, and he is about 6 feet high.

The soil is a black and rich loam, and yields to the fingers. A single horse would draw a plough through it in the spring with entire ease, and the soil is better today than the richest gardens in the old states. Surely this is wonderful. The new farmer may plough the first year every acre of his prairie and raise a crop. Nor is this all. You can raise two crops a year of many things, and of several alternating things, as two crops of beans, one of onions, and after of turnips. There is also beside the grass prairie, the hazel wood prairie. This is covered all over with this bush, and requires more labor to reduce it. It is usually cut off with a bush hook. It is not a large or troublesome bush, and has one advantage that fruit trees will grow upon it, and upon the timber lands, while it is very difficult indeed to raise them on the grass prairies.

All that has been said of the prairie does not half express the wonder of it. Today I saw on the prairie where we tied up at the bank the spectacle of an emigrant wagon crossing the plains of Kansas. It was on the way from Fort Leavenworth on the Missouri above Kansas City for Lawrence, as we supposed, and came on to the Kansas River

some miles above that place. It consisted of a single covered wagon drawn by five yoke of cattle, and was passing through the prairie at the base of the hill and about a mile distant from us. It was an interesting sight, and could not have been a dreary journey to the emigrant by any manner of means, but one full of promise on reaching this promised land. For agricultural purposes this prairie land is the garden of the world, and the country of the prairie will become the granary of the world.[15] It is a singular comment upon this remark that our principal freight up the river was sacs of flour, of which larger quantities also are carried up to Kansas City by boat from different places down the river. Last year's crops were not up to the wants of the people. It will not soon occur again. The question will soon be what shall they do with the superabundance raised.

I have had my curiosity raised a good deal about the Kaws, now called the Kansas Indians.[16] They are the original inhabitants of the territory, and are called the Kaws and so is the river after them, although named Kansas river on the map. They formerly resided on the river at different points and last on what is now the Pottawatamie reservation a few miles west of Topeka and chiefly on the north side of the river. They are now about 30 miles south of Topeka on their reservation. They have refused up to the present time to have missionaries, and are said to be wild and untamed. Their language is not mentioned by either Gallatin or Schoolcraft so far as I know. I am told they shave their heads except the scalp lock, and are a bold and fearless race. Their number is said to be about 800.

About four miles below Tecumseh on the Kansas river and on the north side, we have just passed one of the most beautiful and

striking prairies I have yet seen. I went up on the top of the pilot house at a place where the river widened out to about a half mile in width. Along the margin of the river for near two miles, the trees were wanting. The river banks were a perpendicular wall of sand or loam about 12 feet high, then a perfect floor level of prairie, as far up and down as you could see and extending back from four to six miles, spread out below us. As a dead level covered with its rich carpet of green, green grass, looking like a field of wheat in its green state, when per-

Three chiefs, members of the Kansas tribe, all dressed up for the photographer. They are, from left to right: Al-le-gu-wa-ho, Kah-he-ga-wa-ti-an-gah (Fool Chief), and with his eyes closed, Wah-ti-an-gan. Morgan was particularly interested in the Kansas tribe.

fectly uniform and well filled out and green, it was truly a wonderful spectacle. Then it broke up gently into a hill about 50 feet high, which is as high as these hills ever rise, and you lost sight of it in the distance, leaving a clear line as its crest or summit level.

On the opposite or south side of the river, there was a hazelwood prairie along the margin, and then a rising into hills with here and there the deep green of the grass prairie. On the north side there were clumps of trees in a few places, indicating wet spots, and along the horizon here and there a fringe of trees indicating a creek or water. In addition to these attractions of nature in her attire of centuries, we had the beautiful water spectacle of the Kansas under the light of the declining sun. All these features united in a landscape such as I have never before looked upon, as it now seems to me. The strangest thing of all is that instead of a new country and a soil never disturbed by man, you seem to be in the midst of an old and highly cultivated country, with the meadows in their richest green, or the wheat and barley fields in their growing freshness. You only miss the fences and the farm houses. The Illinois prairie did not make anything like such an impression upon me as do these along the Kansas river.

We are now near Tecumseh which is five miles below Topeka, and we shall reach the latter place about ten tonight, when the trip of the boat and my trip westward ends except five miles or so on to Mr. Jackson's Baptist Mission to the Pottawatamies. We have been three days on the river. There were quite a number of passengers aboard and some of them intelligent. Our progress has been extremely slow, but the whole trip has been greatly to my gratification. On the way up we have seen the Turtle Doves in

pairs as usual, the Turkey Buzzards, the Whippoorwill or Night Hawk, I could not tell which, the bat, the wild goose, the wild duck, the woodpecker, the pigeon, the crow, the blue Jay, the King fisher, the quail and some small birds. There were but a few of each kind, but quite a variety. On the Missouri I was struck with the scarcity of the birds, and the same on the Kansas. The reason is that the forest and prairie birds are different and there is but a narrow belt of forest along the Missouri above Jefferson City and along the Kansas. I saw also today for the first time a prairie wolf. He was about half grown, quite bright and good looking and about [?] as large as a medium sized cat but shorter. He was caught by a boy on the prairie and partly tamed, and he had him in his arms on a horse at a landing where we stopped.

Sunday May 30 [29]. We reached Topeka yesterday morning early. It is a mere cluster of houses[17] but they are well built of brick and stone. The village is laid out on a large scale, and the houses are far apart, but the site is a beautiful one. It is back a number of rods from the river on rising ground, and in the midst of a fine prairie. We can see evidences of greater dryness here. It is seen in the less growth of grass and less greenness. The increase of dryness becomes more and more as you advance west. In time it may become quite a place, but I should prefer to live lower down the river.

I came on to the Baptist Mission[18] about 9 in the morning where I now am with Mr. Jackson and his numerous family of Indian boys and girls. The first thing was to find a conveyance, and not being able to do that, the next was to get my bag carried. While debating this matter with Mr. Chase in front of his hotel, a singular looking estab-

lishment passed on the road in front of us which Chase said was for Pike's Peak. He halted them and they consented to put my bag on their wagon and I joined them. The whole concern was a curiosity and it is worth describing. They were two young men, one about 22 and the other about 25, full size, well built and intelligent looking. The wagon was a pair of old wheels with a good axle, hubs and tyre, but cracked and broken spokes. The thills[19] were two ash poles, looking weak and rickety enough, and upon it they had about five hundred pounds of provisions, enough they said to last them to the Peak and a month after they reached there. The horse was a pony, and the harness aside from a saddle and collar and hames a mere mass [of] strings and straps. They had their tent over the top of the goods, and thus accoutered these young men were about to cross the prairies.

I was astonished, and my inquiries continued to astonish me more and more until I left them. I found one was from Maine and had been in Iowa for 12 years, having been taken there as a child. His complexion was nut brown, but he had a splendid chest where his shirt opened, and a skin as white as snow. He was near six feet high with good features, a pleasant address, a great hearted boy I know. The other was from Connecticut and had been in the west about five years. They were both inhabitants of southern Kansas at the time they started for the Peak. They told me they had materials to make a harness a day in case of accident, and that their two wheeled concern had a great advantage over the heavy ox team in crossing the bad places. Between the rolls of the prairie there are of course hollows, and in them water is usually standing. A man can step across, but the wheels go down into the mud and some-

"Bust," by the prolific and once very popular W. M. Cary, portrays graphically the tragedy which overtook a would-be gold prospector — and which may well have been the fate of the emigrants Morgan met on May 29th.

Tuesday morning, May 31. Mission House, Pottawatamies.

Since I came here I have been very busy, and quite successful. I have worked out my schedule in the Kaw or Kansas language and also in the Pottawatamie, and expect to leave this evening for Topeka, and from there tomorrow morning for Lawrence. Yesterday it was very hot, about like the last of June with us, and there was but little air stirring. I walked about 17 miles during the day, in the morning to see Joseph James [Jo-Jim], the half breed Kaw, and in the afternoon to see J. N. Buraseau, a half breed Pottawatamie. This one last named was educated at Madison University and afterwards studied law in New York somewhere and then taught school at Whiteston [?] near Utica. He is a fine looking man with a mustache and hair cut close. He has written a "History of the Pottawatamie Customs, Manners and Usages of His Nation," and he thinks it will be published this present summer. I have no doubt from the character of the man and from his education that it will be valuable.

times mire. In crossing one of these the Indian pony gave a sudden start, and tore off his harness in a moment. We pulled out the wheels, and in five minutes the harness was repaired, and we were again on our way.

I walked with them five miles to the Mission where I left them. Before leaving we sat down under a tree and I showed them my government map of Kansas and Nebraska, showing upon it the route of Freemont and Gunnison [?] who went on their route almost direct to the Peak, and I cut out the part which showed their route from Fort Riley to the Peak, and gave it to them for their guidance, which they received very thankfully. In travelling one leads the horse and then the other by turns. They make 20 to 25 miles per day and spreading their tent over the wagon at night, they sleep under it. They had two rifles and a musket, and one of them had a rifle constantly in hand. They expected to shoot a prairie chicken each day for dinner. They seemed happy and perfectly self reliant, and spoke to each other very affectionately. They were both unmarried.

I saw some other emigrant wagons on the road during the day. Each wagon was drawn by five or six yoke of oxen and the emigrants rode instead of walked.

I found yesterday that there was a half-breed Kaw, Jo-Jim,[20] who lived about two miles from here, and on going there learned that he was at Topeka for the day, but what was more important to me, that there was a full-blooded Kaw man and his two Kaw women encamped by his house. I hope to get from them the geography of Kansas, and also their system of relationship, but I must take it down in another book, as this is to go in the mail when completed.[21]

Mr. Jackson appears to be a pleasant and kind man and gave me a cordial reception. He is a missionary.

Joseph N. Buraseau (Bouressa), the Pottawatamie from whom Morgan obtained the Pottawatamie kinship data.

Prairie Roads

The main roads over the prairies, although never worked, are about as fine roads as were ever seen, except the crossings of the hollows where there is usually mud and water. These are so slight that a foot passenger can step over easily, but the wagons and horses and cattle sink down. The grass is kept down and the road is hard and without ruts, so easy is it to turn one side if the road breaks up in any place. After being tread down by wagons and teams it becomes very hard and smooth. You would not wish to see better roads with the exceptions above mentioned.

I have [seen] quite a number of the emigrants pass the main road by the Mission since I came here. It is quite a spectacle. They walk of course, as they all have ox teams, but the men ride and the women when they drive except the teamsters. Yesterday I fell in with the largest one I have yet seen. There were six large wagons with white canvas tops each drawn by from four to six yokes of oxen, and they had with them 850 head of cattle they are taking with them to California. I came through them in the morning on returning from Jo-Jim, and we passed them again in the afternoon in going to Buraseau, and at night on our return found them encamped. It was on the whole a fine sight. These cattle were traveling through vast meadows from day [to day] covered with the finest grass they had ever tasted in their lives, and were feeding as they went and growing fat every hour. These wagons went ahead and the herd followed on within a distance of half or three fourths of a mile, followed and watched on each side by drivers. There is however but little difficulty in keeping them together. They find plenty of water in the little creeks they cross, and in the hollows between the hills. I presume the big want of the herd was the privilege of lying down and resting a few days in the midst of the abundance before and around them. At night the emigrants pitch tents around their wagons, shoot some game and cook their suppers and enjoy it right well after marching in this way about fifteen miles per day. As there are no farms, no houses, and but little strips of timber here and there along the creeks and streams and low places, you can see them for a great distance as [they] travel over the hills on their western way.

You have a feeling of home on the prairie, as the fresh green grass pleases the eye and carries with it the idea of plenty. These vast prairies of whom no one can form any idea who has not seen them with his own eyes are the wonder of the continent. They would raise and fat every year cattle enough to feed the whole human race. It is about as if you should collect all the meadow land and wheat fields in the United States when they are most fresh and green and put them into one vast field, without a house or a fence, breaking up into low hills here and there so as to allow you [to see] for miles in every direction as far as the eye can reach. You would then have some idea of a Kansas prairie, which is of the kind called the rolling prairie. In Illinois the prairie is flat with but little roll and you are therefore soon bounded in your view. You cannot on a flat prairie get one tenth part of the range for the eye you can on the rolling prairie. You can see land enough on one of the hills for half a state.

As I have said before, Kansas instead of wearing the appearance of a new state, has every appearance of an old one. It looks older and more finished by the hand of man than any part of our state of New York. It looks just as though you had taken an old country like England[22] and stripped off its fences, hedges, houses and timbered [?] lands and then abandoned it to grow up luxuriantly in grass in every direction. The roads wind considerably of course and the best crossings are rough but their main direction is accurate. This is one of the great California roads. They cross the Kansas river a little way above this, and leaving Fort Riley to the left, go up the Republican bank of the Kansas river. This I believe is not the principal California trail. The one from Fort Leavenworth up Platte river is more travelled and also the Santa Fe road south of this is considered the safest of all. A journey over the prairie looks inviting from this point.

Indian Trails

All over the prairie we came upon Indian trails. They are usually horse trails which consist of two, three, four and sometimes five parallel paths deeply worn in the ground. Three paths are the most usual number. All of the prairie Indians raise horses and those who do not raise them steal them, so that about every Indian man and woman has a horse, an Indian pony. They ride the prairies a great deal and hence these trails. In crossing from point to point you frequently leave the main road and strike across. I met one morning a few Indians riding at full speed[23] along one of these trails with red streamers flying from their heads and they made quite a splendid appearance in the distance. They are frequently out in troops, and when off on an expedition muster in large numbers. The Pawnees come down occasionally to steal horses. Not long since the Pottawatamies lost some horses in this way. They gave chase, overtook and captured two of them and regained their horses. The Pawnees called themselves Kaws to escape. The Pottawatamies sent for some Kaws to speak with them, whereupon it appeared that it was but an artifice. They were then struck on the head, and I saw the scalp of one of them hanging up in the house of the educated half breed, Buraseau. He told me the circumstance with great apparent relish.

The Baptist Mission

The Pottawatamies have a splendid reservation about 30 miles square lying on both sides of the Kansas and they number about 2800 in all. There are two Missions here, one a Catholic Manual Labor School called St. Mary's Mission[24] about 12 miles up on the north side of the river, and the Mission of the Southern Baptists where I am staying. They are both manual labor schools. The children are brought to the mission, fed, clothed and schooled at the expense of the Missions under a contract with the government by which they secure about $75 per head for each one taught during the year. The Mission house is a stone building near 80 feet long with a basement for a kitchen, dining room and store room, a first story for a school room and family rooms for the Mission, and a third story for sleeping rooms. The whole number of children here of all ages, from 4 years to 20, is about 50 but these numbers change from time to time, as some are taken away, and others sent here in their place.

Mr. Jackson, a very sensible and good man, is the head of the establishment, and carries on the farming education of the boys as his particular department. He has a teacher who superintends the school house duties of the children. They teach reading, writing, arithmetic and geography. The children are comfortably clad and fed and appear to be happy and contented. I saw them play at marbles on Saturday, several of them, and they showed themselves thorough professionals. The farm of the Mission contains about 200 acres of which they plough about 100 and the Indian boys assist in its cultivation.[25] Mr. Jackson has several children of whom one, a daughter, was married here on Sunday in the presence of the whole establishment, and it was to the children no doubt quite a spectacle.

Yesterday it was warm with no breeze. Today it is cool with a fine breeze. This morning I am to have some further conversation with the Pottawatamies, preparatory to leaving. I must finish here today. My Indian information of the Kaws is entered in number two, as this is more in the character of a journal which is to go today to Mrs. M[organ] in the place of a long letter. I will perhaps go finish it up at Topeka.

Indian Fashion of Drinking Whiskey

When I sat down with Jo-Jim and the Kaw chief, they had just commenced upon a bottle of whiskey holding near a quart. As we talked they drank. About every five minutes one of them took a wine glass, poured it full, and handed it to the other and then took the same amount itself. This they continued until the bottle was empty. I was sitting at the table asking questions and writing out my schedule, the Indian geography of Nebraska and Kansas, etc. Presently the first bottle was empty, and I hoped that would be the end of it. But lo, as Mrs. Arink[26] would say, the Kaw produced a flask and poured out into a square bottle about one ½ quart more, possibly two, and at it they fell. This was continued for some hours until I expected any moment they would become overthrown, but they stood up under it bravely, and when I left them the bottle was about half finished. I learned afterwards they stuck to it until it was done to the last drop. And the chief started in the evening for his camp, lost his way, fell off his horse, and sometime in the night found his way back to the house of Jo-Jim who found him in the morning outside just emerging from his drunkenness after laying out all night in a hard rain which poured through the most of the night.

To my remonstrance against their drinking[27] and attempt to show them that if they drank moderately they would enjoy it more, the chief asked me through the interpreter why the white men made it if it was bad for them to drink it. I told him we could not prevent their making it, but we considered all the makers to be common loafers and had but little to do with them; that we had passed a prohibition law in our state[28] and were trying to get rid of all ardent spirits. I then told him he was not obliged to drink it because the white man made it. He replied that he should drink it as long as he lived. It was fearful to see the power of their appetites.[29] A wine glass full to each one in five minutes for two hours was about the allowance. I tasted a part of a glass and felt it immediately. They always took down the glass at a single swallow and poured it brimming full. It opened their hearts and tongues and I got with readiness and ease what at another time it would be hard to draw out of a Kaw Indian. They are a wild and untamed race.

Tuesday P.M. I came down to Topeka this afternoon and leave tonight for Lawrence. Tonight is [Pundit] Club night and I shall be far away, but I think I can find an equivalent.

PART II

Early Home of "The Kaws"

With Jo-Jim, a half breed Kaw as my interpreter, I had a day's conversation with a Kaw chief and his wife who was occasionally called in, and with another Kaw who stayed for a time. After working out the system of relationship, we went into other matters. They say they were anciently located at the mouth of the Missouri river[30] and had a town on the north side at the mouth called Ne-bla-zha-ta-ma, or Blue Water,[31] to mark the fact of the clear water of the Mississippi as compared with the Missouri. They also called the Missouri Ne-sho-ja, the muddy river, which I think is the radix of the word Missouri. As the whites advanced upon them they retired up the river and up the Kansas [To-pe-ka] until their home country lay between the Platte river [Ne-blas-ka] Flat River, where they dwelt at the time the Government commenced the removal of the Indians. They are now located around Council Grove south of Topeka upon a reservation assigned to them by the Government.[32] They number 6 or 800.

They are said to be a tall, well formed, wild and fearless race. Those I saw were characteristic Indians. One was a tall, powerful man over six feet with a large mouth, wide set eyes, high nose, knotty forehead, and very dark skin. The other who was a chief, had small eyes, a dark skin, but he was thin and not marked by a high degree of intelligence. I liked him, however, better

and better the more I saw him. His wife was very dark and wild in her look. Her eye glittered but she would not look me in the face beyond a glance. The son of the tall one was a splendid specimen of the wild Indian. He was tall already at 16, with regular features, a bright keen look, and a very dark skin. His hair was shaved pretty close except the scalp lock which was long and braided. This is the Kaw fashion with the hair and is mentioned as an evidence that they are original and untamed Indians. They are the original inhabitants of the territory so far as we know, and have given to the rivers and streams their names. Hence we must look to their language for the geographical names of the territory. Their language, I think, shows them to be Dakota or Sioux.[33] They go west in the spring into the Buffalo country for the hunt which is about three or four days' journey west from this place. It would be a good plan to join them but for the fact that they are at enmity with the Pawnees and some other Indians, who are often in the same region for the hunt, and they fight when they meet. A white man found with them shares the same fate with themselves. Therefore the whites would do better to make a party of their own.[34]

"War Dance in the Interior of a Kansas Lodge," by Samuel Seymour, was sketched on August 24, 1819 near the present Manhattan, Kansas. It first appeared in Edwin James's, ACCOUNT OF AN EXPEDITION . . . 1823, and may be the first sketch to be made in Kansas.

The system of relationship and the vocabulary were taken down principally through Joseph James, Gí-he-ga-zhin-ga, Little Chief. He is half French and half Kaw, and bright and intelligent. He speaks the Kaw which is his mother tongue, so that I feel entire reliance on what I have obtained. He is married to a Pottawatamie woman, and lives in a good log house on the bank of the beautiful Kansas river. He has a second house in which the cooking and eating is done. I took dinner with them and it was very good.

[*Kaw Clans*]

The children [among the Kaws] are of the tribe [clan] of the father, both boys and girls. A man is not allowed to marry a woman of his own tribe. The Koon [i.e., Racoon] and Deer[35] Tribes marry with themselves, and no other tribes but these two. They are not allowed to intermarry inside of second cousins under our system. They are very careful about this. The chiefs have no power to control this question by punishments but custom regulates it. They are clear and sure that the children follow the tribe of the father, and that all inheritance is in the male line. They buy their wives, but the marriage is arranged and agreed upon by the parents without the knowledge of the parties. They make it a regular surprise, and quite an event. Presents are made to the family of the girl. The man who marries the oldest sister is entitled to all her sisters for wives as fast as they grow up [the custom of sororate, widespread among primitive peoples].

Change of Names

The names of each tribe [clan] are kept distinct, and their [personal] names, as with the Iroquois, are often changed. The first name is used through childhood. When

Dances of the Kaws or Kansas Indians

War Dance	Wä-se′-se-ga-Wä-che′	The last war Dance, Sioux dance
Black "	Wä-shä′-ba-Wä-che	They black themselves All men
Flute "	Mo-so′-ja-Wä-che	Music of flutes " "
Passing "	E-lose′-kä-Wä-che	" "
Buffalo "	Ja-po′-lo-Wa-che	" "
W— king "	Ja′-la-Wa-che	Men & women
False Face "	Ja-po′-lä-ga	Men alone
Thanksgiving "	Wä′-ja-wä-che	Women alone
Medicine "	Ma′-kä-Wa-che	" "
Dance for Dead	Wä-Wä-che	Men alone
Scalp Dance	Ne-she′-hä-i-e-Wä-che	Women alone
Kiowa "	Kä-a-wä′-ne-dä-Wä-che	All men. Kiowas (name of)
Brave Dance	Wä-sho′-sha-Wä-che	Danced by man after putting his [?] [?] young.
Track Finding "	Se-la-E′-a-Wä-che	
Hide Dance	No-ho-lo′-ha-ä-Wä-che	All men
Charging "	Tone-ä-uk′-kä-yä-Un-gä-yat-je The first [?] Weas charge or assault and the second [?] town or village. All men	
Private or Family Dance Wa-che′-wa-ke		All women

old enough to go out to war, his name is taken away and a new one given. It is usually done when out with a war party, and done, at the request of the young man, by the war captain. Jo-Jim says his name has not yet been changed and he is thirty years old. He however has no tribe as his father was a Frenchman.

The Kaws have five chiefs in all, one of whom is called the Principal Chief. The office descends from father to son, and this is confined to the tribe or family.

The Pot-a-wat-ta-mies

I have made a failure with the Pottawatamies for want of an interpreter.[36] J. N. Buraseau half breed is a splendid interpreter, as he was educated at Hamilton College[37] and taught school. He is six miles away from the Mission. I saw him yesterday, and made out the schedule. But as I ascertained he had a book in manuscript ready for the press on the "Customs of the Pottawatamies,"[38] and found him averse to giving me much special information, I did not press him but returned [to] the Mission the same night, although I intended to spend the night with him. We went through [the] schedule quickly, and I was so unfortunate as to give him some offence by limiting [?] him on the schedule. He gave it up but I could see [he] was annoyed.

The Pottawatamies are divided into tribes [clans] the same as the Chippeways and have the same law of marriage. The children are of the tribe of the father and the son succeeds the father in the office of chief. I obtained the names of the following tribes which they say are all they have but it cannot be true.[39]

1. Na-neme-wa, Prairie Wolf
2. Emg-wa, Black Wolf
3. Ah-ah-weh, Duck
4. Make, Loon
5. Me-she-ga, Little Turtle
6. Bukh-ke-nok, Great Turtle
7. Sake-se, Deer
8. Ka-gose, Fish
9. Cotch-p, shick-ha, Buffalo

The Pottawatamies number about 2800 and have a grand reservation about 30 miles square. I went up to see an old chief this morning. He moved here from Sugar Creek, Michigan, and said to me through my boy interpreter who could not interpret much, that he preferred Michigan, that he had kindred there still and if he had money enough he would go back and buy him a farm. He was a chief about 60 years old and very fine looking. His wife also referred to her Michigan home, and another to her home on the Wabash in Indiana, which she much preferred to Kansas.

It is painful to hear them express these longings for their ancient homes. They miss the deer and the squirrels and the pigeons of Michigan. They also prefer the forest to the prairie. As they are so far west on the Kansas river, the emigration has not yet reached and surrounded them. This is the westernmost reservation. I hope before the tide rolls upon them they will have become sufficiently advanced in farming to protect and defend themselves. It is of course utterly impossible to preserve the Indian any-

where in his wild and thriftless state. He must become a farmer and make money and throw off the Indian in part. Those alone who do this will be able to save themselves and ultimately will be absorbed in our race. The untamed Indian who refuses to settle and civilize to the extent of becoming tolerable farmers must pass away. It is perfectly clear and certain. They have a great many good and respectable men among them who are anxious to save themselves and become farmers, and I have seen quite a number of such busy at work. They cultivate but a few acres each, and do not seem to look beyond a bare subsistence and the possession of a horse, wagon and house.

I am not at all well today from the overwork of yesterday, or I should attempt to increase my stock of information. My principal effort here has been with the wild Kaws[40] and with them I met with good success. The Ottawas are closely allied with the Pottawatamies and what is true of one is true of the other.[41] I shall endeavor to make it up there.

The Pottawatamies are a good deal scattered as a people. There are almost 2800 here. These formerly were apart; one portion was located on Sugar Creek in South Kansas [Michigan was intended] and the other at [Morgan left a blank space here] in Kansas at the time they were brought together on the present reserve. They were removed into the Indian territory from Michigan and Indiana in 1836. A portion still remains in Indiana and another portion on Lake Huron in Canada, and I think there are some in lower Michigan with the Chippeways. I had a conversation with an old chief about 70 years old, still erect, strong and noble looking. He said he wanted a claim that he might leave it to his children.

He said also that if he had the money he would go back to Michigan and buy him a farm.

[Morgan inserts about six pages of Potawatomi vocabulary at this point.]

On my way to Topeka with a young Indian to carry my bag, we sat down in the timber about a mile from the village to rest and then made the vocabulary. It was made in haste and without as much care as the work deserves. The dialect is far inferior in polish and finish to the Ojibway but very decidedly the same language.

Buffalo Dried Meat

I forgot to mention that I saw a braid of Buffalo meat dried as put up by the Indians. It was cut into strips about two to three feet long and as large as your finger and then braided and dried in the sun. These braids were cooked in some way or pleated into a square sort of an open card of meat about two feet square. I tasted a twist and found it very palatable. They bring home from the hunt which they make both spring and fall considerable quantities of meat in this form. At the time I went to the reservation a small party had but just gone to the west for the hunt. Near Fort Riley and about four days' journey from the reservation they find the Buffalo.

The word Pottawatamie means, according to C. C. Brown of Osawattamie, "Fire Makers."[42] Nau-ka-ni-sie "Women in the Water."

Santa Fe Road

Wednesday evening, June 1, 1859
Left Topeka last night at 11 and rode all night reaching Lawrence at 6½ this morning. It was the only stage each day. This morning we came on the Osawattamie stage 22½ miles to the Ottawa reservation and to

PE-CHE-CO, A POTTAWATTOMIE CHIEF

BY JAMES OTTO LEWIS

This old man was painted by Lewis at Mississinewa in 1827. Like most of his work, the original no longer exists. Pe-che-co is a good example of Lewis' caricature-like style—note the very large nose and the unusual character of the eyes.

INTERIOR OF A SIOUX LODGE

BY JAMES OTTO LEWIS

This illustration, which appears as Plate 73 in Part 10 of the *Aboriginal Portfolio* is really the work of Peter Rindisbacher, a Swiss artist about whom little is known. Presumably executed in 1824, this water color may be, as De Voto has pointed out, the "first actual illustration of a Plains tipi—and yet it looks like no tipi known to ethnology."

this house of the well known Ottawa Jones, a half breed French[43] and Ottawa. In coming we crossed the celebrated Santa Fe Road going from Kansas City to Santa Fe, formerly starting from Independence in Missouri. The Road is about 750 miles from point to point and beyond doubt the finest natural road in the world. It is on the divide between the waters which flow to the Missouri and its tributaries and those which [flow] in the opposite direction. For about four rods not a spear of grass scarcely grows in the road. There are but few or occasional ruts and it is tramped down hard by the feet of thousands of cattle who are constantly travelling upon it to New Mexico and California. We went about a mile upon it and could count along the line of the road in sight perhaps thirty emigrant wagons including six or eight Pike's Peak emigrants on their return.

We did not go far enough on the road to be able to judge it. Of course it is never worked. These roads from the hollows are not easy to travel in a stage. This, however, is far in advance of ordinary prairie roads. Although we hear a great deal about the western emigration we can form but a small idea of the extent of it without being in the country and seeing with our own eyes the number of vehicles and men and cattle who are traversing the country in all directions. Most of the government land is already entered and Mr. Jones informs me that within five years there will not be an acre of government land in the state. The Indians on the Ottawa reservation ask the Government $7.00 per acre for a portion of their land which the Government wished to purchase for the Munsees of Fort Leavenworth. The Government resented the idea of paying such a price for land, and charged them

with a desire to speculate out of the poor Munsees. Which is rather amusing when the land is worth the money and will bring it, and the government has a plenty of land of its own at government prices, which is all they offered the Ottawas.

The Ottawas[44]

This band now numbers about 200 and their reservation is located on the Ottawa Creek, Kansas Territory, south of Lawrence 22½ miles. They were removed in 1836 from Ohio to this reservation. They were originally inhabitants of Canada, on the Ottawa river, I presume, and got from there among [?] our Indians and on the other side of the lake. They have no school, but they have one missionary, Rev. Mr. Willard.[45] Both of their chiefs are members of the church. They have but two chiefs, one of them hereditary and the other elected every two years. When the other dies, they will elect his successor in the same way for two years.

The Ottawas are far advanced, and are now anxious for a school,[46] and to divide up their lands and own them as we do. They have made a treaty to that effect, which the government has refused to accept. That is, the Indians have agreed among themselves, but the Secretary of the Interior has refused his concurrence. They have had their land surveyed and agreed to make a division among themselves without the aid of [the] government. They have about

This photograph was taken in a small Sioux village on a Dakota Sioux reservation before the turn of the century. Dried buffalo meat was a staple in the Plains Indian diet, particularly in the winter months. Smoking and drying were the basic Indian preservation methods.

enough to give them each 200 acres of land, which would secure to a man with a wife and five children 1200 acres of land. Their desire to divide their lands, and the assurance they feel that they can do so and keep their farms,[47] is quite encouraging. I confess I am yet afraid of it, but it may be they could bear it. It must come to that with every Indian nation [tribe], or they must be exterminated. When they can become farmers and each own and sell his own farm, then the stimulus to exertion which they so much need will be applied, and it may make good farmers of a share of them, and thus save a portion. They must also change their government and have a council, and allow no man to sell his land to a white or an Indian without the consent of the Council, which shall be properly inserted in the conveyance.

I believe the time is near at hand when a great effort should and will be made at the call of the Indians themselves to reverse the policy of the government towards them, and to devise some plan for their relief. The Indians are now calling for it themselves, as their best men see distinctly their future extermination unless some remedy is found. They are even discussing the question of a consolidation of all the remnants of tribes as well as the great tribes into one, with a common country and a new form of government. Whether it is feasible one cannot say, but it does not seem to me to [be] possible. A convention of the most sensible men of the several nations has been proposed, and within a year or two we may witness such a convention. Great results would flow from it. Our people would be astonished at the amount of ability and experience and wisdom these nations, broken and scattered as they are, could assemble. They have many intelligent, solid and good men, who would

John Tecumseh (Ottawa) Jones, the famous half-breed Pottawatamie Indian, from whom Morgan obtained the Ottawa Indian kinship system. He was an Ottawa by adoption, an advocate of the Free Soil philosophy by inclination, and a fruitful source of information for Morgan.

not disgrace any public body in the country. They also know the conditions and wants of the Indians, and could give to our people a mass of information in relation to the condition and future prospects, which we at present have no idea of.[48]

[Ottawa Jones]

In riding about four miles this morning to see an Ottawa man and woman in relation to their relationship, etc., Mr. Jones gave me an account of himself. He is a Chippeway[49] by birth—his mother being a full blood—by an English officer. At ten he ran away and went to Detroit and spent five years in the family of an Irish Catholic. Then upon the death of the captain and the marriage of his daughter, he ran away again and went about three miles to a brick yard and went to work for one summer. Then he was invited to go to St. Jo on Lake Michigan, and become a member of the Mission to the Pottawatamies, the establishment of the Baptists called the McKay Mission. He

thus commenced his education and after staying there about two years he, with about nine others including Joseph N. Buraseau, was taken to Hamilton and educated at the Baptist University at Madison.[50] He came west and settled in Southern Kansas with the Pottawatamies on Pottawatamie Creek. He had previously married a Stockbridge Indian woman. On the sale of this reservation, or its exchange for their present one on the Kansas river, he was, through the contrivance of Buraseau and the Catholic priests, cheated out of his improvements, about $1000, and in consequence of this he refused to live with them any longer. The Ottawas invited him to become one of their number and live with them and offered to adopt him and his present wife, an English woman,[51] which was done and he has since lived with them. Buraseau has left the Baptists and become a Catholic.

The free state men made Jones' house their place of resort during the troubles as he kept a hotel. This drew on him the vengeance of the border ruffians and they burned down his house and its contents, took from the person of his wife $800 in money and shot at Jones as he fled from the house.[52] They intended to kill him, but he escaped. His loss as he estimated it by items amounted to $18,000. This the government is bound by law to pay, but they have not yet done it, and continue to put him off. He had a large and fine house. He has commenced a new house on a large scale to cost $7,000. The cellar walls are up, but he has stopped for want of funds. Jones is a Baptist, a member of the church, a gentleman in manner, fine looking, about 60 years old.

[Black Walnut]

The black walnut is the principal timber in Kansas. You see log houses made of black walnut logs, the floors of black walnut, the joice [sic] and shingles and rafters are of the same. The walnut grows along the creeks with the other timber, is the best of all that grows, but it is not very abundant. The amount of timber is small, and it will soon disappear entirely before the large consumption of the inhabitants. They are now thinking of planting locust groves or forests for timber for fire wood.

Tribes [Clans] of the Ottawas

The Ottawas have lost their tribes,[53] except they call themselves after places they have occupied. They call themselves [?] Wolf's Rapids and Blanchard's Forks Ottawas. A part of them lived on Wolf's rapids, a branch of the Maumee River in Ohio, and the other Blanchard's Forks from a fork of the Maumee of that name. The remainder of the Ottawas are in the lower peninsula of Michigan and Canada. There are but 200 here. In all they have about 3000. They are southwest of Mackinaw, near Traverse Bay. At Ottawa Creek in Kansas they are Christianized and civilized beyond any Band I have yet seen. They have given up their dances and all pagan practices and adopted our mode of life by turning agriculturalists. This is the highest evidence of their advancement, although the smallness of their numbers has no doubt exerted a great influence in breaking up their tribal life and ways. And all this has come about, strange to say, without a school or a boarding house among them. Their great want at the present moment is a school for the education of their children. They are now discussing a plan of setting apart a farm and assigning their annuities, about $3000, to the maintenance of a boarding and manual labor school.

The other proposition is to ask the Government to allow them to sell a few sections of their reserve to raise a school fund, but they have but little hope on this head as the government would be afraid to start the precedent [?]. Mr. Jones is very much interested in this question of a school and hopes to bring it about in some way soon. He is a very sound headed, practical man and like his wife a staunch friend to the cause of the Indian. His wife insists, and Jones agrees with her, that the annuity system is a curse to the Indian, and ought to be broken up by the Government; that it would be better to give to them the principal and let them waste it and then be compelled to rely upon themselves, if it could be used for their benefit in no other way than it now is. This is a serious question, and it has been remarked to me at different points in the territory since I came here. The most hopeful feature of the case of the Indian, as it seems to me, is the fact that they are aware of the truth, that if they continue in their present course, their exter-

mination is certain, and that at no distant day. Hence the desire expressed by Mr. Jones for some movement to arrest this result.

An attempt has been made in New York and Philadelphia to organize an Indian Aid Society, whose object shall be to embrace the welfare of the whole Indian family and devise ways and provide means for his reclamation. This is certainly a noble object and worthy of the philanthropists of the country. I hope it will result in something. I tell Mr. Jones the first movement must come from the Indians. They must furnish the facts and statistics of their condition, and show where the defects and hardships of the present system lie, and as far as they can, indicate the true remedy, and that he will then find that the Christian communities of the country will not be idle or indifferent, but on the contrary will come forward to their rescue. The idea suggested by me of a convention of the most intelligent Indians from the several Indian nations to meet in some central city it seems was one that he had thought of and one that had already been discussed. I hope very much that some result of this kind will be reached. Such a convention would be a new and great event in the history of the Indian.

Ottawa Tradition

The Ottawas have a tradition that they came from the East and from another country. But they have no knowledge of their separation from the Chippeways (Ojibways) and Pottawatamies, with whom they are closely allied in language. After they had been apart many years, they formed a league or confederacy. The Ojibways, being the oldest family, or the primary stock, were styled the "Oldest Brother." The Ottawas, being the next, are the "Second Brother" or "Next Oldest Brother," and the Pottawatamies, being the youngest, were styled the "Youngest Brother."[54] They called their confederacy the Na-swä′-bane-zid′, or "three council fires in one." The league bound them not to make war on each other forever, and to join either of the others against their enemy; thus it was in strictness an offensive and defensive alliance.

Sacs [Sauks] and Foxes

I have seen some of these ride by Mr. Jones' but have not met and spoken with any of them. Their agency is about 16 miles southwest of here,[55] and I ought to go there, but have decided not to do so. They are like the Kaws, wild Indians, and as much so as any in the territory. They came originally from Illinois and are Algonquins. They numbered when they were removed to Kansas about 2700. Their present number is but 13 or 1400.[56] In the short space of time which has elapsed since their removal, they have diminished one half. The smallpox has been among them and done its work, but intemperance, exposure and vagrant habits have done their share. Mr. Jones says their habits are very bad.[57] Besides their intemperance they wander about from encampment to encampment off of the Reserve and drag their women and children along with them, and that the hardships they thus encounter destroy many lives. They have never had a school or a mission among them, but have refused both. They have their farmer and blacksmith and their agent and licensed traders among them. Within the last year a Quaker has settled among them as a missionary and friend in general. Some good may grow out of this.

I expect to see the Sacs and Foxes near Iowa Point [the "Missouri group"]. There are some there near the Iowas and I think I can reach them there easier than here. Mr. Jones says there are some fine men among them here and who are in favor of schools and improvements. Mr. Jones is in favor of concentrating the most of the Indians, or as many as will unite as one people into one territory and organize a municipal government on the plan of the Cherokees. This is a grand good plan, were it feasible. Its feasibility will depend upon the extent of the uneasiness now existing among them in relation to their future destiny. If they were ever thoroughly aroused there is no telling how far they might be influenced in such a direction. He suggests a territory farther north in Nebraska.

Today, June 4, is very cool with a north wind, quite as cool as our June. A fire would not be uncomfortable although it is not needed. I slept, however, last night with my window up. It just suits me, and is a splendid climate. This season however is said to be colder than usual. I have seen some hot weather since I came here, but on the whole the weather has been beautiful.

[The Prairie and Its Immigrants]

Kansas is a prairie state and the Indians from the forest states have hard work to get on. There are narrow margins of timber along the streams, and in this timber of course they erect their cabins, and yet quite near together, thus occupying but a small part of their lands. It makes it very inconvenient for cultivation, as it is hard to find timber and prairie near together. In some places on this reservation it is four miles from one strip of timber to another and not a house between. Even the eastern farmer is slow about erecting his house in the midst of the prairie, away from all fire wood and fence timber. They are beginning to do this, however, and hauling their wood from the nearest point where they can purchase it. There are coal seams throughout the state, but no one as yet enters upon the business of raising and supplying coal. In time it will become the principal fuel, and the sooner they get it out, the better for the people. The emigrant Indian tribes from the East have found the prairie a hard country under their mode of life, it being a total change in their mode of life and means of subsistence, although the soil of Kansas is exceedingly fertile.

Yesterday Mr. Jones and myself went over to see Mr. Mills[58] and his mother-in-law, an old Ottawa female and a good woman. They live about four miles away across the prairie. We spent from about 9 o'clock until two in getting out the schedule in Ottawa, and got it out finely as Jones is a perfect interpreter. They were a good deal puzzled at times, but we stopped for dinner and got through well. It is not a little interesting that while they have dropped their tribal [clan] divisions, given up their dances, and joined the church, a great part of them still hold and practice their system of relationships. They also give their children Indian names as well as English ones, but contrary to the ancient practice, they do not now change them.

Peorias

The Peorias, Kaskaskias, Piankeshaws, Weaws, and Miamis are all located together north and east of Osawattomie in the southeastern part of Kansas from the Kansas river but not far south of the center geographically. From Ottawa Creek and Mr. Jones' I went south about 23 miles to Osawattomie, and from thence north east again to Paoli, Lykins Co.,[59] K.[ansas] T.[erritory] about 7 miles, to see Battise Peoria

Morgan was extremely fortunate in contacting Baptiste Peoria, half-breed Peoria, and one of the best-known Indians in Kansas. It was from this amazing man that he learned about the Peoria tribe.

and his son-in-law, Luther Paschal, the former a half breed French and Peoria, with an intermixture of some African blood, and the other a half breed and a good English scholar. Battise is a man of note.[60] He speaks all the languages of the tribes above named, is interpreter for them all, carries on a large farm well stocked, and is principal owner of the stage line from Osawattomie to Kansas City. He talks our language well, but slowly, has been among all the Kansas Indians and is well known throughout the territory as a man of large property.[61] He and his households occupy several houses grouped near together about a mile from Paoli. He gave me the Peoria system of relationship [see *Systems*, p. 288], although it is not as perfect as I intended to have it for want of time. It is the same as the Shawnee, or nearer that than the Ottawa, and the system of the Kaskaskias, the Weaws, Piankeshaws and Miamis is precisely like theirs. These tribes are fragments most of them of the same original band within our historical period and came all of them, I believe, from Illinois and Indiana here. They are all Algonquins, and their language closely allied as a dialect to the Chippewas. Many of their words are identical in spelling and pronunciation, and I think a Chippeway would have but little difficulty in understanding them. It is interesting to notice the close connection or resemblance in their languages. Luther Paschal is a Kaskaskia.[62] I left with him a schedule and letter explanatory and he and Battise agreed at their leisure to go over the schedule again and send it to me completed at some future time. Mr. Crawford of Fort Scott gave me the name of Gen. Seth Clover of Paoli, as the Agent for these Indians, and I am to write to him to see that the schedule is executed and returned to me.[63]

I saw a number of the Peorias and Kaskaskias. They work this land, and are learning to be farmers. The son and daughter of Battise dress tidily and in our style, and are quite good looking, especially the son, who has fine black eyes, and is over six feet tall. His mother must have been a full blood from his dark complexion, and if the young man did not stoop, which is strange for an Indian, he would be fine looking. These several tribes are divided into tribes [clans] like the Chippeways and still retain some of their tribes [clans]. The office of chief descends from father to son and the children follow the father's tribe [clan]. Battise says that their ways, manners and customs are like those of the Shawnees and Delawares. Their number I did not ascertain, as it is easily had from other sources. Battise says this system of relationship is universal among the Indian tribes so far as he knows, and his acquaintance and intercourse have been quite extensive. I inquired if he knew how it was among the Cherokees and he could not inform me.

I passed through the reservations of the Peorias, Kaskaskias, Piankeshaws and Weaws, or near that of the Weaws, and in sight. They are well located and contain as beautiful land as any in the territory. The creeks are more numerous in this part of Kansas, than nearer the Kansas river, and therefore there is a good deal more timber here than in any other part of the territory I have seen. The Osage river runs through some of these reserves, also the Potawattamie creek and the Weaw creek. You see ranges of timber in every direction, and in good quantity.

[*The Indian and the Prairie*]

The Indian likes the woods, and does not like the prairie. We always find his lodge in the timber and never on the prairie, and the scarcity of game makes the prairie country a non-desirable one for the Indian. Before the discovery of the country by Columbus, and before the Indian was possessed of any domestic animal, the prairie must have been an intolerable country to him,[64] and if he came from Asia, he must have dwelt for a long time on the Pacific coast before he ventured to cross the plains, or to attempt a settlement upon the prairies, and when he found his way into the eastern forests, he was sure to work his way eastward as pressed on from behind by advancing tribes. Thus no doubt has been shown on this continent an advancing tide of Indian races pushing each other eastward along the great lakes and up the great rivers which came from the eastward until the advancing column reached the sea or the Atlantic; and when pressed upon they were compelled to turn around and press back the invaders. The breaking through and dispersion of primary stocks must, I think, be accounted for in this way, as the intrusion of the Iroquois into the very center of the Algonquin stock or area.

The prairie is not congenial to the Indian, and is only made tolerable to him by the possession of the horse and the rifle. The prairie neither affords the cover and shelter which the Indian both desires and needs, under their system of guerilla warfare. Even the white man has hardly the courage to build on the prairie in the midst of peace and security where there is not a tree, not a shrub, nor a thing[?] of timber with which to kindle his fire, nor a spring perhaps to slake his thirst. But the rolling prairie like Kansas is well watered, and with copious and running streams. The country is so much thrown up that the water is naturally and quickly thrown into them; besides this they are usually with stony bottoms. Wood, however, is as prime a necessity as water and it is the need of it today which localizes all white settlements along and in the timber margins. With the horse and other domestic animals, the emigrant Indians, as they are called here, have been able to do very well, and have advanced in their condition instead of retrograded. They have had up to the period of the settlement of Kansas the practical occupation of the whole territory, and of the far west for the purposes of the hunt.

[*The Indian's Opportunity*]

The Peorias and their kindred tribes in this vicinity have an excellent opportunity now to become farmers and derive a substantial advantage as agriculturalists by the sure sale of all the crops they can raise. They have also this advantage over the white settlers, that their farms are free and paid for, their cattle and horses the same, and they are perfectly acclimated. They also have natives like Battise Peoria to set them an example of the advantages of thrift and industry. They also have his intelligence and that of a good many others in these several tribes to guard their property, and prevent their abuse by the whites. The Indian has a chance now to show what he is made of, and if he has sufficient intellectual power to turn himself from a nomad or hunter into a settled agriculturalist, he has an intellect and power of control of more value than we are apt to suppose.

I think an amalgamation with the Indians by the white race, or the absorption of the best blood of their race into our own is destined to take place, and that Kansas will be the theater of the first honest and regular experiment. Hitherto the lowest and basest whites have been the fathers of the half breeds. Now we are to see respectable white people marry the daughters of wealthy and respectable Indians and bring up their children with the advantages of education, Christianity and wealth, and these half breeds will then again intermarry respectably with the whites. Our race, I think, will be *toughened physically* by the intermixture and without any doubt will be benefited intellectually.[65]

PART III

Friends Shawnee Mission House
Johnson Co., K.T. June 5, 1859

I left the Peoria Reservation yesterday morning, and after riding in the stage about thirty miles from Paoli, Lykins Co. to Westport in Missouri, and walking about four miles, I reached the Mission about nine in the evening. I found to my great regret that Simon D. Harvey,[66] the Superintendent, was absent with his wife in Ohio, but I found a relative of his, a Mr. Harvey and his wife, with some others at the Mission who gave me a very warm and friendly reception. The first thing of course was my letters from home, which were to be sent to this post office. I found but two—one of the 19 and one of the 21, so that I am still without news for fifteen days; but the last is favorable.

On the way from Paoli we saw a deer run across the prairie quite near to us; and as it is the first one I ever saw on his feet free and wild on the prairie it was to me an interesting sight. I am told that they are quite numerous in this part of the Territory. We also started a prairie chicken occasionally. The day before on our way to Osawattomie we passed over Turkey Creek, which is famous for its wild turkeys, which are seen almost daily to cross the stage road by passengers. The turkey buzzard and the crow

are quite common. In the evening I started out a rabbit and thought of trying [?] him with a revolver but gave it up. He crossed the road quite near to me. He was of a reddish brown color, and of fair size. I saw one some days ago on the Pottawatamie Reservation the day I went to see Buraseau. The whippoorwill is also heard here every night. Of all the birds the meadow lark is the most abundant. He is quite large, larger than a pigeon, of a brownish color with white feathers in his tail which he spreads as he flies. The turtle dove in pairs is also quite common, and the crow is abundant.

The country from Osawattomie to Westport is very beautiful, quite equal to the rest of Kansas, and better wooded than any I have seen except along the Kansas river. At this point, about nine miles above the mouth of the river, and from four to five miles back from the river, the Mission is located just by the edge of the timber, and it is all forest from here to the river, and the same on the other side for four or five miles. This margin narrows as you go up the river until in some places as elsewhere noted the prairie comes out to the river banks and in many places is seen through the timber. There is no end to the beauty and fertility of Kansas. So much splendid land, with bright and genial skies over head, and boundless fertility under the feet can hardly be found in such perfection elsewhere on the earth. There is no part of the country where at this season at least the face of nature is not cheerful and attractive. This present season has been colder than common, with more rain, although there has been but little since my arrival.

Fires in June

We had a fire at the hotel at Osawattomie June 3 in the evening, and again this morning at the Mission June 5, and I found them both quite comfortable. But through [the day] it was warm enough with a good strong breeze.

Prairie Farming

It has been my intention several times to refer to this topic, although I know no more about it than I have seen as I rode along. The first thing after getting up a small house, is to start the plow in the spring. One yoke of oxen is sufficient, but they frequently put on two. The first sod they aim to turn from 1½ to 2 inches deep, just sufficient to turn the grass. The furrow is from 12 to 20 inches wide according to the plow. It is turned over rapidly, about 2½ acres per day, as there is not a stone, except on the edge of the bluffs, that is just at the summit of the highest prairie hills, to obstruct the free motion of the plow. As it is turned and lies in the sun it looks black and rich, but the soil adheres firmly together and lays as neatly in the furrow as need be.

The first planting, I believe, is always with corn, and this is planted with an axe instead of a hoe. They axe it in, as they say, that is, they cut a hole in the sod with an axe, drop in the corn, and then with the handle cover or smooth over the place. Sometimes they use the hoe and drop the corn between the furrows. The best planting is with the axe. The second year they plow deeper, and the third deeper still. It is in the third ploughing that it turns up as mellow as the best garden. I have [seen] the finest wheat, corn and oats growing in Kansas I have ever seen anywhere. The crop looks healthy and vigorous, and better yet, uniform, and not good in shreds and patches.

The last day I was at Jones', he was using a sub-soil plow on a strip of land for the sweet potatoes. This was a mere fancy; the

This sketch, "Breaking the Prairie Sod in Kansas," appeared in HARPER'S WEEKLY in 1868 and was drawn by the fine illustrator Theodore R. Davis. Davis traveled on the plains in the late 60's and his work appeared in HARPER'S WEEKLY until 1884.

ground did not seem at least to need it. But he believes in trenching the [blank]. His men were using three yoke of great fat oxen. After seeing the bony, starved cattle of New York—comparative—it is a pleasure to look upon the sleek, fat, growing cattle of this prairie land, where the pasturage is so rich, sweet and inexhaustible. I have never seen such an abundance of cattle anywhere. Every family has a regular herd of from twenty to 100, or are growing one. It costs nothing whatever to keep them, and that too as fat as butter. The only cost is the value of the animal, and the care of him. And yet, strange to say, such is the extent of the immigration that butter is 2/ per pound, and almost impossible to get at that.

After the field is plowed and planted, and they continue to plow and plant until near the middle of June, they then look to the fencing. They have first a hog law in the territory, which makes it necessary to shut up all swine. They are thus compelled to fence against cattle alone. As timber is so scarce the fences are slight. The common kind is made by setting posts in the ground and nailing to them three strips or rails, all of which is done in the roughest manner. Another form is to drive stakes in the ground at an angle of about 60° and insert from the opposite side another stake through it by means of an augar hole, and then nail on the strips, and allow them thus to rest on the other stakes, thus avoiding the danger of blowing over, or falling apart, to

which the upright fence is liable. In the best timbered portions we see regular black walnut and burr oak rail fences. The black walnut is the most common wood in the territory. In the house of Mr. Jones at Ottawa Creek, the hewn logs are of black walnut, and so were the floors, the joice [*sic*], the doors, and all the wood about the house including the shingles. The time will come when the pine of the East will come here to be exchanged for the walnut, and when it will be profitable to plant and grow it as they do other crops.

It is yet a question whether fruit trees are to flourish here. I have seen fine peach trees growing on the Pottawatamie, Ottawa, Peoria, and Shawnee Reserves and the apple in several places. At Battise Peoria's I saw quite a nursery of all kinds of trees growing thriftily, but the trees of this kind are very few in the territory. They say they will grow where timber has grown, and also in the hazelwood and sumac prairie. The climate is a favorable one for the peach, and indeed they say they can grow everything in Kansas but coffee and cotton.

The Shawnees

This is one of the most celebrated of the Algonquin tribes. They have, from the days of William Penn, had perhaps as large and eventful an intercourse with the whites as any other Indian Nation. They are now far advanced in civilization, and are trying the great and dangerous experiment of dividing up their lands with the unrestrained power of sale in each individual. They sold their reserve to the Government several years ago,[67] reserving a farm of 200 acres for each man, woman and child, which after 8 years each was to have power to sell. It is believed that many of them will make a good use of the encouragement which the ownership of their own land will give them. They tell me, however, at the Mission that quite a number are inclined to and will sell and go down and live with the Cherokees, who have invited them to do so. This reminds me of the fact that the Shawnee Prophet, Elketsana [Elskwatawa] or Tecumseh,[68] went down to visit the Cherokees in his day and claimed kindred with them, as the Iroquois coming west even now claim kindred with the Wyandottes.

As Henry Harvey has written a book on the History of the Shawnees,[69] it will save me the necessity of making many inquiries of a general kind. I have his book. The

Tens-kawaw-ta-waw, the Shawnee Prophet and brother of Tecumseh, as painted by George Catlin. This Shawnee played a major role in American Indian history.

Shawnees here numbered at the last payment 850 souls. To this number must be added the Shawnee Band in the southern part of the state, numbering about 750, and these, I believe, make up the remainder of the race. They had originally, I think, 100,000 acres of land at the mouth of the Kansas on the south side, the best watered land except that of the Delawares on the opposite side of the river in the state. It was no doubt thought to be quite important to displace them when the rapid settlement of the territory began, and the Shawnees appear to have been wise enough to see the necessity of removing or selling a large part of their reserve lest they should find their condition intolerable from the pressure upon them by the whites.

Shawnee Tribes [Clans]

1.	Wolf	M-Wa-wä′	From John Blue-
2.	Raccoon	Tha-pä-ti′	jacket U Käl-ue
3.	Turtle	No-ma-thä′	[cf. *Systems*]
4.	Turkey	Pa-la-wä′	Rabbit Tribe
5.	Snake	Mä-na-to′	
6.	Hare	P-sa-wa′	
7.	Rabbit	Pa-täk-e-na-the′	
8.	T. Buzzard	We-nä′-se	
9.	Panther	M-se′-pa-se	
10.	Deer	Psake-the′	Common Deer
11.	Loon	Mä-gwä′	He thinks it is lost
12.	Bear	M-quä′	
13.	Owl	Me-ath-wa′	

Mrs. Chouteau—Na-ta-wa-kom-se

[The following is a good example of the sort of data that Morgan was trying to obtain.]

Mrs. Chouteau[70] says that the son of my aunt is my son, the daughter of my aunt is my daughter. My brother's son is my nephew, the son of my nephew is my grand son. My brother's daughter is my niece, and his son is my son, and the daughter of my niece is my daughter, and the children of this son and daughter are your grand children. My mother's brother's son is my uncle, and my mother's brother's daughter is my mother. The son of this uncle (my mother's brother's son's son) is also my uncle, and the sons of this last uncle would also be my uncles ad infinitum. But if I were a man, my mother's brother's son would be my uncle and his daughter would be my mother, but the son of the son of this uncle would be uncle also, and so would his descendants.

Neither two men nor two women can call each other Ne-lim-wa, but a man and a woman may. A man's mother's mother's sister's son is his father, but a woman's mother's mother's sister's son is her uncle. The daughter is mother to the uncle and aunt to the man.

Family Names

She informs me further that each of the tribes [clans] have their own family names which are kept distinct, and that one tribe has no right to use the names which belong to another; that these names are so well known that you can, or a person well versed in Shawnee life could tell at once to what tribe she belonged. [This is not uncommon among North American Indians; the Hopi observe this custom in naming even today.] She is of the Wolf tribe and the word wolf appears to be incorporated in her name, a fact to which she called my attention.

They do not change their names at present as a matter of custom when they become of age; but if a person is sickly, it is a common practice to change the name of the person. This would seem to be a superstitious notion that thereby the sickness might be put away. They do, however, change their names even now occasionally, but it is not common. What the ancient practice was she does not know.

The children are not necessarily either of the tribe of the father or of the mother. She said she was named into her father's tribe which was Wolf. Sometimes the children were named into one tribe and sometimes into another. I must make this a matter of further inquiry.

This morning I went to see Anna Rogers, the wife of Graham Rogers,[71] whose house is sketched at the end of this book. She is a half breed, was educated at the Quaker Mission school, and is in every respect a bright, intelligent and even beautiful woman. Her husband is the Head Chief by election[72] of the Shawnees. They elect a Head Chief, Second Chief and Council for one year. The recent death of the Head Chief advanced him to that position. Their house is a fine one, and well furnished and as neat as a pin. She is very industrious, and said as she had her work to do she could hardly spare me any time, but was willing to give me all the aid she could. I went over a part of the schedule and left to call again tomorrow. In the afternoon I went to see Nancy Chouteau[73] who was also educated at the Quaker school, and who is now married to Cyprian Chouteau,[74] a son of the well known French Trader of St. Louis now deceased of that name. His wife is a half breed, speaks our language fluently, and is also a beautiful and even elegant woman. Her eyes, like Mrs. Rogers, are mild but very brilliant and expressive. I went over and nearly finished the schedule and am to call again tomorrow.

[Morgan has a Shawnee vocabulary of six pages here.]

Shawnee System of Relationship

Mrs. Chouteau says that a man's father's sister's son is a nephew, and a woman's father's sister's son is a son. A man's father's father's sister's daughter is his niece, and a man's father's sister's daughter is his daughter, and a man's father's sister's son's son, son's daughter, daughter's son and daughter's daughter are each a grand child. The son of a woman's niece is her son, and the daughter of a woman's niece is her daughter. A man's and a woman's mother's mother's sister's son is their uncle and the son of this uncle is an uncle, and so on ad infinitum. But reverse this, and a man's mother's sister's daughter's daughter would be his niece, and the daughter of this niece would be his grand child. A woman's uncle's daughter is my mother, and her daughter is my sister. My own grand mother (man's) her daughter would be my mother, her son would be my uncle. The son and daughter of this mother would be my brother and sister, but the son of the uncle would be uncle, and so on ad infinitum, but the daughter of my uncle would be my mother, and her daughter my sister, etc. A man's grandmother's sister's son would be his uncle and his daughter would be his mother. My uncle calls my son grandson. My children would be grand fathers and grand mothers to my uncle's children.

I spent a part of the forenoon with Mrs. Chouteau and upon the schedule, which we finished. There is a very great difficulty in determining the relationships between the children of a brother and of a sister, when carried out to remote points. It is very complicated, but yet is understood by the Indian female as far as is needed for all practical purposes, and they seem to know at a glance the order of succession. This does not change the main result of the schedule, but I should be glad to be able to remove every difficulty which stands in the way of a complete elucidation of the subject.

She is quite clear that while her mother's brother's son is her uncle and the son of this uncle is also her uncle and so on ad infinitum, so is her grandmother's son her grandfather, and his son is also her grandfather and so on ad infinitum. But the exact course of this does not hold, except in the last case. She thinks the daughter of a man's niece, and also his son, becomes a grandchild, so that it might occur that a person called grandchild by one person could be called back by such person as uncle, which is an inconsistency. The difficulty, however, is confined to the descendants of a brother and of a sister. Between two brothers, or two sisters, the rule is simple and unconfused and perfectly consistent from first to last.

The Shawnees do not, as the Kaws and Winnebagoes, have terms for the older, next older brother and so on; nor for oldest and next oldest sister and so on, but limit themselves to older and younger brother.

Family Names

It is given to a few only to bestow family names. The father and mother seldom name their own children. Some persons are well versed in the names which belong to each tribe [clan], and these are the persons who are looked to to bestow names upon the children. Among the Shawnees near the Quaker Mission, Ga-che-qua, the mother of Mrs. Rogers is the one who gives most of the names. She is familiar with this subject. The names are all significant. The prohibition of marriage in ancient times extended beyond fourth cousin, but of late is not so rigorous, but Mrs. Chouteau knows of no instance of first cousins marrying. They might as near as third or fourth cousin. The name given determined the tribe, as the tribal names were distinct, but the child is named into the tribe of one or the other. The chiefs do not now interfere in this matter of bestowing names, although they might formerly. The Shawnees now marry into their own tribe if they are not related.

Naming Children

After a child is born, word is sent to the chief of one [?] of the other tribes [clans], and the name comes from one of the other tribes. Thus Blue Jacket[75] is of the Rabbit tribe. He looks to the Wolf tribe. His wife is Owl. She would look to the Raccoon or the [blank]. These other tribes or the chief of the tribe decides to whom—Tribe—the child is to be given, and thus a balance is preserved between the tribes. The names of each tribe are distinct, and any one can tell the tribe of the individual from his name. In case of divorce, there is no law about the children. They can put the children out of the tribe of the father and mother into some other tribe but it is not usual. Each tribe has one or more chiefs, whose duties are confined to the affairs of peace. As they say, or Blue Jacket said to me, the Braves make war, the Chiefs make peace. The son succeeds the father as chief, and it is in the power of the tribe who has the naming power, by naming his children into his wife's or some other tribe to cut off the inheritance.

Religious System of Shawnees

The Supreme Being anciently worshipped by them was a woman, and was worshipped as grand mother, Go-gome-tha-na, our Grand Mother.[76] Some of them in ancient times used idols made of wood. Mrs. Chou-

teau was not able to give much account of the ancient system of the Shawnees, and was afraid to say much about it. They believe in an evil spirit, and in other inferior spirits, but she could not give the names of any of them. Blue Jacket confirms the statement about the worship of a spirit whom they call our Grand mother. They also worship a Great Spirit. But this grand mother they regard as the creator of man and of all plants and animals. It appears to have been the original worship of the oldest branch of the Shawnee Nation called the Chilicothe Band, whom the other bands now call Grand-fathers and they call the others grand children.

Singing and Fasting Festival, Na-ka-mo-weh

At this festival they commence with a fast which lasts through the day. In the evening they get together and sing all night. It is a form of worship peculiar to the Chilicothe Band. They say that their Grandmother sings with them, and that they can hear her. They allow no impure person at this festival, no woman with child, no person in the menstrual season, no drinking person, or who has drunk within several days. This festival is held but once a year, and that in the spring. Dancing with the Shawnees is a mode of worship as with the Iroquois.

Bread Dance (Da-qua-na-ga-weh)

This is the dance at the Spring Festival, which they call the Bread Dance. They dance a great number of dances at this festival, but this I understand is the principal one. At this time they render their thanks to the Great Spirit for his goodness. It is not for the worship of the Woman Spirit, but the Great Spirit. The ceremonies consist of dancing, speeches and a feast. The hunters at their fall hunts cut out the

tongue of every deer they kill, wait a little, then dry it and string it, and these are brought forward on this occasion as a part of the feast. The women have charge of the feast. They are called Ho-ge-ma-wen-gweh, or "Chief's Sisters." The word, Blue Jacket says, is nearly equivalent to Queen. I presume they are analogous to the Iroquois Keepers of the Faith,[77] of whom the female portion have charge of the feast, and with the men have charge of the Festival itself. They also have ball and other games at this Festival.

Roasting Ear Dance (Ne-pa-na-qa-weh)

When the green corn is ripe they hold this Festival, which is observed, like the former, in honor of the Great Spirit, with speeches, games, dancing and a feast. The name of the Festival is from the dance which is particularly set apart for this festival, which is most likely the same as the Great Feather Dance of the Iroquois, which I believe is also called the Green Corn Dance.

Steaming Worship (Lo-tho-wa)

This is a fast, and is followed by the steam bath in a hot oven in which hot stones are placed, and after the person gets in, water is poured upon the stones, and thus a vapor bath is obtained.[78] With this bath is connected some religious rights [sic] to Go-gome-tha-ma, "Our Grand Mother," the chief spirit of the Chilicothe Band of the Shawnees. I could not find out much about it. The person strips except the breech cloth, and no impure person as before named is allowed to participate or even to be present.

Councils

The government of the Shawnees was by chiefs in council. Each tribe had its chief or chiefs, as before stated, and these chiefs in council were the government. They had power to make new chiefs in their discretion and not the people; and on the death of a chief his eldest son succeeded, if free from objections. In the councils of the Shawnees, as with the Iroquois, and as far as I know, with all Indian tribes, unanimity was a fundamental law. At present, the old system is entirely abolished. The Shawnees are farther advanced, if anything, than the New York Indians, a part of whom have tried [?] elective chiefs (Cattaraugas) with poor success.

Present Condition of Shawnees

The treaty [of 1854] under which the Shawnees have divided up their lands is about to take final effect in giving them the power of alienation. Each man, woman and child has 200 acres,[79] which would give to a family consisting of a man and wife and three children a farm of 1000 acres. Mrs. Chouteau informs me as her opinion that about half of the Shawnees will sell and go south among the Cherokees, who want them to come. The remainder will cultivate their farms and become farmers. They certainly have a splendid chance with their land their own, their annuities to assist them to stock and farming implements, and the consciousness that they must work or perish. I hope greatly the experiment will succeed. I think it would have been well to have provided that no Indian should be allowed to sell except with the consent of the Indian Council, and that to be incorporated in the deed. Hitherto the white man could not buy the land of the Indian. He is now about to be subjected to a new temptation, and he will be tried by artifices.

The Shawnees have abandoned their dances on this reservation, and their tribal organization is but faintly preserved. This shows that the Indian life of the nation [tribe], so to speak, is destroyed. The Shawnees are much farther advanced than I expected to find them. There are a large number of sensible and highly respectable men among them. They have also changed their government like the Ottawas, and have given up the rule of hereditary chief, and substituted a Head Chief and a Second Chief, elected by the people once in two years, I think it is, and also a Council, elected for the same time. I have been greatly and agreeably surprised at the progress made by the emigrant Indians in this territory, so far as I have seen them. Each Band or Nation has its prominent and educated men who are familiar with the ways and business forms of the whites, and they will form a strong barrier and shield to the Indians. As the Parker family at Tonawanda up to this time has kept back the Ogden Land Company, so will the Jones, Rogers, Peorias and others watch over and protect the rights of their kindred.

Tomorrow morning I leave the pleasant family at the Friends Mission where I have been so kindly and cordially treated, for the Delaware Reserve and the Mission of Rev. Mr. Pratt.

The Shawnee Friends Mission, Johnson County, Kansas, where the author had a "warm and friendly reception."

I left the Shawnee Mission Wednesday morning, June 8, for Blue Jacket's house about a mile from Shawnee village and three miles from Harvey Mission. Mr. Harvey very kindly went with me, and introduced me, and I then parted with him. He found letters at the office stating that Mr. Simon D. Harvey would be at home next Sunday. I regret very much not to have seen him. At Blue Jacket's I obtained the information which is written down above, and which was written out at his house and in the woods while resting on my way to Kansas River. I there at Blue Jacket's learned that it was pay day or payment as they call it to the Delaware Indians, and that it was to be at the Delaware Crossing. I was then on my way to Mr. John T. Pratt's Mission on the north side of the river, and was but a little out of my way to go to the Delaware Crossing, and I accordingly went. I will reserve a description to the next note book in which I hope to make a good show of Delaware information gained.

After waiting there for about four hours, I left for Mr. Pratt's Mission about seven miles away on foot, after having in the morning walked about seven miles and carried for four of it my heavy carpet bag weighing at least 25 pounds. I had a long and weary walk, having got out of my way, and thus lost near two miles. But on the road I took it was so beautiful that I do not now regret it. Most of the way for about three miles the road was as level as a floor, and overhung with elm trees which interlaced their branches overhead. Most of the trees were elms, but there was also the mulberry then bearing fruit nearly ripe; the wild locust, a large and beautiful tree, and the black walnut and the different kinds of oak, the ash and wild grape vine also grows in these woods. I saw vines as large around as the small part of my arm; but these, I am told, only leave out at the top.

I reached the pleasant house of Mr. Pratt about 7 o'clock, and after introducing myself and my business, he remembered the letter and schedule I sent him and gave me a very friendly reception. His wife is quite agreeable and a lady, and he is a man of education and refinement. I anticipate a pleasant sojourn here for two or three days. I left the Friends Mission with regret; they did every thing in their power to make it pleasant for me and to assist me. But I suffered for want of interpreters and came away with the firm belief that I had left a mine of information behind but half worked, by which I mean, but little worked, only begun.

I saw Tooly,[80] a Shawnee, at the Payment, and he informs me that the Great Spirit of the Shawnees was a woman. I could not get at him at such a place so as to go into the matter. He also agreed that neither a father nor a mother could name their own child. I must write again to Friend Harvey, and ask him to look out for me some of these questions.

PART IV

Baptist Delaware Mission,
Kansas T. June 9, 1859

I left the Shawnee Mission (Friends) yesterday morning and reached here the same evening. I crossed Kansas River at the Delaware Crossing, about twelve miles above its mouth; and was so fortunate in point of time as to be there on Payment Day, which is the annual gala day of the nation. As I had never seen a government payment of Indian annuities I was, of course, very glad that it happened as it did. After spending about four hours as a spectator of this curious scene, I went on to the Mission. Today Mr. Pratt and myself went down again, and spent a few hours, the payment still going on, but so near completed that they expected to finish tonight. We have just returned somewhat fatigued by the ride, as the day is warm. Some account of the payment must be given, although it is one of those scenes which should be seen to be appreciated. The amount paid was universally large, it being no less a sum than $78,000 to something less than 1000 people all told, men, women and children, and was paid in gold and silver. In January 1858 the Delawares numbered by census 988. At the present June census their number is but 941. These figures were given me by Mr. Ford, a merchant of Lawrence, who stops here and is looking after the accounts with the Delawares. I supposed the nation was not diminishing, but rather on the increase.

A modern artist's conception of the Delaware crossing of the Kansas River. Morgan may have taken Moses Grinter's ferry on his way to the Delaware mission.

[*Payment Day*]

The place of payment was centrally located but a most inconvenient place in itself, as it was upon a side hill with very rough ground all around it. The only recommendation was the eight or ten houses which made up the settlement, and furnished shelter for the goods of the traders, who are inseparable from all payments. The number present was large, just as many of the Delawares as could possibly leave their homes, with a single one behind in some cases to watch the premises. About 800 were present and some Shawnees from the opposite side and perhaps 100 white people, including traders and spectators. I arrived about 10 A.M. and the paying out commenced about 1 P.M.

The Indian women were all dressed out in their best attire, as this is the only occasion that ever brings them together as a people. We saw the fruits of the sales of previous years, and some of the present, in advance a few hours of the time of payment, as the traders are eager to commence their work at once. In the first place the Delaware women have usually dropped the Indian skirt, and put on the long dress of the white female. I thought I saw a skirt upon an elderly woman, although it was covered up with a gown. Their dresses are of all colors, and some of them of rich materials. A few were dressed in colored muslin with silk shawls, and looked quite becomingly, but the most of them were, strange to say, dressed in silk gowns, some of which were brocade patterns of rich brocade silk, some were black, these looked the best. Some were crimson and black, some fiery plaid; the most of them were in bright colors. Over these they wore silk shawls of every color and shade, most of them fringed. They were expensive silk shawls of good

materials. Some of them had on two shawls, and some a third arranged as a neck drape. They appeared to have put on all they had, to show it, the quantity of dress being of more importance in their sight than its style, or quality.

Of course their appearance as a whole was fantastic and ludicrous. The dresses were made without taste from scant patterns, and worn without hoops or petticoats, thus giving to the skirt an appearance not to be compared for a moment with the Indian female skirt of cloth and blanket of the same, but these would be too warm for Kansas. I was glad to see the gown upon them, as it is a move in the right direction. At home they may wear the Indian gown, but I doubt it. The Shawnee women, all that I saw, wore the gown. On their heads they tie a silk handkerchief universally. I did not see a bonnet among them.

The color of the Indian women is quite uniform, and is light. It shows that the white blood infused into them in the East has been well diffused throughout. The next cross with the white will make a pretty white child, of which I saw a few and but a few specimens, as the Delawares are quite vigorous against intermarriage with the whites, and also against unlawful intercourse. As a whole, the expression on the face of the women was pleasant and healthful. They look strong, literally cleanly and healthy, although I am told by Mr. Ford that syphilis is among their women to an alarming extent. Their faces would not lead to such a suspicion.

The men were more fantastically dressed than the women, and did not appear half as well. Their fancy dresses were cheap and absurd, rendering their general appearance ridiculous. There were many good faces among them, and also well dressed Indians

who speak our language and have the manners and address of gentlemen. Some of the old men and some of the young men had on colored calico frock coats of the most gaudy colors. Many had vermilion on their faces, thus giving them a low appearance, and I saw a few girls with spots of it in their cheeks. One man I saw with a silver ornament in his nose, which covered part of his mouth. Many of the men wore leggings with a wide side projection, ornamented, and the breech cloth, over which they wore a vest or shirt, and perhaps one of the frock coats of calico above named, with head bands of bead work over the shoulder and meeting in a large bead work pocket on the right hand side. As a body I should think the men inferior to the women.

The Delawares have a million and upwards in the national treasury at five per cent interest. Their regular annuity is $50,000. The present is a part of two payments, I understand, and is larger than usual. There were several stores full of goods, and a great many stands out in the open air with the protection of canvas. The great show of all was in saddles and bridles, of which I presume I saw of saddles alone 150; the price ranges from $15 to 50 dollars, the ordinary being $22 to $25. They are the Mexican saddle, made at Westport, Mo., and the kind usually used in Kansas and this part of the west. It has a high pommel, wooden stirrups usually, which are easier than metal for long journeys, and a well stuffed and quilted seat, with a high rear plate. They are far superior to our eastern saddle for riding.

The assortment of goods was creditable to the good sense of the Delawares, as the supply was adapted to the demand. Grains of all kinds, tin wares of all kinds and at reasonable prices, in fact they could not make anything on this article, wash tubs and washboards, coffee mills and household articles, calico and muslin goods. The chief take in was in the jewelry of which large and flashy assortments were exhibited, some of it looking extremely well; salt pork, flour and bacon were also offered. The trading, however, was not brisk, and I think was pretty much a failure, the reason being that Wyandotte and Kansas City are within easy reach, where they can buy cheaper and at their convenience. The trader's chance lies in the weakness of the Indian before temptation, and his slight regard for money. As the payment was delayed more than a day beyond the time, I noticed some of the Indians commenced moving up to book account in advance, which the traders favored. I saw two of them this afternoon arranging [?] payment in the Indian tents, and getting it, and I have no doubt doubling the amount in footing it up, or increasing it largely. They have to pay for a trader's license $25 to the agent, and unless they speculate in some way, they must make a failure on their sales.

I saw no whisky nor ardent spirits of any kind, and consequently no drunkenness or quarrelling. After it is all over tonight and the payment is over, and the government strikes its tent and moves off with the wagon marked U. S. and the small file of soldiers sent to protect the specie, the whisky will show itself, and the pockets of the remaining Indians who have any money will be picked. There were more white men around today than looked well for the Indian women.

Shawnees Uncles to the Chippeways, etc.

Buraseau told me that years ago the Ojibwas, Pottawatamies and Ottawas took the Shawnees into their alliance, or perhaps what is nearer the truth, recognized an ancient connection still preserved by tradition, and acknowledged the Shawnees their uncles, by which they admit them to be the older stock.

Tribes [Clans] of the Delawares and Descent in the Female Line

Was introduced by Mr. Pratt to William Adams,[81] Wa-le-oak-se, (White man), a very intelligent young man and an Indian. We went out under a tree and talked an hour. I found that the children of two tribes are brothers and sisters to each other, and the children of his sisters the same, and that the children of a brother and of a sister are nephew, and something else to each other, but he thought not uncle. He says the Delawares are now and were anciently divided into three tribes: 1. the Wolf, "round paw"; 2. the Turtle, "unfeathered animal"; 3. the Turkey or fowl, "feathered animal."

That this was a sort of generalization; that the Wolf separated the animals having hair, the Turtle animals without hair, including fish, and Turkey or Fowl, as this means any fowl, the animals with feathers, and these he says are subdivided into a number of others, but he could not give me the names. He said his tribe was that of the Mud Turtle, the turtle that muds himself and then lies in the sun. This was as far as he could go on this head. He says that in old times no man was allowed to marry a woman of his own tribe, and it was the law until within the last generation, but that now is broken over constantly. That he was of the turtle tribe, and so were both his father and mother. He also said that he was entirely certain that in old times *the children followed the tribe of the mother*, and that it is so now where the father and mother were of different tribes. This is a very interesting fact, as it is the first exception, if true, in the Algonquin race which I have found. Mr. Pratt informs me that he understands the children are of the tribe of the mother, and he has been their missionary for twelve years and for 22 years an Indian missionary. I shall verify this perfectly before I leave. The young man also says that the office of chief was hereditary in the tribe, as he thought, and that a brother or nephew succeeded as frequently as a son, but he was not quite sure on this subject. He gave me the names of 16 of the dances, all he could remember, which will be given later.

He said the Delawares thought a good deal more of their relationships than we did, and if there was the least particle of relationship they were glad to find it. He says that in old times near relatives could not marry, but now they married as near as our cousins.

Family Names

We took up this inquiry. He says one tribe has no right to use the names of another tribe, as he thinks, and he also says the names can be readily distinguished from one another, but I must inquire further about this. He seemed to think the same name might be used by another tribe, in which case it would be slightly varied. The real truth about the distinctness of the Indian names constantly eludes me.[82] I shall soon think there is nothing in it.

Dances of the Delawares

1. Old Religious Dance
2. Wolf Dance
3. Turtle Dance
4. Chicken Dance
5. Buffalo Dance
6. Bear Dance
7. Doll Baby Dance
8. Horse Dance
9. False Face Dance
10. Dog Dance
11. War Dance
12. Feasting Dance
13. Dance for the Dead
14. Striking the Stick Dance
15. Buzzard Dance
16. Turkey Dance
17. Duck Dance
18. [left blank]
19. Shuffle Dance

Origin of the Three Varieties of the Human Race

Mr. Pratt mentioned to me a Delaware explanation of the creation of the Negro, Indian and White man, to the effect that the Negro was created first, and was, as we say, a mistake or failure; it was the first attempt at man's creation. The Great Spirit next created the Indian, who was admitted to be a great improvement upon the negro; and last of all he created the white man.

The Good Spirit and the Boil

Mr. Pratt had a boil come on his arm. A Delaware told him he had a good friend, and in explanation said to him that the Evil Spirit had intended to destroy him; that he was followed in his rounds to do mischief to men by a small but good spirit, who continued in various ways to defeat the evil spirit of his purpose, when it was a case in which he wished to save the person from harm. That as the evil spirit was about to put forth his power upon him, the little spirit stepped forward and said to the evil one, "you let me deal with this person," whereupon he took or drew on his invisible bow a small and invisible arrow, and shot Mr. Pratt on the arm, and hence the boil. In the meantime, the evil spirit, seeing the little spirit about to deal with him, passed on, and was thus diverted from his purpose. After doing this friendly act the little spirit at once passed on upon the track of the evil one to arrest and avert as many of his evil deeds as he could by persuasion, cunning or artifice. Thus the Indian said Mr. Pratt had a friend, and this boil was the result of his friendly interposition to save him from a greater evil.

[Delaware Clans]

Conversation with [Morgan's blank], the mother of Charles Johnny Cake.[83] She is sub. 1 Wolf Tribe. Her husband was Turtle. Her children are Wolf.

She confirms the division into Wolf, Turtle and Turkey Tribes, and says these are subdivided. The Wolf has the Bear, the Turtle the Big and Little Turtle, and the Turkey has the Crow. Those belonging to each subdivision to this day refuse to intermarry; but Little Turtle intermarries with Big Turtle, Bear with Wolf, Crow with Turkey. The children of ancient times and now are of the tribe of the mother in all cases. The terms Wolf, Turtle and Turkey are general ones, the word Took-seat, the name of the Wolf Tribe means "a round foot." There is another name for Wolf, Tam-me. The word for Turtle, Poke-koo-rin-go, does not mean any particular kind of Turtle, and so the name of the Turkey, Pal-la-ooh, means any kind of fowl. It appears to be a generalization for haired, non-haired and feathered animals. The subdivisions I must learn from her son.

She mentioned the We-loon-see Tribe as that of the Little Turtle, and also the Crow and the Bear, but could not remember their names. She gave We-saw-hut-ko, meaning

Charles Journeycake (Johnny Cake) was a chief, and a prominent leader of the Delawares in Kansas, as well as being a widely known Baptist minister. His mother gave Morgan information about the Delawares.

"Yellow Tree," as the name of one of the Bands. She appeared to be about 70 years old. She was of the Wolf tribe and her husband Turtle. She said the son did not necessarily succeed the father in the office of chief, but could not explain the succession fully. A brother or a sister's son often succeeded. Captain Ketchum[84] at the time of his death was head chief, a principal chief of the Turtle Tribe of the Delawares. This title or office is hereditary as she thought in the tribe, for she said the Turtles could not have a man of the Wolf or Turkey Tribe for their chief. Ketchum's name was Ta-whe-la-na (Catch Me). He died leaving a son; but was succeeded by John Konner, the present principal or hereditary chief who was the son of the youngest sister of Cap-

NOAPEH, AN ASSINIBOIN INDIAN; PSIHDJA-SAHPA, A YANKTONAI INDIAN

BY KARL BODMER

At Fort Union, on June 28, 1833, Bodmer painted Noapeh ("Troop of Soldiers"),
". . . who stood with unwearied patience to the painter, although his relations frequently
endeavored to get him away. He had put on his best dress, and had, on his breast, a rosette
of dyed porcupine quills, eight or ten inches in diameter." Between the antelope horns
in the headdress are black feathers cut extremely short. Maximilian thought Noapeh
"characteristically Indian." Psihdja-Sahpa was painted at Fort Clark on January 21, 1834;
he was one of three Yanktonais who came to the Fort to persuade the Mandans to join a
war party against another tribe.

THE BEAR DANCE

BY GEORGE CATLIN

This was an exciting and spirited Sioux ceremonial. The dancers appeal to their deities before going on the bear hunt and "dance and sing to the invisible Spirit supposed to watch over the destinies of this animal." The Medicine Man, clad in a bear skin, leads the dance. Several dancers wear bear-bead masks and others bear-fur anklets. All imitate the bear—walking, or eating, or sitting on its hind legs, forepaws relaxed, on guard against possible danger. Catlin saw this dance (it sometimes continued for several days) in a Sioux village on the upper Missouri.

tain Ketchum, and of the Turtle Tribe. His name was Ta-ta-ne-sha. Here we have a practical illustration of descent in the female line, as with the Iroquois. She says each of the three tribes have one hereditary chief, called the Head Chief; that this chief never goes out to war, but stays at home while the Braves go out to fight.

The Delawares call the Senecas Min-gwa-o, hence I think the historical word Mingoes,[85] a name for the Iroquois. The Delawares call the Iroquois and Wyandottes nephews, and thus assume the name of uncles, which is a way to express their seniority as well as original superiority.

I inquired of her about the family names, and was again put at fault. She says the father and mother can name their children as they please; that they ask some one for a list of old names of persons dead, and choose such ones as they like. She thought the names of the three tribes were kept distinct, and then that they were used by these tribes indiscriminately. She said her husband named her children, and gave them all Turtle names, which was his tribe, then followed this up by stating that she did not know as it made any difference, that all used the same names. She referred to the Seneca practice of making a feast when a child was named, but said the Delawares did not do that way.

Winter

Mr. Pratt mentioned a Delaware tradition about the origin of cold and heat and the change of the seasons as follows. In ancient times a married pair fell into disagreement. They lived in the far north region of cold. The wife, finding it impossible to live with her husband, or in resentment for some injury, travelled into the far south, into the region of heat. The husband became weary and lonely in her absence, started to make her a visit. As he travelled southward he carried the cold with him and wherever he went it became winter, or rather winter followed his footsteps. After he had concluded his visit he returned and carried back the winter with him as he advanced to the north. From the most ancient times this visit has been annually renewed.

Indian Persistency

Mr. Pratt mentioned as a recent occurrence among the Delawares, that while a party were out on a Buffalo hunt a few years since, one of them said one day that before he returned he would take a three year old bull buffalo alive. His companions rather laughed at his suggestion as an impossibility, and thought no more about it. This is the age when they are the most ferocious and unmanageable. A few days afterwards this hunter rode up to a herd of buffalo and having singled out a two or three year old bull, he managed to detach him from the

John Gill Pratt was a dedicated Baptist missionary, working in turn with the Shawnees, the Stockbridge, and finally the Delawares. Morgan regarded him highly.

herd and gave him a chase. He followed until the buffalo was about tired out, with his tongue hanging out, and hardly able to move, while his own horse was in the same condition. Leaving his horse and his gun, the hunter, fresh and strong, took the buffalo by the tail and drove him on. He then went up an ascent and down on the other side until they came into a wet place where the buffalo stuck in the mud from weakness and exhaustion. He had thus taken his buffalo, in one sense. He was powerless, and still, except as he made slight efforts to fight. After spending some little time in this situation during which the buffalo was gaining strength and he was losing his, he was so fortunate as to espy and signal one of his party, who came to his aid, and the two, with a rope tied to his horns so as to keep at a safe distance from each of them and between both, they led or drove him to camp and thus the Indian maintained or made good his boast.

Delaware Baptist Mission School[86]

This school, under the supervision of Rev. John G. Pratt,[87] a matron, Mrs. Muse, and a teacher, Miss Morse,[88] is in a very flourishing condition and superior to any I have seen in the territory. It has accommodations for 78 Indian scholars as boarders and lodgers. The number last term was 64, the number the present term is about 50, as they have held back for the payment, and will soon come in now.

The buildings consist of a two and a half story farm house large on the ground, designed for the sleeping and clothing rooms of the school; another of the same size with a wing for a kitchen, designed for the residence of the superintendent and teachers, and is the eating and cooking place for all.[89] Also a large school house with folding doors in the center so as to separate the boys and girls, although they are as yet all together. There are numerous outbuildings, as a farm is carried on in connection with the school of about two hundred acres. The buildings were erected a few years ago with school money belonging to the Delawares, and is supported with funds in the hands of the government reserved for that purpose.

The children are clothed, boarded and taught by the Mission, and the government allows $75 per annum per scholar. They have two terms of five months each, and the children are kept in school about seven hours per day. They study reading, writing, and spelling, geography, arithmetic, with blackboard exercises. The scholars are mostly young, those now at school ranging from 6 to 18 years. They look well and healthy and free from sore eyes, and are decently and comfortably clad. This is the true system of Indian education, beyond a doubt, and this school is by far in the best condition of any I have seen. We see here New England cleanliness, system and good management. I did not visit the Mission School of the Methodist Southern Board among the Shawnees. It is a large and flourishing school, I believe, but complaints are made of the principal of unfairness, of avarice, etc. He has made himself rich and also the Mission, they having secured by treaty between about 2000 acres of land, and at the same time he was active to prevent Friend Harvey from selling his Mission farm of 200 acres, evidently desiring to break up the Friends Mission.

Mr. Pratt commenced his missionary life 22 years ago with his present wife then 20 years of age. He was accepted as a missionary to Burma, but was requested to fill temporarily an Indian Mission then vacant among the Stockbridges near Fort Leavenworth, and went from there to the Shawnee Baptist Mission now closed, and from there to this Mission about 12 years ago. His wife is still young looking [she was forty-five at the time, ed.] and must have been beautiful as a girl. They are very worthy, refined and agreeable, and my short stay with them has been very pleasant indeed. Mr. Pratt is a well educated and superior man.

The Friends Shawnee Mission has done a good work among the Shawnees, but was never, I fancy, a very large school. There are but two boys there at present, but no doubt they have done as much good in proportion to the means employed as any other missionaries. The Friends are well adapted to gain the confidence of the Indian.

[*Delaware: Succession of Chiefs*]

In a brief conversation with Charles Johnny Cake, he informs me that the son never succeeds the father in the office of chief, but that the office goes either to a brother or the son of a sister. But strange to say the Turtle, the Wolf and the Turkey tribes each have several subdivisions, and while it was the ancient law that Turtle must always intermarry with Turtle, Wolf with Wolf and Turkey with Turkey, yet the subdivisions were not allowed to intermarry and in these the children were of the tribe of the mother. Mrs. Johnny Cake, the mother of Charles, would not or could not tell me the names of the subdivisions. Charles would not today under the pretence that it was important to be right and he doubted his recollection of these subdivisions, although he said there were a number of each.

I am very anxious to know. I asked an old Delaware this morning, and he very coolly told me that these questions were too small, by which he meant, I suppose, that it was prying into family matters rather impertinently.

It is by means of these subdivisions with the prohibition of intermarriage that descent in the female line is secured.

Lemuel R. Ketchum [90] says:

The Delawares have three Heads or great chiefs, one for each tribe. This chief is called Sa-ke-ma. It means Principal Chief. It is the name of the office, or the title of the person equivalent to President or King. They also have two subordinate chiefs. These chiefs together are called Ka-ke-um-ha-suk, or the chiefs. The term also includes the three head chiefs, and is used in contradistinction to councillors. The office has no special name. These two are inferior. If the three head chiefs decide upon a measure the two inferior must submit, but if two of the head chiefs and the two inferior chiefs should agree and the third head chief should stand out, the thing could not be done. The principal power is with the head chiefs. The three head chiefs can never go out to war, but the two inferior chiefs may. They are not, however, called war chiefs. Besides these three the wise and experienced men of the nation are called councillors or Ha-ha-che-nowl-se-chick, which means simply councillors. These have a right to speak in a council of the chiefs. They can speak of their own motion without waiting to be asked by the chiefs. Women cannot speak in council.

Religious System

The Delawares believe in a Great Spirit, and in an Evil Spirit. They also believe in the immortality of the soul, and that they all went to heaven. They have one religious festival at which the Gum-win Dance is performed. This is the great religious dance. This is held once a year every fall, after the corn harvest is gathered. The festival lasts seven days. At this festival they have a number of old dances, which are still maintained among the Delawares. This Festival is called the Gum-win, from the dance. This is held for the purpose of returning thanks to the Great Spirit. They have a feast. Men, about 12, go out beforehand to hunt, and get game for the feast, particularly the deer. There is a class of persons whose business it is to appoint the time for holding this council, to prepare the feast, and supervise the business of the festival. They are both men and women, but Lemuel could not give me the name by which they are distinguished.

Marriage

Near relatives are not allowed to marry. First and second cousins are within the forbidden degrees; but third cousins under our system are allowed to marry. The names used by the several tribes are used in common. This seems to be the preferable conclusion. A young lad at the Mission told me that those of the same subdivision of the same tribe can intermarry if not too near of kin, but the fact is that they are all of near kin.

Succession of [Head] Chiefs

Upon the death of a head chief of the Turtle Tribe, the three other subdivisions meet in council to agree upon a successor who must be of the same subdivision of the tribe with the deceased, and is either a brother of the deceased or a sister's son. The second chief has the first speech, and the War Chief last, and enumerates the persons who

have expressed themselves in favor of the person nominated. If they disagree, I have not ascertained how it is adjusted. After the person is agreed upon, then all the chiefs meet in council and perform the ceremony of investing him with his office.

The war chiefs are selected and made such by the Head Chief without consulting the people, but not so with the Head Chief.

The Delawares are very well advanced as agriculturalists. When Mr. Pratt came among them 12 years ago, as he informs me, they were living in bark houses. Now many of them are living in frame houses two stories and 2½ stories high, some with a veranda in front the whole length, and they have good barns and outbuildings. Some of them have herds of cattle from 25 to 100 and have from 5 to 20 swine, sheep, wagons, and all kinds of farming implements. Their future prospects are certainly very flattering if they push on as they have here. Their women are interfered with a good deal by the whites, and they are quick to marry white husbands, as they seem to regard that as advancing. It would be so were their husbands respectable.

With their large annuity of $50,000 per annum, the best timbered lands in the state, and sufficient of them to give them all large farms, there is no reason why they should not become both agriculturalists and respectable citizens of the state. When they become wealthy farmers as some of them now are, their children will intermarry respectably with our white people, and thus the children will become respectable and, if educated, in the second and third generations will become beautiful and attractive. This is to be the end of the Indian absorption of a small portion, which will improve and toughen our race, and the residue run out or forced into the regions of the moun-

tains. There are two cases of *polygamy* here. Two well known Indians have two wives each. The Delawares are opposed to it, and are inclined to make a fuss about it. But I suppose it is an old Indian institution and they cannot make a law against it. If it was contrary to Indian law they would not admit the children of both mothers to annuities. As it now stands, their annuity is a bounty on children. I think the Delawares are tempted by their annuities.

Religious System of the Delawares[91]

William Adams, Del.

The Delawares believe in a Great and in an Evil Spirit. They also believe in a number of subordinate spirits, some of whom are waiting or ministering spirits of the Good and some of the Evil One. Among the waiting spirits of the former are the following.

1. Kaka-sha-ha-no-hase, the Spirit of the Whirlwind. He is represented as having the form of a man and is called Grand Father.

2. O-we-ya-la-so, the Spirit of the Wind. He is represented as having the form of a man, with long streaming hair, so long that it sometimes gets entangled in the trees as he rides along. He is called Grand Father.

3. Pate-hoc-hoo-weh, the Spirit of Thunder. He is represented as having the form of a bird, an Eagle, called Grand Father.

4. Wa-o-tun-oo-wase, the Spirit of Water. She is represented as having the hands of a woman, and the body, but ending in a fish's tail. She is supposed to dwell in every drop of water as well as in every river, creek, lake and stream, and sometimes to be a punishing spirit. She it is in cases of drowning who pulls the person under the water. Hence her name means "Pulling Down far Under."

5. Has-gueme, the Spirit of Corn. She is represented as having the form of a woman, and is called our Mother. She can foretell

about the coming crop. When she rises with her hair combed smooth and shining, and is seen in this condition, it is a favorable omen and indicates an abundant crop. When she rises with her hair uncombed and loose, it indicates a bad crop, or a failure of the harvest.

6. Wa-ma-take-a-nese, the Boy Spirit. He is represented as a little boy, with a bow and arrow, and as a constant friend of the Indian. He is everywhere and always at hand in the most impossible places, ready to assist us in our trials and troubles. He is a servant of the Great Spirit.

7. Ma-mun-da-ase, the Spirit of War. He is represented as having the form of a panther, with a very long tail. He can foretell war about to arise, who will fight, and who succeed. The meteoric stones are dropped by him, and the war will arise in the direction from which the meteor comes, and go in the direction it goes. He is under the control of the Great Spirit, as are all good spirits.

The Great Spirit has the form of a man (name elsewhere). The Evil Spirit has the form of a man with one leg, the leg of an ox. The tradition is that the Evil Spirit was created by the good and was himself originally good, but he originated a contention among the inferior spirits which resulted in a division and taking of sides. In the midst of this contention they all came into the presence of the Great Spirit, who seized the Evil One and as a mark of his disapprobation and as a punishment, he wrenched off one of his legs and placed in the room of it that of an ox, that he might ever afterwards be known and recognized at once as an evil spirit, and then sent him down to the earth with the evil spirits who followed him.

Heaven they consider to be immediately over their heads and a place in which they have a bodily form. It is a journey of 12 days from earth to Heaven after death. They believe as do the Iroquois, that the soul does not leave the body finally at death, but that it revisits the body for a few days before it takes its final departure. For this reason, as Adams says, they bury on scaffolds in the trees, and in a sitting position near the surface of the earth. Last year he made a coffin for an Indian, and his friends made him bore a hole in the head of the coffin, the object of which being to allow the spirit free egress and regress to and from the body.

Heaven is a place of rest. They follow up the path, and the first stopping place is a place where they find a supply of vermilion or red paint. They cannot pass this place without painting their faces. If they have been accustomed to paint on earth, the paint will readily adhere, unless they have been very wicked, and then they pass on without delay. But if not used to painting, or if they have been very wicked, the paint will not adhere, and thus they are detained at this place until the Evil Spirit removes them to a place of punishment.

They say there are seven points of good and evil. If the deceased has four of the points of good in his favor, or more, he is sure to pass on to heaven, but if there [are] four or more bad, he cannot go to heaven but must be placed in a place of misery and unhappiness where he is punished according to his evil deeds. If he was accustomed to paint, it will be more apt to stick, and that is all that is claimed for this meritorious act. There is a second stopping place on the way where the selfish and covetous are surrounded and burned up in the article [on which] they set their store upon earth, and thus are kept out of heaven. They have a belief that mosquitoes sprang up out of the souls of those who were punished by the evil spirit, the wreck, or fragments into which they were cut up were turned into mosquitoes and such evil creatures.

Bad spirits are believed to pass by about day break and good spirits are believed to pass along about dark. For this reason boys are often sent to bed without supper, that they may commune with or be visited by good spirits, the fasting state being thought to be favorable to such communion, and for the same reason are often compelled to get up before day break that the evil spirits may not obtain or exercise any wicked influence upon them.

I am told that the Shawnee Female Great Spirit is in reality the moon, and is worshipped as our Grand Mother or something of that sort; and Isaac Johnny Cake who mentioned this [to] me also said that the Great Spirit of the Delawares was represented and believed to be a brother of the Sun, and that the Moon was the Grand Mother of the Great Spirit; and young Toucey, the Stockbridge, says that there is some evidence of a [?] in of the sun in the worship of several of the Indian races, including his own. The Iroquois return thanks to the sun for heating the earth and to the moon for cooling it, but this does not show a sun worship or anything like it. William Adams is to correspond with me on the religious system of the Delawares, and I hope to find out something definite about it.

Gum-mween

This festival or annual worship of the Delawares as explained by William Adams and of which he is to write to me more fully, is quite interesting. They believe unless they observe it once a year their crops will fail, and they will lose the favor of the Great

Spirit. It lasts 6 days. It may be repeated by another person or family for a second 6 days, and so on until the feelings are satisfied. It has been known to last a month. The meeting is called by one of a certain class, who I presume correspond with the Keepers of the Faith of the Iroquois. They are called A-la-pa-cte, meaning *Dreamers*. The people meet in a large house erected on purpose for this worship and used for nothing else. They build two council fires in the house, and the people assemble by tribes, the Turtles by themselves, the Wolves by themselves and the Turks by themselves. They use belts of wampum and have many ceremonies. It would seem that this council or religious meeting was called by some one person. The door of the house of worship must open to the east.

When they are assembled two singers [?] sit down to two dried and rolled up deer skins, with sticks in their hands to beat time. The leader, who is stationed on the right hand side of the door, gets up and shaking a turtle shell rattle, comes in extemporizing verses which are adapted to the set tune of his choosing, to relate his dream. As he relates his dream in music, he dances, they sing the same time and beat time, and all who enter the dance, dance the religious dance which altogether is called the Gum-mween. This is repeated day by day for six days. But the leaders change. When one has told his dream, he hands his rattle to the next one, who in like singing relates his dream in words of his own making, but sung in an old well known tune of his own choosing.

Before the festival 12 hunters are sent out for deer's meat, as no other meat is allowed. About 9 each morning this meat is served to all. At sundown each day they have an exhortation from the oldest wise man of the nation. Once during the six days, about an hour after night fall, they burn incense by throwing on the fire in the center of the house cedar branches, which fills the house with smoke and then ascends to the Great Spirit. If no one repeats the worship, or when all are done, the people all go out in Indian file, and facing the east, in a united voice they thank the Great Spirit for sparing their lives through the year, and invoke him to spare them until the next Gum-mween.

Mohekunnuk or Stockbridge Indians [92]

Found a family of Stockbridges among the Delawares. They were originally from Massachusetts, but moved from there to a reservation given to them by the Oneidas south of Utica, and removed from thence with the Oneidas to Green Bay, where they now reside. The word Mohekunnuk means "People of the Sea." They are divided into three tribes like the Delawares, the Wolf, the Turtle and Turkey, and each is subdivided, the Wolf into Wolf, Bear and Dog; the Turtle, Little, Greater and Greatest Turtle; the Turkey into Chicken and Turkey. Each

of the principal tribes in ancient times had its head chiefs, three in all. The office descended in the female line, the brother or a sister's son succeeding and not the son. But the son of a principal chief was not passed by as of no account. He was respected as the son of a chief. Their system of relationship is the same as that of the Delawares and other nations. There are about 300 left of the ancient nation.

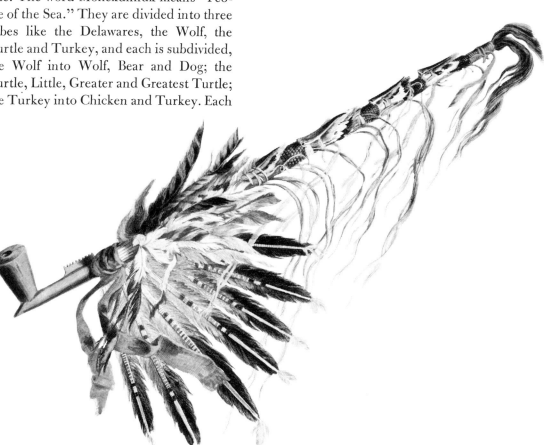

PART V

Po-ta-wat-a-me

I found a delegation of Pottawatamies encamped this morning, June 10, in a lot of Charles Johnny Cake, a Delaware, about a dozen in number with a good interpreter. I went among them and obtained the names of fifteen of their tribes [clans], or to-dems [totems],[93] as they call them, which are given below. They were wary about giving me information but I gained considerable. In the first place, they have *three* hereditary sachems, or principal chiefs. One of these belongs to the Bear Tribe, one to the Sturgeon, and one to the Hare or Rabbit Tribe. These chiefs are men of peace and never go to war. Besides these they have ten subordinate chiefs whom they call councillors. Among these are their war chiefs. The law of marriage they would not give me, but quit upon that. The interpreter, however, would give me all he knew. He spoke of their Medicine Society. They have one among the Pottawatamies. The members are male and female and he thinks they number about 200 members. They take an oath of secrecy on their initiation, and the penalty of its violation is death. Their dances are public, but their initiation is secret. He was not a member, but he thought the society was of a religious character.

They do their business, that is, the nation [tribe], in council of the chiefs and councillors, and unanimity is a fundamental law, as with all Indian nations as far as I am acquainted.

The tribes [clans] they gave as follows:

1.	Wolf	Mo-ah
2.	Bear	M-ko
3.	Beaver	Muk
4.	Elk	Mis-sha-wa
5.	Loon	Maak
6.	Eagle	K-now
7.	Black Hawk	M-ke-tash-she-ka-kac
8.	Sturgeon	N-ma
9.	Sucker	N-ma-pe-na
10.	Bald Eagle	M-geze-wa
11.	Thunder	Che-gua
12.	Hare or Rabbit	Wa-bo-zo
13.	Crow	Ka-kag-she
14.	Fox	Wake-sha
15.	Turkey	Pen-na

The Pottawatamies call the Delawares their grand fathers, and this delegation is here to renew the ancient friendship, a regular Indian visit. There are quite a number of Delawares here also at the house of Charles Johnny Cake and several of them took dinner with us today.

Relative Age of Kansas Emigrant Bands

All the Kansas Indians except the Iroquois, call the Delawares and Stockbridge Indians Grand Father. The Stockbridges call the Delawares Grand Father, and the Delawares call the Iroquois Uncles. The Chippeways, Ottawas and Pottawatamies stand in this order, the first being Oldest Brother to the others.

Kaws, Osages and Quappas

Kaws, Osages and Quappas are parts of one nation, I am told by Benjamin Toucey, who has been among them. Toucey is in Stockbridge. He says they have the same system of relationship.

Wyandotte, June 13, 1859

Wyandotts

Wane-dotte, Wyandotte, Calf of the Leg. The Iroquois gave them this name, and they adopted it. It refers to their manner of stringing jerked buffalo meat [cf. *Systems*, p. 166].

I left the pleasant Mission and family of Rev. John G. Pratt this morning, after remaining there about four days, every moment of which I enjoyed, and reached this place in the afternoon. After tea I called upon Judge Walker,[94] an educated half breed Wyandotte and spent the evening with him. He was a judge by appointment of the Bogus legislature. He has been in the country a number of years, is married to a white woman, and has a fine family of children. He was the person selected in 1839 to locate the Wyandotte reservation and negotiated a purchase of their reserve from the Delawares, who preceded them in the country. There are about 300 Wyandottes here. They are the ancient Hurons of Canada, where about 400 of them still reside near [?] ; but this portion located near Upper Sandusky, Ohio, and were removed to Kansas. He has been with most of the Indian tribes east of the mountains and professes to be well acquainted with Indian affairs. He is intelligent and cordial, and I am to spend the day with him tomorrow. I should note here that I found to welcome my arrival here four letters from Mrs. M. which gave me immense pleasure.

Wyandottes

Wane-dotte, Calf of the Leg. See tribes further on. Matthew R. Walker, Ra-honda-se, Running around tree top. They have seven tribes [clans] and seven principal chiefs and seven war chiefs. 1. Deer tribe, Ca-sken-o-to (Roaming). 2. Turtle, Ge-a-wish (Fire land). 3. Bear, Ah-nu-yih (Stays in trees). 4. Wolf, Ah-na-pese-quat (Bone Gnawer). 5. Hawk, Yun-da-so, (Flying). 6. Snake, Sun-gain-see (Creeping). 7. Fox, Cha-nain-toun-to (Sly Animal).

The principal chiefs come in by inheritance. The head war chief belongs to the Hawk Tribe. He is appointed from merit. The chiefs must be of the tribe they rule. The children are of the tribe of the mother, and no man can marry with his tribe.

The Hurons lived on the north side of the St. Lawrence. Their tradition is that they separated in Canada near Quebec and fought 30 years. From this place the Iroquois drove them up to Lake Huron, where they formed an alliance with Pottawatamies, etc.; thus stated the Iroquois.

Tribes [Clans] of the Wyandottes

They all agree there are 7 tribes, but they state them differently. My last version was from Governor William Walker, a brother of Mathew, and Isaiah a nephew of theirs. The Governor gave them to me as follows:
1. Great Turtle   Ge-a-wish   Fine Land
2. Wolf   Ah-na-rese-qua   Bone Gnawer
3. Porcupine   Ya-ra-hato-se   Tall Tree
4. Snake   Sune-gain-see   Creeping
5. Deer   Os-ken-o-to   Roaming
6. Bear   Ah-nu-yih   Tree liver, stays in trees
7. Beaver   Tso-ta-e   Sly Animal
8. Hawk   Da-soak

The Hawk was one of their ancient tribes, but it has died out. I think, therefore, they should be spoken of as having 8 tribes instead of 7.

Munsees

The Munsees are closely allied to the Delawares. They have the three tribes, Wolf, Turtle and Turkey, with the prohibition of intermarriage in the tribe, and with descent in the female line. This Toucey told me who has lived among them. They are old Connecticut Indians. There are about 50 near Fort Leavenworth, and some I think near Green Bay.

Sun-a-get, a Pottawattomie chief, painted by James O. Lewis in 1827, is a good example of the style of this early illustrator — note the very large nose and the unusual character of the eyes.

Creeks

Walker spent two years with the Creeks. He says they are divided into 7 tribes as follows, which are the same as the Wyandottes. 1, Deer. 2, Bear. 3, Wolf. 4, Hawk. 5, Turtle. 6, Snakes. 7, Fox. As far as the Wyandottes are concerned he must be relied upon as a native Wyandotte. They have these seven tribes. He says the Creeks have the same system of relationship as the Iroquois, and descent in the female line. He has also been among the Comanches as a trader. He says they have 8 tribes as follows: 1, Bear. 2, Wolf. 3, Buffalo. 4, Elk. 5, Deer. 6, Gopher. 7, Dog. 8, Antelope.

He says the old Outigaminies [95] are the present Sacs and Foxes.

Sioux and Dakota

Walker says the Dakotas are descended from the Wyandottes, and that the Dakotas still call them and treat them as brothers. [96] The Wyandottes call them Seune-de-no, hence the French word Soo [Sioux]. It is the name of the man who went off with this band from the Wyandotte family. It means the Man with the Big Stomach. If a Wyandotte goes among the Sioux, they take him to their cabins and treat them well. The Winnebagoes, Sioux and Foxes and Missouris were originally one, and are the original Outigaminies. [Morgan later inserted "not so" under "The Winnebagoes."] See further on under "Origin of Dakotas."

[Winnebago] Medicine Dance

I met Judge Williams [97] this evening and listened among other things to a very fine description of a medicine dance among the Winnebagoes. He is District Judge of Kansas, and has held the same office in Iowa and been with the Indians for 25 years. He superintended the removal of the Sauks and Foxes etc.

He was invited by the Winnebagoes as a compliment to attend a medicine dance, or the Spirit Dance. [98] This is a religious organization which the Judge likens to our church. They initiate with forms and ceremonies each neophyte, and at that time go through with their high religious performances. The Judge says they have mesmerism

and clairvoyance, and thinks they have had them for centuries. They use a long and large lodge a [blank] prepared for the purpose, in which all those allowed to witness the ceremonies are assembled. Adjoining this house is a bark tent built in a conical form as a steam house. They excavate a hole in the ground, heat large stones in a fire to a great heat, and then put them in this hole, and cover them over and seat the initiate over them. He is then covered around with blankets so that none of the steam may escape, after which water is poured on the stones and the neophyte is enveloped in a roasting steam bath. This is the first act, and the object is to steam all evil spirits out of him.

He is then led in to the house, after the steaming process in some instances has been repeated once or twice. He is then blindfolded and led around the house. Presently the singers beat the drum, shake the rattles, and commence singing a tune; then commences the dance, which is joined in by all present who wish to do so. The women are members of the medicine lodge as well as the men, and they join in the songs and in the dance. After the dancing is done, or perhaps he may have stood in the midst of it, there is a suspension of all singing and dancing. Several medicine men then advance towards the neophyte, pointing their medicine bags at him, then drawing them back. This advancing and receding and ejaculating certain words calculated to work up the mind of the novitiate into a regular phrenzy.

Presently they reach him when they hit their medicine bags against his body, he still being blindfolded and at the same time uttering a shrill exclamation. The Judge said the novitiate jumped up and fell flat on his face as if dead and that apparently with-

out design. There he lay without motion or sign of life, and the dance was resumed around them. After a time he was brought out of this mesmeric or clairvoyant state, a medicine bag was put in his hands and he at once had power to strike any one down as he had been. The person who stayed by the Judge was thus struck down. He felt of his arm and wrist and found them perfectly rigid.

They told the Judge before they admitted him to this ceremony that while he was there he must think no evil thought. If he did, his life would be in danger from the spirits. No impure person is admitted to witness these ceremonies, no woman in the menstrual period, no woman pregnant or recently delivered, no intoxicated or intemperate person that is under the influence of liquor is allowed to attend. The proceedings in the sweat lodge were not seen by him as none but medicine men were allowed there. The ceremonies commenced at 8 in the evening and lasted until day break next morning. The Judge confirms my former opinion that this is purely a religious rite, and a religious organization, having but little to do with the uses of medicine proper. The roots and herbs are one thing, but the ceremonies and incantations which are the real remedies are quite another. They call it the Spirit Dance, or the Divine Dance. The Judge informs me that he has witnessed the same thing among the Sauks and Foxes.

[Winnebago Burial]

He also mentioned the fact that he witnessed the burial of a Winnebago some years ago. He was set upon a natural mound and house made over him, food and some personal articles laid by his side, after which the whole was covered over with earth, except a small hole or chimney was kept open from the top down into the house. When the Judge asked what this meant they told him that it was for the spirit to pass through in going out and in.

He never found among them during the long period of his intercourse any evidence of sun worship, and thinks it fell far short of that in which I agree with him.

This morning I had a further conversation with Judge Walker, who is a regular medicine man of the Wyandottes. He says the name of the Spirit of Medicine among the Wyandottes is Mon-ane-tow, who is the same as the Manitou of the Ojibways etc. That this spirit of Medicine is a good spirit etc. He says that the initiations described by Judge Williams are in the presence only of medicine men and women. The people of the tribe are not allowed to be present. That both men and women are members, and are regularly initiated before they can become members. That no oath of secrecy is required, as the Indian knows nothing about oaths, but they initiate on the honor of the man and of the woman, choosing such only as are known to be of good character for integrity. That the Society and its proceedings are secret, except these ceremonies which medicine men perform on patients for their cure.

Walker says that these ceremonies proceed upon the idea that a violent shock of the nervous system, which prostrates it entirely will also prostrate or relax the hold of the disease. They know by experience that by fasting and steaming they so arouse and excite a well person as to produce a shock which will throw him to the earth. This is done at the ceremony of initiation which Judge Williams described. It is done by nervous excitement, and Indian faith in these ceremonies, and is repeated over every initiate as a proof of the possession by medicine men of this marvellous power. He

says there is no sham about this falling down of the person on the floor in a swoon in the manner described. That this is the precise shock of the system to produce which the fasting and the steaming process is resorted to, and all the other ceremonies of the initiation, including the dance.

When a person is sick and incurable by the simple remedies known to the Indians, and the friends become apprehensive for the life of the person, then the medicine men are called in and they go through certain ceremonies, all of which operate upon the nervous system already enfeebled and excited by disease, and tend to bring about that shock or prostration of the nervous system, which when produced is supposed also to relax the hold and power of the disease at the same time. In a word it kills the disease, or breaks the disease, or destroys the evil spirit then in the body which causes the disease, and then if there is constitutional strength enough left to raise up the body from its utter prostration, the patient recovers.

It would seem that they regarded the nervous system or the sensitive part of our nature as the seat of the disease, and addressed their remedies to the sensitive part, that is to the mind rather than to the body, to the spirit rather than to the organs of the body. The medicine system prevails very generally among our Indian races. In fact it is universal so far as we have found out the customs of the remote tribes.

I asked Walker about the cheats practiced by the medicine men upon the credulity of their patients, that is, pretending to take out of a man's back a tooth or a bone. He says that in their practice they want to make money, and the greater the feat they perform the greater the charge they make. Sometimes they charge a horse etc.

Origin of the Dakotas

The Wyandottes claim, as before stated by me, that the Sioux or Dakotas are descended from them. [They belong to different language families: the Wyandottes to the Iroquoian, the Dakotas to the Siouan.] They call the Dakotas *Sun-da-no* [spelled Tan-da′-no in *Systems*, p. 166] and they believe the French word Sioux was made out of this. This was the name of the chief under whom the Sioux separated themselves from the Wyandottes. The word signifies Big Stomach. Walker says the Sioux still have this name Sun-da-no among them as that of one of their original leaders. I have before mentioned the fact that the Dakotas regard the Wyandottes as relatives. There is another interesting fact which has occurred to me in connection with [the] subject, and that is that the Algonquin races called the Iroquois Nah-dah-waig (School-craft 5 p. 193) *Nan-do-wage.* They call the Wyandottes the same. Now in Carver's[99] time or about 1750, the Sioux before they came to be called either Sioux or Dakotas were called *Nan-do-ooipies,* which is substantially the same name which the other nations gave the Iroquois and the Wyandottes. This is worth further inquiry, as this Dakota family has become of late years one of the most important on the continent. The Dakotas call the Wyandottes brothers.

I left Wyandotte Wednesday morning, June 15, for St. Joseph, where I am to find my mail from home, and then determine my future route, or whether I will return at once. I am told that the Iowas have been moved back 35 miles from the Missouri into the interior. I expected to find them on the river, and some Sacs and Foxes with them. Unless I stop and go out to their reservation I shall not find any Indians on the river until I reach the Omaha reservation some 300 miles above St. Joseph. The fruits of my trip up the river do not promise much.

The Missouri river is not beautiful, nor anything very near to it. The muddy color of the water, and the low sand banks covered with cotton wood trees with half concealed sand bars in the river covered with drift wood, does not present a very inviting appearance. In places, however, the banks rise into bluffs and become quite fine, as the bluffs are covered with better timber.

Yesterday afternoon we stopped at Leavenworth City, the largest place in Kansas.[100] It contains about 6000 or 7000 inhabitants, and is quite a smart place. The Fort is about 3 miles above on a government reserve which may have caused the location of the town below. The governor here accumulates stores for Utah and for Fort Riley and I presume for several interior forts, and

from the Fort sends out large government trains with supplies for the interior. Leavenworth is also nearer [?] than Kansas City or Wyandotte, and I noticed a good deal of freight for Lawrence was landed here.

We stopped also about half an hour at the Fort to land some stores. The government has a stores warehouse and open sheds on the river for the receipt and safe keeping of goods, with a fine graded road down from the bluff to the ware house on the river side. The Fort buildings stand back about a quarter of a mile from the river and could not be seen from the boat. I went up the hill to get a view and just as I came in sight of the first building the steamboat bell rang and I returned. The fort is said to be one of the finest in the country and to be located in a place of great natural beauty. I felt a desire to see it as it was for a few years the residence of a lady friend, Miss Charlotte

Saxon, who married Maj. Sibly,[101] the Commandant of the Fort for about three years, I think. We are now drawing near St. Joseph.

Steamer *Twilight*[102] Missouri River Between Iowa and Nebraska, June 17, 1859. We left St. Jo about 12 o'clock at noon yesterday for Omaha about 300 miles above. During the afternoon we passed several promising settlements on both sides of the river. Iowa Point, the last one in Kansas Territory, is quite well situated in the midst of hills and well up from the river. I ascertained that Mr. Irwin's Iowa Mission was located five miles from there, and I am to stop on my return and make him a call for the system of the Iowas and Sauks and Foxes.

The river as it was below is monotonous, but I think there is some slight improvement. The banks of the Missouri from Jefferson City to the point near Nebraska City

Leavenworth, Kansas, as it appeared in 1858. The town was one of the great supply points of the West, and one authority described it: "... coughing steamboats nudging into the wharves, singing stevedores carrying bale after bale ashore, wagon masters supervising the loading of wagons, blacksmiths adding to the din . . ."

are much the same, being five feet or such a matter from the water at this time when the river is full, and perpendicular, consisting of nothing but sand which is constantly falling in and carrying its growing trees along with it. As we advance up the river from Kansas City the bluffs are more frequent, and the country around which is thus brought into view pleases the eye. There is timber however, lining the margin of the river for from three to five miles on each side, after which you find the prairie, both in Kansas and Nebraska, and in Missouri and Iowa. At this point and at various points above St. Jo where the bluffs appear the prairie comes to the river with some straggling timber here and there. As soon as the prairie appears we find more settlements; but yet the country is very thinly inhabited.

This river is a puzzle to me, with its sand banks constantly falling in, thus widening its channel. Why is it that in the course of thousands of years during which time it has been rolling its turbid waters, charged with its own sand banks into the gulf, it has not widened out from bluff to bluff until the river has become a series of shallow lakes covering thousands of square miles of land? All the flood wood in this river, and the quantity is prodigious, is but the growing trees undermined from day to day until they fall into the water. It is said that the channel is constantly shifting and that it is this shifting which cuts away the banks, and that when the channel wears away the bank on one side, it throws up a low bank of sand on the other, and by such means keeps within certain uniform limits. The muddy yellow color of the water which continually forces itself upon your attention when you look at it detracts greatly [from] its beauty as flowing water. You never see

the [?] surface which is always so striking and so pleasing to the eye.

I notice a difference already between the climate of Kansas and Nebraska. There is more cloud here and it is cooler. Besides we had last night a drizzling rain, and had heavy clouds and some drizzle this morning, while in Kansas it pours in tropical style with wind, lightning and peals of thunder.

The steamers on this river are quite large and comfortable, costing about $40,000 each, and they are well manned. The one I am on has about 40 staterooms, a wide saloon and is plainly but well finished. Their speed up the river is from five to six miles per hour when lightly loaded, and about 15 miles per hour going down. On the upward trip they go through the night, but are required by the Insurance Companies to lie by at night going down, as the increased speed by means of the current makes the danger of running aground, and consequently of loss much greater.

The current of the river as elsewhere stated by me is said to be 6 or 7 miles per hour. It is certainly very rapid, much more rapid than the Mississippi. This rapid current shows that the surface descent must be great to the mile. It is well worth working out by mechanical laws whether it is not owing to the yielding material of the banks and of this river that in places there are not deep channels cut through, and in other places great waterfalls. With high and precipitous banks in some places and waterfalls in others you would have a slow and gentle river, with clear and settled water. It is owing to the rapidity of the current and the constant falling in of the banks here and there that the water is able to hold so much mud and sand in suspension. With less velocity to the current the banks would not yield so readily.

The steamers usually stop at St. Joseph, but a few go on to Omaha which is the limit of boat navigation at present from St. Louis. Omaha is between 800 and 900 miles above St. Louis. They could go on to Sioux City if haste made it desirable, and I presume some hundreds of miles beyond. The river continues to be of the same width as at Jefferson City averaging from ¼ to ½ of a mile in width but growing narrower in some places than we saw it below Kansas City. It is a great river, and one is well repaid by riding upon it for days together.

We have passed Nebraska City and are now (June 18) at night near the mouth of the Platte river. The appearance of the country improves as we advance, that is, the timber disappears almost entirely on the Nebraska side, but continues unchanged on the Iowa side. The bluffs along this part of the river are on the Nebraska side, and some of them rise quite high, from one to two hundred feet and the river follows the bluffs. It is here that the prairie comes to the river. The hills are grass hills covered with straggling and [?] with groves of trees and the two united make a very attractive appearance. The river is now in flood, rising in many places within a foot of the top of the banks. It has risen they say two feet within the last 24 hours, and the reason assigned is that we are meeting the melted snows of the mountains several hundred miles away in the north west, in other words, of the Rocky Mountains. It looks reasonable.

Comanche Tribes [Clans][103]

Furnished me by Matthew Walker who said he had been among them. 1, Wolf. 2, Bear. 3, Buffalo. 4, Elk. 5, Deer. 6, Gopher. 7, Dog. 8, Antelope.

PART VI

Omaha City, Nebraska Territory
Saturday, June 19, 1859

We reached this place this morning at 9 o'clock. It is the capitol of Nebraska and most advantageously situated on a bluff a little way back from the river, and mostly surrounded by prairie. The bottom in front of the town lying between it and the river is near a half a mile wide, and as it is an open meadow, it adds to rather than detracts from the beauty of the place. The river is a treacherous neighbor and the people have learned pretty thoroughly the lesson not to build or even buy a farm upon the bottom lands. The river claims the right of shifting its channel whenever it pleases from bluff to bluff. As an illustration there is quite a large and prosperous village on the bluff on the opposite side of the river from Omaha. It is "Council Bluffs." An open meadow without trees lies between, but as the river is nearest to the bluff on the Omaha side, Council Bluffs is at least three miles back

from the river, and it may be more. It can hardly be seen without going up into the city of Omaha.

Omaha must contain about 3000 inhabitants[104] at a guess and Council Bluffs 2000. In my school boy days Council Bluffs in Olney's geography[105] was thought to be on the outer edge of the world, and I little thought that I should ever see it. This is not however the Council Bluffs of the geography. That point was about 15 miles further up the river, and on the Nebraska or western side, and was so named from the circumstance that an Indian treaty was made on the Bluffs many years ago, and the spot was thus named in commemoration of the event. Of the truth of this I have no other knowledge. Omaha is the best situated and by far the prettiest place I have seen west of the Missouri river.[106] It is situated in the midst of a rolling prairie and from the eminence on which the capitol stands you take in a large extent of country on both sides of the river. It bears the same appearance of an old and long settled country as the prairies of Kansas.

Since we passed Nebraska City, the prairie has come to the river for miles together and the forest on one side and sometimes on both has disappeared except as seen as groves of trees here and there. The prairies seem to roll into higher and often into much steeper hills than in Kansas, as an evidence of which I have frequently noticed on the Iowa side that the hills are so precipitous in parts of the bluffs facing the river, that there were slides of the soil so as to show sand denuded of vegetation although the grass was growing all around in

other places. This however may be limited to the land near the river. The country west of Omaha after a few miles becomes perfectly level like the Illinois prairies, and hence must be poorly watered and little settled, will not be as healthy as the rolling prairie. The timber also becomes more scarce as it appears only on the creeks.

It rained hard this morning from daylight until about 10 A.M. with thunder and lightning. About noon it came off hot and clear and down on the river bank where the boat lies there has been little or no breeze, and we have felt the heat considerably.

The Capitol is quite a handsome edifice. The Government appropriated $50,000 to build it, and to this the people of Omaha added $20,000 more. The building is not finished and the money is expended. It is rectangular with four entrances, about 120 feet by 60, with a portico of six columns at each end extending across the entire length of each end and a portico of six columns on each of the other sides, each about 60 feet in width. The building is of brick, painted, two stories high and a high basement, and a fine building for this remote place. The city also has a very large and well built hotel which cost 40 to $50,000 they say. All of the houses show good taste, thrift and the possession of means. I was a good deal surprised to find at this remote point so much life, enterprise and prosperity. Lots 22 feet front by 120 deep on the principal street are selling at $1000. It has been a great place for speculation and my cicerone about the place told me that most of the houses were built with money made out of eastern capitalists in land operations.

Top: Omaha City, capital of Nebraska Territory, as it appeared in **FRANK LESLIE'S ILLUSTRATED NEWSPAPER**, November 6, 1858. Morgan thought it "... the best situated and by far the prettiest place I have seen west of the Missouri River."

Right: The Second Territorial Capitol of Nebraska, built in Omaha in 1857-58. Morgan remarked that it was "... a fine building for this remote place."

Just above here at Florence, 6 miles up, is the headquarters of the Mormons in these parts and the point from which hand cart trains have set out for Utah.[107] Each cart carries 300 pounds of provisions, and to it is assigned four persons usually 1 male and three females, as they go about in that proportion or nearly that, and they harness themselves in by turns and draw it cheerfully and contentedly over the plains. Those who have no means for an outfit stop and work and go out to service, saving every cent that they may sooner get to the promised land, or harem, rather.

I went on to Omaha partly to see as much of the upper Missouri as possible, and partly with hope of finding some Omahas or Pawnees at the village whom I was informed were frequently there. I found a band of Pawnees some thinly encamped near the village and they were over at the boat and squads of them remained about the boat during the day and night. I went down to the encampment, tried to find their interpreter who has the respectable name of John Rogers, but could not find him. Unfortunately for me a theft had been committed the day before by the Shawnees and he for some reason thought best to leave and to keep out of the way. I found a Pawnee who could talk some English and commenced a schedule with him, but I soon found out it would not answer and gave it up, and offered him pay if he would hunt up and bring Rogers to me during the day, which he promised to but did not do.

The Pawnees are said to be demoralized as a nation. Their women are universally prostitutes, they all steal and beg and are idle and profligate. This character is given to the nation and not to the few who wander about. How far it is just to the mass of the Pawnees who remain at their village at home I cannot say, but I should think it must [be] too strongly expressed. The specimens I saw at Omaha were of a low, vile and filthy order. The women were all prostitutes and diseased, some of them clearly. I saw men offer to sell the use of their women for a paltry compensation, which fact proves the entire completeness of the demoralization of this portion of the band.

The Omahas are of as high repute for the unusual chastity of their women as the Pawnees are the other way, and I am told that all the neighboring Indians despise the Pawnees and shoot them down without mercy. They are particularly celebrated as horse thieves and carry their depredations down into the Kansas reservations where I saw at least one of the scalps taken from a horse thief who was caught by the Pottawatamies.

I found an Omaha half breed confined at the house of the Dep. Marshall, Mr. Paige, as a safer place than the public prison. In a drunken brawl he killed his brother in law, one of the Omaha chiefs, and was afterwards attacked the same night by another brother in law, a brother of the deceased chief, and left for dead, after he had received seven knife wounds. His wife who was a sister of the murdered man adhered to her husband, who revived, and she got him onto a horse and carried him to Decatur to save him from the further fury of the Omahas who surrounded his house at Decatur and waited for days to get their revenge, but were prevented by a guard. Mr. Neil was afterwards tried for murder by the United States Court, found guilty of manslaughter and sentenced to 3 years imprisonment and a fine of $250. They were all educated men, and the prisoner appeared quite like a gentleman. He did not talk Omaha, and I could get no information. He said the system of relationship was like the Winnebago and Shawnee rather than the Iroquois after I had explained each. He could not tell me of their tribes. Thus failed my expectations at Omaha.

[Morgan has a six-page Otoe vocabulary here.]

We left Omaha this morning, June 19, at 8 o'clock and came down the river finely [?] about fifteen miles per hour. During the day we have had two thunder storms with hail in the first and a pounding rain in both. I must take back a former remark about its drizzling in Nebraska and pouring down in generous style in Kansas. Nebraska has today redeemed herself. We were obliged to run up to the bank and tie up for the night, and but two miles above the place where I get off. We should have been there in eight minutes. The lightning shivered a tree about two rods from where we tied up this morning, and it was done about five minutes before we touched the bank.

Such is the rapidity of the current in this river that the boats are obliged to turn around and head up stream to land. But for bends in the river which are numerous and which distribute the descent, and but for the yielding banks which are constantly falling in, this river would show waterfalls in some places and deep excavations in others, with a moderate current on the bends. I have remarked upon this before, and am more and more persuaded of the truth of the observation. It is truly a wonderful river. I have been upon it for 800 miles above its mouth in the Mississippi and from Kansas City to Omaha I am quite sure the river will average one half a mile in width.

The steamer on which I now am and on which I went up from Wyandotte to Omaha is a first class Missouri boat with 40 state rooms, and yet this same boat went up last year to the mouth of the Yellowstone river and considerably above it, which is either 1500 or 1800 miles above St. Louis. From Iowa Point which is the beginning of Nebraska the prairie begins to come in sight and continues to increase in quantity up the river until you reach Omaha. Nebraska on the whole makes a favorable appearance from the river.

Otoe Tribes [Clans]

The children are of the tribe of the father, and no one marries into his own tribe. A brother succeeds. If no brother the oldest son comes next.

1, Bear, Moon-cha. 2, Buffalo Cow, Cha or Ah-ro-wha. 3, Eagle, Kra. 4, Snake, Wa-ka. 5, Beaver, Pa-kh-tha. 7, [sic] Pigeon, Lute-ja. 8, Owl, Ma-kotch. 9, Small Elk, Hoo-ma or Ho-dache. 10, Wolf, Shim-ta or Me-je-ra-ja.[108]

Rulo, Nebraska Territory June 21, 1859

Yesterday morning about four o'clock I was landed at Yankton about ten miles above the point and not finding what I expected there I came on to this place where my expectations have been more than met, and the necessity of stopping at Iowa Point avoided.

[Otoe Kinship]

I obtained yesterday the system of the Otoes through an Otoe woman married to a Frenchman; in the afternoon the Yankton Dakota from a native Sioux woman with Charles Rulo as my interpreter.[109] This schedule is perfect and reliable. Towards evening a son of White Cloud, a famous Iowa chief

Notch-ee-ming-a, White Cloud, chief of the Iowas, painted by George Catlin in 1832. The chief, who is "tastefully dressed with a buffalo robe . . . with a necklace of grizzly bear's claws . . . and profusion of wampum strings," was a distinguished Indian leader.

whom I had sent for, came in and I obtained one on the Iowa. His name is Robert D. White Cloud,[110] he talks English perfectly, and is intelligent. I consider this schedule as one of the most reliable in my collection, and I shall alter the Otoe of the correctness of which in places I have some doubts, to conform to it. The difficulty with the Otoe was the want of a competent English interpreter. Dupre, the husband, was a Frenchman. I have obtained the names of the Otoe tribes and also the names of 6 of the tribes of the Iowas. They have eight, but White Cloud could not give me this remainder. He afterwards added two. He thought they had run out; but as I still wanted them he had to give it up; but I shall probably get them today.

I found Mr. Hibbard of Illinois here, a gentleman with whom I became acquainted on my way up the Missouri and Kansas rivers. Rulo is a small village of twenty or thirty houses pleasantly situated on the bluffs with a meadow in front on the river. Last evening we walked out about a mile and a half on the prairie, which here comes to the river, to take another good look. We had a fine view of a large extent of country. It is the same splendid rolling prairie with timber in the distance here and there in thin strips. Not a plow has yet turned the soil where thousands in a few years will live and thrive.

Iowa Tribes [Clans][111]

Pä-ho'-che, Dusty Noses [Name by which Iowas call themselves; see *Systems*, p. 285] 1. Wolf: Me-je-ra-ja. 2. Bear: Too-rum-pe. 3. Eagle: Cheh-he-ta. These formed themselves first. 4. Pigeon: Lu-chih. 5. Buffalo: Ah-ro-wha. 6. Snake: Wa-kuh. 7. Elk: Ho-dach. 8. Owl: Ma-kotch. 9. Beaver: Pa-kuh-tha, extinct. He [White Cloud] thinks they have also the Owl and the Elk. Beaver: Hamilton's notes [112] state that there was a Beaver tribe among the Iowas and the Otoes.

Iowa Dances

1. Buffalo Dance, Cha-wa-she. 2. Otter Dance, Mung-ka-ne. 3. Scalp Dance, Wa-ja-wa-she. 4. Braves Dance, E-rose-ka-na-she. 5. Society Dance, Mun-wa-tan. 6. Feather Dance, Wa-yun-wih. 7. Dance with joined hands (Green Corn), O-ne-ha-wa-she. 8. Ancient Dance, O-kee-hra-ne. 9. Taking the Kettle Out, Pa-ja-doo-tha-weh. 10. Dance for the Dead, Wa-she-wa-he. 11. Night Dance, Ha-ha-wa-she. 12. Medicine Dance, Wa-cha-wa-she. 13. Grizzly Bear Dance, Mun-to-wa-she. 14. Medicine Drinking Dance, Mong-ka-shu-ja-wa-she. 15. Enlisting Dance, O-nei-ha.

This reservation [Iowa] on the river 30 miles by 8 back, was set apart by the government for the half breed Indians of the Yankton and bands of the Sioux, the Omahas, Otoes, and the Iowas. This effort of the government for the half breed class has brought here quite a number of Frenchmen, who as traders had married Indian wives. They have come here with their wives to reside. I saw at Yankton a Frenchman, Mr. Galdy, who had been a trader for 23 years in the Upper Missouri and from him I learned that the system of relationships of the Dakotas was also to be found among the Asiniboines, the [?] and Mandans, the Crows, the Snake Indians of Washington Territory, the Cheyennes. He says all the Indians have it so far as he knows. I learned from him and Rulo and Dupre that the Arickarees [?; same as the undeciphered word two sentences above] and Pawnees were the same people and spoke a different language from the Dakotas. That the Asiniboines spoke a language closely like the Sioux, and that the Cheyennes were unlike the *Dakotas* or Sioux.

Changing Names Among Iowas

The names of each tribe [clan] are kept distinct and no one of the Wolf tribe can by right use a name belonging to the Bear, etc. They have a set of names for childhood, but they are not changed until the person has performed some exploit upon the war path or in other ways, when he may change his own name, or [it] is changed for him. If he does nothing of note he usually carries his boy's name through life. White Cloud told me he had been with war parties when a boy, and that his name had been changed several times, and that he had changed it himself once or twice. His present name is Wa-nye-me-ra (Sitting holding something).

With the Iowas the children are of the tribe of the father and not of the mother in any case. But a man is not allowed to marry a woman of his own tribe. The son succeeds the father in the office of chief, but if not acceptable they take a brother of the deceased, which shows that the office is elective. They have chiefs for war and chiefs for peace.

A new idea was mentioned about certain dances of which he gave me a list of all he could remember used by the Iowas. He saw one of the Medicine dances named, the one in which a kettle of medicine of various herbs was put on and boiled during the night of the dance, and in the morning at break of day they were required each to drink a dose, the effect of which was stimulating and ended as a vomit and cleanser from bile. He said he was not a member of this dance. It was got up by a sort of society by itself and no one not initiated was a member of the dance or could take any part in it. He says several of the dances are society dances; that he had given them horses to get into the one mentioned, but

had not succeeded. He also told me that one reason why the Indians would not let a stranger or white man about these medicine affairs was a superstitious fear of evil consequences or bad luck. The Iowas still continue their dances.

The Sauks or Foxes are about ten miles west of this place on their reserves. I ought to take this chance to go and see them and did partly arrange to go, but could not make it out. I did not go to their Kansas reservation because I expected to find them here and now in my haste to return I leave then unasked of the system of relationship etc. The fact is I have enough schedules to show what the system is of the races east of the Mountains and north of New Mexico in the United States, and merely to multiply these schedules does not strengthen the argument. I seek additional ones quite as much for the vocabulary as for anything else. [But Morgan did not feel this way after he got home. Instead, he made three more long trips, as we know, to "multiply these schedules."]

Geographic Names in Iowa

Platte River, Ne-brak-a, Flat River. The word is in Iowa. Des Moines Run, Neen-ta. Missouri, Ne-so-ja, Riley Water. Mississippi, Nu-hun-ya, Big Water. Kansas River, To-poo-ka, A good place to dig wild potatoes. Nebraska River, Ne-ma-ha, Muddy River. Little Nemaha, Ne-ma-la-ing, Little Muddy River.

The Iowas believe in a great spirit and in an evil spirit. They are not represented as having any particular form. Besides these they have a large number of inferior spirits, some of which are good and some evil. They have the Spirit of Medicine, of Water, of the Bluffs, and of nearly every object in nature. The principal ones only are named.

LE SOLDAT DU CHÊNE, AN OSAGE CHIEF

artist unknown, but probably GEORGE BIRD KING

"The Soldier of Oak" or the "Big Soldier," say McKenney and Hall, owed his name to "a desperate fight, in which, having sheltered himself behind a large oak, [he] successfully defended himself against several enemies." He was a well-known chief, mentioned by Zebulon M. Pike in his *Account* (1810), and was of enough importance to sign a number of treaties.

FUNERAL SCAFFOLD OF A SIOUX CHIEF

BY KARL BODMER

"Mr. Bodmer . . . made a sketch of the stage of a distinguished Sioux warrior, whose remains had been brought from a great distance with pomp, and were covered with a red cloth." The sketch was made on April 27, 1834, near Fort Pierre. Prince Maximilian, like Morgan, was interested in burial customs: "Among the peculiar customs of the Sioux is their treatment of the dead. Those who die at home are sewed up . . . in blankets and skins, in their complete dress; painted, and laid with their arms and other effects on a high stage, supported by four poles, till they are decomposed, when they are sometimes buried." Morgan saw similar Sioux burial stages.

They worship the sun and the moon, and all natural objects, to use White Cloud's language, but on being questioned he said they did not worship the sun as a god or as a spirit in any sense whatever, but recognized the favorable influence of the sun upon nature which was the work of the Great Spirit. They believe in witches and in dreams, and that their Indian medicine men can put a bone in a man's back or take one out.

White Cloud agreed to spend the afternoon with me, but has disappointed me. We were to take up their religious system among other things. I have left with Mr. Brown two schedules, one for the Cheyennes and one for the Sauk and Fox, which a brother in law of White Cloud is to assist Mr. Brown in making out for me. I am quite disappointed in not seeing him again, as in our previous conversations we had been upon other subjects. White Cloud, although a young man, has been in several battles with the Sacs, and frequently out on the buffalo hunt. His adventures are said to have been quite remarkable.

I saw today two Iowa chiefs. One of them was fine looking. He had on deer skin leggings coming up to his thighs, a shirt, a red blanket, an otter skin cap with a tail pendant from the side, a necklace of grizzly bear's claws with a pendant of otter [?] hanging from his neck down his back about four feet long, and moccasins. He was on horseback. I saw him at a store a few moments and was quite struck with his fine appearance. He told me he had been to Washington twice, which he evidently thought was a feather in his cap. The Iowas are not a numerous band, are kindred with the Dakotas or Sioux, and have a fine reserve near Iowa Point and extending to the Big Nemaha river about two miles below Rulo.

The reservation of the Sauks and Foxes is west of Rulo, their village being ten miles distant.

I leave on the next boat for home, and am now writing on my knee on the bank of the river waiting for it at sundown, June 21, but it may not be in tonight in which case it will be here shortly after daylight as they lay up all night going down. I have eleven schedules in my pockets in eleven different languages and have settled the existence of the same system in at least eight or ten others, beyond any question. I shall return quite satisfied with the general results of my inquiries, only regretting that I could stay so short a time in each place. The system of relationship was my main point of inquiry, but I also intended to make their religious system a subject of minute examination. I have not as much material as I could wish. There is a steamer coming up slowly from below, but none in sight from above, and it is growing cool fast and will soon be dark. If nothing untoward happens, I hope to be at home Friday night, June 24.

Steamer *Peerless*[113] Missouri River
From Rulo to St. Joseph, June 22, 1859.
After waiting on the bank of the river until dusk, we gave up and went back to town for the night, and did not get off until this morning at 7. One good result was a second interview with White Cloud which we devoted to the religion of the Iowas.

[Religion of the Iowas]

He says they have but little religion; that they believe in a Great Spirit, Wa-kun-da-pe,[114] and in an Evil Spirit, Wa-kun-da-pesepkun-ye; that they have no names for any of the inferior spirits. They have a name for a spirit or a ghost, Wa-noh-he. They also divide them into good and evil

spirits. All good is the work of the good spirits, and all evil of the bad. They believe in the immortality of the soul, but not in future punishments. They think the soul goes to a place of rest, where it lives in the body as it does here, knows former friends, and is happy.

They address the dead after death. They put on them their best attire, paint their faces, and then some one of the same tribe who is called upon by the oldest son, if a father, or some near relative, then makes a formal address to the body. In burying, the old practice was to bury in a sitting position with the face to the east. The body was put in the ground and over the top was raised a small mound. He insisted that no opening was left in the grave for the spirit to reenter. That for four nights after the burial it was customary to build a fire on the grave. With the body they buried food, and weapons and personal articles of the deceased in the belief that they would be useful to him on the journey.

They also believe that the souls of those who are killed in battle or that are killed in a village, do not go to heaven immediately, but are transmuted into thunder birds. That it is the souls of these departed warriors who make the thunder and lightning, and they are represented as having the form of birds. I did not learn whether their solicitude to carry away the bodies of the slain for burial was caused by this notion on the ground that those who remain unburied are the ones only who become thunder birds, which I presume is the fact.

He says they also regard the buffalo as a god. This seemed so strange to me that I was curious to know in what sense or way. He said the Indian believed the buffalo after being killed and eaten by him had power to cover his bones again with flesh and

come to life again, and that he did thus come to life again after being killed. I suppose this must be a legend to account for their constant reproduction. I was surprised to find that they have no names for these spirits. He said when they gave any names they said Wa-kun-da-he, or Great Spirit or God. I think this word means Great Medicine and that what they mean by Great Medicine is Great Spirit, or a superior power, be that what it may be;[115] and if this is so, their idea of the Great Spirit is very feeble and low.

About their idea of painting the face, he said when they went out to war they painted to represent some animal whose motions and speed they were to imitate on the march. He knew nothing about it as a religious rite.

The Iowas have eight tribes [clans] which are given above, and the Otoes nine. In both cases no man marries with his own tribe, and the children are of the father's tribe. The chief is also succeeded by his brother, or by his oldest son. I asked him whether the ancient system did not give the office of chief to a nephew or a sister's son, and whether this change to the present system was not the result of the interference of the French and English, and particularly of the early missionaries. He said he could not tell, but that the government offices and the missionaries were continually interfering to put upon these chiefs whom they would not recognize in their domestic affairs. I hope yet to find some solution of the enigma about descent in the female line, which the larger part of the Algonquins have not, but which some of the oldest of them have, as the Delawares and Mohekunuks [Stockbridge]. I think it was the original system, notwithstanding what is now history about the succession of sachems in New England from father to son.

The Buffalo and the Buffalo Grass

At various points the buffalo has been made the subject of conversation and I have picked up here and there some information concerning him. Their number is immense. Men who have passed through the buffalo ranges say there are millions of them, that they go in vast herds, and when in motion they carry everything before them; that a [wagon] train if in their way is not able to stop them or turn them aside; they pass through it frequently stampeding the ani-

Left: No photograph ever taken nor picture ever painted demonstrates as vividly the magnitude of the buffalo herds that grazed the West as does M. S. Garretson's "The Herd."

Below: This excellent study of buffalo hunting was done by Felix Darley and first appeared in **GRAHAM'S MAGAZINE.** Morgan, in common with every western traveler, was intrigued by the buffalo and by the methods used to hunt the animal.

mals. That the bulls frequently kill oxen when they are thus loosened and get among them. They say, however, that the buffalo is a timid animal, or what would be more truthful, is averse to a collision with other animals, and moves off when a man comes near him, never attacking a man in the first instance. When wounded he does not always turn upon his assailant, but he does sometimes give chase for a mile or two.

The hunter prefers to hunt on horseback when he rides up and shoots him behind the foreshoulder from the saddle and then reloads in the saddle still pursuing and fires again. They will with an expensive horse ride up within six feet of a buffalo bull with perfect impunity and bowl him over with a rifle ball. When the buffalo is full grown and in good condition it takes a fast horse to overtake him and keep up with him. The Indian still uses the bow in the far west and I have been assured over and over again by those who ought to know, that an Indian will shoot his arrow, pointed with iron, entirely through a buffalo behind the fore

shoulder so that the arrow will go clean through and come out on the other side and stick in the ground. I have heard the Iroquois say that their hunters would send their arrows through a deer in the same way.

The buffalo comes up in the fall within fifty miles of Fort Riley in Kansas, which is 120 miles up the Kansas river, making the whole distance 170 miles west of Wyandotte. In Nebraska he comes within fifty or 75 miles of the Missouri river. The river goes westward somewhat but the buffalo comes further east no doubt because the prairies of western Nebraska are not so much traversed by the emigrant to frighten them away. Their habitat is constantly contracting although it is still immensely extensive.

The buffalo grass is not high, but short, round and wiry and [krinkles, or doubles?] down, and never grows high like the ordinary prairie grass. It is said to be remarkably nutritious for cattle and that it will fatten them faster than corn. It is said that

after the buffalo returns and ceases to crop the buffalo grass, the prairie grass takes its place and works it out. Whether a subsequent cropping would restore the buffalo grass, I do not know.

It would be perfectly easy to hunt the buffalo now in parties from the east, but for the Indians, and then you would be safe were your party large enough. The Indians are at feud and always expect to fight when they meet on the buffalo hunt. If a white man is found alone with an Indian party he is treated as an enemy, as one of their number, and must share their fate. Such an excursion with a strong party, all white, would be glorious, the climate being unrivalled, the exercise health giving and the sport exciting. One would think that a fall would not pass without a number of such expeditions from the east by our hunter characters. We are now near St. Jo and I must end my journal.

This peaceful scene of grazing buffalo was taken by the pioneer photographer L. A. Huffman in northern Montana in 1880.

Steamer on the Mississippi
Between Hannibal and Quincy
June 23, 1859

A word more about buffaloes. In April after the young calves make their appearance, the cow buffaloes with their young separate from the herd and move southward and remain by themselves about three months. As they feed from day to day the cows form a circle with the calves in the center and thus they move over the pasturage from day to day. About July the herds of bull buffaloes go south in quest of the cows. It is at such times that they come upon the emigrant trains, that they rush on without turning aside and when the oxen sometimes stampede in their fright as before stated. The buffalo is also found about 75 miles west of Fort Kenney [Kearney?].

Dew on the Prairie

The dews on the prairie are remarkably heavy and must exercise an important influence on the climate of the west, as it certainly does upon the vegetation. We know of no such heavy dews in the east. It commences to fall immediately after sundown and continues until "sun up" as the phrase is in the west. At Rulo we went down to the river at day light, 3½ o'clock to watch for the boat. Another boat came up the river just as we reached the bank and landed some passengers. One of them remained on the bank and we began a conversation. Presently it began to feel cool and I put on my overcoat. Soon after he began to feel it and raised his umbrella, saying that it came down like fine rain. I noticed afterwards that the rim of my hat was quite wet. In the morning you cannot walk in the grass without getting wet feet and clothes, and in August when the grass is high, as a doctor out in the night occasionally said to me, without getting wet up to the throat even on horseback. There is almost always a fine breeze on the prairie by day and sometimes it continues through the night, but you will always notice a great moderation at sundown. If it blows strong through the night there will be no dew, but if still, or it blows gently there will be the usual amount of dew.

It is easy to see what a great influence these constant and excessive dews exercise upon the grass of the prairie. It is sufficient to support vegetation without any rain. The same heavy dews continue for four hundred miles west of the Missouri river on the route to Pike's Peak which is as far [as] I have inquired concerning it, and without doubt over all the plains, and that it is owing to the dews in these dry regions that that very vegetation is able to live.

The emigrants use tents or roll up in a blanket and sleep on the ground. Of course they could not sleep in such a heavy dew without danger of a chill and of fever. There should be some instrument to measure the amount of precipitation in the form of dew, and I do not know whether there is or not, and then a proper allowance be made in consequence of its uniformity in determining its climatic effect. Much of a heavy rain is of no use to vegetation, but a little dew shed upon the grass every night tells directly upon its growth. Climatic laws are as important in their relations to production as to health.

We are now going up the Mississippi to Quincy about 20 miles up. This river is much superior to the Missouri in size as well as in beauty. Its water is about half as rapid and less than half as muddy, and takes on that silvery appearance which always makes the water look so beautiful. My paper is exhausted and here on the Mississippi ends my journal, very appropriately this 23 day of June 1859.

Quincy, Illinois, from Henry Lewis', DAS ILLUSTRIRTE MISSISSIPPITHAL. Morgan passed the town as his 1859 trip was coming to an end.

Notes of a Visit to Kansas and Nebraska in May and June, 1860

Chapter V PART I

Left Rochester May 23, 1860, for Kansas. Mr. Frothingham[1] who is interested in a village site at Bellmont near St. Joseph started with me. We reached Detroit at 8 P.M., Chicago at 9 A.M. Thursday morning and Quincy on the Mississippi at 9½ Thursday evening. We are now, Friday morning at 7 o'clock, steaming down the Mississippi to Hannibal where we are to take the cars at 10 again for St. Joseph which we expect to reach at 9 tonight and Kansas City Saturday noon. It is pleasant again to see the Mississippi. A great river commands our interest. We slept upon her last night in the steamer *Pike* to which we were conducted on our arrival, as we are to leave early for Hannibal. It rained this morning with thunder and cooled the air. Yesterday it was very hot and uncomfortable all day on the road to Quincy.

Saturday morning, May 26, 1860
We reached St. Joseph, Missouri, last evening at 9 o'clock after three days and two nights from Rochester. The railroad from St. Jo to Atchison, 20 miles down the river, is running and we were sent down immediately and went on board steamer *Black Hawk*[2] which was to leave for Kansas City at daylight. We are now leaving Nestor, Mo. The contrast with last year at the same time is very great. There has been but little rain for six months.[3] In Illinois and Missouri the winter wheat is mostly destroyed and the corn crop is in danger unless we have rain soon. Every thing is drying up. I expect to find the same effects of dryness in Kansas and Nebraska. The Missouri river which last year was full from bank to bank and nearly to the top of its banks, is now low and full of sand bars. The current is sluggish. Last year it was swift, so astonishingly swift that the best steamers could not move [?] to exceed 5 miles per hour going up and about 20 going down. Now the current is about the same or less than that of the Mississippi and does not greatly affect the speed of boats going either up or down. The color of the water is not quite as strong a mud color as it was last year, although muddy enough. There is not as much flood wood moving in the river, in fact little or none, while last year the quantity was great. We expect to reach Kansas City about 2 P.M. which will give me time to reach Friend Harvey[4] at the Shawnee Mission before night, which was my plan on leaving on Wednesday that I might spend the Sabbath with him and go to Paoli on Monday. I hope to have him go with me and to go on horse back. Wrote Mrs. M. [Morgan] today.

Friends Shawnee Mission, K. T.
May 27, 1860
We left Atchison for Kansas City at daylight yesterday morning and about 9 o'clock got onto a sand bar just above Fort Leavenworth and remained there about 3 hours, during which time by means of spars she was nearly worked off, the work being finished by a steamer of the line coming up the river and tugging her off. We spent about two hours at Fort Leavenworth and reached Kansas City about 6 P.M. I got into the stage for Westport four miles inland and there procured livery in the shape of a white mule and was driven out to this place which I reached about 9 o'clock. Friend Harvey was at home this time and received me very kindly, as also did his family which now consists of himself and wife, his eldest son

with a wife and two children, another son, a teacher and two other female members, together with about ten (10) Shawnee children now attending at the Mission.

At 11 today we had a Friends Meeting in the school house, or room of the building. Mr. Stanley[5] and wife and two children were present. They are friends who own a farm near by and are old friends of the Harveys, a very pleasant couple. After dinner we went into a regular talk about the Indians. He has lived with the Sauks and Foxes.

Sauk and Fox Descent in the Female Line

Mr. Stanley says that Keokuk,[6] the principal chief of the Sauks, succeeded in procuring a clause to be inserted in a government treaty that his son should succeed him as chief and that he should be recognized as a chief by the government. They now live in southern Kansas and young Keokuk claims to be a chief and has been recognized as such by the government, but the people refuse to acknowledge him as a chief and have asked the government to consent to his expulsion or disownment. This is one of the many instances of gov-

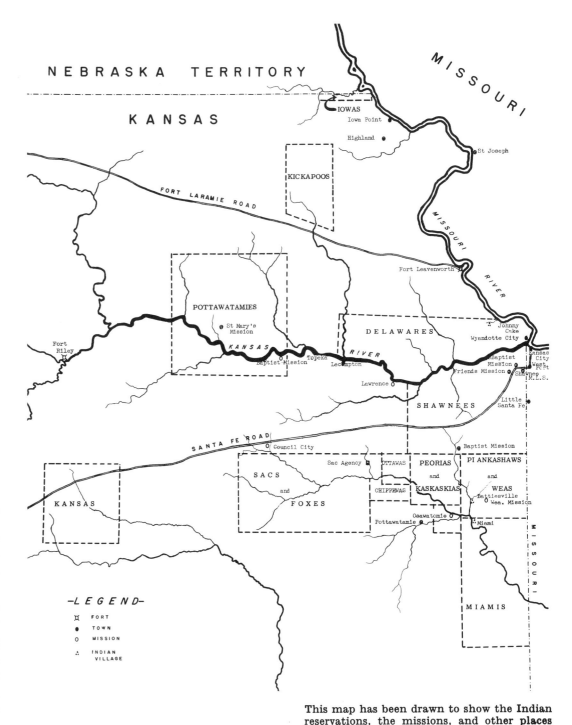

This map has been drawn to show the Indian reservations, the missions, and other places visited by Lewis Henry Morgan in his trips to the West in 1859 and in 1860.

Below: Keokuk on horseback, by George Catlin.

Left: Moses Keokuk (Wunagisa), the son of Keokuk. Keokuk, the Sauk who opposed **Black Hawk**, and who was made chief by the government, was never accepted as such by the tribe. His son, Moses, followed him and was the acknowledged leader of his tribe, the son succeeding where the father had failed.

ernment interference in the appoint[ment] of chiefs. There is no doubt, I suppose, that the Sauks are divided into tribes [clans], that father and son are of different tribes, and that the title of chief descends in the tribe. Hence the forcing in of Keokuk Jr. had the effect of putting over the tribe of his father a chief belonging to another and different tribe which no Indian would tolerate. He thinks the language of the Sac and Fox is Algonquin.[7] (I learned afterwards that Keokuk himself usurped the office, and on that account wished the treaty clause.)

Shawnee Children in case of separation of parents always belong to the mother and she takes them under her exclusive control. Their regulations appear in all respects to be the same as the Iroquois.

Succession to Office among Shawnees

Mr. Harvey says that the oldest son succeeds the father and if there is no son, then the oldest son of a sister of the deceased commencing with an elder sister. There is some mistake here because I think it must be fundamental that when the office of chief is hereditary it must be limited to the tribe and where the son succeeds the son is of the father's tribe and descent is in the male line. When the nephew or a brother, it is in the female line. I intend to make this a matter for further inquiry. This may be modified by naming the son into the father's tribe.

Shawnee Dances

1. Bread Dance, Da-qua-na-ka-wa. This is used in spring and fall to obtain a good spring and before they use green corn.
2. New Corn Dance, Ne-pen-a-ka-wa. Used at the Green Corn Festival. Men and women in both of these.
3. Buffalo Dance, M-tho-tha-ka-wa. Men and women. Used at any time.
4. War Dance, Hik-he-ka-wa. Before setting out. Men alone.
5. War Dance, He-len-he-na-ka-wa. Dance on return. It signifies the dance of the braves.
6. False Face Dance, Path-ka-wa-ka-wa. Dance with false faces and by men alone.
7. Pumpkin Dance, Wa-pe-ko-na-ka-wa. Much like bread dance with singing a little different. Men and women.
8. Wolf Dance, M-wha-wa-ka-wa. This is a begging dance. Every one is expected to give, and when the whole is collected they make a feast.
9. Fish Dance, Na-ma-tha-ka-wa. Men and women. The women enter the dance at their pleasure. None but a female relative can dance with a man. A woman not a relative is not allowed to do so. This is the Iroquois Fish Dance in form, but I do not know as it must be a relative.
10. Horse Dance, M-sa-wa-wa-ka-wa. Men and women. The women stand by the singers and the men trot them into the dance side by side as they go by the singers. A man can take any woman whether relative or not.
11. Swan Dance, Wa-pa-the-wa-ka-wa. Men and women. Two men side by side and occasionally a woman.
12. Bear Dance, M-qua-ka-wa. Men and women. Used in the Bread Dance.
13. Bean Dance, M-sko-che-tha-ka-wa. This is danced with joined hands from the head to the feet of the dancers. Men and women.
14. Rocking Dance, Na-ma-na-ka-wa. Men and women. A trotting dance.
15. Cherokee Dance, Ka-to-wha-na-ka-wa. Dance of the [Morgan's blank] by women alone.
16. Dance for the Dead, Lap-se-ma-te-wa. Dance on adoption of one in place of deceased.
17. Scraping Dance, Lal-ha-ka-wa. They notch a stick and for music scrape a stick along over the notches. This is put over a wood bowl to increase the noise.
18. Squat Dance, Na-na-ma-cha-qua-wa. They squat down and shake like a turkey or chicken shakes off the dust, not all at once, but a few at a time.
19. Bird Dance, Ga-che-ga-pa-the-wa-ka-wa. By women alone. It is a small bird which appears in winter and sings, not a snow bird.
20. Corn Dance, Tha-pa-te-wa-ka-wa.
21. Turkey Dance, Pa-la-wa-ka-wa.

Kahl-we, Blue Jacket [Morgan met Blue Jacket in 1859], Rabbit Tribe (Tail up). He gave me the above tribes [dances?].

[Spirits]

1. Great Spirit, Ma-ya-ta-la-ta-ga, the Creator;
2. Great Spirit, Ta-pa-la-ma-la-kwa, the Master; } one
3. Great Spirit, O-a-si-man-a-too, the good and powerful Being;
4. Evil Spirit, Ma-che-man-a-too, a Bad Spirit;
5. Thunder God, Na-nem-ke, a Bird or Eagle; when he flaps his wings it lightens

Relationships—Shawnee

My mother's brother is my uncle, his son is my uncle again and so on to the end.[8] But my mother's brother's daughter is my mother, her son and daughter are my brother and sister, and the son of this brother is my son if I am a man, and my nephew if I am a woman, and then thus [?] is brought around [?]

Shawnees Salute of Kin

When Shawnees meet they never speak each others names, only the term of relationship. My nephew, grand son as above, are you going etc. They always use the term of relationship. They shake hands now; I think it was the old usage.

Aunt and Uncle among Shawnees

Friend Harvey and myself visited Mrs. Graham Rogers [Morgan worked with her in 1859] yesterday and found her and her sister at home. We ran   [?]   out anew the aunt and her descendants, and the uncle and his descendants, and found that the kink so to speak finally ran out in every case when female succeeds male on uncle's side, but the son of an uncle is an uncle again as far as you may choose to go. But the daughter of an uncle is a mother, her children are my brothers and sisters, and from them the rule is the same as in other cases. The father's sister is an aunt, both to a man and woman, but her son is a man's nephew, and a woman's daughter, and her daughter is a man's niece, and a woman's daughter, and the next generation are grand children. Thus both sides clear out complete and bring the collateral line into the lineal except the son of an uncle. The uncle, as elsewhere frequently stated, is a most important relative, but not more important Mrs. Rogers says than the father. The aunt, on the other hand, is not raised up to a superior position, but rather brought down to an equal, in the rank of her relationship, with a sister, since her son is a man's nephew and a woman's son. This is a new thought which suggested itself to me last night and is worthy of further consideration. One thing I am at least prepared to say, that this Indian system of consanguinity is, in every sense, a wonderful and a splendid system; and a credit to the affections and intelligence of the original race which wrought it out.

Shawnee Office of Chief

A Shawnee chief of the Wolf Tribe [clan] was about to die, he had a son and also a nephew. His son was of the Rabbit Tribe and the nephew of the Fish Tribe. The name of the latter was Kos-qua-the, (sharp). The old chief, whose name was John Perry (La-loh-weh) Bob Tail, called a council and said he wished to name as his successor his nephew. After the death of the uncle the name of the nephew was changed to Tep-a-ta-go-the, (To hear an animal making a noise), a man belonging to the Wolf Tribe. This changed his name from the Fish to the Wolf and kept the title of chief in the Wolf Tribe.

Shawnees Sleep Nude

Blue Jacket says it is still the practice of many of the Shawnees to sleep nude, and was the ancient practice by all. They remove all the clothing except the breech cloth of the men and the waist cloth of the females. He said further that it was still the custom among all the Indian nations so far as he knows.

Miami Nation [Tribe]

Me-ä-me-ä′ -ga [the name by which the Miamis designated themselves according to Morgan's informants]. From Moses Silver Heels [Friend Simon Harvey interpreting]. Wa-yä-tä-no′ -ke: This was an old name of the Miamis. They call themselves by this name now. It signifies lovely or eddying water, out of which the nation sprang or were born [see *Systems*, p. 287].

1. Turkey Tribe [Clan], Pi-la-wa. 2. Raccoon, Ah-see-pon-na. 3. Snow Tribe, Mon-na-to. 4. Sun Tribe, Keel-swa; the word means the sun. 5. Water Tribe; this tribe sprung out of the water when it whirled or boiled around in an eddy in some stream. 6. Wolf, Moh-wha-wa; 7. Panther, Ka-no-ta-wa; 8. Buzzard, Ah-pa-kose-e-a; 9. Loon, Mon-gwa; 10. Eagle, Ken-da-wa.

Marriage

The Miamis as far back as he can remember could marry into their own tribe [clan]. The children belonged to the tribe of the father if he married out of his tribe, and he was of a standing superior to the woman, but if the woman was superior in position of [sic] the man, then they were of her tribe. If a chief died his successor was not a certain thing in any election   [?]   . Wild Cat, a chief of the Panther Tribe, was succeeded by his son in law who belonged to the Raccoon Tribe. His mother was a Miami, and his father a Pottawatamie. The nationality [i.e., tribal affiliation] followed the mother.

Paoli, Peoria Res. K. T.
May 30, 1860

We arrived here last night, and saw [Luther] Paschal and Battise [Peoria, both of whom had assisted Morgan in 1859], also Seth Clover [?] [9] and Allen Ward,[10] an old acquaintance of Friend Harveys. Harvey is with me, I should have said at first. Battise and Clover are about to leave for Kansas City and thus I am again disappointed as to him who is the best Indian authority here; but he has agreed to direct Paschal to do the work for me, and to send for a Peoria woman to aid him. One most important fact Battise has settled for me, namely that in Peoria, Kaskaskia, Weaw and Piankeshaw, my father's sister's son is my nephew and not my cousin, and consequently my mother's brother's son is my uncle. One other thing also he settles, that my father's brother is a father and not a step father and that my step father is the same as father. The last I doubt.

The Peorias, Kaskaskias, Weaws and Piankeshaws have lost their tribes [clans] for many years and marry [?] other. If a Peoria man marries a Kaskaskia woman the children are Kaskaskias; they follow the mother. If a Weaw man marries a Delaware woman, the children are Delawares, and if a Delaware man marries a Weaw woman the children are Weaws. This is the remains of the old system. If a Peoria woman marries a white man, the children are Peorias, but if a Peoria man marries a white woman, the children are aliens. They have no tribes nor recollection of any. I have just worked out carefully the system of consanguinity of the Peoria and am told that the system of the four nations is identical, and the dialectical differences are very slight.

The four bands now number but 187 persons all told. They have $340,000 invested in government funds, 160 acres of land to each person and ten sections of land in common. Their annuity is about $20,000 per annum and gives about $126 to each person. They receive their annuities as one nation, but yet preserve their national [tribal] distinctions. They have lost their tribes

Top: The Medicine Bag Dance of the Sauk and Fox, by George Catlin. In this dance the warriors who have returned from battle and who have taken scalps, dance in front of the lodge of a woman whose husband has been killed. They sing to his medicine bag, which hangs on a bush, and throw presents to his widow.

Center: The Sauk and Fox Slave Dance, by George Catlin. This dance celebrates Indians who pick a master to serve for two years prior to their first war party.

Bottom: Dance to the Berdash of the Sauk and Fox, by George Catlin. A curious ceremony, not yet fully understood.

[clans] they say more than a hundred years ago, marry indiscriminately, that is, there is no barrier but near relationship, and yet their system of consanguinity is still alive in all its forms and fullness. I have made out their schedule today and have succeeded to my entire satisfaction. The words of their nomenclature follow the Chippewa quite closely, or I should say the languages are closely alike but in this deviation, a father's sister's son, they follow the Shawnee, and leave the Chippewa. Before step father was substituted for father, as applied to father's brother, and before cousin was invented as applied to father's sister's son, and used in the place of nephew, the Peoria, Kaskaskia, Piankeshaw, Weaw and Miami must have separated from the original stock, and the Shawnee must have come off before them. The Ottawa and Chippewa and I think the Pottawatamie, are alike.

I am told by Battise, and by Paschal, and the two other Indians named on the schedule, that the system of the four bands is precisely the same, and that the dialectical differences, if ever very great, are now inconsiderable. They all understand each other readily, most of their words being the same, and but a few in which there is any discernible difference.

Battise and General [?] Clover [?] left this morning for Kansas City, but before they left instructions were given to Luther Paschal who behaved so shabbily last evening, to assist us and they also sent up two other well informed Indians, Valley and Mitchel, to aid us and we together made pretty thorough work of it. Mr. Allen Ward, a merchant of Paoli, and an old friend of Friend Harveys, spent the forenoon with us at the house of Battise, where we did the work. He was very kind and gentlemanly, indeed. He has agreed to

furnish me with the Indian geographical [names] of this region if I wish them.

We leave after dinner for Ottawa Jones [a Pottawatamie whom Morgan had met in 1859] which is about 20 miles west of this place. Wrote to Mary [Mrs. Morgan] this A.M. before breakfast. It will leave tomorrow the last day of May, and be about a week reaching its destination.

1. Peoria Indians Pe-o-ri-a
2. Weaws We-a-ta-no
3. Piankeshaw Pe-ank-e-shaw
4. Kaskaskias Ka-ka-ke-ah

They are now amalgamated into one nation. They have lost their tribes [clans] and each nation [tribe] is now about the same as a tribe.

Ottawa Creek, June 1, 1860

We reached Ottawa Jones last evening and leave now in a few minutes for the Sauk and Fox reservation, the Agency of which is 15 miles distant. Paoli is 25 miles from here.

Sauk and Fox Reservation, K. T.
June 1, 1860

Saw-kee, Sauks; Spouting up; Mas-kwa-ka-uk,[11] Red Man, Foxes. The name Fox is a nickname. A real Sauk speaks slow and plain, a Fox does not. The languages are a little different, but the Sauk most prevails. They were different nations [tribes] united by the government. The Foxes anciently were very numerous and were great fighters. They overtook the Sauks, and they united the Sauks taking them under their protection. The fighting propensities of the Foxes made many enemies. Their languages were originally one. There are now more Sauks than Foxes. This from Antoine Gookie,[12] a Menominee, but for nine years interpreter for the Sauks and Foxes.

Sauk and Fox Dances

1. War Dance	Wa-da-sa-wa-ga-wat	Men and women who have been on war parties.
2. Medicine Dance	Me-da-wuk	Men and women
3. " "	Wa-ba-noke	" "
4. Buffalo Dance	Pa-she-ke-wa-ga-wat	Men alone
5. Shawnee Dance	Sha-wa-no-wa-ga-wat	All M. W. & C.
6. Turning Dance	Ka-yo-wa-ga-wat	Men and women in pairs. This is the Seneca Fish Dance.

Sauk and Fox Tribes [Clans][13]

1. Wolf, Mo-wha-wis-so-uk	8. Hawk, Ka-ka-quis-so-jik
2. Eagle, Pa-mis-so-uk	9. Bones, Au-kuh-ne-nate
3. Fish, Na-ma-sis-so-uk	10. Bear, Ma-quis-so-jik
4. Deer, Pa-sha-ga-sa-wis-so-uk	11. Fox, Wa-ko-sa-wis-so-jik
5. Buffalo, Na-mus-sus-so-uk	12. Sea, Ka-che-kom-a-ue-so-jik
6. Thunder, Na-na-ma-kew-uk	13. Sturgeon, Na-ma-wi-so-uk
7. Elk, Ma-sha-wa-uk	14. Big Tree, Ma-she-ma-tak

Tribal [Clan] Names

These tribes [clan names] are very numerous. He said he could continue to name them for a day. They do not now go by tribes except they name their children into those names. Long Horn is a name which belongs to the Deer Tribe; Yellow Thunder, a name of the Thunder Tribe. Ka-ka, Hawk, is among the Hawk Tribe; Black Wolf is one of the Wolf names. Shedding Bear, Ka-po-na; Eagle drawing his nest, Oa-ka-qua-he-; Eagle sitting with his head up, Pe-a-ta-na-ka-hok; Eagle flying over the limbs.

In ancient times no one named into the Eagle would marry into the Eagle family, and so of the others. As far back as we can remember the children were named into the *father's family*.

Children of Father's Tribe [Clan]

It seems above that the children are named into the father's tribe, so Gookie, a Menominee, says of the Sauks and Foxes. But he also says that the nationality [tribal affiliation] follows the mother. That if a Sauk woman marries a Chippewa her children are Sauks. If a Sauk man marries a Kaw woman, the children are Kaws.

Descent of Property

He says if I should die my brothers and sisters and uncles could pitch in and rob my wife. The old law of descent gave my property to the nearest of kin and these were his brothers and sisters and uncles and not his own children. Now they expect their children will inherit, but there is no certainty of it now. The old Indian institution of descent in the female line turns up at every point.

The Sauks and Foxes Salute of Kin

The Sauks and Foxes and Menominees now address each other by the terms of relationship universally and not by their personal names. This is no doubt universal. The Sauks are dark skinned.

Descent of Chief's Office

If a Hawk chief died he could be succeeded by one of the Hawk family, the same of the Bear and of each of the others. They would paint at the grave the device of the Hawk or the Bear and thus the family of the deceased would be known. His oldest son takes his place, and when he dies, the next oldest. If he had no son, and his daughter had a son, he would take it. If no daughter's son, and he had a sister who had a son, he would take it.

Marriage

In the marriage matter the uncle and the brother had the principal management and authority. He says among the Menominees and Sauks the uncle is the principal personage. He can command or order his nephew to go wherever he pleases and he must go. He may take his horse, saddle and bridle, or anything he likes. He simply asks him if it is his, and if he says it is, then the uncle says, "you have had it long enough,"

and takes it away. After the nephew becomes of age, he may retake it in the same manner, by telling his uncle he has had it long enough.

Divorce

If husband and wife separate, the children belong to the mother. In old times they bought their wife, that is the brother and uncle sent presents to the family of the girl; if they were accepted, the girl was given in marriage etc.

Sauk and Fox Skulls

It is perfectly easy to procure skulls in the Sauk country and also in the Kaw and Osage, if it is managed prudently. The graves are heaps of stones, or a pile of timber which can be easily opened at the top and the skull taken out, without much of any labor and without much disturbance. If it had not rained while we were on the Sauk reserve I should have gone with William Turner to a grave where two Foxes were buried together in a sitting posture, who had been killed in a drunken brawl 18 months before. Turner said a few days before he had opened the stakes and saw the skeletons or the upper part of them. I think for 100 [$1.00?] each he would secure me any quantity of Sauk and Fox, Kaw, etc.

Munsees

There are a few Munsees on the Chippewa reservation in Kansas, less than 50 in all. I think their number is 34. They still speak their Language, but it is very near the Delaware and is supposed not to be pure. I procured last night the Munsee system of consanguinity from a Munsee family well qualified to give it.[14] It is like the Delaware, but the language is dialectically different. It is not as harsh and guttural as the Delaware.

They have kindred at Munsee Town in Canada. They were originally from the Susquehanna river in Pennsylvania. They still preserve their separate existence as Munsees, and will as long as one remains. Descent in the female line. See No. 5, First Visit to Kansas.

The Chippewas

The Chippewas who have a reservation here number only 45. They were removed to this from the St. Clair river near Detroit and above.

The old man, Mr. Coonts, said he had been in England, New York, Philadelphia, Quebec, Montreal and most of the states. "And by G-d, there was no comparison to this country; this is a damn big country. We can raise anything. There is no country like it for farming." It is impossible to swear in any Indian language. The old man was lying on his back, where he has lain since Christmas from the effects of an accident, occasioned by the running away of a horse, and bad treatment of broken limbs. He is partly white, and a man of intelligence and a good farmer.

Children follow the tribe [clan] of the father. This is the rule now among them. But yet in case of divorce the mother takes them. They inherit from the mother and not from the father, the father's property going to the brothers and uncles. The nationality [tribal affiliation] also follows the woman, and not the man.

Osage

The Osages, Kaws and Quappas speak the same language with slight dialectical differences.[15] The Osages and the Kaws are both very dark skinned.

The Osages in a large delegation were here about two weeks ago to visit the Sauks and Foxes, about 50 of them. They have a treaty of peace and friendship with each other and they exchange visits to keep it good.

The Osage's Buffalo Hunt

William Turner[16] at whose house we are staying, is a Pottawatamie by birth, but Chippewa by bringing up and his wife is a Chippewa, and daughter of Mr. Coonts. He says the Osages number more than a 1000. That they are the largest and most powerful Indians in the country, and will as he says average six feet in height. They have horses and live on the prairie and may be called prairie Indians. They are moving a good part of the time, particularly during the buffalo hunt twice a year; the first season Turner says is about the first of June, and the second about the first of September, and [they] last about three weeks. They dry the meat and bring back large quantities without salt. Some of it is plaited as the Kaws had it, some of it shaved an inch thick and a foot wide, and it will dry in a day. The air is pure and there are no flies. Both the Osages and the Sauks still prefer the bow and arrow to the gun for the chase, but for the still hunt they use the gun. It is asserted that Osages have killed two buffaloes with one arrow at one shot, the arrow going entirely through one buffalo, and piercing mortally an other. That they often send an arrow entirely through a buffalo I have no doubt.

The fall hunt is chiefly for the pelt, which is not saved in the spring as the hair is shed; but the buffalo is in his prime to eat September 1, and begins to fat [?] about June.

Crees of Canada

Turner has been among them. He says their language is Algonquin.

Sleeping Nude

Turner says all the Indians in the west now sleep nude. They remove all their clothes except the breech cloth and roll up in a blanket. He does not think it is to save their clothes, it is not to air them, as they are usually rolled up and put under the head. It must therefore be for comfort, and the [practice] is continued from habit and usage. The Chippewas, Sauks and Foxes, Kaws, and Osages all do this. Turner has hunted with the Osage, the Kaws and Sauks and they all follow this practice.

Kaw Marriages

If a man marries the eldest daughter of a Kaw, he has the privilege of taking all of the remaining daughters as fast as they grow up, and they all become his wives at the same time. He is not bound to take them all, but may at his election. If he marries the second or any other daughter he has not this privilege. Polygamy prevails more among them than in any other tribe he knows of. The above usage is just the reverse of polyandria, by which one woman becomes the wife of several brothers at the same time.

Kaw Burial Customs

The Kaws still bury in a sitting posture facing the west, arms crossed and knees flexed. A bow and arrow on the left side, a little brass or earth kettle between the legs or feet, containing corn or beans or dried buffalo meat, and their tobacco pouch and pipe. The hole in the ground is about one foot deep, the body is set up erect, and covered with bark, this is then covered with dirt lightly, after which stones are piled up around the body loose so as [to] cover the body fully about one or two feet over their

A Chippewa grave, with a covering of birch-bark. The Chippewa usually buried their dead in a sitting position and built a roof over the grave. Through a door at one end food was placed by the grave; through it one could talk with the spirit of the dead.

head. This is to secure the body against wolves, etc. In the case of a distinguished man the Kaws saddle a horse, lead him up to the grave and shoot him at the grave, and leave him there unburied. Sometimes the saddle is buried in the grave.

Sauk Burial

The Sauk and Foxes still bury about half of them in a sitting posture, the face to the west. Turner has buried a good many. The deceased is dressed in his best clothing and is buried from 8 to 10 hours afterwards. His tribe prepare him for burial, the men the men and the women the women. If he dies early in the morning he is usually buried the same evening, but otherwise he is kept until the next day. From 4 to 6 are appointed to sit up with the body if a medicine man from his lodge. They sing all night, beating a drum slowly. In the morning they appoint four young men to bear the corpse to the grave. When the body is taken up the medicine man with his squash rattle follows the body and sings the death song, as they march to the grave. The family also accompany the body.

After the body is put down the singing stops. The body is set up in the grave and one of their number previously appointed for that purpose addresses the corpse. He generally tells him, commencing with the term of relationship he has to him, as my brother, nephew, etc. The speaker stands behind the back of the corpse on the east side of it. As he talks he throws tobacco in the ground. "When you get to our uncle (a famous man deceased) give him this tobacco, and speak a good word to him in our behalf. That he, the deceased, must not trouble himself about us, as he is now better off than we and can enjoy the society of all who have gone ahead. Speak a good word to our relative (mentioning some deceased relative). You must not come back to trouble us who are left behind, but leave us in peace." This is about the substance of a funeral discourse.

The Sauks and Foxes put in his grave by his left side a bow and arrow (never guns), and a kettle or pan with corn and beans, pipe, tobacco pouch and tobacco, and if a medicine man his medicine bag unless he wills it away. The body is then covered with bark and earth and stone over the top or make a timber house over the grave, so as to make it secure against animals. The grave is about a foot and a half to two feet deep. They march around the grave and then leave for home. There is no wail at the time of the burial, but the wife must always attend the burial. After the body is placed in the grave and before it is covered the wife takes her stand on the north side of the grave, then steps over it and goes due southward without ever looking back, until she gets out of sight of the place. She may then turn and go back to her home. This is now the custom.

About half bury in graves flat without coffin. The grave is from 1½ to 2 feet high, the head is placed to the east, the same articles are put in the grave and it is covered with bark and then with earth and rounded up. Then they make a bark house over the grave. The same forms and address are made and the wife steps across the grave and goes south out of sight.

There is no wail at the grave in either case. The next day the women go to the grave or out in the field and wail with their hair loose and faces blackened with charcoal. It is continued every day early in the morning and late in the evening for two weeks, and then it ceases. They then adopt another person in his place, giving him the same relationship.

They suppose the spirit is able for some time to return and revisit the body and also that it will need food for the journey.

Shawnee Burial Customs

Friend Harvey says the Shawnees after they commenced burying in coffins here always had a three cornered hole cut in the coffin at the end near the head. This was to enable the spirit to enter and revisit the body.

Chippewa Burial Customs

Turner says the Chippewa burial customs are the same or used to be as the Sauks and Kaws. They do not now bury in a sitting posture, but used to do so. He has seen a good many such graves in Michigan. They now bury in coffins with the head to the west, which they no doubt secured from missionaries.

Pottawatamie Burial Customs

Turner says this nation still, about half of them, bury in a sitting posture, the same as the Sauks and Foxes, with the face to the west, the remainder horizontally. The Ottawas the same.

The Shawnee Methodist Mission and Manual Labor School located in the present Johnson County, Kansas.

PART II

Sawk and Fox Reservation
Kansas Territory
May 31, 1860

Chippeway Mode of Naming

Turner says when a child is born a name is selected and at a subsequent feast, which may be four or eight months afterwards, the child is brought to the feast, and is handed by the father or the principal person of the father's tribe to the manager of the feast, who announces the name which is given to him by the person who hands the child. The name of the father and mother is also announced.

At the Sawk and Fox Reservation I obtained the Sawk and Fox schedule through A. Gookie, a Menomine Indian who had for 9 years been the government interpreter for the Sawks and Foxes. A Sawk woman assisted.[17] She had the true typical Indian face, a black skin, small eyes, forehead narrowing as it rose, high cheek bones and invariable [?] solid features.

I also obtained a Menomine schedule from Antoine [Gookie] and his brother Louis together. They talk the Menomine Pure they say and have their mother, a Menomine, with them. They live with the Chippeways and are strays.

I also obtained a Munsee schedule on the Chippewa Reservation of a Munsee family. There are as many Munsees here as Chippeways, about 40 of each and they still cling to their own language and nationality and had their system of consanguinity in full operation and remembrance.

At Paoli we obtained the Weaw, Piankeshaw, Peoria, and Kaskaskia from competent parties.[18] Battise says that in Peoria, which is his language, a man's father's sister's son is his *nephew*, and his father's brother is *his father*. This settles the question that it follows the Shawnee and not the Chippewa. He also said that the other three nations agreed with the Peoria. As the four nations now number but 187 souls, I shall represent them all as having one system, and give the Peoria schedule as the schedule of all. Luther Paschal is a Kaskaskia. He assisted with two others who were Peorias, in working out the schedule. This he did by direction of Battise who as he was going to Kansas City, could not help me, at the request of Gen. Clover [?] put me in the way to get what I wanted.

[The Missions and the Indians]

The following report was copied by me by

ARCHERY OF THE MANDANS OR GAME OF THE ARROW

BY GEORGE CATLIN

The Mandans, whom Catlin found "polite and friendly," were insatiable gamblers, intensely interested in "athletic games." The bow and arrow was not only their basic weapon of war, but their principal hunting device. They were more interested in speed and striking power at close range than in pinpoint accuracy at long range. "The meeting represented here is something like that of an archery club in the civilized world, but for a different mode of shooting." To enter the game a contestant put up an entrance fee—a shield, bow, or similar possession. The object of the game was to put the greatest number of arrows into the air before the first one shot hit the ground. Catlin noted that the Indian "in the attitude of shooting" was able to put eight arrows, one at a time, into the air before the first hit the earth.

MATO-TOPÉ, WITH THE MARKS OF HIS EXPLOITS

BY KARL BODMER

Mato-topé ("Four Bears") was a principal chief of the Mandans, and a brave and distinguished warrior, said to have killed five enemy chiefs. He assisted Prince Maximilian with "very accurate information respecting his own language, and that of the neighboring Indian nations . . ." The red wooden knife in his hair signifies he has killed a Cheyenne chief with a knife; the six wooden sticks, painted red, blue, and yellow, each with a brass nail at one end, signify six musket wounds he has received. The wild turkey feather in his hair stands for an arrow wound; the yellow and red owl feathers at the back of his head are the badge of the "dog band." The yellow stripes on his arms indicate his heroic deeds of war; the yellow hand on his chest shows he has captured prisoners.

the consent of Samuel M. Cornatzer,[19] one of the committee and the present clerk of the Shawnee Council. It tells its own story as shows up in strong colors the first case which ever came to my knowledge in which a religious denomination or missionary board have sought to speculate in hard cash, as well as in land by means of an Indian Mission out of an Indian Nation. The report will speak for itself, of which the following is a copy made by me on the Shawnee Reservation, June 2, 1860.

Shawnee, Johnson Co., K. T.,
May 5, 1860

"To the Honorable Board of Chiefs and Councilmen of the Shawnee Tribe of Indians in Council assembled.

"We the undersigned visiting school committee, visited the Methodist M. L. (Manual Labor) School, and the Friends M. L. School, April 26 last, and would respectfully submit the following to your Honorable Body, as their report.

"At the Methodist M. L. School we found 3 boys and 5 girls, Total 8. We went through the different departments. The boys bed room looked as tho it had not been cleaned for a very *considerable time.* The bedding was dirty and ragged. The only excuse we heard for the disorder was, that they had visitors that day, who of course required their attention. The boys in our opinion (showed) evidence of neglect. The Female department looked a little better, but showed unmistakable evidence of neglect also. We were present at dinner. We saw nothing in the boarding department to complain of. We did not make all the inquiries you wished us to. The appearance of the school reminds us of a remark the present manager at this school made when the Shawnee Council were about locating their school

fund at the above mentioned school. *So we get the money, we dont care.* (Underscored with red ink.) Knowing the deep rooted prejudice among our people against the present superintendent we would recommend the M. E. Church South be petitioned to change superintendents at the next sitting of the Kansas Mission Conference, and that steps be taken to change the present contract with the Methodist Missionary Society at as early a period as possible. We think it not advisable for you to confer any higher power upon said committee till we see some change for better or worse. For under the present state of affairs we would not put a child of our own at the school, and cannot try to persuade others to send theirs.

"At the Friends M. L. School we found 17. This school is not what many desire, and we have no doubt but the Friends themselves desire and would do better had they the means. We need not enter (into) details of what we saw here, for some of you are patrons of, and all of you occasionally visit the school. We need not say more than that this school is kept up entirely by the Society of Friends without any help from the Shawnees whatever. We are forced to believe that they are here only from a desire to do good, and benefit our people. And we challenge any unprejudiced mind to say anything else of them. The Dollar Almighty is not the prompter of this people.

"Let us draw a contrast. At the Quakers we have no money. They have the privilege of staying upon and cultivating what they can of a half section of land so long as they will keep up a school at their own expense. They have 17 children, everything neat clean and order(ly) notwithstanding they have visitors too.

"At the Methodist School we have an

annual school fund from the U. S. Government of $5000.00 and an annual fund for land granted to the Methodist Missionary Society of $1000.00 annually at the M. M. L. School for the benefit of our youth. That is $6000.00 annually, $3000.00 semi-annually, $1500.00 quadrennially, $500 per month, or about $16 per day. A handsome sum indeed we pay the Methodists for attending to their own private business, and entertaining curious idle visitors, instead of attending to the Shawnee children for whose benefit it was placed at this school. They have 8 children and everything in their rooms is dirty and out of order. In all kindness and present friendship we ask the superintendent if he does not receive money enough to pay for keeping things in better order, or has he become as he used to say of employees of the school careless and don't care so he gets the money.

Levi Flint[20]
David Desham } Committee
Saml. M. Cornatzer

N.B. This is a true copy of the report we will submit next Monday."

The Shawnee Treaty was made May 10, 1854, at Washington. G.[eorge] W. Manypenny, Comr. for U. S.

Art. 2. ". . . Of the lands lying east of the parallel line aforesaid these shall first be set apart to the Missionary Society of the Methodist Episcopalian Church South, to include the improvements of the Indian Manual Labor School, three sections of land: to the Friends Shawnee Labor School, including the improvements there, three hundred and twenty acres of land . . ."

Art. 3. Sets apart the int. of $40000 at 5 per cent—2000 per annum for education. Also perpetual annuities before received of $3000 per annum—5000 per annum cash for school purposes.

Art. 6. Provides that the President shall give a patent for the 3 sections of land to the Missionary Society of the M. E. C. South "upon the allowance to the Shawnees by said society of ten thousand dollars, to be applied to the education of their youth, which it has agreed to make . . ."

This Methodist society by a contract made between the Shawnees and them, with the concurrence of the Commissioner of Indian Affairs, agreed to pay in education 1000 a year for ten years. The same agreement also gives to the society for the like period of ten years, the whole income of $100,000 of the invested funds of the Shawnees, set apart for education amounting to $5000 per annum, in cash, which this society now draws quarterly from the government direct, without doing enough educational work to discharge the $1000 per annum payment for the 1900 odd acres of land granted them by the Shawnees, and which was worth four times that sum at the time. Thus this religious society, save the mark, now pockets $5000 cash per annum, without rendering to the nation any equivalent whatever.

The Friends Mission was founded among the Ohio Shawnees 40 years ago in 1822 and when they were removed to this place in 1832 and 4, and became incorporated with their kindred before that time removed to this place, the Mission followed them here and was opened in 1838. Improvement commenced in 1837.

The other Shawnees were removed from Cape Jericho, Missouri, under the treaty made by Gov. Clark in 1825. Cape Jericho was below St. Louis.

The Methodist Mission was commenced in [blank].[21]

Friends Mission, Saturday, June 2, 1860

Friend Harvey and myself left the Sawk and Fox Reservation yesterday June 1, at 12 o'clock, reached Otawa Jones' about 4 and at 5 continued our journey about 17 miles further to [?] where we spent the night in a dirty uncomfortable hotel. Today at 12, we reached the Mission after an absence of five days during which we have worked diligently, and have been very successful. We went out in a buggy wagon, and were thus quite independent to do as we pleased. We have a good time and I found Friend Simon a most agreeable and gentlemanly companion. We have laughed a number of times over the speech of the old Chippewa. Harvey thinks he said, after mentioning the countries he had visited, "By G-d, this is the damndest biggest country of them all. We can raise anything, and have everything we want etc."

Shawnees Sleep Nude; Eskimo

This practice was confirmed to me by Charles Blue Jacket, as universal among the Shawnees in old times and still in use. I may have mentioned it before. There is no doubt, I think, but that it prevailed from the Eskimo inclusive to Mexico, and probably to Patagonia. It shows that the primitive costume of the Red Race was the breech cloth, nothing more nothing less, and it suggests a curious question as to the Eskimo. It has been thought the Eskimo might have been separately derived from Asia from the Asiatic polar family,[22] and that they at least came across the straits. I think the polar family whether on this or on the other side, was originally forced into the polar regions from a warmer latitude by the chances of war and pressure behind. They thus underwent a gradual process of acclimation and adaptation to a northern climate, after which they would migrate as all other races do on lines of latitude or isothermal lines rather. But the Eskimo after all may be directly connected with the North American Indian, and may have been forced northward after the establishment of the Red Race upon this continent. This usage of sleeping nude is certainly very singular as a characteristic of a polar race. It is a custom more natural and proper to a tropical and to a temperate climate than to the Arctic regions. It has only come into my mind that the existence of this custom among the Eskimos and our Indians carries with it some evidence of a common origin. At least it deserves further consideration.

Friend Harvey

This estimable and warm hearted man is about 50 years of age. All his life he has been an Indian man, and he has entered into my work with a degree of warmth and cordiality beyond any other person. My second schedule was from him, the Shawnee, and he had taken the necessary steps to procure the Sawk and Fox when I arrived. He went with me with his own horse and buggy for five days into southern Kansas during which we procured the Peoria, Weaw, Kaskaskia, Piankeshaw, Sawk and Fox, Menomine, Munsee and a final revision of the Chippewa and Shawnee. We also procured the Miami. He gave me his undivided attention and cordial hospitality, and would accept no remuneration of any kind whatever. Such encouragement of my work is of far more value to me than the money saved, and I shall always remember Friend Harvey and his excellent wife and agreeable family with the highest pleasure. At some future time I hope I shall meet them again.[23]

Otawa Jones

I fear Jones, who might do a good deal for the Indian, cares for nothing but making money; and I doubt whether his influence for good is what it ought to be. His wife is smart and would make as thorough a missionary as she does a house keeper.

Steamer *Des Moines*,[24] June 4, 1860

I came down from Friend Harvey's Sunday towards evening to take this steamer for Atchison and St. Joseph. From there I shall go direct to Omaha in quest of the Pawnee first and after that the Omaha.

The Double Walker (Nom-ba-mon-nee), a brave of the Omaha tribe, by George Catlin. This is an excellent example of the famous painter's ability to render portraits. Double Walker was painted in 1832, on a trip that took Catlin all the way to Ft. Union.

Steamer *Emilie*,[25] St. Jo. June 4

We arrived at St. Joseph at 6 P.M. and went on board this steamer who [sic] is to leave tonight.

I found an Omaha Indian on board and who talks English tolerably well. I have inquired about their system of relationship, and find that the language closely resembles the Kaw,[26] and the system also is the same. Tomorrow we are to work out a schedule.

Omaha Original Home

They were originally settled at the mouth of the Missouri river, and that is all he can say of their original location. The Kaws say the same. The Sioux may have taken the northern route toward Lake Superior, while what are now Omaha, Kaw, Osage, Iowa, Otoe, and Quappa may have descended the Missouri, dividing as they went. The *Punkas* speak the same language as the Omahas.

Omaha Tribes [Clans][27]

1. Deer Tribe, Wa-zhes-ta
2. Black, Ink-ka-sa-ba
3. Medicine, Hun-ga
4. Bear, Wa-sa-ba-e-ta-zhe
5. Bird Pigeon (Hawk) probably La-ta-da
6. Turtle, Ka-ih
7. Kaw Tribe, Kun-za
8. Buffalo, Da-thun-da
9. Head, Ta-pa
10. Red Tribe, In-gra-zhe-da
11. Thunder, Izh-da-sun-da
12. Making the seasons, O-mon-e-ka-ga-ha

The individuals of each tribe never eat anything of the kind of the tribal name. [Members of the head clan] don't eat brain.

Omaha Marriage and Children

No one is allowed to marry a woman of his own tribe, but the children are of the tribe of the father instead of the mother. In case of separation, however, they belong to the mother. The chief must be of the tribe of his predecessor.

Names of Individuals of Bird Tribe

Boys names
Gla-don-a-shin-ga   Young chicken Hawk
Ah-bo-zhe-da   Black and Red Bird
Neshe-tare-ka   White Eyed Bird
Ah-hese-na-da   Long Wing
De-ga-map-ha   Neck Bird
Gla-don-noh-zhe   Hawk balancing itself in the air
Girls names
La-ta-da-win   one of the Birds
Me-ta-na   Bird singing at daylight
We-ha-tun-ga   My big sister
Ge-huk-ba-ah-ha   High flying Bird
Wa-ta-ma   Birds Egg

The old father of the tribe gives the names to the children, and one of the chiefs at the next council announces the birth and name of the child.

The names are changed for brave actions such as a successful war expedition. It is then usually done on the return of the party. The names of females are never changed.

The names of each tribe are kept distinct and no one of another tribe is allowed to use them. They are also related to the tribe or the animal itself. Thus all the names above given are of the Bird Kindred and relate to the Bird. The members of the Bird Tribe can eat Ducks, Turkey, Chickens, Geese and no other birds. The tribal bird includes all the other birds, and no one is allowed to eat the animal of its own emblem.

The Omahas believe that if this prohibition is violated the person will turn grey, or swell up, etc.

Omaha Spirits

Wa-kon-da[28]   Great Spirit, Omaha
Wa-na-ha   Spirit of a man which returns
                                              to earth
Wa-no-ha   Spirit of the Wind

Omaha Burial Customs

After death the body is dressed in the best clothes of the deceased and painted. They keep a watch at night before the burial and they neither cook nor eat in the house before the burial. The burial is either the same or the next day. They cover the body with blankets and secure over all a raw hide, and then carry the body on a pole to which it is tied, to the grave, two persons at each end of the pole when the person is heavy. He is carried with his face and feet forward. There is no regular procession, but the relatives and friends including the widow go to the grave. They lament and cry aloud in the usual Indian way, at times before and at the burial. The grave is shallow as the Omahas are averse to being buried deep in the ground. They dig a grave three feet deep and set them up in a sitting position facing the west. (Moody[29] says to the east, that his aunt was so buried; confirmed by graves opened by me), but on further inquiry he says with the feet to the west and the head to the east. They place in the grave a vessel containing corn, meat, bread etc. together with a pipe, bow and arrows and sometimes extra clothing. After the body is dressed and painted, and before it is removed from the house, an address is made over the body by one of the chiefs, in which his virtues are spoken of favorably and his vices reprovingly. After the body is

placed in the grave thus covered, and in a sitting posture, a roof of split timber is placed over the grave so as to make the grave hollow except as occupied by the dead body. The timber is then sodded over with earth. They plant a crotch at each end of the grave, lay on a pole and then set the split logs or timber against it, making a roof which is covered thinly with earth, and thus the body is left. A fire is built the first night after the burial by the side of the grave, and for one night only, and food is placed on the grave for three or four weeks by friends or relatives who visit the grave—as meat and corn. The relatives mourn for about a year.

An Omaha chief was buried about six years ago on the bluff near Bellevue, Sarpy Co., Nebraska Territory, where they then resided. He was buried in a sitting posture.

After the burial was over a fence was made around the grave, his horse was tied inside of [the fence] by the grave, and was then shot. His bones they say are still to be seen there.

Omaha Names

Missouri River, Ne-shoda, Muddy or Riled
                                              Water
Platt River, Ne-blas-ka, Flat River or Wide
                                              Water
Neosho River
Nemaha River, Ne-ma-ha
Mississippi River, Ne-tan-ga, Great River
St. Louis, Pa-he-zhe-da-he-ra, Red headed
                         man's town, Gov. Black
Black Bird Creek, Wa-kon-da-or-gra, Spirit
                                              Creek
Sioux River, Hra, Place of catching
Nebraska Run, Ne-o-bra-tha, Open Run

Omaha Dances

1. War Dance	Na-da-wa-che-ga-ha	Men alone
2. Horn Dance	Ha-rus-ka	" "
3. Mandan	Ma-wa-da-ne	" "
4. Scalp Dance	Wa-wa-che	Men & women
5. Dead Dance	A-ga-ha	Men
6. Buffalo Dance	Da-wa-che	Men, women & child.
7. Womans Dance	Wa-o-wa-che-ga-ha	Men
8. Bear Dance	Ma-cho-wa-che-ga-ha	Men alone
9. Wolf Dance	Ma-kus-e-wa-che-ga-ha	" "
10. Medicine Dance	Wa-h-ba-wa-che-ga-he	Men and women
11. Otter Dance	Wa-shese-ka-wa-che-ga-ha	" "
12. Green Corn	A-hun-ga-wa-che-ga-ha	Men
13. Spirit Dance	Wa-na-ha-wa-che-ga-ha	"
14. Horse Dance	Shun-ga-wa-che-ga-ha	"
15. Big Wolf Dance	Shunk-tun-ga-wa-che-ga-ha	Men and women
16. Fox Dance	Dink-a-ho-da-wa-che-ga-ha	" "
17. Elk Dance	Ah-um-pa-wa-che-ga-ha	Men
18. Hunters Return Dance	A-ha-de-wa-che-ga-ha	"

Sleeping Nude—Omahas

The Omahas are not an exception in this respect from the other nations, but do like them.

This morning I made out an Omaha schedule without any difficulty with the aid of Moody. It is the same as the Kaw, and the language quite the same. This afternoon, Mr. Fontenelle,[30] a half breed Omaha, came on the boat. He talks English perfectly. I read over the schedule to him and he revised it. He is quite intelligent. He lives at Black Bird Hills and knows Mr. Sturges.[31] He says Mr. Sturges has made out for me a perfect schedule. This he wrote me, but why does he not send it?

Wind Storm

This evening, June 5, while we were a few miles below Nebraska City on the steamer *Emilie* we had a regular wind storm. It nearly amounted to a tornado. It had been exceptionally hot during the afternoon, and when it commenced blowing, it created waves of considerable size. The boat went up to the bank and tied and laid by an hour. We are now so far up the river that the timber is scant.

Pawnees

Fontenelle says the Pawnee is a radically different language from the Omaha; that it agrees with the Arikaree. He thinks the Omaha is remotely connected with the Dakota, and that they were originally one.[32] He has given me information of a Mr. Allis at St. Marys about 30 miles below Omaha, who has been a Pawnee interpreter. I shall stop there tomorrow.

Bellevue, Sarpy Co.
Nebraska Territory
June 6, 1860

Our boat reached this place, which is twenty miles below Omaha, about 3 o'clock P.M. I went immediately to the house of Rev. William Hamilton,[33] and found him at home. His family consists of a wife, two pleasant grown daughters, and one girl. I think there are some other children who are at school. Mr. Hamilton came out in 1837, as a missionary of the Presbyterian Board to the Iowas and Sawks, and was located for some fifteen years at that place, Highland, where Mr. Erwin [Irvin][34] now resides. He learned and made a grammar of the Iowa language which has been published, 150 pages.[35] He was connected with the Omaha Mission at Bellevue until the Omahas were removed to their present home at the Black Bird Hills and he was there until the Mission was opened. On account of the health of his wife, he gave up his connection with the Board and located at Bellevue, where he carries on a farm, and officiates at the Presbyterian church as pastor. He is evidently a man of superior sense and integrity. His children were born in Kansas.

Rev. Samuel Allis, Cerro Gordo P.O., Mills Co., Iowa

I came over this morning to the house of Rev. Samuel Allis[36] on the Iowa side of the river near St. Marys and about four miles from Bellevue, where I am now writing. He was the first missionary of the American Board, or Presbyterians, to the Pawnees, and remained with them for a number of years as their missionary. I came for the Pawnee system of relationship. Much to my regret he went on Monday to the Pawnee village distant about 60 miles inland and

westward to attend the Payment as government interpreter. He has held this office for 9 years. His wife and oldest son were also away from home for the day, but will return this evening. They both talk the Pawnee, as also a son now at home, and his brothers and sisters were born at the Pawnee village. They have also in the family a Pawnee woman who of course must know their system of consanguinity. I am waiting for the return of Mr. Allis and expect to stay here tonight. We went out with guns before dinner and fell in with three Frenchmen, one of them has a Brulé Dakota wife at St. Marys two miles below here. He also speaks that language and gave me most of their terms of relationship. I am going down at 4 P.M. to secure the remainder. This will make it a good day for me. He gave me the name of Simon Mills,[37] who has a Blackfoot

The Reverend Samuel Allis, distinguished Presbyterian missionary to the Pawnee Indians. Morgan stayed with his family in Mills County, Iowa, in 1859. Allis spent a dedicated, useful life, to the benefit of the Indian.

wife, who went down to the Half Breed Reserve about six weeks ago, and is now there. He also gave me the name of Joseph Tesson,[37] a half breed Sheyenne, and of Edward Glode,[37] who has a Sheyenne wife now on the Half Breed Reserve. This determines me to stop at Rulo where I may hear of them.

Assinaboine and Dakota are alike; Pawnee and Arickaree Do. Ponkas and Omaha are alike in language, Sheyennes different. Sonton, Dakotas or Mississippi, Yankton or Missouri. Riggs Dakotas, Sonton, Rulo Dakotas, Yankton, Brulé Dakotas, Burnt Thighs, etc [blank] Pawnees, Arickarees and Pawnee Picts west of Arkansas on Red River are the same. Sheyenne and Arapahoe Col. Sarpy says are the same.

Hooded Dove[38]

The Allis family have a pair of hooded doves male and female, which interested me a good deal. They were of the size of the common dove, perfectly tame, so much so that I held one on my finger; color white and light chestnut, head and upper part of neck white, with short and close plumage, tips of wings, tail, lower part of breast and between legs white, remainder of back, wings and breast light chestnut, toes bright red, and a little tinge of red around eyes and at root of bill. The most remarkable feature was the rise of the plumage around the neck, except a narrow space in front below, and in the form of a hood, the rise being abrupt and about half an inch high, crossing the neck on the upper side and gradually descending the neck as it passed around and disappeared on the under side. The hood is at the commencement of the chestnut plumage of the neck. I have [not] seen the bird before or seen it figured, and for that reason noticed it quite minutely, as it sat on my

finger with some reluctance, and afterwards sat at roost upon the well curb. It coos like the turtle dove, but unlike this dove does not refuse to mate again. Mrs. Allis had two pair, of which the male of one and the female of the other died, after which the widow and widower united their fortunes, and now have two young ones in their nest and two eggs unhatched. I have arranged with Master Otis Allis to send some of these eggs to Prof. Baird[39] should he wish them, and also the eggs of the little wren which is common in western Iowa and Nebraska.

Fan Tailed Hawk[40]

Saw this hawk in Nestor, Iowa, and in Nebraska on the Missouri. It is about the size of a pigeon hawk or a little larger, white head, white breast, and brown back and wings as near as I could determine while it was ? -ing over my head, tail forked in a very pointed way, and wings also pointed so as to give the bird a slender and angular appearance.

Brulé Dakotas

I fell in with a French Creole who has a Brulé wife at St. Marys as before stated. I went down there in the afternoon and completed a Brulé schedule,[41] which now gives me three of the seven Dakota bands, namely the Sontans [Santees, or Isaunties] by Riggs, the Yanktons procured by myself at Rulo, and the Brulé procured as above at St. Marys in western Iowa on the Missouri. Bought a pair of moccasins of her, elk and buffalo skin.

Pawnee System of Relationship

On the return of Mrs. Allis and her son we made an attempt at the Pawnee, and could not complete it even with the aid of the Pawnee woman.[42] But I was able to ascer-

tain that the children of brothers are brothers and sisters to each other, and that the children of two sisters are the same, but about the children of a brother and a sister I could not ascertain. There is no term for aunt, therefore a father's sister is a mother, and probably her son is a brother, but on this point I could not make any certain progress. Col. Peter A. Sarpy of St. Marys told me that the father's sister was a grand mother, and a man could marry this grand mother. If there is no aunt, then a woman has no nephew and niece, and a woman's brother's son is her grand son. But the mother's brother is an uncle, and consequently a man has a nephew and niece. I think I can nearly write out this system, but at all events I feel sure Mr. Allis will be able to do it for me with the aid I shall now be able to give him.

I stayed with this pleasant family which consists of a mother, two sons and one grown daughter and also an orphan girl brought up by them, and the Pawnee woman besides the Rev. Samuel Allis now absent as before stated. They refused compensation for my entertainment, and I left them Friday morning to return to Mr. Hamilton at Bellevue, well pleased with my visit: I am to write to Mr. Allis on my return, and to send him a schedule and they say he will attend to it for me.

I returned about three o'clock, June 8, to Bellevue, and shall remain here until Saturday morning when I go up to Omaha to meet the boat on which I am to return to Rulo, where I shall make a desperate effort for the Blackfoot and the Sheyenne and also try at Omaha again for the Pawnee.

PART III

Bellevue, Sarpy Co., Nebraska
June 8, 1860

Omaha Graves

As I crossed the Missouri this morning at the ferry in a small boat, I inquired about the burial place of the Omaha chief mentioned to me by Otis Allis. He said it was Elk Hill which overlooks Bellevue, and I think the chief's name was Big Elk. The ferryman also told me that just on the bluff back of their house at the ferry on the Nebraska side were a large number of Omaha graves, some of which were made since he had been there about six or seven years ago. We arranged to go up with a shovel and examine some of them, which we did. On the bluffs about one hundred feet above the river, among a thicket of sumacs we found them, quite a large number, the most of them had fallen in and were open; some had been looked into perhaps by whites and some were still unbroken. A broken glass bottle lay upon the top of one of them which was a large and comparatively recent one. This we decided to open as I wished to see the mode of burial, and of the construction

of the graves. I had before learned that the Omahas did not put earth upon the body, but found an open grave and roofed it over.

The mound over this grave was about six feet long and four high above the surrounding earth, with weeds growing, but not thickly, over the top. I shovelled off one side of the roof until I came to the timber which consisted of round sticks about four inches thick set close together, and at an angle of about fifty-five degrees. After clearing away the sticks, we found a large open chamber or grave, perfectly dry and roomy, and on the floor covered with blankets or quilted coverlet was the body sitting up in the same position in which it was deposited there. An excavation had been about four to five [feet] long from east to west and about three feet wide from north to south and at least four feet deep; stakes were then driven in at the head and foot with a fork about two feet above the ground or three feet perhaps. After the body had been wrapped in a blanket after it was dressed in its clothes and painted, it was set up as we found it, a pole was placed in the forks, the sticks of timber against it from the side of the grave to this pole, after which the earth was covered over it to the depth of two or three feet.

After opening the grave we found a tin pail near the head which we took out, and found the corn or food whatever was deposited in it had decayed, leaving a mould at the bottom. It was a two quart pail. We then lifted out the skeleton and found it was that of a boy or a girl about twelve or fifteen years of age. It was not so far decayed as to fall to pieces, but remained together, neither did it emit any smell; the moccasins were on his feet, the wrappings around his face, and the remains of the blanket or coverlet over all; the flesh, how-

ever, was gone and the paint could yet be seen on the head. A pocket book of leather containing some printed paper or certificate of fine quality was found in the grave and also a glass bottle which would hold about a pint. No other articles were found. We returned the body to the grave, and covered it up with earth, although we did not attempt to restore the roof.

This grave and mode of burial was at least in good taste and respectful and respectable. The roominess of the grave, its dryness and the freshness and smoothness of the earth walls made a favorable impression upon my mind as to the good taste of the mode of sepulture. To my great surprise this body was placed with the feet toward the east and the face in the same direction, or a little diagonally, so as to make it face north east, but it was nearly due east.

We next examined a large grave which had caved in on one side by falling through of the timbers showing a deep cavity, while the roof on the other side was entire, with about two feet of earth above its ridge pole which was still unbroken. The young ferryman stepped into the grave and partly shovelled it out. It contained two skeletons of full grown persons, but evidently buried at different times, and several years apart, in doing which, or making the last burial, the grave was opened on the south side and new timbers put in for the roof on that side or closing the grave, which accounts for the falling of the north side while the other still stands.

The length of the grave was east and west, the same as the former one and all the others we examined, and the first body we came upon was in a sitting posture, with the feet towards the east. This we could see after the skull and main bones of the body had been removed, by the direction of the leg bones, which run to the east or north east. This skull although sound, began to show signs of decay or exposure to the air. It is a skull of a man I should think by the length of the other bones, and of a full sized man near six feet high. The lower jaw we did not find, and most of the upper teeth are gone. The Omaha skull I have brought with me as also a piece of a whet stone found with his bones. A bottle also of glass was thrown out.

The other skeleton was of equal size, but of more recent burial. The hair was still on the head, a part of it in braids. The large ear ring was still in its place, held to the side of the skull by some of the ligatures of the ear, and the winding cloth. The face was wrapped around with a blanket or belt which appeared to have blocks of different colored silk in it, ornamented with beads. The paint also about the head was yet fresh. The under jaw of this skull was found, and I have this with both skulls in my carpet bag. They are both fine specimens. There was so much earth in the grave over the bodies that we did not clear out the graves and did not find the articles buried with the bodies. The bones were returned and covered with earth. These graves are about a mile above Bellevue, on the west side of the river. The Omahas were removed from this place several years ago to their present reservation at Black Bird Hills near Sioux City about 200 miles above here, and for that reason we felt more at liberty to do what we did. [Morgan has three small sketches here showing "end view," "side view," and "bottom," respectively.]

In the evening I attended a public meeting of the citizens of Bellevue upon a land question and was much pleased with the intelligence and spirit manifested by those present. The sale of the land in question was to be made the next day at Omaha and the meeting adjourned to meet at the land office at Omaha at 9 o'clock June 9, and a large number agreed to attend.

Omaha, June 9, 1860

I came down this morning from Bellevue to Omaha, the capitol of Nebraska, with a merchant of the former place. Mr. Hamilton refused remuneration. My visit to his house was very pleasant, and I shall remember them with pleasure. A two hours drive brought us to this place, which has not changed much since I saw it last year. I called upon the son of S. B. Woolworth[43] and also had a conversation with Col. Peter A. Sarpey[44] of St. Marys, Mills Co., Iowa. He is one of the American Fur Co. and has long been a trader among the Indians. He

Colonel Peter A. Sarpy and his trading post at Bellevue were familiar to all who journeyed up the river or were in the fur trade.

talks several Indian languages and among others the Pawnee, but as he was a little intoxicated[45] I could not make any gain upon the Pawnee system of consanguinity except in one thing which he stated to me, namely, that while the children of brothers and the children of sisters were brothers and sisters to each other respectively, in the next degree down they became half brothers; that is our second cousins were half brothers.

Hamilton's Manuscripts

Before I left, and [at] my request the Rev. William Hamilton placed in my hands a large amount of manuscript[46] matter which he had prepared during twenty three years of missionary labors among the Iowas and Omahas. I know not the contents, but I understand they relate chiefly to their religious notions. I am to hold them subject to his order and shall give him credit for any material which I may use.

At Omaha I made another unavailing effort to find a Pawnee interpreter. I found a small band here of 8 or ten and went out to their camp among the willows. Not a soul of them could speak English except a few words. I bought a Pawnee deer skin, or elk skin, quiver, bow, sheath and five iron pointed arrows and two blunt ones, and a bow for about 13/. They were nude to the waist, the men, and the only child among them was naked. Their skins are a dark bronze color, and look well, their forms are round, plump, and well developed. They paint, some of them shear the outside hair, keep a little long and in the center of that a scalp lock left of hair neatly braided. This Pawnee boy wore his hair precisely as the young Kaw did whom I saw at Topeka.

A drunken fellow came down to the landing and commenced fooling and then annoying this boy by taking his bow and arrows, and shooting them, then slapt him on the side of the face. After which he wanted him to turn a somersault, and did it himself to show how. He then took hold of the boy to make him do it, and got him down on one knee; the boy remained there in a quiet and most dignified attitude, merely putting his hand over his face, and then submitted himself without resistance to the indignities offered. Among so many whites he did not think he could resent.

Steamer *Omaha*, June 10, 1860

We left Omaha last evening about six o'clock and ran down to Council Bluffs, where we tied up for the night. This is about twelve miles below. Tomorrow about noon we shall be at Rulo, where I intend to stop for the next boat, with the hope of obtaining the Blackfoot and the Sheyenne, and perhaps the Hun-ga-lal-la [Ogalalla] Dakota. I think I shall need the three days I shall have to wait, but if I can get neither it will be a bore.

Work of a Tornado

In the preceding journal I mentioned a wind storm we were in last week. Tuesday or Wednesday, I think, June 5. We found the track of this tornado as we ascended. The force of it seems to have been spent in and near Bellevue and across the river in the direction of St. Marys where I saw large trees torn up by the roots and others twisted off at the stump, fences blown down etc. At Bellevue the hail fell in large quantities from the size of a bullet to that of half the size of a hen's egg, Mr. Hamilton informed me. Others said there was now and then one as large as a hen's egg. A brick livery stable was blown down, the side walls however were but 8 inches, or a link [7.92 inches], thick and therefore insecure. A

brick house enclosed but not finished was blown down. A frame house sitting on pins was moved forward ten feet and set down slanting; another house was moved off about three feet. Nearly every glass in the west end of the houses in the village was broken in. Mr. Hamilton's garden and farm was a perfect desolation. His raspberry bushes were literally cut to pieces, not a leaf nor a berry remained. His small fruit trees were stripped of their leaves, and the bark cut through and slipped around by the force of the blow, so as to show on one side the naked wood as much as the bark which remained. All the vegetables in the garden were cut down to the ground. His wheat fields and corn fields on the flat east of the house and between it and the river which lay in the range of the storm were cut down to the ground. As the wheat had commenced to head, not a bushel will be saved. The corn may come on again. I have never witnessed destruction to be compared with this from a storm. At Omaha one or two buildings were moved off of their foundations, and the State House was unroofed on one side partially. But the corn and grain fields between Bellevue and Omaha did not suffer as much as at Bellevue. I rode up to Omaha on land, and saw the state of the growing crops.

Climatology

The air is dry, and as the breeze is constant and verging always to fullness [?] , its dessicating effects must be great upon vegetation. I am still inclined to think that the dews do a great deal towards saving the grasses and the crops from the effects of dryness or the drying winds. The present season has been dry, and I am told that the dews have not been heavy the present year. I took a cold the day I went to Paoli, and

increased it at the Sawk and Fox Reserve, and have not really got clear of it yet, as I have made small additions from time to time. I should think the present season must have been a bad one for persons inclined to pulmonary difficulties.

Kansas and Nebraska do not look as well as they did last year at the same time. The prairie grass is short and has not the rich green it had last year, and the corn does not look as well. Nebraska has not suffered as much as Kansas and corn looks better in the former than in the latter.

Butter is selling at Omaha at 1/– per pound, and eggs at 10 cents per dozen, potatoes 30 cents, corn 30 cents. Meat is also abundant and cheap.

Frontier Men, Their Estimate of the Indian

The ferry man at Bellevue was a large rough man with red whiskers and yellow hair. He was from Michigan, and had been in Nebraska several years. He said when he came here he had a good deal of sympathy for the Indian; but that he had got over it. That they are a wild, untameable and thieving set. That they would rob and kill as opportunity offered. That there was no use of talking about doing the work of saving them by missionaries. That he knew Rev. Mr. Hamilton, who was a good man, but that he did not think Hamilton with his experience had any confidence in their reclamation. He said old Col. Sarpey had the right view of the matter, and without quoting Col. Sarpey's language, [?] a short and energetic method of taming the Indian, which has a true French cast, it was in substance that the only way to tame the Indian was to put white blood in his veins.

The ferry man further said that when he first established his ferry the Omahas used to visit the graves on the bluff and wail and

howl like wild animals, and that after he had heard it a few times, he went up and told them if they did not quit it he would kick their damned a-s into the river. I put this down just as he said it at the risk of its vulgarity for this, and the remark of Col. Sarpey, have caused me [to] laugh outright every time they have come into my mind. This conversation took place while we were at the Omaha graves.

I afterwards met Col. Peter A. Sarpy at Omaha and stated the ferryman's version of his remedy for the cure of the Red man and he at once accepted it as correct. He said if you attempt to domesticate a wolf, he will snap at everything which comes near him, and do what you will he is always a wolf. So with the Indian. And the only way to tame him is to put in the white blood. He thought the government could not do a better thing than to send men among them for that purpose, etc. He was tight, I should say, at the time we had the conversation.

I think a most important idea lies in here and it is one which has occurred to me before; and that is, whether after all it is not in virtue of the white blood already taken up and distributed among the emigrant nations the improvement we see among them has come to pass; and that but for this blood all efforts would have been unavailing to introduce agriculture among them. I can hardly think this is true and yet it may be.

Pawnee Jo

Col. Peter A. Sarpy said if I would send my schedule to Pawnee Jo, in his care at St. Marys he would see that Jo had it. He says he can read and write and could furnish what I want. He is also called Joseph Sarpey,[47] which will be the proper address.

Sheyenne

Col. Sarpey said he had been among the Sheyennes; that he found he could not converse with them although he tried Sioux, Kaw, Winnebago etc. He thinks it must be an original language. He says the Sheyenne and Arapahoe are the same language. It may be that they are off shoots of the Algonquin.

He says the Snake[48] Indians speak a language unlike all others he knows, and that they are intelligent and respectable Indians.

Rulo, Nebraska
June 11, 1860

Tesson [a trader mentioned later] says the Arapahoe are derived from the Blackfeet or the Blackfeet from them. The Sheyennes say they came from the east of the Mississippi river. They say they crossed

Left: An early photograph of part of a large Cheyenne Indian village. Morgan was never able to visit among the Cheyennes, confining his travels to the relocated tribes, and to those who lived near either the upper Missouri or the Red River.

Right: Black Hawk, as he appeared in a lithograph published in New York in 1833. This troublesome Sauk, never friendly to Americans, precipitated the tragic "Black Hawk War" of 1832. As a direct result of this unhappy conflict, the Sauk and Fox were removed from the Mississippi Valley to Kansas.

two large rivers, Mississippi and Missouri.

On the death of a man [among the Sheyenne, probably], his brothers take his property, including his wives. The oldest brother has the first election and he can take them all, with the horses etc. if he chooses. If he does not, the next brother and so on to the last. A woman may ask the privilege of choosing any of the brothers which she will take, which is always accorded her.

Marriage among Sheyennes

If a man marries the oldest sister, he is entitled to all the sisters if he chooses to take them [the sororate]. There is the same ceremony performed for each one. The man sends a present, usually a horse. If they do not wish to part with their daughter, the old folks, they send the horses back. If willing, they accept the horse, and other presents made. The father of the girl receives nothing, but the presents go to those the father sees fit to give them to. Then the brothers of the girl give several horses to fit out the girl. Usually two or three horses are given by the groom, and eight or ten are sent with the girl. She then goes to meet the family of the groom, a blanket is spread where they meet, and she gets into this blanket [and] is carried home by the friends of the groom. She is dressed and painted, and they have a feast. The girl then returns to the house of her father. Her family then provide a wigwam and furnish it and she is taken there by her husband.

In case of separation the father takes the children if he wants them. The uncle is not of much account among the Sheyennes. Adultery is punished by cutting off the nose and putting her [to] death, and pay no attention to it. It was the ancient law, but now the law is more lax.

Among the Sheyennes adults, there are five women to one man, which Tesson says is owing to the constant fighting of the men. They are always at it. He says the women never die, they dry up and blow away, the country is so healthy. I put this in as a specimen of his mode of talking. He lived among the Sheyennes about 29 years.

Sheyennes Have No Tribes [Clans] [49]

So says Tesson, and the son succeeds the father. The government agents interfere and make chiefs and then set the right person aside. Tesson says that [they] have been greatly demoralized by this means. If the son is too young, then the brother takes it.

Black Hawk [50]

Tesson says he was a Pottawatomie and was raised among the Sawks as an orphan. He was not a chief but made himself a chief by his bravery. This may account for his wishing it inserted in the treaty that his son should succeed him as chief.

Uncle

An uncle among the Sheyennes will correct his nephew when the father would not. A boy will strike his father and the father will not resent it, but the uncle would return the blow.

Sheyenne Mode of Burial

The Sheyennes now bury on a scaffold and never in the ground except in cases of a murdered man. After the flesh is gone they wrap them up in a package and the family carry them around for several years, as they are moving Indians without any settled home, and at some proper time they bring together all of these bones and bury them, not in one grave, but where they please.

Sheyenne

Me-hu-na-ve, Great Spirit

Tesson is now forty nine years of age, and has spent most of his life among the Indians. His first wife was a Sheyenne, and his present is an Ogalalla Dakota. This makes his authority of the highest value on the manners and customs of the Indians.

Sheyenne Schedule

Procured the Sheyenne system although not as yet quite perfect. I am to go out to Tesson's house tomorrow which is ten miles from here, and complete it through his sons who are Sheyennes through their mother and who speak the language.[51] Tesson's present wife is a sister to White Cloud, and an Iowa and not a Dakota as stated before. It is clear that the Sheyennes are of Algonquin lineage.

Sheyennes Sleep Nude

Tesson has been among the Sheyennes for 23 years and also among the Sawks, Otoes and Ioways, Omahas, Punkas, Yanktons, Tetons, (Sioux or Dakotas west of Missouri), Sontes (Is-sa-te, white tooth) East Dakotas, Arikarees, Gros Ventres of the Prairie, Mandans, Blackfeet, Crows, Nez Perces, Sand Pitch (off shoot of the Snakes), Snakes and Root Diggers (who are the same), Utahs, Apaches, Navahoes (he thinks they are Iowas), Monkeys [?] , Arapahoes, Comanches, Kiowas, Kaws, Chippewas, Osages, Pottawatomies, Delawares and Shawnees, Munsees and Pawnees. He is Sawk and French, Chippewa and Menomine and speaks nine of these languages including French, English and Spanish. Among all these nations the practice of sleeping nude prevails, as to the men. They take off all but the breech cloth. The women of all these

nations strip with the exception of the skin cloth or skirt except the Mandans, Arikarees, Pawnees, Crows and Snakes, Blackfeet and Gros Ventres of the Prairie, who strip entirely naked before retiring and then roll up in a blanket. The men of these nations do not remove the waist cloth.

The Indians say it is not healthy to sleep in clothing and that in the winter they do not feel the cold as in their clothes. Two men will not sleep skin to skin no matter how cold it may be. This he says is the general rule.

The Creole at St. Marys said he had been among the Sheyennes some years and that the men always strip off to the breech cloth, and roll up in their blankets. He says all Indians do it as far as he is acquainted.

Son-in-law and Mother-in-law

It is a singular fancy of the Red man that true modesty forbids all intercourse between the mother-in-law and son-in-law after that relation is formed by the marriage of a woman's daughter. [This "mother-in-law taboo" is widespread, not only among the North American Indians, but in other regions of the world as well.] The idea is that after a man has lived with the daughter as his wife, the daughter is so much a copy of the mother that true delicacy requires them to avoid each other. The Choctas carry this to excess as stated to me by Mr. Byington.[52] Tesson says that among the Sheyennes it is [?] to excess. That the son-in-law never enters a place where he knows his mother-in-law is to be, and that it is the same with her; and if enticed to enter by deceit, the son-in-law turns away his head and refuses to look at her. The Otoes are an exception. But aside from them all of the nations mentioned as far as he had observed have the same custom.

Marriage of Kin

None of the persons described as relatives on the schedule in any of the nations whose systems I have obtained will intermarry except such as are related by marriage; cousins and brothers for as many degrees out as they can be traced, and these never marry. Col. Sarpy mentioned to me that uncle and aunt intermarry among the Pawnees, but I do not credit it yet. Among the Sheyennes they are very strict on this custom. Tesson knew a case in which cousins had married. The fact was thrown up at them frequently and made such a means of annoyance that they finally separated from this cause exclusively.

Bathing

The northern Indians Tesson says, particularly those who sleep entirely nude, usually in the coldest weather, roll up their clothes in their blanket and go to the river and plunge in and wash themselves before they dress daily.

Tesson says that a woman would be ashamed to have it said that her husband had to go and get himself a bucket of water. She takes a personal pride in his exemption from all drudgery.

Dakota Tribes [Clans]

Tesson says there are no tribes or clans,[53] but they have parties or societies as follows.
1. Bear Party, Ma-to-o-ko-la-cha-ke-che-ap
2. Horse Medicine Party, Sun-ka-ka-pa-zu-ta-o-ko-la-che-ap
3. Strong Heart Party, Chan-ta-ta-za-o-ka-la-ke-cha
4. Fox Party, Taw-ka-luh
5. Wolf Party, Shun-ka-ha-o-ka-la-ke-cha
6. Buffalo, O-ta-tank-a-o-ka-la-ke-cha
7. Owl, Plume, A-ha-pa-o-ko-la-ka-cha

8. Elk, A-ha-ka-o-ko-la-ke-cha
9. Turtle, Ka-ah-o-ko-la-ke-cha
10. Eagle, Wa-be-la-o-ko-la-ke-cha
11. Dog Soldier, Shun-ka-a-keteh-tup

These are not tribes in the Indian sense. They are elected men and women, but mostly men into these parties, societies, or lodges. They are not consanguinei, but friends and each society is numerous in members. Many Indians are Masons and from the nature and objects of these Indian Societies they call them Masonic societies as that fraternity among the whites comes nearest to expressing it.

Joseph Tesson

Tesson gave me some little account of his life and I should have been glad to have had the whole of it, as a sample of a trader's life. But he was something more than this. He turned Indian first and trader afterwards. He ran away when a boy and went to the Sheyennes. He learned their language, took an Indian wife and became a Sheyenne chief, which distinction he earned on the war path. He said he went the whole figure, wore the breech cloth and the blanket and shot and scalped and stole horses. He said he had killed a good many Indians, he ventured to set the number as high as sixty but with how much truth I cannot state. When he had followed this life for about twenty years he says he came back among the whites and was worth about $60,000. That he was now running down again although he had good farms and horses and cattle and village property at Rulo. His present wife is a sister of White Cloud, who is an Iowa and not a Dakota as before stated by me. White Cloud's mother was an Otoe, but the children follow the father's nation in this case, not a little to my surprise. Tesson is good looking, and far more French

than Indian.[54] He speaks 9 languages including English, French, and Spanish, and is evidently a man of strong purposes and quick intelligence. He is well spoken of at Rulo.

The Fur Company

Samuels[55] says the Fur Company control everything in the Indian country, and that they ruin any Indian agent who will not yield to their policy and views.[56] He says the goods sent into the country by the government are not distributed to the Indians, but are placed in the forts or posts of the Company, and are by them distributed and that they require the Indians to pay for them in furs. Of course he cannot be well informed how this business is managed, but it is the impression of all that Col. Vaughn[57] has been a mere speculator in Indian money and goods for years, and that the whole system is rotten through and through. The Indians on this reserve[58] complain of their agent. They say he is a mere speculator out of their affairs. That men are now cutting and carrying timber from the reservation down the river on shares by his permission. They also say that when the Indians make representations to the government they are not believed as the agent usually denies whatever they state. When I tell them that they make too much of a man of the agent, who has really no power over them, by inviting him to interfere with and decide upon their affairs, they say they cannot help this. That if any of them denounce the agent, they in turn are denounced by him, and as their payments come through his hands, they are afraid to come into collision with him. I am well satisfied that what has before been stated would be wise, and that is to separate from the Agencies the paying powers. Let the Agents prepare and

authenticate the rolls of each nation, and let a separate paymaster sent annually from the Department make all these payments. This would reduce the power of the agents and cut up by the roots the great source of abuse, which is speculation in Indian payments. It is impossible to escape all abuses, or to make the affairs of the Red men easy of management, but if the complaints which any man may hear on the Missouri and west of it are one quarter of them true, it is time the whole system was overturned and reformed. All connection with this Fur Company ought to cease. For years they have had the contract to carry up the Indian goods, and have had more to do with the government than was good for the Indian, as this connection apparently with the government must give them undue power and authority over the Indians of the northwest where the operations of the company are carried on.

Prairie Wolf

I saw a prairie wolf this morning for the first time. He was quite large, much larger than I expected to see. He seemed to be half larger than the largest sized fox, and ran with greater fleetness. White Cloud saw him run into a thicket, and he took down his gun and went out to fire upon him. The wolf was too wary and ran out and across the prairie. Robert [White Cloud] fired at forty rods but did not hit him. He was of a reddish brown color, and I should have taken him for a timber wolf, although Robert called him a prairie wolf.

Blackfeet

I went up this morning to White Cloud's to see a Blackfoot halfbreed, the daughter of Augustus Hamel a French trader and a Blackfoot woman, and the wife of John

Samuels, a Kentuckian who has been for some years a trader. Samuels says if I will write to Mr. Hamel at Sioux City he will make out for me a complete Blackfoot schedule. I will do this on my return. I have procured through this woman and her husband a tolerably correct Blackfoot schedule which I shall use unless I can secure a better one.[59]

It shows that the Blackfeet are Algonquin and are nearer allied to the Chippewa than the Peoria branch. She has been away from the Blackfeet some years, although she talks this language to her child. Her husband and she talk English principally. I think she understands the Blackfoot system, and with a good interpreter would have made it out well. As it is there are some doubtful answers. But it is perfectly clear that they have the Indian system of relationship.

Blackfoot Tribes

The Blackfeet live in camps, and each camp has its chief, who controls its movements. They have no villages, and raise no grain of any kind. They are strict nomads moving from place to place, and staying in one place but a short time. They have horses and they follow the game. The Blackfeet have no tribes [clans] in the sense of the other nations, as each camp is made up of many lodges, and of persons who are not related by blood. It would seem that the prairie Indians have been demoralized by their hard mode of life, and by being forced back as they have been by our advancing race into the prairie which the Indian never liked, and until he obtained the horse, could not occupy. The Blackfeet as Algonquins must have originally had tribes.

Polygamy

Among the Blackfeet polygamy prevails, and also the same custom of assigning all the sisters to the one who marries the oldest if he elects to take them. This polygamy they say is a necessity of the case growing out of the disproportion between the sexes. Life is long in this most healthy part of the world, and as the men fall in war constantly and in fights and casualties of all kinds, the women soon come to be the most numerous as this means becomes a sort of necessity to replenish their numbers.

The weather has come off warm today, but it is a very delightful day, and the country in the rear of Rulo presents a magnificent prairie spectacle, the same which I described last year. As I went over to White Cloud's this morning about two hours and a half after sun rise the grass was still covered with a heavy dew, and I was obliged to keep close in the road to keep my feet dry. It was a still morning, the first in several days, and the night had been still. It was at this place that I was so much struck with the amount and effect of this precipitation last year.

Hunting buffalo, from an old print. Instead of running parallel to the animal, this hunter approaches him head on, firing a heavy caliber pistol as he passes. Since a wounded buffalo could be very dangerous, those riding behind the hunter probably disliked this method.

Otoe and Iowa Descent

If an Iowa man marries an Otoe woman, his children are Iowas because descent is in the male line, and if an Otoe man marries an Iowa woman, the children are Otoes. White Cloud's father was an Iowa and his mother an Otoe, and Robert is an Iowa. This no doubt runs through these with the Kaws, Osages, and Quappas and perhaps the Winnebagoes. Robert D. White Cloud tells me that he can understand the Winnebagoes from the resemblance of their words to the Iowa. [Both belong to the Chiwere division of the Siouan language family—along with Missouri and Oto.] He regards them as a cognate nation.

Buffalo Hunt

White Cloud says that the Indians still prefer the bow and arrow to the gun for hunting buffalo. That the animal is easily killed, and the arrow does it with great certainty and that they can fire, or rather shoot, from the saddle much easier with the bow than with the gun. That the motion of the gun is liable to be unsteady, and therefore to shoot over, while with the bow they have no difficulty. They also prefer to hunt on horseback, as they must follow the buffalo as they hunt. They usually advance at the rate of ten to twenty miles per day, cutting, drying and packing their meat as they go. All these nations, I find, expect to go out for the June and September hunts. The hide in the spring is good for shoes, and for tent covers and for rawhide. In the fall the hide is preserved with the hair on for robes. The only drawback is the constant fighting of these Indians with each other, which endangers the lives of those who engage in the hunt. Robert says the Navy revolver is the best weapon for the buffalo hunt.

PART IV

Rulo, Nebraska Territory
Richardson Co., June 13, 1860

Conversation with Charles Martin, Trader

I have been a trader for the last twenty years in the employ of the American Fur Company, and have visited and lived among the following, Dakotas, Otoes, Omahas, Pottawatomies of Council Bluffs, Pawnees, Arikarees (Ah-rik-a-ra), Gros Ventres below Yellowstone, Assinaboines, (they call themselves Da-ko-ta), Crows (Up-sa-ro-ka, which means a crow), Sheyennes, Snakes (Sho-sho-nee, which means snake), Utah (U-taw they call themselves), Arapahoes (Ah-rap-a-ho they call themselves which means tattoed breast), Ban-aks and Kaws. All these nations have their signs by which they indicate their nationality, thus the Dakota make a sign of cutting the throat by drawing the hand across the throat. Their sign is rendered by the trader in English as "cut heads." The Sheyennes are "cut arms," and they make their sign by drawing the hand or finger two or three times across the left arm. The Crows make their sign by working their hands up and down like a bird. The Dakotas are as follows, who all make the same national sign. 1, Yank-ton (Lower Band). 2, Yank-ton-ais (Upper Band). 3, Pa-bok-sa (Cut Head, Pa-head, and Bok-sa, to cut). 4, Wa-ze-koo-ta (One who shoots in the Pine). 5, Se-a-sa-pa (Blackfeet, these are Blackfeet Dakotas and not the Blackfeet of the Maps [?]). 6,

Onk-pa-pa. 7, Cha-ha-nump-a (Two Kettle Band). 8, Min-e-ko-zhu (Farming near the Water). 9, E-ta-zip-shne (One without a Bow). 10, On-ga-lal-a (Rovers and always moving camp). 11, She-cha-hoo (Brule Dakota, Burnt Thighs). 12, Son-te. The above are given in Yankton dialect.

These are in three great divisions. 1, Son-tee. 2, Yank-ton. 3, Te-tons. The Son-tee are one. The Yankton consist of the Yankton and Yank-ton-ais. The remainder are all west of the Missouri and are called Tetons. This is their own classification.

The Assinaboines make the cut head sign. The Blackfeet raise one foot and touch the bottom. The Snake first points his finger to himself and then waves his finger from side to side and ahead to imitate the motion of a snake. The Arapahoe touch all the fingers of the right hand upon the breast several time in quick succession to show that they are pricked or tattoed breasts. The Pawnees pass the hand edgewise over the center of the head from front to rear to show that his head is shaved, with hair along the center. The sign for a white man is the hand drawn quick across the forehead horizontally to indicate that he wears a hat. The hat is the sign of the white man. Arikaree the same as the Pawnee. The Nez Perces make the sign of the pierced nose by touching the two sides of the nostril.

Talking by Signs[60]

There is a regular language of signs by which all the most western Indians can make themselves understood for all ordinary purposes. Martin made for me the signs for quite a long conversation. For crossing a mountain the closed hands were brought together and then stretched out horizontally to indicate a range, and then one hand is passed over the other at right angles curving upwards to indicate a crossing. That he met a white man on horseback would be made by the sign of the hat, and then two fingers in a fork on the other hand to show that he was on horseback straddle. If a mule, a motion would be made to show large ears. Martin says that without any Indian language and with these signs, he could go through these nations and travel with them and have no difficulty.

No Words of a Profane Kind

There is no swearing in an Indian language. The worst saying they can make is "you are a dog." "You are nasty" is another.

Marriage

Among all these nations the brother has most to say about the marriage of his sister. If the girl is applied for by a poor fellow, he says, "you will not marry that poor rascal. You must marry someone with plenty of horses, that he may give much horse to hunt buffalo with; or that white man and I shall always have a blanket and good clothes and horses etc." This is the way especially with the Dakotas and the Sheyennes.

Martin confirms my former position that the Indian woman has no passion, no love in our sense.[61] She is quiescent and submissive to her husband from duty, but without active passion. Martin says that the women are not attached to their husbands in the general sense of that term as one friend is to another, and perhaps it is because of the precarious tenure of the relation. A man may put away his wife and take another whenever he pleases or have several wives at once. After the birth of a child there is a substantial separation of husband and wife for a year. The children nurse, when polygamy permits, sometimes for six years or seven, as long as they please or until they

Charles Martin, as sketched by Rudolph F. Kurtz in his journal. Martin was a familiar figure along the Missouri; Kurtz met him in 1851. The information he gave to Morgan is indicative of his extensive experience among the Indians.

are shamed of it. That is, the boys nurse as long as they please; the girls are usually weaned at three years. I saw a boy stand on his feet and nurse sometime in Kansas last month. It was on the Sawk and Fox reservation. He must have been three years old. Martin says that where there is but one wife, the children are weaned earlier. Polygamy prevails very generally. He has known an Indian with 14 wives. He has had four at a time himself. The number of wives shows a man's wealth and influence, and not from passion. He says the Indians call the month of January the rutting month for human beings, such is the meaning of the name of the month.

An Indian never whips his wife, nor scolds her, nor pets her, but he simply says I don't like you any longer and I will throw you away. Sometimes he gives her the lodge and some horses and leaves her in it. Sometimes he sends her back to her relations. Complaints are made to the relatives on both sides but no quarrel results. She takes the children usually because the husband does not want them. The woman is not dis-

honored by the divorce. Another man will take her with her children just as quick if she is a proper woman and desirable.

It is clear from Martin's account that a man is expected to buy his wife with presents, usually of horses in the prairie country, and this necessarily begets an expectation and a desire to speculate or profit by the marriage of the girls in the family to which they belong.[62]

Indian Women

Martin has had a large experience with Indian women and mentioned to me many facts which it would be perhaps injudicious to note down, although I sought them and wished to know. He says the Indian woman never or rarely kisses her children, and never her husband unless asked to do so. He says he never knew an Indian woman to have a foul breath; they are also modest and retiring, and universally industrious. He is entirely positive that they know nothing of love, and cannot be made to manifest passion. They are always the same passive and passionless creatures, but acknowledging

THE INTERIOR OF THE HUT OF A MANDAN CHIEF

BY KARL BODMER

This is the interior of Dipauch's house. He was a distinguished Mandan who furnished Prince Maximilian with information about Indian religious beliefs, legends, and traditions. The picture was painted in November, 1833, at the Mandan village of Mih-tutta-hang-kush near Fort Clark. Four strong pillars at the center support the roof; the inner wall is formed of a number of posts, and from the tops of the posts rafters run to the four center supports. Between the posts the wall is filled in with shorter posts. On the outside the hut is covered with a kind of mat over which is hay, and over that, earth. In the center is the fire, and around the four center posts the owners' various pieces of property. The beds are by the walls, and "they consist of a large square case, made of parchment or skins, with a square entrance, and are large enough to hold several persons, who lie very . . . conveniently and warm on skins and blankets." Maximilian thought the Mandan houses "spacious, tolerably light, and cleanly."

MIH-TUTTA-HANG-KUSH, A MANDAN VILLAGE

BY KARL BODMER

This was the large village near Fort Clark. It was about 150 to 200 paces in diameter, built in a rather irregular circle, and was once surrounded by a palisade. The houses were close together, with an open space in the middle of the village, and a religious emblem, "the ark of the first man," in its center. At the north end of the open space was the medicine lodge. Among the huts were many scaffolds, some several stories high, upon which corn and meat were dried. The women in the foreground seem to be returning in their bull boats from a successful hunt for firewood.

the principle of obedience. Martin says the Indian woman really prefers an Indian husband to a white husband, as they like and approve of the Indian's ways and deportment the best; but they prefer to marry a white man from such motives as the certainty of more and finer clothes than an Indian can provide, and perhaps a more comfortable home and fewer hardships, but the Indian nature and temper is better adapted to her. I was surprised at what Martin said about the attachment or affections of the Indian female other than the passion of love. He says they do not become attached to him even. That if he is brought home wounded she does not manifest the least sensibility, and if he is killed she is not much affected by it. We know the Indian suppresses all emotion. If a relative returns after a hunt, or a war excursion or a long absence when he enters his home, no word is said of welcome or of pleasure. If married his wife takes off his moccasins, washes his feet and oils them if sore. She then sets food before him. After [he] has eaten, and not until he has eaten, it is polite or proper to speak to him. Then his friends and relatives begin and ask him the questions where he has been, what he has seen and what he has done, and he gives his account in due form over his pipe. Martin admitted that he was always contrary and exacting with his wives, and this I think accounts for the want of even a moderate affection for him which he discovered. The Indian female, well treated, must I think become attached to her husband, and strongly interested in his welfare.

Color of the Skin

Martin says the face and body where exposed to the sun on the prairie becomes quite dark, but that covered parts of the body of dark faced Indians are light. Speak-ing of the Sheyennes who have but little white blood in them, he says, none he says, the uncovered parts of their bodies are as fair as the back of his hand which was of a buff brown color. He is French Canadian, with blue eyes and chestnut hair. This is lighter than I expected. He says the forms of the Sheyennes, Crows and Sioux women are very fine, and as he says very beautiful. He seems to think the Sheyennes are about the finest Indians on the continent.

Indian Beard Plucked

Martin says he has seen Sioux and Sawks and Pawnees who had not a particle of white blood in them with heavy beards. It was plucked on the sides, and the eyebrows were plucked. The moustache was full. He says they sit for hours and work at it on their arms and face. The Indian says the white man's hair stinks, and that he is hairy like a dog. Martin says if they did not pull their beards they would become full in time. He thinks their scant beards are their own work, and besides they like to paint their faces. He says his Indian wives were continually pestering him to cut off his beard, which is yet a very full and flowing one. They said it was ugly and dirty. "You have too much to pull, but take a razor like a white man and shave it." They said "you are a good looking man and if you will shave you can get any young girl you like, etc."

Original Indian

Martin says that the three things which spoil the Indian are: 1st, the preacher, 2. the agent, and 3. the soldier. That the Indian who has seen neither, nor whisky, is a noble looking fellow, good hearted, proud and manly. He is honest, truth telling, hospitable, the best kind of a neighbor, all like brothers, and stand by each other. They fight every nation with whom they have no express treaty. These are broken by stealing horses and by retaliation. After the introduction of soldiers, and agents, and white people among them they were abused in all ways. They were made drunken, they were taken as wives and then abandoned. There are about 1,000 half breeds around Fort Laramie, and as many around Fort Randall and Fort Pierre. By these abuses the Indian is cowed down and oppressed. He also retaliates upon innocent white people for the wrongs done him in such ways as these.

At the Forts the officers high and low expect to have their Indian women, and the soldiers who are loose and free to do as they please, do the same. In this way the Indians are debased and demoralized, and learn to look upon the white man as treacherous, or at least as a devastator and the worst possible results flow from it. As to the agent I am more and more inclined to the belief that the agency system is a failure, and of but little benefit, and the only remedy I can see is to reduce the number, and leave the Indian to depend more upon himself.

Missionaries

As to the missionaries, I am not prepared to go to Martin's extent, and make the evil effects of their intercourse exceed the good.[63] I am surprised, however, to hear the traders, who are French Catholics it must be remembered, as far as they have any religion, bear their united testimony against the missionaries, and also some of the half breeds who are the descendants of traders. I think the first and greatest blessing now which we can give the Indian is the *English language*. With this he can depend [upon] himself, and make himself understood, and show his mind to the white man. The boarding school is the only instrumentality by which this can be effectually done, and therefore I am for the missionary and his school; but as to the agent and the soldier I agree with Martin. The Agents are opposed to the missionaries and it is because they are observers of each other.

I notice that all of these Missions look out well for themselves when a reservation is broken up and a band is moved to a new home. Thus the Methodist Manual Labor School among the Shawnees secured three sections of land, the Friends Mission half a section, the Presbyterian Mission at Bellevue among the Omahas secured a section of land which covered about half of the village site. Mr. Hamilton told me that the Board had expended $25,000 at Bellevue, and that they had or would realize from their real estate received from the Indians about $20,000 which was the amount they had expended upon the new Mission building at Blackbird Hills.

At Highland the same Board had secured a section of land which is quite valuable, and I was told also that they had managed to secure Iowa Point which was a valuable village property, besides. How this was done I know not. They also told me that the children were compelled to work hard and so much of the time that the school did them but little good. There was a strong prejudice against it for this reason. It is painful to hear and see so many and such constant evidences of mistrust in the Indian mind, of white people and their motives.[64]

[Charles] Martin

Martin gave me some account of his life, but it was too meagre to insert. He said if you take 20 white men there will be at least one soft head among them, but of 20 Indians, not one would be soft. He thinks the old Indian before the advent of the white must have been the happiest man on the earth. He was evidently a great admirer of Indian life and had a real love for it.

Martin must be 60 years old or at least 50. He brought his first wife whom he married 16 years ago down with him to this point, where she lived until last winter in January. He is now a widower and alone. His son, 15 years of age, is now in Montreal at school. I should have been glad to have seen more of him, as he is a man of intelligence and observation.

Steamer *Emilie*,[65] Missouri River June 14, 1860

We are now going down the river towards St. Jo at fair rate, and shall be there shortly after midday if we meet with no hindrances. I got up at day light, and went down to the bottom to watch for the boat which cannot be seen in time to reach the bank from the hotel. The boat came around the bend an hour after sunrise, and I had just time to make the landing and get aboard. My journey now is homewards, as my work on the Missouri is done for the present year. I may not go immediately home, but to St. Paul, Minnesota first, if I find favorable letters from home at St. Joseph.

Nebraska Ball

I omitted to mention that night before last a ball was given at Rulo. It was got up on short notice. A young man was sent to notify the girls, another to sweep out an empty store and arrange the seats, and another to notify the two village fiddlers. At 9 o'clock all was ready and the dancing began, first with one and then with two cotillions. Then [to] secure fair play, the gentlemen were numbered from one to sixteen or fourteen, and as all could not dance at once they were called by number and made to take their turn.

Among the girls were several half breeds, French and Dakota. They were well dressed in English fashion not omitting hoops, talk our language well, and two of them were educated at St. Louis. I joined the dance so far as to dance three times, of which twice was with these French and Dakota girls, Mrs. DeGray and Miss Somebody. They are good dancers and have the manners of ladies. This was my first dancing west of the Missouri river.

Consumption [Tuberculosis]

Martin says that consumption increases among the Indians as they adopt our life. He thinks it was unknown until trading posts were established among them, and that by sitting in rooms made over-hot by fire, and then going into the cold and sleeping in their cold damp huts, they take the violent colds which lead to consumption. He says it takes about three years, to use his language, to pull an Indian down. The Indian women at Riley living in houses, and without wild game, think they are not as well as they were up the river.

Prairie Burial Customs

The Indians of the Prairie above named bury their dead upon scaffolds or in trees, usually the latter. They dress and paint them and then tie them up in skins or blankets and place them in the fork or crotch of a tree, or on a scaffold made of poles. A man who has been murdered in the nation is for some special reason buried in the ground and only such according to the ancient custom. The Dakotas and Sheyennes (pronounced Shi-anns) are beginning to bury in the ground under the example and teachings of the whites.

Right: Omaha scaffold burials. Although the Omaha often buried their dead in a shallow grave in a sitting position, they also followed the custom of the Plains tribes of scaffold burial. The scaffold construction indicates that this photograph was taken about the turn of the century.

Left: Dakota Sioux tree burials, from the original negative of the photographer David F. Barry. After the body had been dressed and painted, it was wrapped and placed upon the scaffold in the tree. Later the bones were recovered and buried.

Indians Who Live Exclusively upon Animal Food

Martin told me that the Crows, Sheyennes, Blackfeet, Assinaboines, Arapahoes, Snakes and Pa Utas [Paiutes], follow the buffalo and consequently live in camps. They have no villages and raise nothing whatever. They live exclusively upon animal food. The Dakotas and Pawnees raise a little, or cultivate a small amount of vegetable food, but it bears but a small proportion to their whole subsistence. Since the Indian has had the horse, and only since then has it been possible for the Indian to occupy and live upon the prairie. He must follow the buffalo as he ranges from place to place, and this he could not well do, and move his camp without this invaluable domestic animal. Before the discovery and the introduction of the horse by the Spaniard the Indian must have turned away from the prairie as impossible of permanent occupation, except in the season of, and for the purposes of the hunt.

Buffalo Hunt

Upon this interesting topic I have procured a few additional facts from Martin, Tesson and White Cloud, all of whom have been buffalo hunters.

The buffalo cows drop their calves in April and May, and in the fall as early as October the cows with their calves begin to separate from the male buffaloes and they keep distant and apart from fall to spring. They live and rove over their pasturages not far apart, but in distinct bands; and if during the period of their separation a stampede or fight occurs by which they are intermingled, they separate again as soon as quiet is restored. The cows with their calves feeding together and the bulls by themselves.[66] In the spring in June the bulls are fat and in fine condition while the cows from the tendance of their young through the winter are still poor. In the latter part of July the buffalo bulls are on the race, the rutting season lasting from six weeks to two months. It is at this time when the males are seeking the females that they stampede [immigrant wagon] trains which happen to be in the line of their march. At such times the herd press forward and carry everything before them.

It is said that the cows seek the same places each year to drop their calves unless driven out by the Indian.

In hunting as before stated the bow and arrow are still preferred by the Indian to the gun. It is sufficiently fatal and more expeditious. There is no doubt that an expert Indian will send his arrow entirely through a buffalo.[67]

The Indian has his running horse for the buffalo hunt as well as the saddle horse. The former is lead until the herd is neared, when the Indian hunters endeavor to come upon the herd by descending a ravine. When they come near they prepare and mount their running horses as they call them, and dash at a bound among the herd, and give chase. It is no uncommon thing for a hunter to kill five, ten and even fifteen buffalo in a three mile chase. Martin said he knew an Indian to kill 17 in less than two miles with nothing but the arrow and the aid of his horse.

After the slaughter is over, they cut up and pack the meat, using every part of the animal but the head, and not, as Martin says, killing wastefully. They eat enormous quantities of the meat, so much as to make the boys deformed by their large and disproportioned abdomens. One ordinary or large family will sometimes consume a buffalo a day, so Martin said, with evident exaggeration.

There are no buffalo west of the Rocky Mountains, and therefore none in Oregon or Washington Territory. Their range is from the mountains to the Missouri and Fort Riley and from north of the Blackfeet to the Cherokee country south.

St. Joseph, June 14, 1860

We arrived here at noon, and expect to leave at four P.M. If we make our connections this will bring me to Niagara Falls Sunday morning, and home Sunday evening. It is very warm here and for that reason I go tonight.

Quincy, Illinois
June 15, 1860

We reached Hannibal at 8 this A.M. and went immediately on board the *Di Vernon* [?] a splendid Mississippi steamer, nearly if not quite equal to the *New World* and *Hendrik Hudson*,[68] and were soon under way. The distance is but twenty miles but as it was up stream it required an hour and a half to make it. It is a beautiful day and the ride up was delightful. It has often been claimed that the Missouri and Mississippi below the mouth of the former should have [been] named as one river, because of their greater united length. The Mississippi is the great river after all, as well above as below the Missouri, and it is right as it is. The Mississippi water is brackish or the color of brackish water, while the Missouri is the color of muddy water, and the best color of the two. We are obliged to wait here until five and a half this evening which will bring us to Suspension Bridge[69] [at Niagara Falls] Sunday morning, if we make no breaks, and here I will end, as I did last year on the steamer in the great river.

The mouth of the Missouri River as seen from the Illinois bank of the Mississippi. Morgan was more familiar with the Missouri, which may explain his preference for muddy water rather than the "brackish" water of the Mississippi.

The steamer **DIE VERNON**, which Morgan boarded at Hannibal; he found it to be a "splendid" vessel.

Reached home Monday evening, June 18, 1860, after an absence of four weeks less one day and found my family well, with the following new schedules: Miami, Peoria, Piankeshaw, Weaw, Kaskaskia (the four last in one), Sawk and Fox, Menomine, Munsee, Kansas Ojibwa, Shawnee, revised Omaha, Brule Dakota, Ogalalla Dakota, Sheyenne, Blackfoot and Pawnee.

Journal of a Visit to Pembina and Fort Garry on the Red River of the North July and August, 1861

Chapter VI   PART I

Steamer *Keokuk*, Mississippi River
July 7, 1861

I left home July 4 inst. at 7:55 P.M. and reached La Crosse on Saturday morning at 10 o'clock. We were at Detroit at 7 A.M. Friday, at Milwaukee at 11 P.M. Friday. We were obliged to remain at La Crosse until 9 o'clock Saturday morning at which time we left for St. Paul. The weather yesterday was extremely hot and oppressive, but in the evening the breeze was cool and refreshing. During the night it rained, and this morning it is cool and delightful.

This is my first sail on this part of the Mississippi. For some reason this river always awakens pleasure whenever I first see it after an absence, unlike any other great river. It is truly a magnificent river, which may well inspire respect.

This morning about 6 o'clock we entered Lake Pepin, and emerged from it about 10 o'clock. It is from 30 to 40 miles long, and from one and a half to three broad. There is no special reason for calling it a lake, unless it be to specialize the scenery upon it

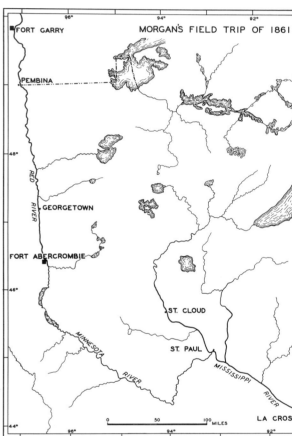

which is very fine. There are high bluffs on either side. I should judge from 300 to 500 feet, and the river occupies the space between them, there being no bottom lands between. Near the crest of the bluff particularly upon the Wisconsin or east side, the limestone crops out in perpendicular ledges of solid walls, making a very grand appearance. The naked rock exposed I judge to be from 100 to 150 feet perpendicular, at the Maiden's Leap, so called, which is on the east side and about half way. This particular cliff may have been 1000 feet long by 150 high at the highest point. The rock is of a yellowish color, and wears the appearance of masonry somewhat. This is the rock over which they say an Indian maiden leaped to escape some intended wrong. I think I have seen the legend.

I am on my way to Pembina on the Red River of the North to visit the Assinaboines, Crees and such other Indians as I can find them married to traders or half breeds. I ought to find Blackfeet, Gros Ventres, Minnetarees, Crows and possibly Athabascas as well as Dakotas and Chippewas; but we shall see. It is the season when large numbers are away on the hunt, and for this reason I should have delayed my visit about two weeks, but for the necessity of my going to Lake Superior[1] on my return. Still I hope for some results of importance. If I can find the Assinaboines, and work out their relationship and old institutions in full it will pay me alone.

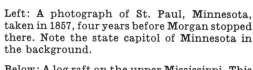

Left: A photograph of St. Paul, Minnesota, taken in 1857, four years before Morgan stopped there. Note the state capitol of Minnesota in the background.

Below: A log raft on the upper Mississippi. This raft is smaller than those Morgan saw, even though only part of it appears in the illustration. The larger rafts were nothing less than traveling villages; all the comforts of home were available.

Left: Map of Morgan's field trip of 1861 to Pembina and Fort Garry on the Red River.

St. Paul, July 7, 1861

We reached St. Paul at 2 P.M. The city, which is very pleasantly situated upon a bluff on the east side of the river, contains about 12,000 inhabitants.[2] The Mississippi bends at this point, and flows nearly east and west, so that a small settlement on the right bank of the river is rightly called West St. Paul. It is a prairie country all around, but yet extensively wooded, as is also the whole of Wisconsin through which we passed. I am told there are patches of heavy timber in different parts of both Wisconsin and Minnesota, running eccentrically without regard to water courses, and ranging from ten to twenty miles through and from forty to sixty in length. There is one above this point crossing the Minnesota river, and running north and south 16 miles wide by 60 in length, and about 30 miles west of the Mississippi.

Rafts of Logs

We passed today about seven large rafts going down to St. Louis, as was supposed.

Their size may be judged by the number of men required to manage them. On them I counted 20 men to each, on two 30 each. The logs are arranged lengthwise with the river, and are secured by cross poles attached to the logs by inserted clasps of tough splints, and sometimes with ropes, making a solid platform of timber one story only in thickness. At each end are secured on a pivot long paddles, or blades of board attached to the end of a pole, the former about ten feet long and the latter near twenty feet. Of these oars I counted seven

at the ends of two, and nine at each end of one. As seven of these point up stream and seven down they use them to move the raft out or in from shore, working them together for the same object. In this way they are able to guide it toward the shore, or out into the current. They keep the raft on the shallow side of the river as near as possible so as to be out of the way of the steam boats. On each raft were one or two shanties, and one or two boats. They float down with the current perhaps 2 or three miles per hour. I counted in one raft twenty lengths of logs, and think it was one of the smallest. The logs were of medium size, but they covered a large area. No doubt they have a jolly time.

I found some traders here [St. Paul] just in with their trains from Pembina. They come here with their furs. I ascertained from Mr. Tate[3] that a Mr. Rune [or Rerne?] who lives near Fort Garry has a Blackfoot wife, and talks several languages. Also that a Mr. Bird, a half breed Cree, who lives 8 miles below Fort Garry talks the Gros Ventres and Chippewa. He thinks I can get the Cree easy, the Blackfoot, the Chippewa and the Assinaboine. He thinks Bird talks the Crow. Fort Garry is the head quarters on the Red River, and not Pembina. I shall go at once to Fort Garry and spend most of my time there. I can return either in eight or sixteen days. If I find it profitable, I will stay the 16. A Mr. Barnard,[4] a missionary near Pembina, was also named to me as full of Indian knowledge. I must find him. I also saw Mr. Colville,[5] editor of a paper at Fort Riley. He is to return on Wednesday and I expect to see him then.

We leave at 4 o'clock tomorrow morning, and shall not be at Georgetown on the Red River until sometime on Friday. It is very hot here today, more so than at home when I left. It was also very hot on the river last night.

St. Cloud, Monday, July 8, 1861

We left St. Paul at 4 A.M., breakfasted at St. Anthony's Falls at Minneapolis, and after a warm ride reached St. Cloud at 8 P.M., a distance of 80 miles. This village is situated upon the west side of the Mississippi and is a straggling place of six or eight hundred inhabitants, all wide awake and good natured. Of our party is Joseph James Hargrave,[6] a nephew of the chief factor at Fort Garry, William Mactavish, on his way to the Fort where he is hereafter to reside. He is a son of a former factor of York Factory. He is an agreeable companion, and it was a fortunate incident that we met at St. Louis [St. Paul] as we did.

Train Dogs, Half Wolf

I saw a large brown and red dog at the hotel, so wolfish in appearance that I inquired his pedigree. I was told that he was half wolf and was raised as a train dog for the sledge to drive on the snow in the winter, and that such dogs are raised and kept at Georgetown for this express purpose. In the rutting season the she dog is taken into the woods, tied and left. She is there found when the heat is upon her by the wolf, at which time she is neither offensive to him, nor he to her, and the result is a cross breed dog of the kind I saw.[7] I could not determine at Georgetown any confirmation of this statement. It is also said to be a mule [i.e., a sterile hybrid], but the truth of this is not perhaps settled. The wolf dog I saw was as long and as high as a medium or perhaps full sized bull dog but lighter in build. The ears were erect with a slight inclination to lop one at a time; but when he rose upon his feet and moved, both were erect. The forehead was long and the nose medium, and the expression wild and untamed. The whole expression was more that of the large timber wolf by whom he was sired, than of the dog his mother. I spoke to him but he did not move a muscle, while a cur dog lying near him wagged his tail without being spoken to, with the true sympathy and good breeding of a domestic dog. The fore legs of the wolf dog reminded me at once of the "splendid tractors" mentioned by Dr. Kane[8] as belonging to one of his Eskimo dogs. They were strong and long furred combining strength with swiftness of foot. His hair was long brownish red, of unusual length and without sleekness.

They hitch four to a light sledge tandem, and drive them 45 to 60 miles per day, carrying one man, with his provisions and blankets to sleep out on the prairie, and also provisions for the dogs for the journey, which consists of one pound of pemican per day to each dog. This pemican, which consists of dried and chopped buffalo meat over which melted buffalo fat is poured, is fed to them once a day and at night when the day's work is done.

The snows are thin and crust over, so that a person who knows the route moves with great rapidity. The dogs require beating to secure submission. They are often used between Georgetown and Fort Garry. Whether they are raised in the manner stated I consider at least doubtful.

Kandotta,[9] July 9, 1861

We left St. Cloud at 6½ and reached this place at 7 P.M. a distance of 65 miles. We had a fine breeze and a cool and comfortable ride, with a pleasant English woman, Mrs. Cook,[10] who resides where we stop to dinner tomorrow, as a fellow passenger. We came along the valley of the Sawk river crossing it three or four times. It is a narrow stream with a swift current and clear water.

From another passenger, and Mrs. Cook, and Mr. Stearns,[11] our landlord at St. Cloud, I learned a good deal about the means of Indian subsistence in this part of Minnesota, and the upper Mississippi. It combines many advantages which place it above any other portion of country west of the Lakes and the Mississippi. In the first place, it is filled with innumerable lakes large and small, and intersected with numerous streams, all of which abound in fish. Many of these lakes are on the government military map of Nebraska, and many are not. Some of them cover from half an acre to twenty and forty acres and some several times as large and have no outlet. They are fed by springs, have a hard bottom, are free of grass or canes and full of fish. Out of one of these small lakes Mr. Cook last week took a pike weighing 16½ pounds, in whom was another pike weighing 2½ pounds, through the ice. Having used up the other fish they were living upon each other most likely. In these lakes large and small are found the pike, pickerel, bass, sun fish and carp. In the Red River are found sturgeon, cat fish, pickerel and carp, and in the Mississippi pike and pickerel principally above St. Anthony's Falls.

Means of Subsistence

In the same region were found the buffalo, elk, deer, prairie and timber wolf, black bear, otter, raccoon, badger and fox. These were abundant and about all used for food by the Indian. In game were wild geese, several kinds of ducks, swan, partridges, pigeons, prairie chickens, curlew or great snipe (of whom I saw one yesterday), wood cock, and pelican and sand hill cranes. There are no wild turkeys. Among berries and fruits were the following: red, yellow and brown plums, about the size of the damsons and a grand plum growing on a low bush, grapes, frost and early, artichokes, ginseng, gooseberry, white and black, strawberries, raspberries, red and black, black berries, cranberries, huckleberries. Of nuts, hazel nuts, butternuts, acorns, no chestnuts, beech nuts nor walnuts.

Pomme de Terre, July 10

We reached this place at seven P.M. [according to Hargrave, they reached Mrs. Cook's farm about noon where they stopped and had dinner] after a ride of 65 miles, mostly through prairie, but with a strip of woods 6 miles wide and some corduroy road. This river is a small one and empties I believe into the Otter Tail river near by. The station consists of nothing but a house and barn but the country is settled in places. We met at this place six passengers from Fort Garry going to St. Paul. They informed us that the boat returned on Monday last and when it came back to Georgetown it was to lie up some time waiting for freight, they said 10 days.[12] This is the first ill news we have received.

Fort Abercrombie, July 16, 1861

We reached this place about six o'clock P.M. after riding 60 miles. The Fort is situated on the west side of the Red River which is crossed here by a government ferry. I presented to Col. Day, Commandant of the Fort, my letter from Dr. [Joseph] Henry. He received me very cordially, and invited Mr. Hargrave and myself to take up our quarters in the Fort for the night.[13] Col. Day is about 60 years of age, gray and fine appearing. We found him very pleasant and sociable.

Lakes of Minnesota

Some parts of Minnesota are full of lakes. Their number is prodigious and they are a positive feature in the landscale of the prairie. Between Pomme de Terre and Dayton where we crossed the Otter Tail River, we passed and counted fifty-one of these lakes on a continuous distance of fifty-eight (58) miles. We rejected from the count, which we scored on the ribs of the coach top, all lakes which covered less than ten square acres of ground. The number thus rejected were a third or half as many as those we counted. These lakes vary from ¼ of a mile in length to two, three, four, five, seven and ten miles in length. But one however was ten miles long, Pelican Lake, and perhaps but one or two over five. A few of the smaller contained grass, showing they were shallow, but the most of them were clear, clean and rather pretty lakes, with the prairie extending to the shore and the shore in some places lined with beach pebbles.

These lakes are in the hollows made by the roll of the prairie. Some of them are fed by springs, and have no outlet. Others have outlets into each other and finally into the Otter Tail or the Sawk rivers, the former water running through the Red River into Lake Winnipeg and Hudson Bay and the other into the Mississippi. From the roll of the prairie those lakes only came into sight which were within two or three miles of the stage road. I have no doubt that within four miles of each side of our route, that as many more could have been counted as we recorded above. These lakes are well stocked with fish. We saw them in numbers at the crossings, such as carp and pike, and we were told by all alike that they were full of excellent fish. Mrs. Cook told us of their taking one in the lake near her house a pike which weighed sixteen pounds.

I have been thus particular about these lakes for this reason, that their fish as a means of Indian subsistence is an important element in the history of this region, and made it a most desirable one to the Dakotas who held it at the discovery, and to the Chippewas, who by the recession of the Dakotas have now come into its posesssion. There are literally thousands on thousands of these lakes in Minnesota. One man

A Dakota Sioux burial, by Seth Eastman. This fine study shows the body wrapped and about to be placed on the scaffold by the deceased's relatives.

asserted that they covered a quarter of the state. This of course is an exaggeration, but I think they may cover about one thirtieth part of the state where they are the most numerous. They are also a great resort of ducks, of which we saw a number.

Sand Hill Cranes

These cranes are brown and white, and are said to stand up breast high to a man. We saw three of them near Pelican Lake, standing and jumping up and down in the prairie grass near the brow of a hill. They were half a mile off, and looked very large. We also saw a flock of pelicans on the lake, but they were too far away to be made out distinctly.

In the evening the Col. sent for his Dakota interpreter Louis[14] and we obtained

through him and another half breed who was half Sis-se-ton the Sis-se-ton-wan and Yank-ton-a Dakota system of relationship. Louis confirms the fact that among the Dakotas and Chippewas they sleep nude rolled in a blanket, and that two men will not sleep skin to skin.

Marriage Customs of Dakotas

Louis says they buy their wives, but that none of the kindred named on the schedule are allowed to intermarry, except those related by marriage. A man may marry his brother's widow, but he is not obliged to do so. This may have something to do with the fact that the sons of a man's brother are his sons. Col. Day's son says that the Ogallala Dakotas do not intermarry among themselves, but go to another band for a wife. Louis says the Sissetons intermarry with Sissetons, and Yanktons the same.

Georgetown, July 12, 1861

We left the Fort about 8 and arrived at Georgetown at seven. This place is located on the Red River at the point which Burbank and Co.[15] think will be at the head of navigation. We found Burbank here and ascertained from him that we must wait here ten or twelve days for the boat to make her next trip. The boat will tie up next Monday, but as there is no freight here the delay is for trains of freight to arrive which is now on the way from St. Cloud. This delay will nearly destroy the results of my expedition as I must return with the boat, and she will remain at Fort Garry but two days.[16]

Dakota, its meaning

This word, pronounced by the eastern bands Dakota, by the western, Lacota, signifies united, or bound together, and refers to the seven council fires. The league was

between seven bands only, and as there are now a dozen or more, the additions are subdivisions of the seven, or some of them.

1. Me-da-wa-kon-to-wa[17] Spirit Lake Band
1. Sis-se-to-wan   Sis-se-to-wan, on schedule
3. Wa-pa-to-wa
4. Wali-pa-ka-ta   Leaf Shooters
5. E-hank-to-wa   (Yanktons)
6. E-hank-to-wa-na   (Yanktona)
                          E-ank-to-wan on schedule
7. Te-to-wa

Out of the Tetowa, or Tetons, came the Ogallala and Brulé Dakotas and perhaps some others. Riggs[18] will be able to furnish full information upon these points.

Cheyennes

The Dakotas call the Cheyennes Shi-ya, which means the people "who speak an unintelligible tongue."[19] The Cheyennes in Kansas are still known to them by the name Shi-ah. G. W. Northrup,[20] not the one from whom the steam boat on the Red River was named, but a Yankee hunter from Oneida County, New York, who now lives here, says that the Dakotas informed him that the Cheyennes many years ago lived at the great bend of the Cheyenne river which empties into Red River above Georgetown. Northrup says he has seen on the north side of the river at the bend the traces of embankments and pit holes in the ground which appear to have been excavations for habitation, since caved in. As a further confirmation of the fact that it was the ancient seat of the Cheyennes he says that the Dakotas call the river Shi-ya-Wo-tu-pe, from the Bear's Den Hillock to its mouth. The word Wo-tu-pe signifies the place "where they planted," from Wo-ta to plant, while from the Hill above [?] to its head, they call it Grizzly Bear's Den River. This would seem to mark the fact that the first which the Dakotas knew of planting was from seeing it at the villages of the Sheyennes, which was thus made the basis of a name for the river where they planted.

Dakota Burial Customs

They bury upon trees or scaffolds, but when a death occurs to one of their number away from home, they bury now in the ground flat wise but he thinks with the head towards some hill, or religious place, known to their religion. He says he has noticed them in smoking take out their pipe and point the stem in the direction of such a hill, as it seemed to him. He thinks they may have more than one.

[A half page or more on the northern extension of the prairie, according to Northrup, is omitted here.]

Train Dogs[21]

I can find no information here about the train dogs. No one is able to satisfy me that they are raised as stated before. There are several large and fine specimens here, which are used in the winter as train dogs, but they appear to be simply a breed of dogs procured from the Indians, and raised from themselves.

Shooting Arrows Through Buffalo

Northrup is a regular buffalo hunter. He says the Indian will send his arrow into the buffalo to the feather, unless bones interfere, and then that by the process of running the arrow will work itself through and out on the other side. He says the Dakotas so explain it to him and he thinks they never do shoot their arrows through, as formerly recorded by me.

[Morgan has here 16 pages of vocabulary of the Cree of the Red River.]

Crees of Pembina Mountain

There is a family of Crees encamped here from Pembina, at work for the Hudson's Bay Company on a ware house, I believe. The women are half-breed Crees and talk French and Cree. The [husband?] of one of them is pure French and has been 40 years in the service of the Company, the other is a half-breed Cree. They are married to a mother and daughter, and they all live in one tent. From them I have obtained the Cree system of relationship, but in some respects imperfectly and the following additional information.[22] There are four bands of the Crees, and they occupy from Rupert's land and Hudson Bay, to the Red River and west of it.

1. Na-he-a-wuk — Crees of the low or swampy lands
2. Sa-ka-we-ne-wuk — Crees of the Woods
3. Mas-co-ta-we-ne-wuk — Crees of the Prairies
4. Me-che-ne-pe-we-wuk — Crees of the Lakes and Rivers

Their tribal [clan] divisions they say have disappeared;[23] at all events they do not know of any tribes among them which are kept distinct. They still mark their tents with signs to keep them distinct as follows:

1. Ah-misk, Beaver; 2. Kee-hu, Eagle or Falcon; 3. O-hoo, Owl; 4. Wa-pe-su, Swan; 5. Moose-tuse, Buffalo; 6. O-je-jak, Sand Hill Crane; 7. Ap-pe-see-moa-soo, Jumping Deer; 8. Ap-pe-sets-see-koose, Antelope; 9. Wa-wa-ska-soo, Red Deer; 10. Moo-shwa, Moose; 11. Mus-kwa, Bear; 12. My-he-kun, Wolf; 13. Ma-ga-sese, Fox; 14. Mish-tan-usk, Badger; 15. Ke-kwa-ha-gan,

Wolverine; 16. Ma-gwa, Loon; 17. Mis-ke-nake, Turtle; 18. Moo-ga-ha-su, Bittern; 19. She-keeb, Duck; 20. Kee-na-beek, Snake; 21. She-she-kwa-o, Big Snake; 22. Ah-dik, Rain Deer; 23. Ne-kik, Otter.

Red Lake Chippewas

About a dozen Chippewas from Red Lake came in yesterday [to Georgetown] on horseback, each with a gun, and say they are going over the river to hunt elk. As this is about the size of an ordinary war party it is thought they are after the Dakotas. I tried this morning to talk with them through an interpreter, but could not get much from them. Their name for the Dakotas is O-po-nuk.

They gave me the following dances: 1. Wa-wen-che-gwa, Dance for the Dead; 2. As-sen-e-ope, Medicine Dance; 3. Ka-wa-skin-ne-ka; 4. Moo-oa-mo, Dance for the Dead.

Cree Tribes [Clans]

On further conversation with the old Frenchman he says that Great grandfather, grandfather, father and son all mark their tents with the same mark. This is some recognition of the fact that there are tribes of the Crees. [But the tent marks could represent personal totems.]

Cree Marriages and Polygamy

Cousins marry among the Crees and half brothers. The women say also that on the Saskatchewan own brothers and sisters marry, but that they are uncles etc. Polygamy is general among the Crees. Some men have ten wives. One chief has fifteen, but these are extreme cases.

If a man marries the oldest of several sisters he is entitled to all of them as fast as they grow up [sororate]. No one could marry either of them without his consent. He is not obliged however to take them. A man however is required to take his sister-in-law as a wife after his brother's death and the woman must take him as her husband [levirate]. So a woman if unmarried must take her sister's husband as her husband after her death whether she be older or younger than her deceased sister; still he is not obliged to take her, which is perhaps because a man has power to put away his wife.

Wives are bought. The man who desires a certain woman takes a horse to the girl's mother and leaves it. He then asks her for her daughter. If the mother likes him the girl is delivered over whether she is pleased or not. She must yield to the custom. He takes her to his house and she is his wife without any further marriage ceremony. If the mother does not like the match she refuses her daughter, but does not return the horse. The horse is hers at all events, from which it is to be inferred that the horse is the price of permission to make the proposition.

The word *Pembina* appears to be from Ne-pe-me-na-ne-se-pe which means the Pembina berry, a large red berry which grows on a bush on the Pembina river.[24] The above is the Cree name of the river.

Cree Dances

1. War Dance	Na-too-pi-ye-se-moo-win	Men alone
2. Scalp "	Ka-ma-che-ma-hu-m-wuk	Men and women
3. Conjuring "	Ne-pa-gwa-we-se-moo-win	" " "
4. Buffalo "	Moos-toos-oo-se-moo-win	Men alone
5. Chiefs "	O-kee-che-tow-se-moo-win	" "
6. Partridge "	Pe-he-ya-o-se-moo-win	" "
7. Discovery "	N'-da-wa-tow-se-moo-win	" "
8. Warrior "	O-ge-che-sa-te-moo-win	One man

PART II

Georgetown, July 18, 1861

We are still detained at this point on Red River, and it will be nine or ten days before we shall get away. The Hudson's Bay Company have taken up a large tract of land at this place, have established an agency here and erected several buildings.[25] Mr. A. H. Murray[26] is resident Agent here. He has been in the service of the Company since 1843, and has traveled extensively over their territories and our own, having been from the Gulf to the Arctic Sea. For health he says McKenzies river surpasses all other places on the continent. He says there are no diseases there. I have talked with him about the prairie area in the Hudson's Bay territories and obtained some information which I will now record.[27] We used the map published in the *Journal of a Boat Voyage Through Rupert's Land,* by Geo. J. Richardson, 2 vols., London, Longman, Brown, Greene and Longmans, 1851, illustrated.

[Morgan arrived in Georgetown on July 12 and remained there until July 28. We learn much more from Hargrave (p. 57) than from Morgan about how the latter occupied himself during this time. "The resources of the country were not great," says Hargrave. "Morgan, having questioned all the people about the village who could throw any light on his researches, sought occupation of a general nature. After a few walks with his gun, the only reward of which worth mentioning, was a hawk he shot one afternoon, he turned his attention to books. Fortunately I had brought with me Mr. Wilkie Collins' *Woman in White*, then newly published. In a short time this popular production completely dispelled Mr. Morgan's *ennui*, and interested him so much that he attended to nothing else. He looked on the circumstances of the story with a legal eye, and criticized them as if they had been of actual occurrence; alternately burning with indignation at the complicated and successful rascalities of the Machiavellian Fosco, and shaking with laughter in contemplation of the 'fantastic tricks' of the monomaniac Esquire of Limmeridge. I presume the unusual nature of the plot had struck his legal mind with unusual force. The volume I possessed was perused by many successive delighted readers . . . but to none, I believe, did it convey nearly the same measure of entertainment as to Mr. Morgan. . . ."

Morgan and Hargrave had many discussions together. " 'The Theory of Democracy,' on which our conversations often turned," says Hargrave, "was a subject which I was confessedly slow to apprehend. Mr. Morgan was good enough to admit he liked me the better for 'supporting the cause of European institutions,' on the ground that adhesion to the government of one's own country, in the presence of citizens of other states, was a high public duty, incumbent on all men. He prophesied, however, that a few years' residence in America, during which I should enjoy the advantage of inspecting the working of New World institutions, would insensibly bring me round to his view of the case, and, meanwhile, he agreed to differ" (p. 53).

Morgan had many conversations with Mr. Murray and others, also, regarding central, northern, and western Canada, its climate, topography, flora, fauna, and Indian tribes. Later, in *Systems*, he cites both Alexander Murray and his wife, "a quarter breed Cree . . . and an educated and accomplished lady," on the Kutchin tribe and other subjects (pp. 207–8, 237–38). He obtained the kinship system of the Cree of the Prairie while at Georgetown with the assistance of Mrs. Murray (*Systems*, p. 286).

Morgan whiled away many an hour, during his stay in Georgetown, recording information received in his conversations with Murray and others, and in copying extracts from George J. Richardson's *Journal of a Boat Voyage Through Rupert's Land* (2 vols.; London, 1851). Since these entries deal with the oral and published accounts of others, we omit almost all of them here; they would number about 12 pages of typescript.]

Prairie Area

I have found here [Georgetown] several traders and *voyageurs* who have been twenty, thirty and forty years in the service of the Hudson's Bay Company from whom I am gaining information from day to day of the country and the location of the native races. [We omit about five pages of the information that Morgan obtained in this way.]

An old Frenchman tells me that he crossed the mountains from the head of the north branch of the Saskatchewan to Vancouver. After passing the summit it was twelve days journey to Vancouver, seven days through a rough, rocky and wooded country, through which they went mostly by water in canoes, then five days over prairie to the water. From thence it was one day by water across the channel to the island. He thinks the prairie[28] does not extend far northward at this point. Another

says that it is prairie between the two branches of the Saskatchewan, but from their junction down it is forest.

Cree Indians

The Crees are on both branches of the Saskatchewan to near their heads. They are at Red River, at Fort Churchill [?] , at York Factory where they are mixed with Chippewas, and at Moose Factory. The latter are called Swampy Crees. They appear to be a widespread people, and must be numerous.

Sussees [Sarsi]

The Sussees are still known by this name. They live on the head waters of the north branch of the Saskatchewan and from thence to the mountains. They speak a dialect of the Blackfoot, or a cognate language, Mr. Murray thinks. They number about 2000. More likely Athapascans. [They are.]

Dakotas and Chippewas

There are no Dakotas east of the Red River, and no Chippewas west of it, except as they are mixed in with the Crees. [But there were Chippewas in North Dakota at this time.] The Red River country is here called the neutral ground between them. The Chippewas however are settled much nearer to the Red River on the east side, than the Dakotas are on the west. At Red Lake a few miles south east of this place, there is a settlement of Chippewas called Red Lakers. The small band of ten or twelve who encamped here last Saturday were from Red Lake. Each had a horse and a gun. They were going ostensibly to hunt elk on the west side of the river, and southward into the Dakota country; but it was thought here that it was a war party and that they were after scalps. Their appearance on horseback was quite picturesque. Tuesday morning they swam their horses over the river and soon after mounted and rode away. The men rode over in a canoe and the horse swam by its side, having been driven in without difficulty by those behind. As Indians they were inferior specimens. There were two among them who appeared well. Of one of these, the oldest, I procured the black stone pipe, by giving him one of red clay in exchange.

Georgetown, July 21, 1861

Last night I procured from Mrs. A. H. Murray the system of relationship of the Cree of the Prairie.[29] She was born on the Peace river. Her grandmother was a half breed Cree. She is nearly full blood,[30] but has some of the Indian characteristics, and so have her children by Mr. Murray. She talks the Cree perfectly, and we had no difficulty in filling out the schedule. This makes two schedules taken here. I cannot yet ascertain whether the first is the Cree of the lowlands or of the Woods.[31] Tonight I

am to have the Cree of the lowlands,[32] or the Swampy Cree as it is familiarly called here, from one of Mrs. Murray's domestics.

I have seen here several times a very old Chippewa woman. She is living with some half breeds in a bark tent near by. Mr. Murray says she is over 100 years old. I should have said that Mr. Murray is one of the chief traders of the Hudson's Bay Co., and is at present stationed at this place. He is very polite and intelligent and furnished me with the volume on the Hudson's Bay Co. from which the foregoing extracts were taken, and also Richardson's work in two vols. which I am now reading. The old woman I intend to see with Cline [unidentified] as interpreter, and see about the ancient descent of the office of chief.

For two or three days I have been unwell, not seriously, but enough so to be careful. It is warm here, and there is malaria[33] in the atmosphere. All this region was under water in the spring, and there is a small swamp in front of the houses here and another in the rear. It is easy to smell the im-

purity. Besides this there are no springs here and we are obliged to use the river water. My tongue is furred up wonderfully, and my bowels distended. I have been dieting, or rather starving, for three or four days. It is Tuesday and we may not get away until next Monday, and I am anxious to keep up until I can get away from here at least.

I find that Caldwell's[34] mother-in-law is a Flathead woman, who talks some English, and her daughter, his wife, talks English perfectly. I must see them.

Georgetown, July 24, 1861

Yesterday we heard from Mr. Burbank[35] and the train of freight for which we are waiting. They will not come before Saturday the 27, and we shall probably get away Monday morning early.

Red Lake Chippewas, Male Line

There are two tents of Red Lake Chippewas here, and among them is one old woman said to be 100 to 110 years old. She is evidently extremely old, but she walks off quite smartly. One eye is blind and the other nearly so. She informed me through an interpreter that her husband was a great chief etc. In answer to a question she said she belonged to the Sturgeon tribe [clan]: that her father was of the Sturgeon tribe and her mother of the Snake, Ke-na-big. This then tells back for 100 years that the

Wooden structures above Chippewa graves. This photograph shows a typical Chippewa graveyard, where the dead are buried in a shallow grave and then protected by a "dog house" structure which is placed over it. Like the Omaha burial, a small door makes it possible to place food inside the structure.

children are of the tribe of the father, unless we are to suppose that the rule has been changed in her day. Cline obtained from her the names of half a dozen Chippewa dances, which I will take down by and by.

Cree Tribes [Clans]

This subject I have had up again with several persons, and cannot find the least trace of a present division into tribes. Neither can I learn that they have any tradition or recollection of a former division into tribes. If they ever were so divided they have given it up. They live with the Chippewas, that is mixed in, and know of their tribes, but deny having anything of the kind among themselves. They mark their tents from father to son with certain devices of animals, but that is the extent.

Chippewa Dances, Red Lake

Dance for the Dead	Wa-wen-che-gwa	
" " " "	Moo-sa-mo	
Medicine Dance	As-sin-ee-ope	
	Ka-wa-skin-ne-ka	
Scarf Dance	Ka-ma-je-wuk	Men and women (from old w.)
Religious Dance	Me-da-we-wat	Men and women
Magic Dance	Wa-ba-no-we-wat	Men alone
War Dance	Na-to-bi-ne-u-sim-o-wat	" "

Kutchin Dance

Murray says the Kutchin dance on the extreme point of their toes, and not as the southern Indians do by laying down the heel. They also squat and dance on their toes. He says their dances and their music are of a superior kind.

Kutchin Burial Customs

Mr. and Mrs. Murray were four years among this people on the Yukon river. He went there to establish a post, the first among them. They live entirely upon fish and game, except wild berries or strawberries, blueberries, which are abundant.

They have seven months of winter to five of summer. If a death occurs in the winter, they split a pine log, hollow it out, dress the body and bury it horizontally in the ground, with all the personal articles of the deceased. They build a timber house over the grave and cover all with earth. They leave an opening in the end of the grave in which to place food and tobacco, and for the spirit to go in and out. They believe in the immortality of the soul, and have the same idea of our Indians that the soul revisits the body.

In the summer the women have a musical lament for all their dead. They turn over their canoe, sit under them and sing their mourning songs the night through. Mrs. Murray says their songs and their music are very fine and impressive. She says their singing is superior to that of the southern

Indians. They also address the dead at the time of the burial and afterwards. Mr. Murray says they are a superior class of Indians, in their ways, habits and appearance. They leave an opening in the grave for the spirit to go in and out.

Chippewa Burial Customs

Mr. Murray described a Chippewa burial. It is precisely like the Omaha. They bury in a sitting posture with the knees flexed, but cover the body with earth. They then build a roof over the grave, and make a door in at one end. This is opened frequently to place food on the grave. They also address the spirit of the dead night after night, build a fire at the grave, sweep away the dirt from the ground etc. Mr. Murray mentioned the case of [a] woman who visited the grave of her daughter in this way at Pembina, night after night, taking food to the grave and placing it inside through the door. She also talked to the spirit of her daughter, and kept the ground swept clean.

Kutchin Sleep Nude

The Kutchin wore when he visited them skin clothing chiefly reindeer dressed with the hair on for winter, and without hair for summer, the hair worn inside. They wore regular pantaloons secured around the waist, the legs attached, and the shoes sewed fast to the legs. Over this was a coat, which came below the pants and was pouched in the center before and behind. (See Richardson's plates which were from Murray's drawings.) The women wore pants with shoes attached, the same as the men. Over this they wore a sort of frock, coming down nearly to the knees, square in front, and pointed behind. It is the finest Indian costume worn by any American Indians.[36]

At night they denude themselves of this clothing and sleep in skin blankets or robes, and after the establishment of the post among them by Mr. Murray, they substituted blankets. They did not wear the breech cloth, Mr. Murray thinks, but he is not sure. As fast as they substituted European clothes, they put on the breech cloth the same as other Indians. He does not know whether the Eskimos wear the breech cloth, but he thinks they do not. He has never seen the Eskimo.

[The Kutchin][37]

The Kutchin are of light complexion, a shade or two lighter than the Crees and northern Chippewas. They have regular and rather handsome features. The men are full size and well made, and average five feet seven or eight. The women also are fair and proportionate size. Mrs. Murray thinks they are undersize. They are quite warlike and fight without covert or concealment unlike southern Indians. Polygamy also prevails among them. The rule also prevails that if a man marries the oldest sister he is entitled to all the sisters as wives as they grow up. Murray mentioned one case where a man took his own daughter as a wife. Many of the men have no wives, in consequence of so many having more wives than one, although he thinks there is no disparity of sex as to number. Mr. Murray has seen most of the Indian nations from Texas to the Arctic Sea, including the Snakes, Crows and Rocky Mountain [?] and he places the Kutchin ahead of them all in intelligence and personal appearance. He says they are great rascals. They are not very numerous. He thinks about 3 to 4,000. He thinks they are not divided into tribes or families [clans] as the Chippewas are, but he is not sure upon this point. He says they are great wrestlers and are very frequently engaged in wrestling as an amusement. Whether they wrestle for their wives he did not state. Now and then one has gray eyes, and Mrs. Murray says some of them are freckled.

Ku-tchin Nursing Their Children[38]

They nurse their children for a long period. Mrs. Murray mentioned one case which came under her observation of a boy of ten years who still nursed his mother. He was old enough to go out to hunt with bow and arrow but still continued the practice. Mrs. Murray knew this woman, and saw her frequently at the fort. This was her only child, and she had borne none since he was born. That she was able to continue her milk for ten years is a remarkable fact. She mentioned the case of another woman who still nursed her youngest child who was about six years old. She said she had also seen a mother nurse two of her children at once, the oldest not being weaned when the next was born. She says they nurse their children as long as they need it, and that the time may average three or four years, if no other children are born in the meantime. They were among the Kutchin on the Yukon about 15 years ago for 4 years. Their oldest daughter was born there. He took his wife to the post when first married from Peace river. I have seen an Indian boy in Kansas, a Chippewa, stand on his feet and nurse while his mother sat on a stool. He appeared to be about five years old.

Mr. Murray says many or some of them [i.e., the Kutchin] have curly hair. It curls naturally, and falls in ringlets over their shoulders. Their eyes are black and not full. Instead of being round they are long disproportionally horizontally, and narrow instead of wide set.

He says they do not wrestle for their wives as far as he knows. Their complexion is very light, the most so of all the American Indians seen by him, and he has seen the most of the varieties. Their hair is not finer than that of other Indians. Their beards are light, or wanting in which respect they agree with the other Indians.

When their feelings are hurt they cry,[39] though grown or even old men. He mentioned a case where he came near losing his life through a vicious interpreter in this wise. He made it [a] rule to close the fort at 9 o'clock P.M. Those who wished to stay were allowed to sleep in the fort. Those who desired to go were required to leave at that time. On one occasion they refused to go, the interpreter having ordered them out without saying that those might stay who wished to, which gave offence, and they refused. Murray took a pistol in each hand, and although he had but two men against 60 or 70 and told them to start or take the consequences. They then left. The next day they induced him to go into the Store House to trade, and when he got there he found they intended to shoot him. He succeeded in disarming the one who was about to make the attempt, and in forcing the others out. The next day an explanation was had, and when the chief, Sevia, (figured in Richardson's book) found how near they had come to taking his life under a misapprehension, he cried abundantly. He said at other times when he refused to sell them goods on credit, they would cry because he refused to trust them and thus showed a want of confidence.

Consumption and scrofula are the prevailing diseases. He knew one man who died of consumption who was as white as a white man. I think he said the Fort was on Red River. They build round top wigwams

TAH-RO-HON, AN IOWA WARRIOR

BY GEORGE BIRD KING

Tah-ro-hon lived on the Missouri above Fort Leavenworth and made a name for himself as a warrior at an early age in combat with the Sioux and Osage. He was a signer of the treaty of St. Louis in 1837 and, as provided in the third article of that document, visited Washington, where King made this portrait.

for winter, but in summer, live in the open air. They turn over their canoes and sleep under them.

PART III

[Divisions of the Cree]

Na-he-ah-wuk, Crees call themselves; meaning lost.

1. Mus-ko-ta-we-ne-wuk   Crees of the Prairie
2. Sa-kow-we-ne-wuk   Crees of the Woods
3. Mus-ka-go-wuk   Crees of the Low Lands

Mus-ko-ta-wo   Prairie or Plain
Sa-kow   Woods or Thickets
Mus-kage   Swamp

[Morgan has here a two-page list of geographical names in the Cree language.]

Cree Language[40]

This language is divided into three distinct dialects, and although the people are greatly intermixed, so that this is not at present a political division, yet the three forms of speech are recognized by them, and it is observable readily. They are called   1. The Prairie   2. Woods   3. Swampy. The first is the highest and most finished dialect. I have obtained from Mrs. Murray a Prairie Cree schedule of relationship, and from the wife and mother of Mr. Ohlson,[41] who are half breed Crees, and reside at Pembina Mountain 30 miles west of Pembina, a

schedule of the Crees of the Woods. On the basis of these dialects the people now speak of themselves as Crees of the Prairie, Crees of the Woods, literally of the thick woods, and Swampy Crees, or Crees of the lowlands. Mrs. Moore from whom I obtained a schedule of the Cree at Sault St. Mary last year[42] I remember said she was a Cree of the Lowlands, so I think I have the three dialects already. I cannot ascertain the number of the Crees, but from their wide distribution, and exclusive occupation of certain large areas, I should judge they might number 5000. Mr. Murray thinks they may number 10,000.

[Indian Languages]

The permutation of consonants in Indian languages it is barely possible may be governed by a law equivalent to that discovered by Grimm in the Indo-European Languages. I have noticed it in a large number of languages, but have never made it a subject of examination with a view to recording results. I have just taken a good specimen of it in the Cree dialects as follows.[43]

Ne-ya	Mine	Cree of the Prairie	We-ya	His
Ne-la	”	” ” ” Woods	We-la	”
Ne-na	”	” ” ” Lowlands	We-na	”
We-a-wou	Them	” ” ” Prairie	Ke-a-wou	Your
We-la-wou	”	” ” ” Woods	Ke-la-wou	”
We-na-wou	”	” ” ” Lowlands	Ke-na-wou	”

Indian Mounds

He [Murray] says the water works at St. Louis, or the reservoir, is upon an Indian mound.[44]

He has also seen a mound, about fifty feet in diameter on the north side of Rainy Lake River, and about ten feet high out of which bones and pottery had been taken, and which the Chippewas said belonged to a race who preceded them in the country.

[We omit here four or five pages of data on the Indians of the Northwest coast obtained from Timoleon Love, a fellow passenger on the *Pioneer*. According to Hargrave, Love "was by profession a gold miner, and had practised his business in the fields of California . . . His reasons for leaving those thriving localities he certainly did not make very clear . . ." (p. 61).]

I am much struck with the combination of natural advantages for Indian subsistence afforded by the Puget Sound country. It is unsurpassed along the whole western coast of America, and no matter whether the first inhabitants were cast upon our shores near Bering Strait, or on the coast of California, this locality would draw to itself inhabitants, and rapidly multiply them, so as to make a point, an initial point of extensive migrations.[45] It is not a little singular also that the geographical features of the country would make it most convenient to people the Atlantic Coast, from that Portion of the Pacific coast, by way of Saskatchewan and Missouri.

[We omit two pages of notes on the Indians of Oregon obtained from Mr. Love. It is probably not without significance that Morgan does not cite Love in *Systems* although he obtained and recorded a great deal of information from him; he does, however, cite Murray extensively.]

Georgetown, July 22, 1861

The wagon trains containing the boat's freight have arrived this P.M. and we have received notice to go on board the steam boat tonight. Although I have been detained here 15 days I have turned it [to] some account and if I had more time at Fort Garry I should be quite content.

Steam Boat *Pioneer*,[46] Red River, July 25, 1861

We left Georgetown this morning at 6 o'clock, with about 40 tons of freight, with a barge carrying a portion of the freight which is to go as far as the Rapids 70 miles below, where the goods are to be put on board and the barge left. The water is now low, and this is the first trip the barge has been used. The boat which is a small stern wheel steam boat draws when loaded about 3 feet. The river is narrow with a current tolerably strong, but safe and navigable. There are numerous tributary streams flowing into it, the outlet of Otter Tail lake contributing the most water, and the outlet of Red Lake the next or perhaps an equal quantity. Below the latter point, the channel is large and full enough at all seasons for a large steamer. They are now building a new steam boat at Georgetown, which is to be ready for next year.

Hunting Season

This river has been famous for elk and wild goose game. The elk and geese are yet

The **ANSON NORTHRUP**, later known as the **PIONEER**, which took Morgan to Pembina.

abundant, and the best time to hunt them is from Sept. 1 to the middle of October, chiefly for the reason that the mosquitoes who make the country intolerable in July and August cease their terrific work about the first week in September. The buffalo also in the regular migrations are in this vicinity in October. All things considered, I think Georgetown must be a good point for the hunt at the time mentioned. If a person came in his own conveyance from St. Cloud, so that they could stop among the lakes on the route to Georgetown they might find good duck, curlew and chicken shooting on the way, with an occasional chance at a bear, sandhill crane and fox. There are no deer in the country. It will be necessary west of the Red River to look out for the Sioux, who might endanger a small party of two or three.

Initial Points of Migration

Upon this point I am becoming deeply interested, for I think the light is dawning upon this singular question.[47]

Upon the Atlantic and Gulf Coast from the St. Lawrence to the Rio Grande, there is no point or district of country which in a permanent degree abounds in Indian subsistence, and which, when occupied, would become populous, and thus an initial point of migration. From the Rio Grande to the Mississippi it is on the whole a poor country for the Indian without the horse. From the latter point to the St. Lawrence it is much better. From Chesapeake Bay to the St. Lawrence, the deer, the moose, the bear and the smaller animals, as well as the furred animals become more abundant, as well as the fish, while from the Mississippi to the

Chesapeake the climate was milder, with more natural forests rendering less subsistence as well as clothing necessary, so that the entire region from the M. to the St. L. may be said to have possessed about equal advantages.

On the west coast this is not the case. East of the great range of the Rocky Mountains from Mexico to Peace River, we have the prairie in the interior of the continent, a country incapable of occupation to any considerable extent without the horse. Beside this, the margin of inhabitable country on the Pacific is rendered still narrower by the Sierra Nevada range which coming near the gulf of California extends northward to Oregon, where the range of the Cascade Mountains becomes a continuation of the chain, and those draw nearer to the coast until they disappear in the coast range (I think) near Queen Charlotte's island or Dixon's Entrance. Between the Sierra Nevada and the Rocky Mts. we have the great basin, a sterile plain. Between the Cascade Mountains and the R. M. we have a mixture of prairie and woodland more favorable for Indian occupation, as the Cascades are penetrated or traversed by the Columbia river and its branches, and by Frazer's river and its tributaries. Hence from the Gulf of California to Queen Charlotte's island, we have a narrow belt of land some two thousand or more miles in extent, which for a long period would have contained the original inhabitants, if they had been cast upon the Pacific shore at any point between Bering Strait and the Gulf of California.

Now the most remarkable fact in the character of this region is this, that the Puget Sound and the Vancouver Island district, or in a larger sense the country from the mouth of the Umpqua to Queen Charlotte's Sound offered means of subsistence for the Indian, conditioned as he was and has remained to this day to a degree unequalled by any other district or area upon the whole continent of North America. In fact it is so far in advance of any other, as to give it an actual and positive preeminence. There is no district or country on the Atlantic, St. Lawrence, or the Great Lakes to be compared with it, and on the west coast it is so far superior to any region to the north or the south of it, that in its ability to sustain an Indian population it has actual advantages in the ratio of three or four to one, and perhaps even higher. California is a good Indian country for subsistence.

As a necessary consequence of these premises it is a matter of little consequence upon what part of the coast the first inhabitants landed, they were of necessity a coast people for a long period of time, and sooner or later would have come into the occupation of this region. From the moment they peopled it the question of subsistence would tell upon their increase in numbers. Here they would multiply for the first time into a numerous people as compared with other coast localities, and thus become the chief center of population on the Pacific coast. We have but to reflect upon the simple fact that the Indian never has been able to increase to a dense population any where upon this continent. So far from it that the thinness of population is one of the chief characteristics in the vital statistics of the Indian family, to see clearly that the question of subsistence governs their increase, as it does that of all peoples. And further that in the hunter life it is more precarious than in any other form of society, far more so than in the strictly nomadic life, for we know that with flocks and herds nomads are capable of rapid multiplication. We have also the striking confirmatory fact, that at the present time, the Puget Sound-Vancouver district is the most populous Indian area by far on this continent, and such has no doubt been the fact for centuries. The Hudson's Bay Company estimate the Indian population in their territories east of the mountains at 55,000, west of the Rocky Mts., 80,000. (See Testimony in Hudson's Bay Company Case 1857.)

It would seem therefore to be an unavoidable inference that if the inhabitants of this continent spread from the Pacific Coast eastward, the initial point of their migration was from the region named. This point being settled, the route or line of migration is evident enough for there are but two, one by way of the Saskatchewan, and the great lakes to the St. Lawrence, the other by the Columbia river and the Missouri, the Mississippi valley; and in my article[48] on this subject which I roughed out before leaving home I think I have shown that the Algonkins went in by the former and the Dakotan nations by the latter route.

[We omit here five pages of data obtained from Mr. Love on the "Root Digger Indians," and other tribes of the northwest; also an account of a Chinese burial in California. We have not been able to identify Mr. Love, but he gave Morgan the following information about himself.]

Mr. Love was born in Gaward Co. Kentucky, Oct. 1, 1827. First went to Missouri in 1845. Then entered the American army and served through the Mexican war. After that went to California and has been there since. He has kept a journal since 1846, which he has agreed to give me a copy. He is to leave it with Hargrave if it is at the Fort, otherwise he is to send it down to him and Hargrave has volunteered to copy it for me.

[We omit two or three pages of data obtained from Love, on the prairie and its flora in Mexico and in the west generally, and a Cree vocabulary of three and a half pages.]

Steamer *Pioneer*, July 30, 1861

We are now on the rapids about 70 miles below Georgetown. Yesterday morning the boat grounded and the whole day was spent in getting her off. She is now shifting her load to the barge which was brought down in tow to help her over. The water is now low. These rapids, as they are called, are simply a place where the river widens out, which makes the water shallow and more rapid. There are also occasional islands. This continues for ten or fifteen miles, after which the river becomes quite narrow as above, in some places hardly wide enough for the boat to turn around. It is a very narrow river, and its navigation precarious except in high water. In the spring it is very high. This spring it rose 35 feet. There was a deep snow on the ground which went off with a rain, and made a great flood nearly as large as the one 20 years ago. We saw trees on the bank yesterday skinned of their bark on the river side at least 30 feet above the present line of the river.

Crees

Angus McKay has been for 25 years among the Crees, and talks their language, and knows the differences in the three dialects. He is a Scotchman and one of our passengers. He was also with us several days at Georgetown. From him I have obtained a good deal of information of the Crees, and a Swampy Cree schedule.[49]

He thinks the Crees all told number from 7 to 8000, not more. The bulk of them are now on the branches of the Saskatchewan and between them. They are also at the Albany district around James Bay.

The chiefs are elected for their bravery, and there is about 100 in all. Each of the principal chiefs has an average of 50 lodges under him. If he turns coward, the band depose him and elect another. A person may leave one band and join another. The son does not necessarily succeed his father. If he has acquitted himself well as a brave, he is likely to be elected, otherwise not. A chief after he is elected has power to appoint four or five assistants or under chiefs, who are at all times subject to his command. He may send one out in command of a small war party to scalp or steal horses, and they must oblige. If any difficulty occurs, the chief is expected to adjust it. There may be a council if the matter is important. The chief directs all the movements of the band under him, and when any of their rules are violated he calls the offender to account and directs the mode of punishment. He is a man of war as well as of peace.

No Tribes [Clans] Among the Crees

McKay says the Crees have no tribes as the Chippewas have. The nearest thing to it originates in this wise, and is called Pa-wa-gun (something dreamed about). If a man dreams of a snake, or wolf, buffalo, dog, eagle or any other animal, he at once adopts it as his tutelar divinity or guardian spirit. It becomes his Man-e-too. If he falls into trouble or is in doubt what to do he invokes this guardian spirit by some conjuring process for aid and confidently looks for an indication from it by dream or otherwise to govern his conduct. He marks this animal upon his tent or lodge and his Man-e-too is thus known to all. The Crees have no word for God or Great Spirit in the general sense, and Man-e-too does not convey that

meaning or sense, but is far more limited as stated above.[50] The son does not adopt the same mark after his father unless he dreams of the same animal or thing, in which case he does if he adopts the same. The old Frenchman states the contrary, as I have recorded farther back.

Pembina, Saturday August 3, 1861

We were detained on the rapids [Goose Rapids], as they are called, about seventy miles from Georgetown 2½ days. The river there is wide, shallow and more rapid than in any other part of the route. The boat grounded repeatedly, and was hauled off with hawsers and capstan. Most of the cargo had to be shifted to the barge.[51] Besides the one spot where we lay nearly two days there were other bad places called shutes which caused some detention. The whole distance of difficult navigation in the low water of this season is about 15 miles. On our return we are to stop the boat below these places and go up by stage to Georgetown. From the last place to Pembina the river is quite respectable, the current is slower, the river wider, and the banks in some places quite beautiful.

Buffalo Hunting

The most expert and successful buffalo hunters in America are the half breeds of Pembina, and of Selkirk Settlement around Fort Garry. These half breeds, who number with their wives and children some 10 or 20,000, are Frenchmen, Scotchmen, Orkney Islanders and their wives and children from Cree and Chippewa mothers. Their collection at this point is in part the result of the operations of the Hudson's Bay Company and the character of the country. In the first place it is the first band fit to settle westward from the Canada line and the true point of inlet, to the west and north west from the Red River, and has a natural connection with the U. S. for purposes of trade, the natural inlet to this region being by way of St. Paul or Lake Superior at some future time.

The hunt is their main reliance of animal food, hence they fit out regular expeditions three times a year to provide themselves, and go in brigades for protection on the plains. About 500 persons, men, women and children, with about 150 hunters, make a full brigade. They take about as many two wheeled carts, that is 500, drawn each by a single ox or cow, and sometimes by a horse to carry supplies and bring back the results of the hunt. These carts are made without a particle of iron in them and will be described elsewhere.

They use trained horses, which are called buffalo runners that are not used at all until the hunt commences, when they are saddled and mounted for the chase. They are so well trained that the rider has no occasion to touch his bridle, and can give all his attention to loading and firing from the saddle. The chase usually lasts from 1 to four miles, rarely more than three miles after they come up with the herd and charge it among them, and it is expected that each experienced hunter will bring down from 5 to 8 buffalo in a single chase. McKay tells me that he has known one man to bring down 21 in a chase of 4 miles; 15 buffalo is not very uncommon, but the results of course greatly vary.

The first hunt goes out June 15, about. At this time the hide is useless for robes, as the hair is thin and whitish, but they are useful for leather and pemican bags. This is the hunt for pemican meat. The second hunt goes out about Sept. 10. The hides are then fit for robes. They are bare from Feb-

ruary to first of October. They dry the meat and make pemican at this hunt also. The third and last for the year goes out about Oct. 10. This is for fresh meat, which they use partially dried, in the fall. They put up large quantities of pemican which they sell to the Hudson's Bay Company and which is their main reliance as meat at all their posts, aside from fresh killed game. The manner of making pemican will be described elsewhere.

The buffalo move in regular courses or lines of migration, but do not appear at regular intervals. The hunters believe they move in great circles, which is probable. The rutting season commences about July 20 and continues to about August 20. The calves are born in the latter part of March, and fore part of April and some as late as the fore part of May. While the calves are growing, and in fact through most of the year except during the rutting season, the bulls and cows live in herds apart from each other, except that each herd of cows always has a few bulls among them. This separation is well authenticated, and has been often remarked upon.

The gun preferred by the half breeds is the flint lock single barrel shot gun of the Hudson's Bay Company. Few of them will use the cap gun from the loss of time in putting on the cap. In loading they pour powder from the horn which is secured around the neck into the partially closed hand, then into the barrel, throwing away the surplus; the ball which is previously put in the mouth is then put into the barrel, after shaking down the powder, and the ball is then shaken down, and gathers powder enough from being wet to keep it in the barrel. In the meantime the horse has been pursuing a second buffalo, and as soon as he rides up he lowers his gun and fires the

gun at the same instant. There is no capping of the gun, and no use of the ramrod. All of our Indians, or at least the Missouri river Indians, prefer the flint lock gun, the Dakotas especially.

They sell their robes to the Company for $2.50 each and when bare for $1.25 each, and their pemican for 6 cents.

PART IV

Steamer *Pioneer*, Below Pembina

August 3, 1861

We stopped at Pembina about an hour. At this place I received my first letters from home down to July 10.[52] It was a very great pleasure which can be better imagined than described, were this the place for the latter.

Pembina consists of about a dozen log houses, and is located at the junction of the Pembina and Red Rivers. Besides these houses, which are on the west side of Red River, there are several wigwams on both sides of the River, occupied by Crees, Chippewas and half-breeds. The principal village of the Crees is at St. Joseph or Pembina Mountain, thirty miles west of Pembina. The importance which Pembina has gained lies in the fact that it is the central point of an extensive half-breed settlement along this river where the traders and adventurers in the Indian country have congregated with their Indian and half-breed wives and children. The post office and cus-

Red River ox carts on 3rd Street, St. Paul, Minnesota, in 1859. Sometimes called "Pembina carts," these vehicles were a familiar sight between Pembina and St. Paul. Travelers frequently noted the size of the wheels, or the amount of freight the animals could pull, but they always remarked upon the horrible noise these carts made as they bounced and rolled on their 500-mile trip.

tom house are here, and this is the point from which their cart trains start for St. Paul, and to which they return, and from which their buffalo robes and furs are sent to market. The boundary line [between the United States and Canada] which we passed some half an hour since, is about three miles below Pembina, and is marked by a post. About four miles below Pembina is a post of the Hudson's Bay Company surrounded by a picket, with a cluster of bark lodges in front of and around it. In front of it and along the river bank we saw perhaps fifty men, women and children, in all sorts of costumes. Many of the children were nude except the breech cloth, and with long hair down their shoulders, ran along the bank after the boat. Occasionally we saw a man nude with the exception of a blanket and breech cloth, their copper colored skins looking clean and well. The hunting brigade had not yet returned, but some of the traders who join the expedition traveled about 1000 miles. They ride and their loaded carts still standing on the bank.

Pembina Carts[53]

These carts are made without a particle of iron. The wheels are larger than those of a common lumber wagon and consist of heavy filleys of wood put together in a circle with pins inserted in the ends of each. The hub is large and strong and so are the spokes and axle. A pair of heavy fills from three to four inches square are inserted in the axle, and upon this is placed a platform of boards about six feet long by four wide, and upon this is placed a rack about four feet high. This rack is simply a frame of the size of the platform with round sticks inserted up and down sufficiently near to hold the load, and large enough to hold as much as a single ox or horse harnessed in, can draw. It is a very simple, cheap and sensible wagon for the prairie. It can be bought new for about $10, is easily repaired, and does credit to their ingenuity.

Their cattle are trained to the harness, and will make journeys of hundreds of miles over the prairie with ease and comfort, going from fifteen to twenty miles per day. The ordinary range of the buffalo hunt is about 400 miles, and they take as many carts as persons usually. The amount of loading an ox will draw from day to day I did not ascertain, but I should think from the carts which arrived from Georgetown loaded while we were there, on their way back from St. Paul and Pembina, was about 500 pounds. Tate says 8 to 900. 50 odd of these carts crossed the river in one day at Georgetown. The distance from Pembina to St. Paul by land is about 500 miles, and these when they reached home would have traveled about 1000 miles. They ride and travel in these carts as we do in wagons.

Pemican

Pemican, as is well known, consists of dried buffalo meat pounded up into small bits and then mixed with about an equal amount in pounds of buffalo fat melted. It is a Cree word, *Pe-mili-kan*, from *pe-mili*, "grease" and *kan*, a "sort," a "kind of something," hence its literal meaning is "a sort of grease."[54] Their word for fat is *we-in*. The pemican is in great demand or rather a prime necessity to the northern Indians, and especially to the Hudson's Bay Company. It is the ordinary provision of the trader, traveller and even hunter when on his journey, as it contains the largest amount of nourishment in the smallest compass, and with the least weight. The Company keep a stock of it at all their forts and posts, and take the surplus of the Indians each year, as well as encourage its production.

It is made on the field where the buffalo are killed. As soon as the hide is removed, the animal is cut up and carried to camp in carts. It is then shaved into thin sheets, and spread out in the sun to dry, without washing and without salting. The fore shoulders and hind quarters, and all the lean save the rib pieces and the thin belly pieces are thus cut up. After it is cured in the sun, as far as it can be, a fire is built, and when the wood is reduced to coals, a frame of cross pieces of limbs is built over the fire, and the meat is placed over the fire until it is thoroughly dried. After that it is broken or cut up into small pieces, and these are placed in a buffalo skin and pounded with a flail, until it is well pulverized; the flail consists of a heavy stick attached to another which is used as a handle, a common farmer's flail. The fat of the bull buffalo is then melted and a quantity equal in weight, or near in quantity, is poured on to the meat and the whole is stirred up and thoroughly mixed together. The buffalo sac is then sewed up, and when it cools, the pemican is made.

They put it up in sacks which will weigh about 100 pounds. To make such an amount requires the meat of three buffaloes, and the fat of as many more. The Company pay them for it delivered at their posts, but 3d sterling per pound, or 6 cents of our money. $2.50 for the robe of the fall hunt and $1.25 for the robe of the summer hunt, which is nearly without hair, and 1/- sterling for the tongues. At this rate 3 buffaloes net the hunter about $14.25 or about $5 each including the labor of taking and curing it, rather a poor return. We have had it daily on the boat. Not bad eating.

Buffalo Hunting

In No. [Part] 3 some facts are given on this subject. McKay, who has hunted buffalo often, says it is not uncommon for a hunter to get mixed in with the herd, and carried along with them for hours before he can work his way out. He said he was in one for three hours; that the only danger was of the falling of his horse as he was rubbed against and pressed upon on every side, that the buffalo did not notice him nor the horse in the least, but there was danger of a buffalo striking his horse with a side stroke of the head when he was pushed against one; that the bull buffalo especially was addicted to jumping himself half around, showing a desire to use his horns when too much pressed upon. That when moving or moving rapidly they become so much packed together that it is extremely difficult to get out. He was obliged to keep on with them, beat them off with his gun, and look out for the bulls. If the horse falls, it is of the last necessity for the man to stick to his horse. If buffalo stumble upon him, those behind will then turn out. Lives are sometimes lost in this way, not by the attacks of the buffalo, for they are not so dangerous, but from being trampled under foot.

One hunter told me he thought the buffaloes paired in the rutting season, but this is not at all probable. The cows are usually preferred by the hunters as their meat is more tender, and at certain seasons they are the fattest. While the calves are suckling the males are preferred as they are then the fattest. In organizing a brigade two or three of the most experienced hunters are appointed captains. They also appoint a major and a number of constables to execute the laws and rules which govern the brigade.[55] When a herd is neared the runners are saddled, guns loaded, and they get as near as they can under the cover of some hill. Before the word to charge is given the excitement becomes very great, and shows itself in the singular form of wetting themselves. They start all abreast, perhaps 100 horsemen at the word of command, and then each man takes his own course.

The chase is usually over in 15 minutes, during which time they have run three miles, after which each man claims his buffalo. Then commences all kinds of cheating and claiming each other's buffalo, an abuse which they find it impossible to correct. It is difficult to know your precise track, and amid the clouds of dust raised, it is easy for unfair hunters to impose upon their associates and find others to swear to their claim. It requires a fleet horse to keep up with the buffalo, and the herd get out of your reach about the time your horse is exhausted. The cows run the fastest and soon lead the bulls. The horses are so well trained that they can be governed by the motions of the body. Robert Tate, a passenger on the boat, and a resident near Fort Garry, is a hunter. He said his horse, after he shot the first buffalo, fell to one side [a] little until the ball went down the barrel, when he turned again for the herd and when he had singled out an animal rode at once to his side. That he had no need to use the reins. He says it is a very dangerous business. The badger holes in the prairie often throw the horse. There is also danger of shooting each other when so many are firing right and left in the dust and confusion, that it is not uncommon to hear bullets whizzing near you. He says two, three and four buffalo in a chase is doing remarkably well; that of a 100 who join in a chase perhaps 25 will [not] overtake the buffalo at all, and some of those who do will be left behind. That the buffalo is very fleet, and it takes a good horse at the top of his speed to overtake one. A good runner is worth at the settlement from $100 to $250.

He says the hoof of the buffalo is so worn down at times as to show that they have travelled thousands of miles. That during the rutting season the noise of a herd of large size, if you put your ear to the ground, sounds like thunder, the deep bellowing of the bulls.

He also confirms McKay's statement that the hunters are sometimes closed up in the herd and carried some distance before they can get out. He knew one man who shot 14 buffalo while thus shut in, taking the precaution to shoot over the backs on each side of those nearest him, so as to be out of the reach of the wounded animal. After they fell those behind tumbled over them in all sorts of confusion. The large number shot at times by hunters in a single chase was the result of fortunate circumstances. He only chased three in a single chase last fall.

The carts carry from 8 to 900 pounds, and ten are estimated to load a cart with dried meat. They leave the neck and some of the other coarse parts.

He says the buffalo which come from the south of the Missouri are smaller than those north of it and that the hunters can tell them at once. Love denies this.

Fort Garry, Tuesday August 6, 1861

We reached the Fort Sunday morning, August 4. And as I am compelled to return with the boat, and can have but two days and nights to do up my work here, I went immediately to the Fort[56] with my friend Joseph J. Hargrave, to call upon the chief factor, William Mactavish, who is an uncle of Mr. Hargraves. We found him an elderly and fine looking gentleman, and as I came

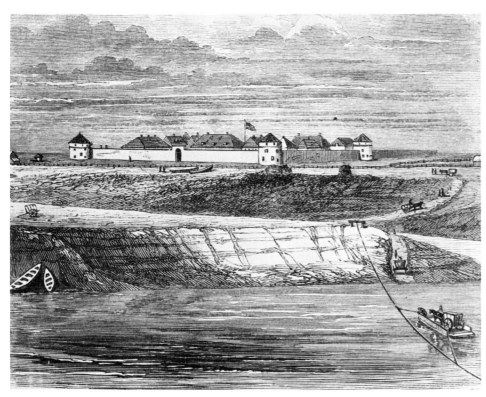

Fort Garry, from Heard's **HISTORY OF THE SIOUX WAR AND MASSACRES OF** 1862 **AND** 1863. The interior was a quadrangle in which was included the chief factor's house. Morgan thought it ". . . quite a commanding establishment."

with a letter from Dr. Henry I was received very politely and invited to dinner. This I declined being anxious to get off immediately[57] to Mr. Birds or Jimmy Jacks twelve miles below the fort where we expected to secure a Blackfoot schedule, and perhaps a Chipewyan. I found it impossible to hire horses, as they were out to pasture on the prairie, which fact I mentioned to Gov. Mactavish, whereupon with a curl of the lip he said he supposed it was difficult. He knew I expected to return with the boat and had but two days and nights to do my work. I hoped he would offer me horses, or at least send out a man to hunt up a pair for me at my expense, but he said nothing, and as dinner was announced he invited me to dinner. I excused myself on the ground that I had taken an early dinner, and left. I afterwards was told that the Governor had a large number of horses in the stable and in the pasture near by, and thinking on the whole that his courtesy was rather scant I left the Fort to shift for myself.

After some efforts at several places to hire horses I walked down to Robert Tate's[58] three miles. He had offered to get up his horse and go with me, and I thought I could walk on with him until we could pick up a horse. Tait at once gave me his horse, and his brother, David Tait, got up his horse and away we went to Mr. Birds,[59] or Jimmy Jacks,[60] 12 miles below the Fort, and

stopped at John Taits an uncle of theirs who received us very kindly. They are Orkney Island[61] men, of the warm hearted and intelligent kind. Supper was prepared, and Bird who happened to be there was called in. We then crossed the river in his canoe to his house and went to work. His wife was a Piegan Blackfoot, and was for some [years] U. S. Government interpreter for the Blackfeet. A fine looking and intelligent half-breed he is too, a natural son of Chief Factor Bird,[62] now deceased. We worked out the Piegan schedule complete.[63] After this we went to another house and called up an Assinaboine woman and worked out their system.[64] It was now nearly twelve o'clock at night and I was so near exhausted that I came near fainting away. The door was closed to this house when we went in and I was smoking black tobacco. Altogether it was too much for me. The fresh air brought me out again and we recrossed the river, at 12 o'clock and went to bed at John Tait's. We agreed to return at daylight and work out a Chipewyan with another woman near there but did not effect it until 7 o'clock and finished at nine. Then we returned to the steamboat stopping at Robert Tait's to dinner. For all this kindness, and use of horses and hospitality they would not accept of the slightest pay, and they were unremitting in their efforts to aid me. God bless the whole of them.

In the evening I obtained from Mrs. Ross an imperfect O-kan-a-kan schedule[65] assisted by her daughter, Mrs. Green, and Mr. Caldwell,[66] a son-in-law and editor of the Nor-Wester. We were at his house.

This morning, Tuesday, I have procured at the Nunnery of St. Boniface on the east side of the river the Red Knife or Mountaineer system,[67] one of the Athabascan family, making two[68] in that language.

PART V

[Probably written on board the *Pioneer*
on the return trip.]

Fort Garry[69]

The proper name of this district is Selkirk
Settlement [also known as Red River Set-
tlement]. It was founded by Lord Selkirk[70]
about 1820 who, it appears, was the principal person concerned in founding a rival
Fur Company to operate against the Hudson's Bay Co. About 1825, the two companies were in open war at the points where
they came in contact followed by bloodshed. An arrangement was then made by
which the two companies were consolidated,
and Lord Selkirk received a large indemnity. I think some 80,000 pounds sterling.
From about four miles above Fort Garry,
which is located at the mouth of the Assiniboine River, on the north bank, at its confluence with Red River down to the Fort
and from there down to the lower Fort
Garry, which is about 18 miles below, there
is continuous settlement on both sides of
the river, all the land being occupied by a
farming population.

The company limit their grants to 2
chains[71] wide on the river, with the privilege of extending their occupation as far
out on the prairie as they may desire to go.
As a consequence of this limitation to each
person, the houses are mostly located on
the bank of the river, and have cultivated
land in their rear divided off by fences. As

the river winds, the greatest irregularity
exists. The houses are not on a line, and
there is nothing but a crooked path in front
of them along the river bank and no passage for a horse or wagon in front of them,
except on foot, with rough crossings over
the gullies and impassible interruptions
here and there. The main road, which is
wide and handsome, is laid out straight
and back on the prairie, some distance
from the houses, with but few houses upon
it, as they prefer to be near the river. If
there was a river road following its windings as well as the present public road made
straight from one Fort to the other, to cut
off the windings, it would be quite a picturesque settlement.

I went down the river twelve miles and
all along the route the river portion of the
land was under cultivation, and the houses
quite numerous, there being one on nearly
every claim of two chains. These houses are
small, of log, and a few of them plastered
over with mortar, and whitened with lime.
Mr. John Tait's was one of the best we saw.
It had two wings, was whitened with lime,
and looked quite neat. It was 12 miles
down. His lot in front was enclosed to the
river and went back through a lane to the
public road about a quarter of a mile distant. At this season the weather is quite
hot, nearly as much so as in New York, but
it lasts only two months, and the average
temperature is reduced to about 32° by the
severe winters, during a part of which the
thermometer stands at 40° below zero.
There is an air of pleasantness about the
district which must please any one at this
season of the year.

There is a great abundance of cattle, and
a good deal of wheat, barley, potatoes, and
summer vegetables growing on these narrow farms. They have no market for their

surplus, and raise only sufficient for home
consumption. Wheat last year was worth
7/ per bushel or 80 cts., which is certainly
a fair remuneration, but I think the crop
was short. Prices are high for all necessaries
which are not the product of the country
from the great expense of transportation
from St. Paul, about 500 miles distant by
land, making the round trip for carts 1000
miles.

The settlers are called Half Breeds, although there is a large sprinkling of pure
white blood. Many of the original Orkney
Island Scotchmen, carried to the country
by the Company and by Lord Selkirk, are
still living. Robert Tait's father went into
the country in 1812. His wife, still living,
is not more than ¼ Indian, if more than ⅛.
She doesn't know the Indian in the least
and is a large strong woman with a very
kind and pleasant face, which would inspire any one with respect. She has borne
15 children by her husband of whom 13 are
now living, which is some testimony to the
healthfulness of the country.

Fort Garry consists of about a dozen buildings including the chief factor's house, arranged in a quadrangle with buildings also
in the centre surrounded with a wall about
15 feet high, the front part of which is of
the light colored limestone of the country,
and about one third of the side walls. At the
corners are round bastions rising above the
walls, and in the centre of the front wall
and of the rear wall are the principal gates
which are of stone, carried above the top of
the walls, giving to it quite the appearance
of a fortress. There are also side gates or
doors through the wall, at least there is one
on the side next the river. It is on the whole
quite a commanding establishment. Although the houses inside are plain wood
structures, some of them plastered and

whitened, and others sided and not painted, and others of squared timber and not painted. The lower fort is said to be the finest structure.

The bishop's church and house are about three miles down the river. The church was finished as far as at present 23 years ago, and has stood with the walls up and no roof ever since. On the east side of the river stands the Catholic Cathedral, also roofless, as it was burned down last winter.[72] It was said to have cost 50,000 pounds. It could have been built in Rochester with less than that number of thousand dollars, but the stone had to be carried about 16 or 18 miles, which may explain the cost.

Near the Cathedral is a Nunnery or Convent of St. Boniface,[73] a large frame building two stories and a half high and capable of accommodating some 200 persons in their way of packing. I went in this morning, saw the Lady Superior for a moment, but could not converse with her as she spoke French only. They say the Catholics out-number the protestants. The Catholics have a Bishop (Tarshe)[74] and the Protestants (Anderson).[75]

I met Archdeacon Hunter[76] at Mr. Caldwells. He is quite a pleasant gentleman, and has been in the country a good many years.

At the Fort I was introduced to a Capt. Smith, I think, of the British Army. He has a company of soldiers stationed at the Fort, which I believe are maintained at the Company's expense.[77] Sentinels also are stationed in and outside of the Fort.

The Indians loiter around and in the Fort at all times of the day and evening. They come in from all points around to trade. All around the Fort there are wigwams of bark and some of canvas filled with Indians, some of whom I suppose reside there permanently, and others are tempo-

rarily encamped while trading. Their appearance is rather dirty and squalid. There were some exceptions. Mostly they are Crees. There are some Chippewas. The Cree language is the prevailing language of the settlement. With this language you can travel from this point through the Saskatchewan country to the mountains. There is also a large sprinkling of French, particularly among the settlers on the East side of the river.[78]

Corn will not ripen at Fort Garry. The wheat may be good, and they say it is, but we saw no good bread. The flour is dark and the bread heavy. They use a good deal of unleavened bread, but it is very hard.

Red River

This river from the junction of the outlet of Red Lake is a fine river, and navigable at low water. It is about half as wide as the Hudson. The prairie comes to the river in a good many places, but the banks are so

high at the present stage of the water, that you cannot see off on the prairie at any place from Georgetown down to Lake Winnipeg. Above Red Lake river, the channel is narrower, in some places barely wide enough for the boat to swing around. At Georgetown, I think it is not more than 150 feet wide. There is a rapid called Goose Rapid, about seventy miles below Georgetown, which affords the only serious obstruction to the navigation at low water. Dredging would correct it probably. The forest skirts the bank of the river, and in many places the willow appears on the margin of the river in the place of the wild poplar or cotton wood. The forest proper is most of the distance a few rods back from

Chippewa dwellings on the Red River. This photograph was taken during the Canadian Red River Exploring Expedition of 1857-58 by H. L. Hime. Birchbark was used extensively by the Chippewa, not only for housing, but for such articles as eating utensils.

the bank, with weeds and grass growing on the bank, sometimes coming down quite near to the water. It looks refreshing, it is so green and thrifty. I have noticed none of the coniferous trees from Georgetown down. There are places above where patches of pine are found, particularly on the outlet of Otter Tail Lake.

This river is exceedingly winding. It is rare to see in sight at any one place a part of the river one mile in length, before it disappears at both ends around a turn. Near Fort Garry the river becomes nearly as wide as the Hudson, and there may be places near there where from one to two miles of the river may be seen at once, but certainly not more. Color of the river water is yellowish, bordering on the brick red, if it was a few shades deeper.

Prairie

The prairie follows down the river to lower Fort Garry, which is about 12 miles from Lake Winnipeg. It becomes a mere narrow strip a few miles back opposite John Tait's, 12 miles below Fort Garry, he said, I think, three or four miles. On the west side of the river it continues to be open prairie, due west from Mr. Tait's. Here then is the north east border of the prairie south of the lake.

Aurora Borealis

I saw a magnificent aurora night before last as we were crossing the Red River in a canoe about 12 at night. It spread over a large portion of the northern sky, and consisted of broad sheets of light. It was unlike any former one seen by me.

[We omit here a two or three page record of conversations Morgan had with Timoleon Love and others about the beaver and his mode of life.]

Sussees [Sarsis]

The Sussees I am told speak a dialect of the Chipewayan.[79] They are now nearly extinct, the whole number being about 80. They have always been great fighters, and have thus been gradually exterminated. They are in alliance with the Blackfeet, but the Crees fight them.

Blackfeet. Marriage of Sisters

Jemmy Jock[80] tells me that among the Blackfeet, the man who marries the eldest sister is entitled to all the others as fast as they grow up, provided he is a good man, and uses the first wife well. If polygamy must prevail at all, why is not this the most respectable form in which it can exist? There would be less strife and jealousy, and the children would be near blood relatives. The Piegan, Blood, and Blackfoot speak dialects of a common language. The Blackfeet are divided into tribes [clans], with the usual prohibition of intermarriage.

Chipewyans, or Athabascans

All of these nations speak dialects of a common language and they are prototypes [?] of the Eskimo on the east and north, the Crees on the south, and they are believed to extend to the west coast. They have no tribes [clans] as near as I could ascertain from the two Mountaineers[81] or Red Knife women, and from the Mackenzie River woman who lives near Jeremy Jocks. Kennicott[82] will settle it.

Their system of consanguinity is a stumbler and cold water on the original supposition that the system in its complexity is unusual upon this continent.[83] It comes down, if I have obtained correct schedules, to the simplest form of consanguinity which can be made, almost identical with that of the

Sandwich Islands. They have no terms for nephew, niece, or cousin. My brothers' and sisters' children are my children, and the children of brothers, of sisters, and of brothers and sisters, are all alike brothers and sisters to each other. Yet they have an Uncle and Aunt. I am disposed to doubt the correctness of my information, although my informants are half breed native women. If I recollect Kennicott's schedule, it does not agree with this. I shall regret leaving Fort Garry without receiving such information as would place it beyond a doubt.

Buffalo Calves

At Fort Garry I saw three young buffalo born this Spring, one female and two males. They are suckled by two cows delacted by the Governor for that purpose and are designed to be sent to England. They are rather shaggy coated, but good looking animals and quite tame. The neck drops down a little from the shoulders, and the foreshoulders are slightly elevated, but I did not see anything on the male buffalo which looked like the rudiment of a rump. They have mild and pleasant faces.

Limestone

There is an entire absence of stone from Georgetown to Fort Garry. At Prairie Mountain on the west side of the river about 18 miles northwest of the Fort they find a good building limestone, very light colored, and I presume magma [?]. It is mottled with a yellowish color. They also find in connection with it a flint sand stone which they call granite. On the east side of the river about 12 miles from Lake Winnipeg, and near lower Fort Garry, they find a limestone of the same character, streaked with yellowish strips like veins. It makes a very pretty stone dressed for window caps, etc. They use the two kinds in the Bishop's church now building, the walls of Fort Garry, and the Catholic cathedral on the east side of the river.[84] I have specimens of each kind for Ward's[85] collection.

Pembina, August 7, 1861

We reached Pembina this morning about 8 o'clock. This place amounts simply to nothing.[86] I was under a wrong impression about the place. The real settlement on our side of the line is at St. Joseph, 30 miles west at Pembina Mountain. For my purposes Fort Garry was the place to visit. The weather is cooler than it was going down and the country along the river wears a cheerful appearance under the bright summer sunshine. We are making good progress and expect to reach Sand Hill, 40 miles from Georgetown, tomorrow night. There we expect to be met by a stage.

Mr. Henry McKinny[87]

He is a fellow passenger on his way to St. Paul. He is a merchant at Fort Garry and goes Sept. 18 up the Saskatchewan, and near the Beaver Indians to establish a store. Mr. Frank Hunt,[88] said to be a fine scholar, goes with him, and he has kindly offered to take up my schedules and get Mr. Hunt to try it for me. I am to send some schedules to Mr. Hargrave to be forwarded to him by the winter [?] express.

Blackfoot, or Piegan Tribes [Clans]

Pe-kan-ne. Rich People. Piegans

1. Skunk Tribe	Ah-pe-ki-e
2. Web Fat "	Ih-po´-se-mä
3. Inside Fat Tribe	Ka-ka´-po-ya
4. Conjurers "	Mo-ta´-to-sis
5. Starving "	Kä-ta´-ge-ma-ne
6. Never Laugh "	Kä-ti´-ya-ye-mie
7. Blood "	Ah-ah´-pi-ta-pe
8. HalfDriedMeatTribe	E-ko´-to-pis-taxe

No man was allowed to marry a woman of his own tribe, and the children were of the tribe of the father.

Wild Geese, Eagles, etc.

We saw large flocks of wild geese in the river as we went down, and shot at a number. We could not stop for them.[89] We got one only on board and had him for dinner. They are very large. They go out on the bank or dive, and afford an easy shot. We must have been within five or six rods of several. A few only flew down the river. Ducks also are numerous. We shot at several. Also we saw the blue winged teal, a large and fine duck. Eagles also are numerous, white heads and tails. We saw at least twenty, and their nests on the tops of dead trees as large as a bushel basket. Pigeons go over frequently in small flights. This river used to be famous for duck, goose, and elk shooting in the river. The boat tends to drive them away.

This afternoon I shot a wild goose from the deck of the boat. He measured five feet three inches from tip to tip of wings, and weighed ten or eleven pounds. I have taken his legs and head as a trophy.

Schedules Obtained[90]

1. Sis-se´-to-wan.	Dakota.	Sisseton.	Fort Abercrombie
2. E-ank´-to-wan	"	Yanktonian	" "
3. O-jib-wa, of Red Lake			Georgetown
4. Mus-ko-ta´-we-ne-wuk	Cree of the Prairie		"
5. Sä-kow´-we-ne-wuk	" " " Woods		"
6. Mus-ka´-go-wuk	" " " Lowlands		"

7. Yase-ka´-pe (A stone)	Assiniboine	Fort Garry
8. Pe-kan´-ne	Piegan Blackfoot	" "
9. Tä-mä-tin-na	MacKenzie River Indians	" "
10. Täl-sote´-e-na	Red Knife or Mountaineers	" "
11. Iroquois of Two Mountains		Pomme de Terre
12. O-ken-a´-kan	Oregon Imperfect	Fort Garry

Drying Fish

We have just passed, near the Red Lake River junction, an encampment of half breed Crees from Pembina engaged in drying and smoking sturgeon for winter use, and making fish oil. There were about 30 of them, men, women, and children. This sturgeon is taken with nets set across the mouth of Red Lake River. They are now running down into Red River, and from there to Winnipeg. I should judge from the size of the head that they would weigh 40 pounds. The flesh is cut off in a thin shaving, the whole size [?] of the fish split, and laid out flat. These thin strips are then hung on a frame of poles arranged in a triangle, the apex of the angle forming the peak. A smoke is built underneath, and thus it is smoked and dried at the same time in the sun. The oil is fried out of the fattest parts of the fish, and the head, and is put in pails.

We saw fish bladders inflated and drying, the manifest object of which was to contain oil, although not over strong. I could think of no other use for them. They would hold a gallon easily. The appearance of the whole party was squalid in the extreme. Their entire subsistence I suppose is animal food, and this is their season of plenty. They also cure buffalo meat in the same way, cut or shaved into thin strips and dried in the sun without salt. The number of children was large, and I noticed the same fact at Selkirk Settlement. An Indian came on board today with his wife and seven children, the oldest not over twelve or thirteen. I saw one child, about 12 years old almost white, and with a remarkably pretty face. The fate which awaits her is sad to think upon. Aside from the hardships of her fate, it may be aggravated by vice.

[We omit a page-long passage about horse-stealing among the Blackfoot, as recounted by Timoleon Love.]

Moschetoes [91] Musquitoe

I intended somewhere to speak of the Moschetoe and I will do it here and now. I have seen this insect in all parts of the country, but I think on the Red River he reaches his highest estate in size, in numbers, in activity, and perseverance. This must be the centre of his habitat, the very region where he was created, and all others are degenerated specimens. [92] In the woods around Georgetown they are in perfect swarms, and will drive any man out of the woods in five minutes unless he has the hide of a rhinoceros and is toughened to their stings. They are the same on the prairie, but as there is more air stirring on the latter, they are not so bad. We slept under moschitoe bars all the way from St. Cloud to Fort Garry, but it was an insufficient protection. They will hide inside by day and work their way through the bars by night and the incessant hum outside dispels sleep.

On the boat from Georgetown down the river we suffered most as the boat laid up at night. The cabin was at once filled with them in swarms. The smudge was kindled at once at the front door, and often brought into the cabin until it was filled with smoke. Traces of gun powder were laid on the floor and fired until the room was filled to suffocation, and yet we all preferred the smoke to them. The smoke bewilders and deadens them and they light for the time being on the ceiling. It would be literally covered in places and they would fall upon the table, and cover the bottom of the candlesticks with those who scorched themselves in the fire. As soon as the smudge goes down they recover. I can understand now why the Indian builds his fire in the centre of his wigwam, and lives in the smoke until most of the old Indians become blind, which may be from this cause. He is right if he must live in the woods or on the prairie.

One night going down it was hot and they got in upon us so thick that Mr. Hargrave and myself got up from sheer necessity, got the watchman to make us a fresh smudge, and sat down in the smoke to refresh ourselves. On the way to Georgetown my hands were a mass of sting points, done through my gloves. My face and forehead and neck were blotched with swellings, and my ears burned with their stings. Still it is not so all the while. When it is cloudy and still they are the worst, and before and after a rain. But when the wind blows they are down, and also when it is cool. At evening they are worse than by day. The extent of their range is about coextensive with the continent from Mexico nearly to the Arctic Sea. Mr. A. H. Mung says that on the Yukon River which empties into Bering Strait they are worse far than on the Red River. Can that be possible? Their legs are half an inch long and I am sure I have killed some whose legs would measure nearly, if not fully, ¾ of an inch. They are all around me as I write. August 8, 1861 at 7 P.M., near Red Lake outlet, Red River.

Journal of an Expedition to the Rocky Mountains by the Missouri River in May, June, and July, 1862

Chapter VII

Editor's note: This was by far the longest and the most fruitful of Morgan's western field trips.

The Missouri River country was a romantic land in those days: a land of adventure, of hardship and privation for many, trade and fat profits for others, whisky for all, and not infrequently sudden death. First of all, of course, there were the Indians. Some were trying to settle down and live the white man's way. Others were determined to resist his encroachment and continue their old life. Disturbed and displaced by white settlers, the Indians fought among themselves; the powerful Sioux were the dread and scourge of many a community, red and white alike. Then there were the traders and trappers, many of them French, the "mountain men" with their buckskin clothing, dusky wives, and half-breed children; the isolated traders in their posts, tempering their loneliness with whisky; a few missionaries and Indian agents; and a less frequent military post. Coffee and sugar were a dollar a pound; three cups of sugar and one cup of coffee for a dressed buffalo robe. And every summer the ascent of the steamboats, bringing news of the outside world, new faces, fresh supplies, and a welcome break in the year's routine.

Morgan was greatly impressed by the Missouri River and the region through which it flowed. Years later, in *The American Beaver and His Works*, he devoted some twelve pages (pp. 205-16) to the topography, geology, flora, fauna, and scenery of the region, and, of course, to the great river itself.

Many people—explorers, military men, missionaries, artists, and scientists, but above all, trappers and traders—had ascended the Missouri River before Morgan embarked at St. Joseph in May 1862. Beginning with the nineteenth century we will note some of the more significant expeditions and travellers.

First of all, of course, was the expedition of Meriwether Lewis and William Clark, 1804-6. Their contributions to ethnography have been summarized by Verne F. Ray and Nancy Oestrich Lurie in the *Journal of the Washington Academy of Sciences*, Vol. 44, No. 11, pp. 358-70.

In 1810 and 1811, John Bradbury, a Scottish naturalist, made a collection of plants for the Botanical Society of Liverpool on the Missouri. He went up the Missouri as far as the Mandan villages. "Next to Lewis and Clark's journals," says Thwaites, "we have no better ethnological authority for the Western Indians of this period than Bradbury" (Reuben Gold Thwaites, ed., *Early Western Travels*, Cleveland, 1904, v, 14).

Henry M. Brackenridge accompanied Manuel Lisa, the great pioneer in the fur trade, on a trip up the Missouri in the spring of 1811 as far as the Mandan villages; he returned the same summer in the company of his friend, John Bradbury. Brackenridge's journal is in Vol. vi of *Early Western Travels*, pp. 1-166.

Manuel Lisa established a fur trading post at the mouth of the Big Horn in 1809. The American Fur Company—John Jacob

A map of Lewis H. Morgan's trip up the Missouri River to Fort Benton in 1862.

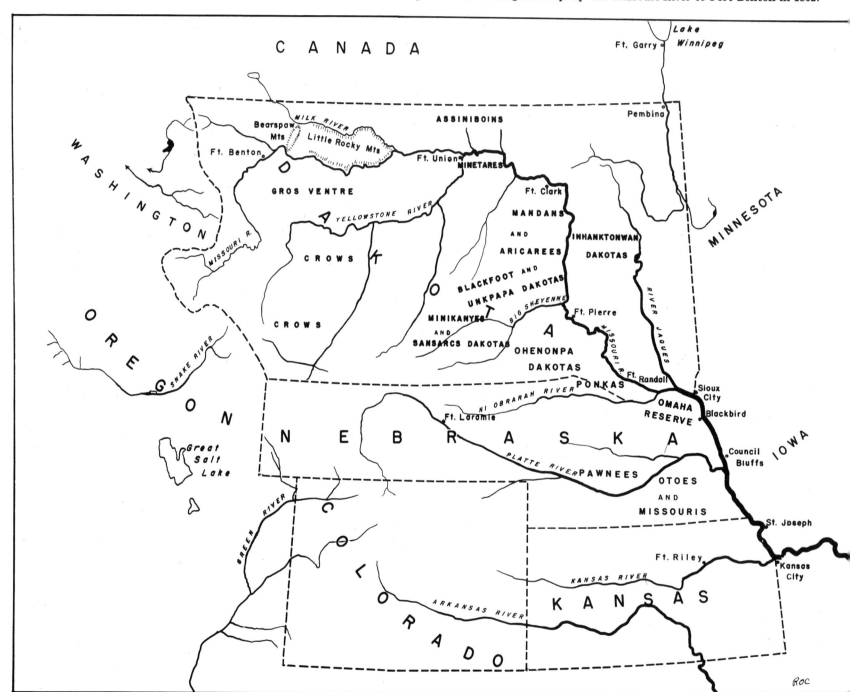

Astor—established an office in St. Louis in 1822. Twelve years later, the western department of this company was sold to the Chouteaus and their associates who virtually dominated the fur trade of the Missouri until 1866. Hiram Martin Chittenden's *The American Fur Trade of the Far West* (3 vols.; New York, 1902) is a rich source of information on this subject, and we have drawn upon it frequently. The personal narrative of Charles Larpenteur, *Forty Years a Fur Trader on the Upper Missouri*, edited by Elliott Coues (2 vols.; New York, 1898), likewise has been of great value in forming a realistic picture of his era, 1833–72.

Major S. H. Long took the first steamboat, the *Western Engineer*, up the Missouri in 1819 on a scientific expedition.

Father Pierre-Jean De Smet, s.j., first ascended the Missouri River in 1838 to found a mission among the Potawatomis, and in the decades that followed he became one of the best-known figures in the region.

In 1843 the great naturalist, John James Audubon, went up the Missouri as far as Fort Union. His primary purpose was to obtain data on the quadrupeds of North America, but his journals (*Audubon and His Journals*, by Maria R. Audubon, 2 vols.; London, 1898) contain many valuable ethnographic observations as well as comments upon the traders and trappers. He met the Alexander Culbertsons, James Kipp, and other characters encountered in Morgan's journal.

Turning to artist-ethnologists, we may mention George Catlin first. Catlin went up the Missouri River in 1832 on the *Yellowstone*, the first steamboat to navigate the Upper Missouri. He visited and painted among several tribes, but paid particular attention to the Mandan, who, by the way, he thought might have been an amalgamation of Indian and a lost colony of Welshmen. Catlin's work, both his paintings and his ethnographic account, has been severely criticized by Audubon[1] and Kurz.[2] In *The Indian Tribes of the United States 1851–1857*, edited by Henry R. Schoolcraft, Catlin's account of a Mandan ceremony is branded as the product of his "fertile imagination." Catlin appealed to James Kipp, a trader who had lived long enough with the Mandan to have mastered their language, and to Prince Maximilian, who had spent a winter with the Mandan, both of whom vindicated Catlin.[3]

In 1833 and 1834, Maximilian, Prince of Wied, and his artist companion, Karl Bodmer, went up and down the Missouri River. Maximilian has left us much valuable eth-

George Catlin, the famous painter of Indians and the West. A number of Catlin's works appear as illustrations in this book. William H. Fisk executed this portrait of Catlin in 1849.

Right: Father Pierre-Jean De Smet, S. J., the famous Catholic priest and indefatigable worker among the Indians, who was one of Morgan's fellow passengers aboard the SPREAD EAGLE. This photograph was taken about 1863 by Gustav Sohon.

nological data, and Bodmer scores of remarkable paintings (*Travels in North America*, by Maximilian, Prince of Wied, Vols. 22, 23 and 24 of *Early Western Travels*, edited by Reuben Gold Thwaites, Cleveland, Ohio, 1905).

A Swiss artist, Rudolph Friederich Kurz, journeyed up the Missouri in 1851, returning in 1852. His journal contains much information of ethnographic and historical interest.

Thaddeus A. Culbertson, a younger half brother of Alexander, has left us a vivid account of his *Expedition to the Mauvaises Terres and the Upper Missouri in 1850* (his journal, edited by John Francis McDermott, has been published by the Bureau of American Ethnology, Smithsonian Institu-

Meriwether Lewis and William Clark. The Lewis and Clark Expedition from the mouth of the Missouri to the Pacific Ocean, 1804-6, was the first step in the opening of the Far West.

tion, as Bulletin 147, 1952). His primary objective was to obtain specimens of fossils for the Smithsonian Institution, under the direction of Spencer F. Baird, but his observations and report contain much anthropological information also.

Occasionally a trader has taken the trouble to set down on paper what he has learned about Indians during many years of residence among them. Such a one was Edwin Thompson Denig. He entered the upper Missouri fur trade in 1833, and spent twenty-three years among the Indian tribes of that region. He had at least two Indian wives, one of whom was an Assiniboine named Deer Little Woman. He knew Audubon, the Culbertsons, Father De Smet, Larpenteur, James Kipp, Kurz, and many others whom we shall meet in the pages that follow. His published writings are as follows: (1) *Indian Tribes of the Upper Missouri*, edited by J. N. B. Hewitt (Washing-

ton, D.C.: Bureau of American Ethnology 46th Annual Report, 1928–29), pp. 345–628; (2) "Of the Arikaras," John C. Ewers, ed., *Bulletin of the Missouri Historical Society*, Vol. 6 (1950): No. 2; (3) "Of the Sioux," John C. Ewers, ed., *ibid.*, Vol. 7 (1951): No. 2; (4) "Of the Assiniboines," John C. Ewers, ed., *ibid.*, Vol. 8 (1952): No. 2; (5) "Of the Crow Nation," John C. Ewers, ed., Bureau of American Ethnology, 1953, Anthropological Paper No. 33, *Bulletin 151*, pp. 1–74.

Francis Parkman was in St. Louis in 1846 on his way west. He went up the river to Westport where he left the Missouri to turn west. The picture that he gives in *The Oregon Trail* of these frontier towns, the emigrants to the Far West, and of local Indian tribes is an excellent prelude to Morgan's first journal, written thirteen years later.

The Missouri River was the veritable blood stream of the Northwest in the 1850's

and 1860's, and most of the contemporary chronicles of that region deal with this great waterway. Numerous steamboats plied its waters and much of the romance and adventure, as well as the bustling and profitable trade, centered about these craft. Phil. E. Chappell has given us a picturesque "History of the Missouri River," together with a list of the steamboats that navigated her muddy waters, in *Transactions of the Kansas State Historical Society, 1905–06*, IX, 237–316. And we have found Hiram M. Chittenden's *History of Early Steamboat Navigation on the Missouri River* (2 vols.; New York, 1903) an invaluable mine of information on this subject.

Of the 1862 voyage of the *Spread Eagle* there are several accounts and partial accounts besides the journal of Morgan. Father De Smet, who was a passenger, tells a fellow priest about the trip in a letter, published in English translation in *Life, Letters and Travels of Father Pierre-Jean De Smet, S.J.*, edited by Hiram M. Chittenden and Alfred T. Richardson (4 vols.; New York, 1905), II, 783–88. Henry W. Reed, agent for the Blackfeet, and Samuel N. Latta, agent for the upper Missouri, also were passengers on the *Spread Eagle*, and speak of the trip in their reports for 1862 (*Report of the Commissioner of Indian Affairs for 1862*, pp. 322–25 and 336–41, respectively). The Montana Historical Society has in its archives diaries of two men who were passengers on the upstream trip of the *Spread Eagle* in 1862; in 1956 they were as yet unpublished. One is by A. H. Wilcox, "Up the Missouri River to Montana in the Spring of 1862." Wilcox left the *Spread Eagle* at Fort Benton. The other is the "Diary of James Henry Morley in Montana 1862–1865." Morley was one of the several gold-seekers on the *Spread Eagle*. He left the boat at Fort Benton and went, with two companions, into the mountains to work a mine. These two journals are both interesting and informative and we cite them from time to time.

In addition to these two diaries the Montana Historical Society has a third account of the *Spread Eagle*'s trip up river in 1862 by Colonel Jirah Isham Jones, who was one of her passengers. It consists of two printed pages; the source of publication is uncertain. It appears to have been written from memory some years after 1862, since it contains an error and some discrepancies with other well-established accounts. He speaks of the *Emilie* as the *Emerline*, and he dismisses the race between the *Emilie* and the *Spread Eagle* by merely observing that the former outdistanced the latter, "waving a fond goodbye as they passed."

PART I

Steamer *West Wind*,[4] Missouri River
Near White Cloud, Nebraska,
May 1, 1862

I left Rochester April 28 for St. Joseph, Mo. where I expected to take the Steam Boat *Emilie*[5] for Fort Benton and the Falls of the Missouri. This boat was advertised to leave between the first and fifth of May. It is a boat of the American Fur Company which goes up once a year under a charter in part from the Government to take up several Indian Agents and the goods sent by the government for distribution among the Indians. The Secretary of the Interior, Hon. Caleb B. Smith, gave me a letter to H. W. Reed,[6] agent of the Blackfeet, requesting him to take me with him, as one of his party (he is allowed 5) and to afford me all the facilities in his power for the prosecution of my inquiries. Mr. Reed has invited me to go with him and thus the preliminaries are adjusted for a trip to the Upper Missouri which I have long desired.

Having learned from the St. Louis papers yesterday that the boat would not leave until May 5, which would bring her to St. Jo. about the 11th, I decided to go up to Omaha again to see the Pawnees, having on two former occasions[7] been at Omaha for the same purpose without success. If I fail this time, I shall stop on my way down and go over to their village. To save that necessity I make the present trip. We reached St. Jo. last evening, April 30, at 9 P.M. and left in the steamer at 10.

The Mississippi and Missouri are both now in flood. The Missouri is higher than it was in 1859 when I was here. It is earlier in the season than it was then and the grass has not yet started on the plains. In about two or three weeks there will be a great change in the appearance of the country.

The Narragansetts (*Female Line*)

Yesterday I conversed with a half blood Narraganset[8] woman with two Peqwa [Pequot][8] children in her charge who were going to Paoli,[9] Kansas, where they reside with the Weaws. She was about 60, talks our language fluently, and was quite intelligent. She says both the Peqwa and Narraganset languages are extinct so far as she knows. Her great grandmother on the mother's side was a Narraganset, which makes the same. She says descent among them was in the female line and that it was the same among the Peqwas and she thinks it was so among all of the old New England tribes. She knows no language but the English, but I think she must talk the Weaw nevertheless. I talked with her about the feasibility of uniting the fragments of the Algonkin nations in one nation. She thought it could and ought to be done. And as to a state for them she thought the New York Indian Lands in Kansas were the best.

[Morgan here gives, in about 500 words, the gist of a discussion he had with a man who lived in California about the Sierra Nevada topography and Indians, especially their means of subsistence.]

St. Marys, [Iowa] May 2, 1862

I left the boat at this place to visit Rev. Samuel Allis,[10] for many years Pawnee interpreter, in the hopes that I could secure all I desired as well in this manner as by going to Omaha. The boat landed me about noon and in due time I found my way to his house.

The Pawnees

The Pawnees are divided into four principal bands: the Grand Pawnees (Cha-we), the Republican Pawnees (Kit-ka), the Tappa Pawnees (Pe-ta-ha-we-rat). These speak the same dialect. And the Pawnee Loups, Skee-de (Wolf), who speak a different dialect.[11] All these now reside on the Pawnee Reservation. The Pawnee Picts [Wichita] live near the country of the Osages. Mr. Allis knows nothing about them. The Arikarees speak a dialect of the same language. [Arikara and Wichita were Caddoan-speaking tribes.] The Pawnees told Mr. Allis that they had lived from time immemorial on the Platt, the Nemaha, Salt Creek, on the North, or Republican, fork of the Kansas.

They do not claim to have lived on the Missouri. They claim once to have owned all the land west of the Missouri from the Platt to the Kansas. The Loups went off from the principal band and went south of the Osage River where they remained for many years. The Republican Pawnees once occupied the Republican fork of the Kansas. They do not know where they came from. They say that there are the sites of their villages still known to them on the Nemaha, Salt Creek, and on the Platt and Republican fork of the Kansas. The Keeches, so-called by the Pawnees, who now live in the west end of the Indian territory somewhere, are cognate. They live near the Pawnee Picts, south of the Osages and the Comanches.

Tribes [Clans]

He [Allis] thinks they are divided into tribes.[12] The marks which he has seen on their robes and lodges are the Eagle, Bear, Beaver, Owl, Buffalo, Deer. The son succeeds the father as chief. He was unable to give me any information upon this question. He never saw but one burial. They excavated a grave or trench and then dug an opening in the side large enough to insert the body under the undisturbed earth, laid it in horizontally, covered it with a mat, and deposited by its side a number of articles, filled up the trench and raised a mound over it.

Pawnee Matting

He [Allis] showed me a specimen of their work in a floor matting made of a species of rush. It was coarse but strong, about two or three yards wide and five yards long. It was stitched or woven on bark threads and very creditable work. With instruction in the art of manufacturing and with reeds of a supe-

Pawnee earth lodges. This photograph, by the admirable pioneer photographer William H. Jackson, was taken in the Pawnee village at Loup Fork, Nebraska, 1869-70. The variety of housing adopted by the various Indian tribes seems to have interested Morgan.

rior quality they might produce an article which would have commercial value. Among all our Indian nations the industry of the woman is proverbial, and if it could be encouraged in the direction of domestic manufactures, the products of which were purchased by government factors at such prices as would reimburse the money an incalculable benefit would be conferred upon them. The women would then support the whole of them. And after a time the men would unite with them in the labor. I talked with Mr. Allis about the Agency system as at present organized, and its results.

Indian Agency System

Mr. Allis agreed with me that the Agency System was a failure. His observation confirmed mine that many of them are dishonest, some incompetent, and but a few really useful. He is not at all satisfied with Mr. De Pau[?][13] the present agent of the Pawnees. He says he has sold the crops raised on the Indian farm, which ought to have been distributed among the Pawnees; that he has hired out the threshing machine, purchased

by a former agent, to white settlers at different places, and that finally a team became frightened while drawing it, and ran away with it and pretty much destroyed it. He says the Pawnees are annoyed by the settlers, and that the licensed trader system is not well managed. He thinks there should be two, and but two, traders licensed, that the Indians may have the benefit of competition, and that a better system would be one something like that of the army settlers. He said he could not get the agency. He did not try as he knew it was impossible. It was a political race as usual between several applicants.

About the religious system of the Pawnees—he knew but little as he had never studied the subject. It was an element worship with medicine and conjuration. They have no term for Devil, and are very superstitious. For want of time I could not take it up further.

This morning at 4 o'clock I left his house,

after a pleasant visit, and reached the bank of the river in time to hail the *West Wind* which left Omaha at 3, and I got on board at 6 A.M. The boat will reach St. Jo. tonight, and I am now thinking of stopping at Iowa Point and going to Highland, the Iowa Mission, for two or three days, as the *Emilie* does not leave St. Louis until May 5.

Highland, Kansas, May 6, 1862

I stopped·at the Point at 8 P.M. and after some effort found a team to take me to Mr. Irwin's at Highland some five miles distant which place I reached at 10 o'clock, and found Mr. Irwin[14] at home and up. He received me very cordially, occupies a large and well furnished house, and has at this time about twenty boarders. He disconnected himself from the Iowa Mission about two or three years ago for the purpose of founding an Academic institution for boys and girls at this place, and went East at the time of the meeting of the Board at Rochester, with the hope of securing some part of an endowment. In this he did not meet with much encouragement. Single-handed he has gone on, and established quite a school of about 65 scholars, using the basement of the church as a school room. About 20 of the scholars are from other villages and Western Missouri and these he is obliged to take into his own family and board in which he is succeeding well. He has two or three competent teachers, Mr. McElroy,[15] Principal, and Miss Paxton[15] at the head of the female department. Dr. Paxton,[15] now upwards of 70, assists some and his wife, a fine looking elderly lady, whom I met last night, teaches music. She went to Beirut as a missionary two years before Dr. DeForest,[15] as the wife of Dr. Dodge,[15] who died soon afterwards. Some time afterwards she met her present husband, Dr. Paxton, at

Jerusalem and they were married, and remained, I think she said, some time in that country as missionaries. For many years they were settled in Kentucky, then in Indiana, to which he removed six years ago from slavery considerations and came from there here. She said [she had] commenced life with the hope of being a missionary in the East, and found herself near the end of it on missionary ground in the West.

Mrs. Irwin is an excellent woman, but greatly burdened with the cares of this large family. She has four children—one son married. The school established by Mr. Irwin is a valuable one, and will do great good. It was much needed, and deserves encouragement and aid. Mr. Irwin is wide awake and cheerful, and well calculated for the post he has taken.

[Morgan has a 10-page vocabulary of Grand Pawnee, Blood Blackfoot and Minitares or Gros Ventre terms here, the same words in each language.]

Iowas

Yesterday I went to the Iowa Agency and village, saw Ma-ha, one of their chiefs—a fine looking man, No Heart, so often mentioned by William Hamilton in his journal, now head chief of the Iowas, as the successor of the 2nd White Cloud. I saw the blind interpreter Elisha who is quite intelligent, and a large number besides. The Iowas who numbered 830 when Mr. Irwin came among them 20 years ago (in 1837) now number 300, and are not increasing. During the last two years they have made great progress in farming, house building, fencing, and raising stock,[16] which if it continues will tend to increase their numbers. They have now but 25 sections of land, which gives but a small farm to each family, but they are giving up the hunt and turning to agriculture.

Blacksmith Shop

This was a grand thought in favor of the Indians. I visited the Iowa Blacksmith Shop. There are two men there employed and paid by the government who do all the work required by the Indians free of charge, such as shoeing their horses, mending their wagons, plows, domestic utensils, and whatever else they can do which the Indian requires. This is an undoubted blessing of the highest and best kind. The Agent has a house built by the government and a council house, which is all well perhaps if he is required to remain on the reservation. The Iowas still hold to their Indian costume with a number of exceptions. Robert D. White Cloud[17] lives on this side of the Nemaha, but he was at work rail splitting three or four miles from the Agency and I did not see him.

Burial Customs of Iowas

They used to bury formerly in a sitting posture, and they still use this mode, although in some cases they adopt our method. I visited yesterday two of their burial grounds, and saw about twenty graves. The most of them were hollow graves, like those of the Omahas opened by me, with a roof of timber, covered with earth. A number of them had grave posts about four feet high at the north end of the grave, and near it a flag staff 15 or 20 feet high to which some kind of a flag was attached.

White Horse's Grave and Post

He died last February, and was buried on the summit of a high swell of the prairie a mile East of the Agency. A picket fence was built around the grave and on the north side was a grave post. [Morgan has a sketch of the grave posts here.] The post was round and about six inches thick with the bark stripped off, the head or top painted with vermilion. On the north side was a row of red marks seven in number showing the number of scalps he had taken. On the left was a similar row of eight which showed the number taken by his friend who put up the grave post. On the side next the grave was a representation of an Indian on a horse in red paint to indicate that it was the grave of White Horse. To the right of this were five or six devices in the nature of heads, which showed the number of heads he had cut off. Near by was a flag staff 15 ft. high with a white flag and a cross in the center still flying from the top. Near the foot of the grave post was a bundle of about a dozen sticks some 6 inches long, and tied around with a string. These showed the number of persons who had together mourned at the grave, and cut their arms so as to draw blood and I believe the red stain still visible on each stick was that of each person. Some of the graves had a frame of timber around them like this [small sketch], others like this [small sketch], slabs standing erect, and others with round timbers on the top, and little or nothing on the side. The mounds raised over the graves were about four feet high and several long and wide. I saw bundles of canes and sticks at other graves. The one first described I wished to bring away, but as it was in full sight of a number of houses I did not think it prudent. This morning Mr. Irwin mentioned the name of an Iowa which means "Bury me in the fork of a tree."

Iowa Descent of Chief's Office

Elisha the interpreter told me that the office of chief descended in the tribe [clan] and usually but not always from father to son. The two White Clouds, father and son, are head chiefs, but Robert, the son of the latter, was set aside and No Heart was made chief in his place. They are all of the same tribe, and of course related nearly. When No Heart dies, Robert may yet get it. He has a right, as Elisha said, to be a chief. The Iowas tell Mr. Irwin that they divided from some other people on the Red Banks, but do not know where the Red Banks are unless on the Upper Missouri.

Omaha Earth House

Mr. Irwin described to me today the Omaha earth house. They were often fifty feet in diameter, made of poles interlaced with willows next to which prairie hay was placed, and upon this sods of earth, making a wall two feet thick. Such houses would last fifteen years. Large posts were set in the ground about 8 feet high above ground and inclined slightly inward. Between these smaller ones were set, and willows interlaced horizontally from the ground to the top. [Morgan has a sketch of the ground plan here.] Within were placed in a smaller circle another set of poles rising three or four feet higher than the outer ones for the roof. Rafters were then laid from the top of the outside wall to and across the string [?] pieces which rested upon the forks of the inner poles, leaving an opening in the center large enough for air, light, and the exit of the smoke. The roof was interlaced with willows, covered with prairie hay and earth as before, and thus a commodious and durable house was constructed. The door way was low, about 6½ feet high, and approached by a covered way which extended out some 20 to 30 feet [two sketches here]. Around the side were raised bunks or platforms for beds, covered with skins. The long door way was designed to keep out the cold as well as the heat. I saw at the Iowa village three old-fashioned Indian lodges. They were round and at least 20 feet high by about fifteen on the ground covered with canvas except the opening in the top.

Agency System among the Indians

I have made this a subject of inquiry both with Mr. Irwin and Mr. Williams who is in charge of the Iowa school. The evidence increases that it does but little good, that it is not only a failure but disgraceful for the immorality and dishonesty with which the business is managed. It is a position of great temptation for the agent to speculate in the funds which pass through his hands, and the opportunities are numerous enough. At the Iowa Agency (Mr. Burbank) there is a school and improvement fund $5,000 per annum, the annuity about $7,000. The improvement money is spent on a school near the agency which is now said to be doing well,[18] about 25 scholars, and on the Blacksmith Shop before mentioned. There is no Indian farm now carried on here. The first abuse is in making out the census or pay roll. This is done three or four months before the annuity is paid and tickets are given to the heads of families, corresponding with the classification of persons on the roll. So that each Indian knows how much he will draw on his family ($22 each). Mr. Irwin mentioned that in making out the roll sham names are sometimes introduced, e.g., Noheart and Wolf. Chief secured a ticket for himself—including his family, and a separate ticket for his wife and a sham family. This they told Mr. Irwin and said they took the tickets because the agent and traders told them to. They were in debt and the agent and traders took this method to aid them. Thus they were made dishonest and also placed under obligations to the agent and traders.

Another method is to include deceased members of the family, e.g., if he has but four in his family he will secure a ticket for seven or eight. When the roll is paid these Indians are required to sign a false receipt, and the agent certifies that it is correct, when he knows it to be false. Remedy for this is to require the agent to swear to the census and punish the perjury. A proper oath can be framed. Mr. Irwin says he has known a number of times a census of four and five hundred Iowas returned when but 300 could be found.

The next abuse is in the system of licensed traders. At present the Iowas have one licensed trader who is a brother of the agent, Mr. Burbank. He has a hand in the census and all the affairs of the agency, and is substantially a partner of the agent. He always knows when the annuities are to be paid, that is, he knows some months in advance, and is the first to know. It is generally understood here that the information comes from the chief clerk in the office at Washington. If this is true, he receives fees from all of these agents and is hand in glove in all these rascalities. As soon as it is known when the payment is to be made, the traders begin to give as large credits as the Indian desires up to the full amount of his ticket. The store is open through the year, but the credits are not large until near the time of the payment. The credits thus given usually amount to the entire annuity. A few sometimes get a little, but the most of them not a cent, besides being a little in debt on the next year.

Payment day. The Indians assemble. The agent calls by heads of families and the Indian responds. His ticket is compared with the roll (this census or roll is never sent to Washington until after the payment is over) and if right the money is counted out by the agent and laid on the table. The trader sits there and says you owe me just this sum and without any account or settlement he takes the money and puts it into his trunk or bucket. The Indian makes his mark on the receipt and leaves without touching the money. Another Indian presents a ticket calling for $80. The trader says you owe me $90. I will take this and you will owe me on the next year. The Indian signs the receipt and walks away.

The Indian has no account, keeps none and does not seem to care anything about it. He buys a number of articles and cannot keep the sum of them, but with a bill he might be made to understand it. The wares sold are partly useful and partly trinkets, and the profits of course very great. We went over some of these prices. It is evident that the Indian cares nothing for the annuity, but most for the credit, and the whole thing is so managed as to make it of little use. Licensed traders ought to be prohibited on the old reservations if there are villages near, or the number should be increased so as to make one a restraint upon the other. After the annuity is paid the pay roll and receipts are sent to Washington.

Indian Farms—Experimental

The government has spent a good deal in opening experimental farms among the Indians. The one of the Iowas was an unsuccessful experiment. Several thousand dollars were spent in opening the farm. A large appropriation was made for this purpose. Afterwards $1600 a year were spent for seven or eight years in carrying it on. It contains 660 acres, something more than a section, and is immediately east of the Mission House, in one of the choicest farms in Kansas. Above 200 acres were fenced and improved, several small buildings erected and the property could have been sold in three or four different years for $25 per acre. This is the general testimony at Highland, including S. M. Irwin. It took about all the farm raised besides the $1600 to carry it on. The Indians got no benefit of the crops, and none from instruction. It was a failure in all respects.

The Department at Washington directed the advertisement and sale of the farm for the benefit of the Iowas to whom the proceeds belonged. Vanderslyce,[19] the agent, held on to it until his term was about out, although opportunities are known to have occurred to sell it at $25 per acre; and finally when the reaction set in on the price of land, he advertised it for sale in accordance with the instructions sent him long before, but was careful to do it in such a way that no one should know that it was to be sold. It was not known at Highland, about three miles from the farm, and the nearest village, nor at Iowa Point, nor anywhere else. On the day of sale a friend of the agent stopped at Highland on his way to the sale but said nothing. He was one of the persons selected to bid. The farm was sold for $1500 to a friend of the agent, and a few days afterwards it was consigned to Mr. Vanderslyce for $2000, who now owns it. There were several men at Highland able and willing to pay them two or three times this sum for the land had they known of the sale, among them Mr. Johnson, Genl. Bayliss,[20] and probably Mr. Irwin. In this manner the Iowas were defrauded of a valuable piece of property by the agent, and that Vanderslyce is admitted to be one of the best agents the Iowas ever had. Think of that! This is so moderate a piece of iniquity that even now he passes as an honest man.

The trust lands of the Iowas which were worth $10 per acre on an average, were sold by the government at a valuation ranging from $1.50 to $2.75 per acre. They were seized by Squatters, and the government refused to interfere and thus allowed the Iowas to be despoiled. So much for experimental farms, and the history of this farm is the history of all.

Kikapoo Agent

Under Buchanan, Dr. Badger[21] was agent and his brother-in-law was the trader. Now the brother-in-law is the agent[22] and Dr. Badger is the licensed trader. Here we have the same simple and effective system in operation to make a sure thing of the Kikapoo annuities and improvement money.

When Vaughan[23] was agent of the Iowas, his son was a partner of the trader. The Iowa farmer received a salary of $600 from the government. He lived seven months in Missouri and five here. The blacksmiths do not always get the amount the government allows. Thirty per cent discount to the agent was the rate at the Kikapoo agency and is probably about the rate upon all the rest.

St. Joseph, May 9, 1862

I came here yesterday from Highland by stage 24 miles. Mr. Branch,[24] Indian Superintendent, is at St. Louis and also Mr. Reed [agent for the Blackfeet]. The steamer upon which we are to go up is the *Spread Eagle* and not the *Emilie*. This boat is advertised to leave tomorrow and will be here next Wednesday or Thursday. Of course there is no certainty about it until she actually starts. I shall thus lose about 15 days, and if that proves to be all shall be content.

On my way here yesterday we passed through Wathena, on Peter's Creek, five miles from St. Jo. It was the site of an Iowa village and named after an Iowa chief. It

was located on the bottom land of this creek in the timber and about 1½ miles from the Missouri. This is doubtless a sample of the sites of Indian villages in the Missouri country. They go back from the river on the creeks into which the few fish found in this river run, and are thus easily taken. They still take in this river cat and buffalo fish and some other kinds. Thus it continually turns up even in this poor fish country that fish are not lost sight of.

Fish in the Platte River

I was told yesterday by a person who had crossed the plains by the Platte and had been on the Arkansas, that fish in moderate amounts are found on both rivers, and are much sought after by the Indians, that he had seen the Indians near Fort Laramie place fish on the fire and ashes to roast without skinning, scaling, or even removing the entrails, and when sufficiently cooked, they were eaten in this condition. One man had four wives, and it was the business of one of them to do the fishing for the family. There is some game beside the buffalo almost all the way across the prairie, but without the horse, it would be extremely difficult for an Indian band to migrate across it.

Camash Root

There is a small white onion found on the prairie from the Missouri to the mountains. In all probability this onion and the Camash Root west of the mountains are one and the same. [P.S.] Not so.

I found at St. Jo, Thomas and Joseph Penney,[25] and Mr. Woolworth, a son of S. B. Woolworth[26] of Albany.

I have also learned here that the Crows have been transferred to the Fort Laramie Agency, and that it is doubtful whether we

meet them at the mouth of the Yellowstone: not so. They have since been retransferred.

Judge Hewitt[27]

I have met here C. C. Hewitt, Chief Justice of Washington Territory. He resides at Olympia and is about to cross the plains. He is an able man. He has agreed to do some work with my schedules of which I have furnished him some.

I have also given W. W. Thayer of Buffalo, who goes with him, two [schedules] for the Shoshonee on his way out.

PART II

[We omit here two pages of notes on Mound Builders and on the prairies of Ohio and Indiana.]

Steamer *Spread Eagle*,[28] May 15, 1862

Mr. H. W. Reed, agent of the Blackfeet, arrived at St. Joseph Monday evening, May 12. He is a Methodist clergyman, 59 years of age and a very agreeable gentleman. His appointment is an excellent one. He invited me to accompany him in pursuance of a letter from the Secretary of the Interior requesting him to take me with him. He has treated me with great courtesy. This morning the boat arrived at St. Jo and we left at 12. We expect to reach Fort Benton about July 6.[29] It is a trip up requiring about 45

days. The boat is loaded with adventurers for the newly discovered mines in Oregon and Washington, and there are also Indian traders and one or two have their Indian wives on board. We shall no doubt have a merry time.

Pawnees

The licensed trader of the Pawnees is aboard. I saw him several times at St. Jo. He is about 25. The Pawnee annuity is $20,000 cash, and $20,000 in goods. This year they received but $15,000. He said he sold them in goods last winter $12,000. Their annuity was paid to them in the Spring. Thus he received the greater part of the money. He said he got his pay at the time the Pawnees received theirs. That it would not do to let the money go into their hands, as in that case he would not get his pay. He took it of course as the Iowa trader did, above described.

Pawnee Farm

The Pawnees have a farm of 1000 acres cultivated by the agent. He understood $20,000 per annum was allowed to the agent to expend upon this farm, $5,000 quarterly. This seems large. He said the crops were distributed among the Pawnees. [Rev. Samuel] Allis said the agent sold the last year's crop. I understand the agent[30] of the Paw-

nees is now in some trouble with the Government. No doubt like most of the agencies, this of the Pawnees is conducted iniquitously.

Father Peter John De Smet[31]

I find on board this well-known Oregon Missionary. He is a Belgian by birth, as he informed me, a noble looking man and about 61 years old. We had a long conversation today. He now lives at St. Louis, and is going up to Fort Benton with stores for the Catholic Missions west of the mountains, but he does not go over. He goes south among the Crows and thence to the Arickarees, and thinks of going into the Comanche country before he returns.[32]

[Morgan records here two or three pages of data obtained from Father De Smet on camas root and the method of cooking it, the gum pine trees of Washington and Oregon, caious, or biscuit root, etc.]

May 16, 1862, 8 P.M.

We are now about 50 miles below Omaha tied up for the night. Now for a few words about the boat and passengers. The first is a good one, well manned and furnished, under the command of Charles Chouteau, Jr. and grandson of Pierre Chouteau, founder of the American Fur Company. The boat takes up the goods of the company for their trading posts, and also the goods of the government for the several Indian agencies. We have a good table, and four excellent minstrels who at evening give us an excellent concert. The passengers are a mixture.[33] There are some fashionable young men in quest of health and pleasure. Some

Below: This curious drawing shows Father Pierre-Jean De Smet being welcomed at a Sioux village in October, 1840. Father De Smet was highly respected by the Indians, and here he is honored by being carried in a buffalo robe from his camp to the village.

adventurers for the gold mines[34] in Washington and Oregon. Some independent traders who reside in the Indian country and have Indian wives. Some traders and trappers in the service of the Fur Company. They play cards and smoke and chat and on the whole are well behaved and happy. The boat is in a cheerful mood. There is some gaming going on but not of a serious character, and some drinking, but no drunkenness as yet. The trip now promises to be a grand and a pleasant one.

We expect to be from 40 to 45 days in going to Fort Benton. After we get above Sioux City, we shall be beyond settlement, and consequently beyond wood yards, after which the boat stops at night, and the men cut wood in the night for the day. This will be continued all the way up. We shall also overtake the *Key West*[35] about Fort Pierre, which is to take us from the mouth of the Yellowstone, or 100 miles above where the *Spread Eagle* stops, on to Fort Benton some 500 miles above. This boat we must keep along with us, and it will cause some delay, as it is a small boat and not as fast as this.

Among the passengers, besides Father De Smet, are Maj. Culbertson,[36] a retired trader who now lives at Peoria, Illinois. He has with him his Blackfoot wife[37] of the Blood Nation, and two fine looking half blood children. They are going up to visit their kindred and return in the summer. Mrs. C. showed me a photograph of her daughter at home, now 18. It is a very beautiful face without a particle of Indian in it. The one on the boat, about 12, is a very handsome child, with bright eyes, brunette complexion, and hair slightly dark. She will make, when educated, a woman to command attention anywhere. She talks the English only, having never learned Blackfoot. The Major is wealthy and will give them every

advantage.[38] They will of course both marry white husbands, and ten to one their children will show the Indian characteristics stronger than they do, from the strength of the Indian physical peculiarities. I obtained today from her a part of a Blood Blackfoot schedule and we are to finish it tomorrow.

Col. Clarke,[39] an independent trader, is also on board. He has a Blackfoot wife, and lives in the Blackfoot country with 7 children. He talks the language and is a man of intelligence. I expect to obtain a good deal of information from him.

A young Mr. Brown of St. Louis is on board. I was introduced to him by Col. H. B. Branch.[40] He is a brother of B. Gratz Brown,[41] a Republican politician and a candidate for Congress.

Mr. Dawson,[42] chief factor at Fort Benton, is also on board with his Blackfoot son, a bright half-breed boy who looks very much like [Mr. Dawson]. Mr. Dawson is a gentleman in his manners, a Scotchman, and carries the air of a Hudson Bay factor.[43]

There are a number of others aboard whom I may mention from time to time as I make their acquaintance.[44] This will do as an introduction of the company.

Father De Smet

He told me today that he was one of 23 children born of the same father and two mothers, himself being one of fourteen by the same mother, and a twin at that. His twin was a sister, and she died when he was a boy. His grandfather was born before 1700, his father in 1735, and he in 1801, thus they represent three centuries.[45] I had another long conversation with him today on his Indian missionary life and he made for me a Belgian schedule.[46] He is a most delightful gentleman.[47]

Department of Indians

I heard from [space left blank] that a son of the Secretary of the Interior was in New York buying some of the Indian goods on board. I hope this is not so. If it is the Indian department is sinking into the vilest depths of infamy.

Sunday, May 19, 1862, Above Omaha

This morning I received painful intelligence from home, of the dangerous illness of my daughter, Mary.[48] My wife informed me in her letter of May 5 that she was taken unwell with a sore throat on the evening of that day, and this is all I know of the nature of the malady. I requested her to telegraph me if she was no better, care of H. B. Branch, St. Joseph, and expected to receive it before I left. But not hearing, I requested Col. Branch to forward it by telegraph to Omaha in case one came. We reached there this morning early and there I received it. It was from Mr. G. H. Ely,[49] stating that she was sick, that they were hopeful, but that I had better return. It was now the 5th day after its date and it must have reached St. Jo. immediately after I left. This is the 15th day since her illness began, and I could not reach home under six or seven days from Omaha, travelling night and day. I felt that the crisis was already past and that my darling child was even now no more, or recovering.

What to do and what duty required I could not distinctly see, and I resolved to continue on the boat to Sioux City, and decide at that place whether I would abandon the trip or continue it. My fears are of the worst. Indeed, I see but little if any hope whatever that my child is now alive, and the thought that I was not with her, that in her distress and suffering she must have frequently called for me, fills me with inexpressible grief. "Why does not Papa come," would be her natural and frequent call; and am I never to hear that sweet voice again, which for seven years has been such sweet music to my ears!

I should have felt more confidence in her recovery from her natural vigor, sound constitution, and uniform health, but for the remarkable fall which she had in the Spring from the upper bannisters through to the floor of the lower hall at least 14 feet. She was saved from death by becoming so poised over the lower bannister that she fell upon that on her bottom and thus slid down to the floor. Dr. Moore[50] examined her and pronounced her uninjured, and she was soon as well as ever apparently and has been since. This occurred three or four months ago. I fear this attack has some connection with the fall and if it proves to be a brain disease in any of its forms, I shall feel confirmed in this supposition. She is a precious child, sweet tempered, affectionate, and of surprisingly quick intellectual powers. Her loss will not only be irreparable, but will destroy our family. Its light and life are gone, and we are both of us miserable for the remainder of our days.

This is the first time I have ever been called to contemplate the death of one of my own children as near, and I confess it unmans me; and this burden of suspense I must carry for days and weeks before I shall know the result. It is dreadful to think of it. I shall be found deceiving myself with delusive hopes, when there is no hope. Even at this moment I almost know that she is dead, and yet I will not quite believe it. And my poor wife, who has witnessed her suffering and felt all her pains. I am not by her side to share them and to watch the pillow of my precious little Mary. Ah, my darling, your

memory and the recollections of thousands of your childish acts come rushing upon me and fill my eyes with tears. How can I part with you! It wrings my heart with agony. God's will be done. This conclusion we all alike reach at last.

Monday Morning, May 20, 1862

I feel more composed today, but although I deceive myself with hopes, I feel that there is none whatever. The telegram was dated the 14th. This was Wednesday, the 8th day. Thursday the 15 was probably the crisis and if she sank under it she probably died on Friday, and in that event this day is the day of her funeral. How sad and solemn the thought. I cannot pursue it. Her last act which I remember besides her good-bye was to hand me the rivet which binds the gun barrel to the stock, which but for her I might have left. I had intended to dispose of it in the upper country, but now I shall keep it. For several days before I left she used to come up to me and say "Papa I don't want you to go away." Precious child, she is cut off in the blossom of life. I know there is no hope, and I must yield to the dreadful truth, and yet I do not know that she is dead. The telegram says we are hopeful. That is all I have to found a hope upon.

I think now I shall go up to the Yellowstone where this boat stops and give up my trip to the mountains on the *Key West*. I ought to return to my wife now at once, and were it merely pecuniary ends I was seeking I should do so in a moment. But the peculiar circumstances under which I am here are such that I ought to go on.

Sioux City, Iowa, Tuesday, May 21, 1862

We have just reached this village of perhaps 1000 inhabitants[51] at 10 A.M. This is the last white settlement on the river. I

have just mailed three letters to my wife, written the 19, 20, and today.[52] She will receive them about the 4 of June and it will be the first knowledge she has that I received the telegraph. She now thinks I will not be back before August 1 from my Omaha letter which she will receive today. She must now be utterly miserable. I have written to her that I will return with this boat, which will bring me home not far from July 1. This will relieve her to some extent. I hope she will go to Albany [where her parents lived]. It is the best thing she can do. I dread leaving this place. I think it my duty to go on, but am not entirely clear that I am doing right. I ought to be with my wife and children in this distressing time. I hope she will feel that I am doing right. For 30 days at least the suspense must continue, then to be followed by a certain knowledge that the worst has happened.

Black Bird

We have this afternoon passed Black Bird Hill[53] where the Omaha Reservation is established. It is on the West side of the river and is a high range of hills back from the river. Black Bird was an Omaha chief who lived and died here some 40 years ago [ca. 1800]. He had a trader with him by whom he was induced so to act as to keep all other traders away. He asked the trader to procure for him the greatest medicine of the whites, and the trader procured for him a quantity of arsenic. As he had conceived a dislike for the trader he invited him to a feast and gave him the first dose in his food. The trader died, and while dying they danced around him. After this, he conceived the idea of destroying his personal enemies among the Omahas. He invited them to a feast, having first poisoned the kettle of soup. After they had all feasted, he

This photograph of a Blackfoot cemetery is from Francis', **SPORT AMONG THE ROCKIES**. The cemetery was near the Blackfoot Agency on Badger Creek, and presumably this view was taken in 1888.

made them a speech. He said he had the power of life and death, and that he had but to say the word and every secret enemy of his would die. Soon after they began to sicken, and all of those who had feasted died, of whom there were twenty or thirty.

Not long after this he became jealous of his wife, to whom he was strongly attached. She was young and beautiful and he killed her with a tomahawk. Being seized with remorse, he resolved to starve himself. He steadily refused all food, and died of starvation. Before his death he directed his followers to lash his body after death upon his best horse, and take [them] down to a high bluff on the river, and bury both horse and man together. This was done. The horse was buried alive with Black Bird upon his back and a large mound raised over both horse and man. The reason he gave was that he liked the white man and wished to be near the river to welcome every white man who ascended the river and passed the bluff where he was buried. Father De Smet once resided with the Omahas near Black Bird Hills. He had often seen the mound. He gave me the above narrative[54] and said further that for twenty years the Omahas

kept a flag flying from the staff on the mound or by its side. The Iowas plant a flag staff near the grave now as elsewhere noticed.

[Father De Smet gave Morgan the addresses of a number of missionaries and said he would write to them to help Morgan with his investigations.] He also gave me a Flathead Grammar[55] just published. I have just learned that he is a count by birth.[56] His father was a count, and although a younger son, he takes the same rank with his father under Belgian law. He ran away when he came to this country from college at the age of 21.[57]

Blackfoot Burial Customs

When the head of a family dies it is a common practice to make a scaffold about four feet high in the tent where he died which is high enough to protect the body from wolves, then place the body on it and cover it with blankets and leave it with the contents of the tent just as they were at the time of his death. Stones are piled around the tent and timber with them in such a manner as to make a strong enclosure against wolves, and thus the body is left. It is also customary when the friends desire to do honor to the dead, for as many as are disposed, to throw on their blankets upon the body as an offering of friendship. When Lame Bull, a Blackfoot chief, died a few years ago, he

was placed in this manner in his tent and the offerings in blankets amounted to half a bale (30).

If young man dies he is often taken into a ravine and covered with earth and stone. Sometimes he is placed in the forks of a tree. They do not bury in a sitting posture. It is also often customary to shoot horses and leave them by the grave. Since the Fur Posts have been established among them their principal men have a strong desire to be buried at the Fort (Benton). One chief who died at some distance from it desired his people to open his body and remove the viscera except his heart, and then take the body to the Fort which was done. In such cases they are buried in coffins in our way. Another chief requested that he might be buried at the Fort, and that no horses should be shot. He gave his best horse to Major Culbertson in a peculiar manner. It was to be his to ride, but not to sell. He was to keep it, but not to own it.

Shawnee Tradition of Heaven

Father De Smet told me the following which he had from a Shawnee who was a Catholic. He said that the residence of the Great Spirit was upon a high mountain in the midst of a large and beautiful island. He dwelt upon the summit. From the top issued numerous streams which, descending on all sides to the plains became beautiful rivers, which abounded in fish. The plains between were covered with cattle of all kinds, and with game. The plains were full of flowers, and roots and berries. Here the good and saved Indians resided in the midst of abundance. This island was surrounded by water, and was reached in one place only by a tree of supernatural length, on which the departed spirit was obliged to cross. Near the centre was a grape vine bearing delicious grapes. As the spirit approached it he became anxious to reach the fruit. If his life had been upright and good, his step was firm; he reached it in safety, and soon crossed to the island which his eternal happiness was secure. But if he had been wicked when he approached the grape vine his anxiety to reach it became equally great, but he was sure to lose his footing and fall into the rushing waters beneath by which he was borne onward to a cold and barren and desolate country, where he was doomed to wander forever in a state of misery and famine.

Half Wolf Dogs

Father De Smet also told me that while encamped once near the woods a slut Indian dog came out of the woods with a prairie wolf and while the wolf stopped, the slut came to his camp and he fed her after which she returned to the wolf and they both returned to the woods. Afterwards he ascertained that the same dog belonged to an Indian camp nearby to which she afterward returned. In the Upper Country they all believe that the wolf and the dog cross,[58] but I have not yet heard of an authentic case. The wolf dog, so-called, is not a hybrid, but they are fertile *inter se*.

Blackfoot Marriage Customs

The Blackfeet sell their wives, or perhaps it would be fairer to state that presents are expected, and presents introduce the affair. The oldest brother has the disposal of his sisters, and if there are no brothers then the father. When Culbertson obtained his Blackfoot wife he sent nine horses to his wife's eldest brother. He told his men to hitch them at his lodge, and to ask for the girl as his wife. She was sent to him and the next day the brother returned nine other horses

as a present to Culbertson. It is customary for the brother to distribute the presents among the relatives, and for the same relatives to return presents to the groom. In this case the marriage was one which gave great satisfaction to the girl's family, and hence the manner in which it was acknowledged.

Presents of equal value are not always returned. Sometimes if the presents made by the suitor are of little value, they are not accepted and the girl is not sent. [If] his presents are not accepted, he may then add to the number and thus finally succeed. If after a marriage the husband does not use his wife well, or the family are disappointed in the man, it is not uncommon for the brother or father to go to the lodge and direct the girl to go home again, which she does. If the husband begs for her again, sometimes she is again given to him and sometimes not. In case of divorce the children belong to the mother if young, if grown there appears to be no certain rule.

Polygamy

This prevails among the Blackfeet. Unless a man has at least three wives, he is not considered to be of much account. The more he has, the greater the influence and respectability. Among the Blackfeet, Col. Clarke says the women are in the proportion of 3 to 1, which is accounted for by the killing of the men in fighting. Adultery is severely punished. They also whip their wives. Clarke says this produces discontent and jealousy. If a man marries the eldest sister, he is entitled to all the remaining sisters as fast as they grow up. The girls are marriageable at 14 and 15. He is not obliged to take them but is entitled to the election. If presents are made from time to time to prepare the way to get a wife, they are not returned if the application fails. If a wife is taken back by the family, and they finally decide not to return her on the husband's request, the presents are returned.

Love Unknown

Culbertson says the women know nothing of this passion in our sense, or the men. They all wear the breech cloth, that is the men.

George Catlin painted the Sioux Beggar's Dance at the mouth of the Teton River while on his expedition up the Missouri. In this dance the braves are begging for presents.

Dakota (Yankton) Dances

1. War dance	Wä-ke-ta′	wa-che′ -pe	men and women
2. Buffalo ”	Tä-tän′ -kä	”	” ”
3. Medicine ”	Pa-zhu′ -tä	”	men & women apart
4. Scalp ”	Wa-chä′ -pa-hä	”	” ” ”
5. Bear ”	Mä-to′ -ä	”	Men alone
6. Fox ”	To-kä′ -no	”	” ”
7. Strong mans ”	Chä-det-in-za	”	” ”
8. Elk (no bison) female	Ha-khä′ -kä	”	” ”
9. Deer	Tabi′ -chä	”	” ”
10. Snake	Son-deli′ -Kä-dä	”	” ”
11. Horse	Shum-gä′ -kä	”	” ”
12. Owl	Me-wä′ -ta-nee	wa-che′ -pe	Men alone
13. Hot Water	Ha-o′ -kä-wä′ -za	”	They jump into a kettle of hot water and then run and dance where they please
14. Concert	Ha-o-kä′ -wä	wa-che′ -pe	Whistles; they use drums, pans
15. Mink Dance	A-ko-zun′ -ä	wa-che′ -pe	Men alone
16. Prairie Dog	Pees-pe′ -zä	”	” ”
17. Elk (horned; male)	Ome-pä′	”	” ”
18. Fish dance	Ho-hä′	wa-che′ -pe	Four or five men lay down and imitate a fish out of water.
19. Half-Man	E-hä′ -ke-sä′ -ne	”	They paint one half with white clay and the other half black to represent a man split in two front and rear.
20. Spirit	Wä-nä′ -ge	wa-che-pe	Men and women
21. Moon dance	We-wä′ -kä	wa-che-pe	A man and woman cut themselves

and cry and dance for five days fasting. They cut through the skin of the breast and ty in a string. This they do before they go to war [?] sometimes. They ty the string to the top of the lodge each of them, the man facing the woman.

22. Wolf dance	Shun-gä′ -ka-do-wä′ -pe		Men alone; they imitate the wolf

trotting; dance before going to war. They use the drum (kettle), whistle, gourd rattle. Whistles are made of the large bone of the wild turkey, in the hollow of which they place small sticks.

23. Frog dance	Mä-tä′ -pe-kä	Wa-che-pe	Men and women
24. War Dance No. 2	E-ka-pä′ -o-ho-zä		” ”
25. Horse ”	Wä-huh′ -pa	Wa-chunk′ -ä- Gä-hä-pe	M & W

Putting boughs on the head. In this dance they cut willows or boughs and trim their horses heads and their own. Then ty up the horses in one place and then the men dance around them.

Arickaree Numeration

The Arickarees count by twenties above that number. A man has ten fingers and ten toes, and when they wish to say 100 they say five men. An hundred dollars are five men: an hundred buffalos are five men in number, or five people, and the same form is used for a greater or lesser number where it can be expressed by twenty. For less numbers or fractions they use the parts of twenty which are named by numerals, or as in other Indian languages.

This morning I sat down with Mr. Dawson, who is the Factor of the American Fur Company in charge of Fort Benton, to work out the Arickaree system of relationship. He was several years among them and long enough to learn their language sufficient for trading purposes, but he could only answer four questions. This language is not accessible as yet, except to make vocabularies. None of the Arickarees talk English, and the traders have but a partial knowledge of the language. The Arickaree [language] is the same as the Pawnee, with a marked difference in the accents.

Gros Ventres of the Missouri

Yesterday I took up this language with Peter Askew, a French trader of the Company, on the boat, who lives with them and has for several years. He talks their language well no doubt for a trader, but he could not give their system of relationship except in the most imperfect manner. I doubt whether I shall be able to get it. Not one of them talks English, and it is the same with the Mandans who live with them. The latter number about 200 and the former about 500. We shall stop at their villages. There is another interpreter there who is a half blood and he may be able to give me the system. Mr. Dawson has kindly offered me his aid both with the Arickarees and Gros Ventres.

Near Yankton, May 24,[59] 1862

As we ascend the river we find timber, but less in quantity. For the last 60 miles the bluffs have been higher and many of them are of a whitish color. There are appearances of limestone formation, but it is soft, and would crumble under the fingers, the same as that which I examined at Sioux City for the purpose of taking a specimen to Prof. Ward.[60]

The Weather

At Omaha it was warm, but soon after leaving we had a shower, and since then it has been cool. We have had fires in the cabin morning and evening and a part of the time through the day; and a part of the time on deck an overcoat has been useful. It is just cool enough to be delightful. The prairies are well grassed with young grass, and the trees are in full foliage. But for the weight of anxiety on my mind which for hours each day weighs me down, I should find great enjoyment in this expedition, and it will increase in interest as we advance. I am deceiving myself with false hopes and they give me more relief than I am willing to allow at other times. My return as I approach the certainty will be terrible enough. I dread to think of it.

Burial on Scaffolds

At the mouth of the Niobrara we saw for the first time scaffolds on the bluff on which bodies were placed. The distance was about a mile and we could not see distinctly. They appeared to be about 6 or 8 feet high and there must have been four poles arranged in a rectangular form, and the body placed

on cross pieces and covered with blankets or buffalo robes. The principal object would seem to be to secure the body from the wolves as they penetrate graves made in the earth. These scaffolds were on the south or west side of the river and above the Niobrara, or "Running Water." There were three of them, and they appeared like this [small sketch here].

On the same side of the Missouri, near the Ponka Agency House and a half mile below the mouth of the Niobrara, we saw several graves on a bluff about the same distance off, covered with quite large mounds of earth. All of these I presume were Ponka graves. Three or four miles further up on the north or east side of the Missouri we saw the first lodges of the Yankton Dakotas. About a dozen lodges in two or three clusters. On the bank were 40 or 50 Indians looking ragged and tattered.

On the bluff, which rose fifty feet from the river by a gentle ascent, was a solitary grave like a marquee tent [small sketch], the angle of the side, or the descent, being quite steep. It looked like an Omaha grave with a roof over the empty grave which contained the body, and the whole carefully covered with earth. It appeared to be six feet high at least. It is evident that they bring the bodies of the dead to the highest bluffs on the river, and then inter or scaffold them on the most conspicuous point

they can find. They do not select the highest rise of land, but a high spot. In the places named the hills roll along the bluff so as to present serrated summits, and the graves and scaffolds occupied the summit of the small rounding hill on which it was placed. They are very conspicuous from the river, and are no doubt the same on land.

Punkas

We landed just above the mouth of the Niobrara to leave the Punka goods, but as the agent was not there they were taken on to the Yankton landing. Several Punkas were there and one fortunately came on board. I took him in charge and obtained the Punka relationships through Catherine, a Yankton girl aboard.[61] It agrees with the Omaha and the lower Missouri nations.

Punka Tribes [Clans][62]

O-a-te-a′min, Mash [?] people, Punkas call themselves.[63]

1. Many people   De′ -a-ghe′ -ta
2. Grizzly Bear   Wä-sä′ -be
3. Elk   Na′ -ko-poz′ -nä
4. Skunk   Moh-kuh′
5. Buffalo   Wä-shä′ -ba
6. Snake   Wä-zhä′ -zha
7. Medicine   Noh′ -ga
8. Ice   Wah′ -ga

The Punkas now live on a reserve on the Punka River and between it and the Niobrara. They are not very numerous. They are dark skinned like all the Indians of the prairie. Catherine procured the tribes, acting as interpreter through the Yankton, which he understands partially. He counted and named the tribes on his fingers in the order in which they are stated, and I think they are given accurately. The name of the first tribe was "Many People" as near as we could ascertain.

PART III

Yankton Agency,
Thursday, May 22, 1862

We reached this place about 9 P.M. and remained over night. It is beautifully situated on the north or east side of the river, but in a region almost entirely destitute of timber. There may be, and probably is, timber back in the vicinity but we saw none. The location was selected and the buildings erected by Mr. Redfield[64] who was agent under Buchanan. He invited me to go up with him in 1859, but it was in July and I could not wait. I left St. Jo. three days before he arrived, about.

A large amount of goods were left here for the Yankton Dakotas. He has about 1000 acres under the plow, and said he hoped to plough another 1000. Mr. Burleigh is the agent,[65] and his brother-in-law, Mr. Foulk, the licensed trader. He has his whole family with him. I was introduced to his wife, sister, and mother. The land is excellent. He has 50 yoke of cattle, a large number of horses, and all sorts of farming implements. The amount appropriated for this farm is [large], $20,000 or $30,000. Whether this is annual, or to start the farm I do not know, but I so suppose, and he may have from $8,000 to $10,000 per annum to carry it on. The field is fecund. I think I heard that a saw mill was attached to the Agency. If so there must be timber near.

There are quite a number of buildings such as the Agent's house, storehouse, store, etc. This money is not entirely wasted. He pays the men 50¢ per day and he said quite a number had come in to work. He would need 40 or 50 to open and start the farm, after which he could get on with less than half the number. In this case the crops could not be sold, as there is no market, and the Indians would get them by distribution. He said he intended to offer to any Indian who would enclose a few acres that he would plough it, assist him in building a house, and give him a cow. This would be a good plan. It had previously occurred to me.

There were a number of tents on the bottom under the bluff, perhaps 40 or 50. They were round tents of canvas, smoked brown at the top. They came in large numbers to see the boat, perhaps 250 in all. They were dressed in all fashions, some in blankets of different colors, all dirty and most of them ragged. Some in buffalo robes. Some were painted. Many had feathers in them. And a few were well dressed in their best costume with good blankets, quivers of arrows on their shoulders, and a bow in their hands. The bows were common, but the arrows were good, pointed with a triangular point of sheet iron filed sharp like the Pawnee and Iowa arrows. Several had fine pipe tomahawks, others pipestone pipes with long handles 2½ feet or 20 inches long, perhaps. On the whole, their appearance was that of great poverty and scarcity. The country is poor in game, except they go on the plains for buffalo, and they cultivated nothing I think until this farm was started. The Indians on this river must have a poor chance in the way of subsistence.

Yankton War Dance

To manifest their pleasure at the arrival of the goods the warriors last night gave to the boat a war dance. At dark they built a fire of chips and old barrels about ten rods from the boat and soon after began. The drum was made of sheet iron about 2½ feet in diameter and 14 inches high, like a tub over the top of which a skin was stretched. Nine men sat down on the ground around it. Each with a drum stick and all beat the drum in concert, singing at the same time the war songs one after the other.

At first half a dozen dancers took their station between the fire and the drum and commenced the dance. They grouped themselves together and danced not around in a circle, but confusedly and as each was inclined. The step was much the same as the Iroquois, on the heel and not on the toe. They either struck the foot down flat or touched the toe first, and then brought down the heel, sometimes twice, down on one foot and then the same on the other. The step was not particularly a good one. The songs were much the same as the Iroquois. The music and dance of all our Indians are *sui generis*. They came out of the same brain and temper of mind. So far as I have witnessed them this is emphatically true.

The warriors shout as they dance in concert with the music. They displayed considerable activity, and endurance as the same persons had continued near two hours at the dance when I left them, and how much longer they continued it I know not. I left them at 11 P.M. They perspired freely and took turns in squatting on the ground around the drum. The number of dancers increased from time to time until the largest number was eleven. Some were young, but the most were elderly.

Their costumes were all unlike except that all wore moccasins and all had more or less feathers on the head. The most origi-

ME-NO-QUET, A POTTAWATTOMIE CHIEF

BY JAMES OTTO LEWIS

Lewis painted him at the treaty of Fort Wayne in 1827. Me-no-quet was a distinguished Pottawattomie chief, whose village was near the town of Menoquet, Indiana. The chief is in a traditional pose, holding a tomahawk and pipe and wearing the inevitable government medal.

nal article was a large hump of feathers, tails, and other ornaments attached to the waist and standing out behind against the butt. Out of it emerged three, four, and in one case I think five sticks about 12 or 15 inches long tipped with feathers or red worsted strings which projected back and upward and made quite a singular appearance. The one most dressed had on a headdress of turkey feathers, black at the band [small sketch here], white in the centre, and black at the tip, with an end piece to each feather standing out, and tipped with worsted, such as I have seen figured. It branched out from the head quite wide [small sketch here]. He carried a gun and had four points out behind [small sketch here]. He was over six feet, and a good dancer. Others carried a tomahawk, others a bow and some arrows in the right hand.

At times they would some of them dance around the drum, but the most of them kept between the fire and the drum. Once the warrior with the great headdress danced alone and then made a short speech. It called out applause. There was no music but the drum and singing. One man was stationed near the fire to feed it with chips, and another near often joined in the song and sometimes started a new one. When the tune ended the dancers stopped and stood until the song commenced again, but in the meantime the drum beat time.

It is unlike the Iroquois war dance in several respects. There were no speeches by bystanders, as is quite common with the Iroquois. They did not walk around a common center between the tunes, but the step and attitudes of the persons [?] were much the same. As performed it was much inferior to the Iroquois War Dance. They seemed to enjoy it very much, and it was on the whole a wild scene.

Fort Randall

This morning (Friday, May 23) we reached Fort Randall,[66] and there put off the goods of the Punkas. It is a U. S. Fort located on the west side of the river, and now has a company of volunteers doing garrison duty. The buildings are around a square which covers 8 or ten acres and are quite numerous. It is pleasantly located at a point where the river is well timbered with large cottonwood trees below the fort, the largest I have seen on the river.

As we go above Fort Randall the timber almost entirely disappears on both sides. An occasional island or bottom has a scanty stock, but it is mostly a treeless region. The Indians use the small willows for fuel of which they need but little in the summer. What they do in the winter I cannot see. The country is but sparsely inhabited by them. It is in effect an unoccupied country and will remain so for some years to come. A pastoral people who moved with their flocks and herds and became partially barbarous[67] would thrive on these boundless plains and that may yet become their use.

Yankton Scaffold Burying[68]

Just above Fort Randall on the east side of the river were a dozen lodges on the second bottom. We saw six scaffolds on the bluff back of, and below, them. They were quite conspicuous on the top of the highest ground site, but perhaps half a mile back from the river, standing in relief against the horizon. There were also one or two mounds or graves nearby. About three miles further up, upon a large bottom, were twenty or thirty lodges near some timber. Their horses and cattle were pasturing near them and their appearance was quite picturesque. They were canvas tents,

round on the ground and conical with the sticks which constituted the frame projecting from the top. They were also Yankton Dakotas. Nearby on the bluff we saw scaffolds and some mounds. They say we hide away our dead in the ground, while they keep theirs in sight, and thereby in memory. It is however a very careless mode of burial, as the frame of poles will soon give way, and the bones will then fall to the ground and become scattered. I could not learn that they gathered the bones after they were cleaned and preserved or burned them.

[A few pages of topographical notes, "Bluffs and Bottoms," and some notes on how to cook camas root, obtained from Father De Smet, are omitted.]

Buffalo Trails

We saw yesterday buffalo trails coming down the bluffs to the river. The sides were furrowed with them. They come to the water in the evening to drink and march in single file, sometimes marching in this way for ten miles. They often stand on the sand bars for a long time probably to escape mosquitoes. Their trails are all through the prairies. They are about ten or twelve inches deep, and a foot wide. Out on the open prairie these trails are the best guides of the traveller. They show they were marching and not feeding. If they approach or tend toward a ravine, you will be sure to find the best crossing and the best ford. If they tend towards hills or mountains you may be sure there is a pass, and the best one to be found. They are the pioneers of the routes of travel.

When they feed of course they move like any herd. They make great circuits to find grass and seem to know where to be at the best season. I have never yet seen a good

Buffalo coming to drink in the upper Missouri, painted by Karl Bodmer, who accompanied Maximilian, Prince of Wied, on an expedition up the Missouri in 1833-34. His paintings constitute one of the most important surviving records of the Far West before it was subjected to the pressures exerted by civilization expanding from the East.

account of their changes with the seasons. The hunters say when the herd travels or migrates they follow a cow who is a sort of Queen Buffalo and if she is shot the herd is thrown into confusion. The Indians have strict laws against firing the prairies in their hunting ranges as it drives the buffalo out of their country. A hostile neighboring nation often fire their prairies for this purpose. The Flatheads cross the mountains to hunt buffalo in the Crow country. Of course they fight when they meet, as no nation will allow another to hunt in their territories if they can prevent it.

[Six pages on the beaver are omitted. Most of the data was obtained from trappers; some from observation.]

50 miles below Fort Pierre,[69]
Monday, May 27, 1862

We are now, 9 A.M., tied at the bank cutting wood. At Cedar Island, we took on the last cord wood. We now cut our own wood, both for this boat and the *Key West* which is behind us and a slower boat. They stop at places where dead cottonwood trees are found and they are able to turn out for chopping and sawing from 50 to 60 men. The trees are felled with the axe then sawed with crosscut saws about 12 feet long, split, and carried to the boat until a sufficient quantity is taken on. Afterwards it is all sawn in two a second time and split into cord wood. Yesterday we stopped from 11 A.M. to 4½ P.M. to wood.

The Appearance of the Country

From Fort Randall to Fort Pierre, Clark says the country is the finest on the river. The bluffs are much higher than below and the timber less. We always see some timber, but in places for miles the banks are bare. The timber is confined to the bottoms which

here are quite narrow. The bluffs are from half a mile to a mile apart. The amount of timber is very small. How civilized man can ever inhabit any portion of this magnificent country I cannot see. Yesterday the small boat obtained a buffalo; four bulls crossed the river after we passed and the men shot two of them and secured one. Buffalo were seen this morning from our boat.

[Morgan has two or three pages of data, obtained from Father De Smet, on the salmon cultures of the northwest coast, and on the use of the acorn in the Rockies and the Cascades.]

Beaver Slides on the Missouri

We have seen these quite frequently. They are found on the bottoms where the bank is three or four feet high, usually bordered with willows [Morgan has a sketch of the slides here. Plate XXIII, "Beaver Slides," in *The American Beaver and His Works*, was undoubtedly made from this sketch.] They are slants cut down the bank at an angle from 45° to 60° about 8 inches wide, **down** which they run into the river and by which

they get out. The banks are perpendicular and thus they are a sort of necessity. They are readily seen and look about like a buffalo trail on the hill side.

Elk

This morning we started out a drove of elk from a clump of timber on the margin of the river. They ran up on a little swell on the prairie bottom and there stopped. At this point I saw them. Twenty-five were counted. They were about ¾ of a mile away and made a fine appearance. They soon disappeared.

[A few pages on the beaver and on "Timber in Iowa" are omitted.]

Above Fort Pierre, Friday, May 30, 1862

Last night I dreamed of returning home, and finding my daughter Mary restored to health. Dreams are interpreted by the contrary. May this prove an exception. I find a secret comfort in it. Dreams descend from Jove, was the Greek aphorism. In this sense they would promise good [word torn out].

We reached Fort Pierre Wednesday[70] evening at 7 o'clock, May 27. Several miles below the Fort we came in sight of the tents of the Dakotas who had come and formed two large encampments near the Fort. Some seven bands come to this place to receive their annuities in goods, the Brulés, Ancpá-pás,[71] Two Kettle, Yanctonais, Metakozees,[72] Blackfoot Dakotas, and one other. We remained at the Fort until last evening at 7. Some of the bands arrived during the

"Beaver slides along the Missouri," plate XXIII, from Morgan's THE AMERICAN BEAVER AND HIS WORKS. The curious vessel being paddled by the Indian is a rather poor representation of a bull boat (see the illustration on page 156).

night and yesterday until there were present some 500 to 700 in all. They had large numbers of horses. The men were comfortably clad most of them in buffalo robes, others in blankets, and a few in dressed skins. The men were large on the average. Many of them over six feet, but the women were inferior, with soiled and dirty blankets, and generally a squalid appearance. Their life is evidently one of great hardship and incessant labor. As we were obliged to land 2½ miles above the fort owing to sand bars, which were on the opposite side of the fort from their tents, we did not probably see all of their women. They are usually more numerous than the men. These we saw were about half as many as the men.

The Dakotas are still roaming bands and maintain an independent spirit. They are not entirely friendly to the government or to the whites. After the Trent affair,[73] they became restive, it is said here, under the instigation of English emissaries, and thought of going to war with the whites, but gave it up. It is more likely under the influence of the French traders who are all secessionists, which shows in a general way that the entire French Catholic element of our population is unfriendly to our government. Their position and influence wanes before the advance of eastern men, and awakens a hostile feeling.

The Indians at this point are under the control of these men. They conceived a dislike to Latter,[74] the agent, at once, and the council was an unfriendly one.[75] They refused to receive the goods, alleging that the wild bands, who refuse to receive goods lest they should thereby compromise their rights with the government, threaten to kill them if they took the goods.[76] This however was mere pretence. They refused to take them of this agent, and he directed

them to be stored at the Fort until they had agreed among themselves when they were to have them; but as soon as this was settled, they were delivered by Chouteau[77] to them at once, and they received them, I have since been told.

Latter has but little firmness, and failed in dealing with them for the want of it. They demanded the goods of the Arickarees as indemnity for recent spoilations by them not two weeks ago, and said they would take them from the boat if they were not delivered. They said a good many other impertinent things to the agent,[78] which he took without a proper and manly reply. On the whole it was quite a shabby affair for the government side. Next year this agent will have trouble.[79] The interpreter demanded $100 for interpreting for the day. He is not connected with the Company, but lives with the Indians. He is a Frenchman, and they refused to have any other. He was obliged to employ him, but what he paid I did not learn. The Indians were greatly under his control.[80]

The council was quite spirited. Six or seven chiefs, one for each band, came forward and stood or sat before the agent who was sitting on the ground, and made a speech of about ten minutes. They spoke in a loud and energetic manner and with great fluency. Many of the points they made were good, and evinced much shrewdness. It was interpreted by periods. Each one spoke for his own band. The agent, instead of replying to each, stood up and replied to all at the close in a very common place manner, noticing but two or three of the numerous points made. So that the special parts of each chief's address received no answer. The Indians were seated around in a half circle four or five deep with the women standing in the rear. The men applauded

their chiefs when they said what pleased them with the exclamation "How," which means good. They also say this when they shake hands. Before speaking each chief shook hands with the agent, with Chouteau who sat beside him, and with the interpreter, and then began. He also closed with another shake.

In the morning a band arrived from the plains and made their *entre* in Indian fashion. They walked nine abreast, singing in concert a song. Behind them were others on horseback and in the rear a troop of horses followed, from which those walking had dismounted. The chief was in the centre of the front row. They halted near the pile of goods, and waiting for a little time for some one to receive them, and not being met by any one, they dispersed. This is probably their form when they make a formal visit, and particularly when they arrive after a council is opened.

The goods were carried ashore, the bales opened, and the goods separated and piled up in seven piles, one for each band. Those in boxes were divided by boxes. They consisted of blankets, red, white, and blue, factory-ticking, red calico, powder, balls, a few guns, pilot [?], coffee, sugar, sheet iron, camp kettles, and tobacco, and they were left in this shape for them to take and divide among themselves. Under their system of communism, they would be well distributed, and all would share as long as anything remained.

Receipt for the Goods

The agent is required to procure the receipt of the chiefs for the goods. This I understand is rarely given, and never by these Indians. The clerks show the goods to the chiefs, ascertain the name of the head chief of each band, write his name, and make his mark on the invoice. Latter has such receipts for all these goods, duly executed by the chiefs, although the chiefs know nothing about it and refused to receive the goods from him.

Burial Scaffold

On the rising ground below the bluff about half a mile back from the landing there was a single scaffold, and I went back to examine the mode of burial. Four poles were stuck in the ground about four feet apart one way and about five the other. They were three inches in diameter and six feet high out of the ground, and forked at the top. Two poles were secured in the forks the long way north and south and parallel with the course of the river, with raw hide strings; two others were secured in like manner across, and upon these were laid 8 or 9 poles of the same size parallel, and upon the top of these at the north end was another cross pole, secured by raw hide. The poles which formed the floor of the scaffold were some of them tied with similar strings to the four upright poles, in such a manner as to secure the scaffold firmly against a strong wind.

The body was still upon the scaffold, although so far decayed that the leg bones were visible on raising the side of the covering. It was dressed, and covered with the remains of a buffalo robe and a blanket, and in its present condition it was difficult to see which was the outside covering. The head was to the north. The body was lashed to the scaffold with raw hide and also with a hemp rope, a part of which was still visible. There was one pole outside of the crutch on the west side and the body was placed on the west side of the scaffold, leaving room by its side for another body. What appeared singular was an open box or coffin

Above: Fort Pierre, by Karl Bodmer. Built in 1833-34 by the American Fur Co., the fort was purchased by the government in 1855. It was dismantled in 1857, and another Fort Pierre was built nearby in 1859. This painting is of the first Fort Pierre.

Below: A Blackfoot woman on her way to a ceremonial council pulling her child on a decorated travois. This photo is from an original Forsyth stereo.

at the foot of the scaffold, with a mass of decayed and tattered blanketing by its side and a few small bones, and near it was a grave in which the earth had settled below the surface level, so as to show the exact size of the grave, and it was shorter than the coffin referred to, but large enough for the body on the scaffold, which appeared to be that of a youth, if we judge by the length, although the leg bone which I saw under the covering was large enough for a man. It seemed clear that the body had been taken out of the ground to be scaffolded or had been brought there in the box we saw.

Near their tents was a scaffold, Father De Smet told me, on which the body had been re-covered with a new blanket. It was a former burial by one of these bands, and on their return they had taken this method of testifying their affection for the remains. They would uncover themselves to do this and suffer from the inclemency of the weather to cover more warmly the remains of their dead.

Dakota Dogs Made Useful

They have large numbers of the wolf dog, who grows large and fat. They say they often kill and roast them.[81] They also make them carry burdens when they move camp. I saw several of them in the harness. Two poles about ten feet long are secured on their back with a piece of buffalo skin as a mat and held by a single strap around the neck. There are thus a pair [of] fills[82] with the ends trailing on the ground, forming a triangle about six feet apart at the hind end. Just behind the dog there is a rim of hickory in the form of an ellipse, about three feet by two covered [by] a net work of raw hide, which is secured across the fills, upon which they fasten the burden.[83] I saw two or three thus bearing burdens of faggots of

wood. I also saw several empty, ready to receive their loading. There were also horses who had a similar but longer pair of fills attached to their saddles, with the same ellipse but of larger size attached across them just behind the horse's tail. In this way a horse could draw quite a large load. I saw other horses with two bundles of sticks one balanced upon each side of the horse. They no doubt when they move camp carry with them a considerable amount of fuel in this way.

Antelope

We saw yesterday the first herd of antelope. They were standing on the top of a roll of the prairie. Seven of them only, looking at the two steam boats which were near each other. They were quite frightened and after a few minutes scampered away, but soon reappeared on the top of another hill for a moment for another look and then disappeared. It is characteristic of the antelope when frightened to stop and look at the object and often go towards it. The hunter often avails himself of this and by raising a red flag, the antelope to see what it is will approach within fifty yards of it, and look

at it, by which the hunter secures a sure chance to kill him. They appear to be taller than the largest size dog, about the size in outline of a year-old calf. They are said to be superior for eating to the buffalo, as the latter is to our beef.

PART IV

Above Moreau River, May 31, 1862
We passed the mouth of the Moreau this morning. It is a small stream at the mouth, but is said to be twice as large further back. Last night I dreamed of returning home and finding my daughter restored to health. I saw with perfect distinctness, both my wife and her. She looked taller, but thin, and very beautiful, and both received me

with great affection. The excitement was so great that I awoke. May this dream for one be realized. It is the second of the same kind within a week. But the night before I dreamed of returning and seeing my wife alone, and of finding a confirmation of my worst anticipations. I awoke in great distress of mind.

This morning we saw the first herd of buffalo, about 70 of them, quietly grazing upon the prairie on the opposite side of the river. They were about two miles off, but with a glass could be distinctly seen. About half an hour afterwards we saw on the same side (the south) the largest herd of antelope we have yet seen, about 100. Through a glass, we could see them with perfect distinctness, although some two miles off. I could see them raise their heads to look at the boat and then resume their feeding. They are quite beautiful.

Minnetares or Gros Ventres[84] *of Missouri*

The morning after we left Fort Pierre we took on board two warriors of the Gros Ventres who were down upon a foray against the Sioux. We found the whole party were 24 and that while we held our council they captured 12 horses and made off. These two were discovered and pursued. They had no horses and took to the willow thickets on the river where they were surrounded. They expected to be killed. They threw off blankets, moccasins, everything but the breech cloth, the knife, and the gun. They were able to conceal themselves. They were fired upon, but the balls went over them. The Sioux came within a few yards of them and they drew their knives, expecting to be killed, but intending to kill as many as they could. Darkness and rain came on and they thus eluded their pursuers. In the night they made up

Fort Clark, by Karl Bodmer. Named for William Clark, this fort was abandoned in 1861. It had been built in 1831 by the American Fur Co. and was well known to all of the early travelers.

the river and in the morning hailed the boat from the bushes and were taken on board at day light. They would have swum the river, but they saw men on the opposite side. Thus their lives were saved. It was a narrow escape. They went down to steal horses, and this is a sample of the risk they run. They had no horses, and if detected there were at least 300 Sioux well mounted and every one of them would have been taken, unless they escaped as these did. They took advantage of their occupation with the payments, and thus succeeded as far as we know. They think the remainder got off with at least 12 horses.

Yesterday afternoon while off an island in the river, one of them sat down on the after deck before several of us and gave an account by signs of the expedition. 24 of

them set out from the Minnetare village 4 or 500 miles above in skids to go down the river. A skid is a small boat with a light frame of willow covered with the skin of a buffalo entire.[85] It is thus watertight, and will carry four persons if they understand the boat. They went down the river five days. When they came to this island where they encamped, and left their boats. He counted the days on his fingers, and to indicate a day put his thumb and forefinger together to represent the sun, and then passed it over the sky from east to west and then with a throw of the hand he indicated its setting. He turned down one finger to

Indian bull boats on the Missouri, a detail from a painting by Karl Bodmer. The bull boat is one more example of the way in which the Indian used the buffalo. The Nebraska State Historical Society, Lincoln, Nebraska, has a bull boat on display in its museum.

indicate one day. This he repeated five times to indicate five days. The seventh day they reached Fort Pierre and the Sioux encampments. For the Sioux he drew his finger across his throat, for the number of horses taken he put two fingers across a finger of the other hand, which means a man on a horse and with his fingers counted the number. To show that they encamped on the island on the fifth day he pointed to it and then bent his head one side and shut his eyes. The remainder of his adventures, especially the pursuit, he acted out in pantomime much of which I could not understand. To show that he saw and hailed the steam boat he put up his hand and then threw up his fingers, first on the right and then on the left alternately, twice on each to indicate the puffs of steam from each pipe alternately.

With Jeffrey Smith,[86] a trader who was taken on board with his load of buffalo robes as before stated and who lives at the Gros Ventres or Minnetare village, I obtained of them a vocabulary and their system of relationship. I ought to have stated before that I have obtained from Mr. Culbertson on board the Blood Blackfoot[87] and at Fort Pierre the Uncpapa and Blackfoot Dakota.[88]

Monday Morning, June 2, 1862
Yesterday at 6 P.M., we passed the mouth of Cannon Ball River. It takes its name from round ball like substances found embedded in the soft shale or clay rock which forms its bluffs. They are of different sizes and appear to be perfectly round. We saw them on Missouri bluff near the mouth of the river. As we stop only at the bottoms to wood, I had no chance to secure specimens. Tomorrow we shall reach Fort Berthold, 750 miles above Fort Pierre. Fort Union is 2200 miles above St. Louis, and Fort Benton is 850 miles above the latter, and New Orleans 1200 below St. Louis,

giving 4250 miles of navigation on this great river.

Yankton Experimental Farm

At first I thought this farm might be an exception as the crops could not be sold, and the Indians would get them. But on further inquiry and thinking, it must be placed with the others as a swindle. I heard Mr. Burleigh[89] say that he had received $20,000 for the farm the present year, and $18,000 which was a suspended payment of this on a previous year. He was bragging of the manner in which he carried his point at Washington. His brother-in-law is the licensed trader, and has a store which I visited. It was an ordinary but a fair stock. I have just heard from Reed, who got it from Latter [Latta], the agent of the Upper Missouri Indians, that the brother-in-law has just sold out to a third person and this person has agreed to pay Burleigh $2,000 for a license to trade. Burleigh said he did not intend to spend his time there for $1500 a year, but intended to make money out of it.[90] I heard Burleigh say that he did not do as Vaughn[91] did, get the Indians to work on the farm and pay them nothing, but he paid them 50 cents per day. He had about 40 and expected more would come in. We saw the farm, about a thousand acres ploughed and partly surrounded with fence. He said he intends to have 2000 acres under plow. How does he pay all these men, that is the question. Not in money, for they have no use for that and know not its value. I do not know, but if inquired into it would probably appear that he paid them in potatoes at 4/ per bushel, in corn at market rates, in goods where they make their own rates at from 100 to 600 percent profit. Thus the Government pay 4/ per day in cash, and the larger the number of men the more profitable the business; the money, ⅘ of it, goes into the pocket of the agent. He will probably report an average of 100 men through the working season.

Potatoes in Oregon

Father De Smet carried the first seed potatoes to Oregon. The first year they retained the entire crop for seed. The second year they distributed them to the Indians and planted them largely at the Missions. The aggregate crop was 10,000 bushels. They are now generally cultivated by the Indians and much esteemed.

Price of Buffalo Robes

A buffalo robe is worth wholesale at St. Louis $4.00. They pay the Indians at Fort Berthold for a good robe already dressed and ready for market three tea cups of sugar and one of coffee=1½ pounds of the former and ⅓ pound of the latter=in value, at cost, 26 cents and a days transportation, about 38 cents. A robe is the standard of value in the Indian country and they know but little of the value of money. They will exchange a ¼ eagle in gold for a 2/ piece readily, if they happen to get the former.

Hoe of Shoulder Bone of Deer [92]

The Arickarees still prefer the shoulder bone of the deer to the hoe for cultivating corn. They think iron affects the taste of the corn. They also still prefer the earthen pot to boil their corn to the iron pot which they say affects the taste of the food. They still make earthenware on the old plan. I must secure some specimens.

Whipping Children

Mr. Dawson says the Indian women never whip their children or very seldom. He has seen them whip a girl, but never a son.

They think a person is wanting in affection who does this. They do not plunge them in water, but let them cry it out, or quarrel it out.

[We omit here a page or so description of Cannon Ball River Buttes.]

English Language among the Indians

Dawson agrees with me that the English language is the greatest blessing we can give the Indian family. It brings their minds in contact with ours face to face, and enables to appreciate their intelligence. It also enables them to learn from us, and to defend their rights. The grown Indians are averse to speaking our language. One reason is that they have no words to express some of our vowel sounds and the same with our consonants. We must take the children and that brings us at once to Mission schools. I taught the two Gros Ventres on board to pronounce a number of English words Saturday evening. It was amusing. Some sounds they could not make, e.g., father was pronounced pader; mother, moder. Some were easy, e.g., daughter, daw-ter; grandson, gran-ne-son. Chin, chin. Chair, chair, Ear, ear. Our language must be more difficult to them than theirs to us. (I write part of the time and now with the boat in motion which shakes the boat through and through, and will account for the difficulty in hand.)

Arickaree Relationships and Tribes [Clans]

An Arickaree came on board this morning and I tried with Mr. Dawson to procure their system, but Mr. Dawson does not talk the language well enough now to put the questions. He has promised Mr. Pierre Garreau at the village to do it. They have tribes.

[Two pages on the beaver omitted.]

June Rise of the Missouri

We met the rise yesterday, and today the evidences are abundant in the flood wood and quantities of bark and small sticks which cover the water. A stick placed or stuck in the water last night showed a rise of two inches. It is probably more since we started. This rise is occasioned by the melting of the snows in the mountains and will continue through this month. The boats rely upon it in this annual expedition to go up and down, on from this point. It gives a full channel and carries them over the sand bars and also enables them to cross from point to point in the bends, which they say saves 200 miles between Fort Union and St. Louis. A cool damp wind came down with the rise which they say follows it and last night I had quite an increase of my sore throat which has been slightly affected for about a week. There has been a good deal of it on the boat.

Pumice Stone or Volcanic Scoriae from the Rocky Mts.

This morning F. De Smet picked up for me on the bank of the river in the flood wood, a piece of pumice [93] stone or scoria which floated down from the Rocky Mountains to this point. We are now about 40 miles below Fort Clark and have stopped at this place to wood, at a place where the spring flood left a large amount of drift wood. This pumice is found in the mountains abundantly, and is also picked up on the river as far down as this. It is very porous and will float on the water. Father De Smet has often seen it in the Rocky Mountain range precisely like this. It may therefore be regarded as a genuine specimen from the head water of the Missouri.

Kin' -ne-kuh-nick' [94]

This is very generally smoked by the Indians of the Missouri. It is the inner bark of a red willow which grows abundantly with the common willow on the river. It is a bush and has a white flower [probably red dogwood].

Minnetarees—No Tribes [Clans]

The Minnetarees have the Bear, the Small Dog, the Big Dog, and some other bands, but I could not learn that they had any tribes. Smith says they have not. [95] They are not cognate with the Dakotas, as has been supposed. Some of their numerals appear to be Pawnee. Their language is said to assimilate with the Crow. Mr. Dawson says that the Crows and Minnetarees can talk with each other fluently without an interpreter. [96] It is also said that the Gros Ventres of the prairie and the Arapahos are the same. Dawson says that the prairie Gros Ventres are supposed to be an old Comanche band who broke off and came north.

Minnetaree Religious Ceremonies

I examined last night the back and breast of one of the Minnetaree, Mä-ish [Hoop Iron] (Gros Ventre before mentioned who has been with us for five days on the boat) to see the scars made by incisions with the knife. On his back there were four [scars] 8 or 9 inches apart below the shoulder blades. These cuts were an inch apart, two on each side. They run a knife through to the hilt, and make a cut nearly two inches long. Through this they pass a string, and keep the skin and muscle loose with a stick. The two strings are then attached to the skull of a bull buffalo, which has dried and bleached, and drag it behind them at a dis-tance of ten or twelve feet, for a distance of a quarter and half a mile, crying as they go, step by step, to the Good Spirit to give them success in the buffalo hunt, or in horse stealing of their enemies, or on their war expeditions against their enemies. This is a meritorious act in a young brave, and many of them perform the ceremony. Peter Askew [97] told me he had seen them drag three and even four skulls in this way.

They have another practice of a similar kind. They make similar incisions under the skin on the right and left breast, but not so deep and large, run strings through, and tie them to a pole at a distance of several feet, and they go round the pole drawing the string tight, crying as they move in this way around the pole for success against their enemies, or in the chase. This they continue until the skin often tears out. The greater the strain upon the string the greater the self infliction of pain, and the more meritorious the ceremony. This is nearly equal to the hook swinging of India, and done much in the same spirit. I saw five or six cuts of this kind on each breast. He must have tried it several times. He is a young man about 28. When a boy undertakes to draw the bulls skull too young and shows signs of faintness or exhaustion, he is re-

Indian Sun Dance (young men proving their endurance by self-torture), by Jules Tavernier and Paul Frenzeny, appeared in HARPER'S WEEKLY, November 13, 1875. The late Professor Taft said this was one of the earliest illustrations by a witness of the Sun Dance, and that it was made near the Red Cloud Agency in May-June, 1875.

leased with honor by the present of a blanket or robe by one of his relatives, and the merit is the same as if he had gone to the proper distance, or for the proper length of time. Who the robe goes to I did not learn.

Minnetaree Mourning

The other man has his hair braided behind into about a dozen plaits or strings which present a flat surafce about ¾ of an inch wide. These are spotted over with white earth so as to show a check work of black hair and white earth. It is quite striking and looks like feather work. There are also round braids by his ears and in front of his ears earthed in the same manner. They prepare it in some way to make it adhere for months and keep it on until it wears off. This shows that he is in mourning for some relative. An Arickaree on board has a large plaster of white earth as the parting of the hair on the forehead and daubs of it on different parts of his blanket. This shows that he is in mourning.

Minnetaree Dances

1. Scalp Dance Su′-da-se-sha
2. Buffalo ″ Ka-sip′-a-mä-ker′-e-sha
3. Tobacco ″ O′-pa-ker′-e-sha
4. Elk ″ Mä-no′-ka-ker′-e-sha
5. Bear ″ Näk-pit′-ze-mä Ker′-e-sha
6. Medicine ″ Hoo-pä′-ma-ker′-e-sha
7. Enemy ″ Mi-hä′-we-il′-ha-se-kä
8. Grass ″ Me′-kä-gîk-she-ze-sha.
Women alone
9. Goose ″ Me′-rä-ih′-ka ″ ″
Mä-te, a small boat. Mä-te-she′-she-she, a steamboat. The last describes the puffs out of the steam from the two steam pipes.

Minnetarees—No Tribes [Clans]

I have tried again but cannot find that they have any tribes. They have bands. 1, Black

Mouth. 2, Full Dog. 3, [blank] these are the chief. 4, Fox. 5, Big Dog. 6, [blank]

Tuesday, June 3, 1862

We are now about 30 miles below Fort Clark at the Square Hills as they are called. For twenty miles below this or from 10 to 20, the river is wooded on both sides which is novel. These hills are striking. [Sketch of same.] These hills are on the west or south west side of the river and covered with grass to the summit.

Vermilion

On the west side of the mountains there are beds of vermilion. F. De Smet has visited the beds where the Kootenays obtain their supply. It is simply a red earth. They carry it home in bags, reduce it to powder, mix it with grease or animal oil, and thus use it. Vermilion River near Sioux City has beds of the same earth to which the Dakotas repair for vermilion.

First Buffalo Killed

Today, June 3, we killed our first buffalo, [98] and I have just witnessed the process of cutting him up Indian fashion. Shortly after dinner we saw two bull buffalo standing on the edge of the river under a perpendicular bank about five feet high. They had gone in after water and could not get out, or had swam across and come against this bank; the former is more probable, as the river was more than half a mile wide, with a sand bar on the other side which they would not be apt to cross. There are over thirty men with rifles on board, and they immediately went to the upper deck. The *Key West* was about five rods ahead of us and less than ten rods from the shore. They had the first shot and dropped one of them, but he got partly up again. A moment after

a volley from our boat brought down the other, but they both rallied, and they poured into them shot after shot, until they were finished. One of them got into deep water and along the boat and turned ashore. As soon as he raised his fore quarter he was killed, and floated off down the river. The other was drawn with a rope and tackle on to the steamboat, not yet dead when the rope was put around his neck, but he was dead when they began to hoist him. He was a monstrous fellow with his old coat partly shed on the hind part of his body. The hump was not so much of a rise as I supposed, the effect being in part produced by the long shaggy hair on his shoulders, head, and neck. He would weigh undressed 8 or 900 pounds, and was in fair condition. The running [?] season commences in June, and the flesh is strong, but as the cows are now dropping or nursing their calves and are poor, the bulls make the best meat and are chiefly used at this season, as the cow is at all others. The head of a bull buffalo is truly formidable. We could see the glare of their eyes distinctly as we came within six rods of them.

The cutting up was done rapidly, and Indian fashion. A Greek young man, born as he told me at Athe-ne (Athens), about 23 years old, who had spent three years in the mountains in the service of the American Fur Co., took the lead, assisted by a Frenchman. They placed the buffalo on his belly, extended his hind legs behind him, and left his fore legs under him, and began without cutting his throat which they never do. They cut the hide along the back bone, and stripped it down rapidly to the belly, and then cut off the half and spread it on the deck to receive the meat. (The hide is worthless at this season for robes.) The first move was to take off the two fore legs,

The Minnetaree Scalp Dance, by Karl Bodmer. Here in excellent detail is one of the most interesting and spectacular of the Plains Indian's dances. Morgan saw a similar scalp dance, and noted that the movement was the "up-and-down-on-the-heel-step."

which was done in a moment, as there is no bone attachment whatever. They cut a handle in the flesh, then run the knife in a semicircle around below the hump, and deep enough to separate all the attachments. When the two parallel cuts were extended from the semi [circle?] down the legging of the leg, and the knife was passed along underneath, off came the leg without showing bone or socket. Next the knife was run along the side of the backbone, and the hump piece was taken out. This was done on both sides. Next the flesh around the thigh bone was cut out. Then the hams were cut off, that is the fleshy part. After this with a stroke or two of an axe the spine or backbone was cut through aft of the ribs, and with a few more the back bone was

struck as far as the neck, and the ribs were divided on the back. The animal was then turned on his side. Next the tongue was taken out. The head was turned so as to bring up the under side, after which the skin was cut down under the throat and an incision made, and the tongue was quickly removed. All of these pieces were deposited in a pile on the half part of the skin. They next split the cartilages of the ribs on the back, and took off the ribs on one side, cut out the liver and heart, which were saved, and threw the remainder overboard, with one of the rib pieces, which next to the hump, is the best part of the meat. This is the process when the buffalo are plenty, and the whole is not needed. This half of the body was full of blood, and as the Indi-

an cannot hang up the animal to allow it to flow out, they reach the same end in this way. We have had buffalo meat for two days. The two Minnetarees and one hunter spent the night on land two nights ago, and came back with three back loads.[99] They killed but one.

We have seen small bands of buffalo daily for several days, and today three or four bands on opposite sides of the river, also antelope and a gray wolf, who stood on the bank for a moment within rifle shot, and then ran back lazily on the prairie. Turkey buzzards are seen daily, wild geese, a few ducks, and occasionally a pelican. We have met two dead buffalo, killed by the boat *Shreveport*[100] a few days ahead of us, or mired in crossing the river.

As we are now where the buffalo abounds, we did not stop to pick up the buffalo just killed and which could easily have been saved by the yaul.

Fort Clark, June 4, 1862

We reached the site of Fort Clark[101] yesterday about 5 P.M., and remained until this morning to wood from the timber of the abandoned Fort and Arickaree village by its side. We are now on our way to Fort Berthold which is 65 miles above.

Arickaree Dirt Village

This large village, now abandoned, is situated on a high and perpendicular bluff, partly rock, about 60 to 70 feet above the river. The bluff forms an obtuse angle, which was the site of the village and it is conspicuous for some miles above and below. Last year Fort Clark was burned, whether by accident or design I know not, and the Fur Co. abandoned the post. The Arickarees then decided to abandon their village and move up the river near Fort Berthold, and near the Mandans and Minnetarees with whom for some years they have made common cause against the Sioux. The ruins of the village are quite interesting. Here for the first time I have seen the dirt houses of the Upper Missouri, and they far surpass my expectations. Many of them have fallen in leaving only the side walls standing, but several were complete just as they were left, with strings of corn still hanging and broken articles of various kinds. Their personal articles were of course removed. We saw several axes, ladders, skids, and I have quite a number of relics which will be enumerated below. The houses were built to ac-

commodate several—perhaps ten or fifteen —families. They are round, all the large ones, about 40 in number, and by measurement are 40 feet in diameter. [Sketch of ground plan here.]

Twelve posts 6 or 8 inches in diameter and five feet high are firmly set in the ground about 3½ feet inside of these in the circumference. Under these, cross pieces are secured in depressions cut in the uprights. Against these so as to form a sort of triple joint, twelve others are braced in, which are set in the ground 3½ feet back and so as to form a slope. Round timbers and slabs are then filled in so as to make a wooden wall around the circumference. Four large posts 10 feet high are then set in the form of a square in the centre. They are about 8 inches in diameter and twelve feet apart. Upon the top cross poles are secured. This and the side wall supports the roof which is first a frame of poles 3 or four inches in diameter, which rest on the side wall or against the cross poles, and they also rest upon and extend beyond the four central cross poles, so far as to leave an opening in the centre about 4 feet in diameter. These roof poles fill the space which constitutes the roof. Straw or hay is then spread over the roof and also upon the slightly inclined side wall, and then the whole, both side roof is covered with a thick coat of earth several inches in thickness, and when done it excludes rain and light and cold. Light comes in through the smoke hole in the centre and through the door of which there is but one. It is a portico of timber about five feet high, five feet wide, and twelve long, made of poles on the sides and top, and fitted close so as to admit the least amount of cold in winter. [Sketch here, "Side View—Interior."]

This is divided into as many compart-

ments as there are families in the house. Mats or screens made of willows are hung up between each family. These are made about 10 feet long and six feet wide, the willows being placed parallel the long way and bound together with three courses [of] raw hide strings, each of which is passed over and under each willow. We saw large quantities of them. The wooden corn mortar is set in the floor and rises about two inches above it. It will hold about three quarts of corn and is shaped, the cavity, like an urn [small sketch]. Sometimes there are two or three in one house. Beside the dirt houses there were a number of hewn log houses and huts mixed in with the round ones. The village covers about 5 acres of ground and is compactly built. There is no order in their arrangement and consequently no streets. They are 6 or 8 paces apart and so placed as to cover, with the scaffolds about to be noticed, the whole area. Hence in going through the village you go round and round on segments of circles. This village contained when deserted about 900 souls. When Mr. Dawson first went to this post, they numbered 2400. This was 10 or 15 years ago. All of the Arickarees resided at the village. There was also a small Mandan village a short distance above.

Scaffolds for Drying Corn and Meat

These scaffolds are more numerous than the houses, and more conspicuous in the distance [sketch here]. The drawing fails to show it. It is two stories high, a set of poles for each. The first story is a scaffold covered with cross poles and over all a willow matting. Above this rise three frames consisting of two uprights and one cross pole each. They were doubtless used for drying corn and meat. I shall ascertain.

These scaffolds occupy the spaces between the houses and fill them with the exception of foot paths. At a distance the village looks quite as much like a collection of scaffolds as of houses.

Caches

We saw large numbers of these open and empty. They dig a hole in the ground five or six feet deep, and shape it like the interior of an urn [small sketch]. The soil is firm and they look neat and capacious. I measured one six feet deep and five feet in width at its greatest diameter. They are usually outside of the houses, but we saw a number inside in the floor of the house. The floor was slightly depressed below the level of the ground about as much as the removal of the sod and packing the earth would give.

Fire Place

This was in the centre of the round house, about 4½ feet in diameter, dug out about six inches and lined on the rim in some cases with stone. One fire served all the families and gave light and heat for all. This was a great item of economy, where timber and wood are so scarce. The village is on the south side of the river. There was no timber near the village except on the bottom opposite and a few miles above. They could raft wood down from above, pick up flood wood, and get it from the opposite side on the ice in the winter. They use their dogs a good deal for hauling wood. These houses must be very warm in winter and cool in summer.

War Post and Medicine Stone

In the centre of the village was a small circular open space, where the war post and medicine stone, painted with vermilion, were still standing. I took out the post and now have it. The medicine stone was a boulder of granite.

Arickaree Graves

Just out of the village is the burying ground. The Arickarees did not scaffold the dead but buried them in the ground. The most of the graves, and there are hundreds of them visible, are on the segment of a great circle. Others are grouped together. They wrapped up the body, dug a grave, and put it either in a sitting posture or doubled it up, I do not know which. I saw the size of some of the graves. They could not have extended the body and I could not tell whether it was an empty grave and timbered roof like the Omaha, or the earth was placed upon the body. I shall inquire. There was one scaffold of a Sioux, and but the one.

The best or most conspicuous grave was that of an Arickaree chief who was killed by the Sioux a few years ago. A large mound was raised over the grave about four feet high and oblong about six or eight feet. There was another grave close beside it and mound over it. On the top of the chief's grave were two bull buffalo skulls, side and side, their horns wound with red bands, and the forehead of one spotted with vermilion. The soil or sod was cleared off for a space of five feet around the mound and lined with a circle of buffalo skulls of which I counted 17. They made about two thirds of a circle and were on the side of the chief's mound and to show that they were placed there for him, and not for the adjoining mound.

Ladders

We saw a large number of fine ladders with which to mount to the scaffolds near the houses. They were usually a forked tree as follows [sketch]. The small end was placed upon the ground and the two ends against the frame of the scaffold. Depressions were cut in the wood for the rounds and they were firmly tied with raw hide strings. It was a strong and respectable ladder. The one described was 11 or 12 feet long and had 9 rounds.

Specimens Obtained in the Houses

1. Corn mortar and pounder. This I took out of the floor.
2. War posts of the Arickarees. This I took out.
3. Elk horn robe dresser. Given to me by a young man who found it.
4. Elk horn moccasin smoother. Mr. Culbertson took from a rafter.
5. Buffalo horn spoon.
6. 4 Stone grooved [?] pounders. These I picked up in the houses.
7. 1 Tomahawk of iron.
8. 2 Baskets, 1 old knife [?], 1 Bone object not known, bead [?] mesh [?].

[Morgan published a description of this village and its culture, prefaced with an historical account, under the title "The Stone and Bone Implements of the Arickarees," illustrated with 6 plates, 25 figures, in *Twenty-first Annual Report of the Regents of the University of the State of New York* (Albany, 1871), pp. 25-46.]

Fort Berthold,[102] June 4,[103] 1862
We reached the Fort last night at 9 o'clock. On our way up we stopped to wood at a deserted winter village of the Arickarees 12 miles below the Fort. There were the remains of 30 or 40 round dirt houses, built in the same manner as those described and about of the same size. They wintered here to be near game and fuel. They keep their horses in winter inside these houses [for] safety and thus man and beast were

Distribution of goods to the Gros Ventres, by John Mix Stanley, was sketched in 1853, while the artist was on the upper Missouri as a member of Isaac I. Steven's party looking for a railroad route to the Pacific. Stanley traveled extensively, and his work constitutes an important contribution to our knowledge of Indians and the West.

warmed by [the same] fire and covered by the same roof. We saw the evidence in the houses themselves. In the Spring they returned to Fort Clark to plant. Their scaffolds and the timber frames of these houses were some of them taken for wood. We took 50 cords at Fort Clark and as many here, and it was but a small part of the whole.

The Minnetaree, or Gros Ventres, village[104] by which Fort Berthold stands is a large village of dirt houses, like that of the Arickarees below and is situated on the east or north side of the river upon a similar bluff. [Morgan has sketch here of village and river.]

The bluff is about 60 feet high, nearly perpendicular on the southwest side, and quite steep in front. It stands back a few rods from the river and is surrounded with pickets about 8 or 10 feet high, set close together with openings or gateways here and there. In the centre is an open place with the war post, surrounded by a timber [?] in a circle—so as to shut it up. The medicine stone is there, but I saw only the post. The houses looked very comfortable, roomy, and were kept tolerably clean. Not over two or three families occupied the same house. Several of them had bedsteads, and iron pots and tinware. I shall go over it again on my return. Back of the village were a large number of scaffolds for the dead; about ¼ of a mile back from the pickets they commenced, and extended along a mile up and down, and quite a distance back on the prairie. I think I saw at least 150 standing.

Minnetare Scalp Dance

Soon after we arrived the people who crowded the bank commenced a scalp dance on the top of the bluff in front of the pickets. They used two drums, like tambourines, which were beat by the dancers themselves, and they danced in a ring from right to left about 30 in all, one-third of them women. They all danced. The women sang in a sort of chorus, with their voices an octave above those of the men. The step was the up-and-down-on-the-heel-step. They were celebrating the taking of the Sioux scalp we heard complained of at Fort Pierre. The last war party had not returned. This morning I met the 3 who took the scalp, painted and dressed, coming through the village towards the boat, and walking side and side, singing their exploit. The dance, the song, the music, and the step among all our Indians came out of one brain.

This morning the council with the agent[105] was held on the boat, and was not concluded until we left at 2 P.M. The best looking chief among them was a Mandan. The latter are now incorporated with them. The speeches were taken down by Mr. Risby [?],[106] who has promised to let me copy them.

Minnetares or Gros Ventres[107]

The Minnetares are well formed, and their women, some of them, quite well looking. The latter are far superior to the Dakota women in personal appearance. Still they work hard. Their village life ought to abridge their labor, particularly as they cultivate the same garden beds from year to year, and as they can make subsistence faster in this way than by the hunt. The Mandans, all that remain, about two hundred, live with them. The finest looking man I saw at the council or in the village was a Mandan chief. They and the Minnetares have been compelled to recede up the river by the advancing Dakotas, and the time is not distant when they will be forced to the mountains. The Crows have invited them and the Arickarees to join them in the Yellowstone country, and make common cause with them against the Dakotas. The Minnetare village contains about 1500 inhabitants.

Travelers meeting Minnetaree Indians, by Karl Bodmer. Morgan saw the Minnetarees or Gros Ventres when he was at Fort Berthold. While the Indians were reflecting certain aspects of advancing civilization in 1862, the Minnetarees quite possibly still appeared much as they did to Bodmer in 1833-34.

PART V

Arickarees[108]

This people are also receding before the Dakotas. The maps show their old villages at different points down the river. They have occupied from the Kansas River to their present village, about two miles above the Minnetare village on the south side of the river. They moved last year from Fort Clark to this place and thus abandoned 65 miles of their country to the Dakotas on the Missouri.[109] We stopped at their village yesterday, and held a council, and the agent gave them their goods.[110] Their new dirt village is back on the bluff about half a mile from the river. The Minnetares wished them to settle on their side of the river, but the Arickarees refused. They said they had always lived, and their ancestors before them, on the west side, and they preferred it. They make winter camps on the east side, but keep their permanent home on the western.

Government Aid in Farming

Although for years agricultural Indians, [the] government has given them no aid. If the Government would send to the chiefs on loan a dozen plows and 25 yoke of oxen in trust to be used in ploughing their lands it would be a sensible aid.[111] Beauchamp,[112] a Canadian Frenchman, married to an Arickaree, the father of Bliss [?] B., the handsome boy,[113] with F. De Smet, would be a good instructor, and $200 a year would be ample pay. The same should be done for the Gros Ventres or Minnetares. They are called altogether by the former name.

Friday, June 5,[114] 1862
This morning the *Emilie* which overtook us at Fort Berthold came up behind us and attempted a race, but the captain wisely declined, and allowed him to pass.[115]

Beaver in the Water

Yesterday I saw for the first time a beaver swimming in the river. It was in the middle of the afternoon, and he was not more than two rods from the boat. He was going up stream and close to the bank. He remained above the water, showing his head and fore shoulder a little, but none of the remainder of his body, and no part of his tail. As he dove he showed the most of his body, turning it under in a curve, but his tail did not come in sight, nor did he make the tail stroke. He remained above the water until one third of the length of the boat had passed him. He was full grown. We continue to see an abundance of beaver cuttings on the banks.

Name of Book

It should be entitled "Systems of Consanguinity and Affinity of the Human Family." The first includes blood kindred, the second marriage relations. "Consanguinity and Relationship" is faulty since the latter includes the former. One is general and the other special, whereas both should be general or both special. The former are both special, cover the whole subject and are those used in the Roman civil law.

BUFFALO DANCE OF THE MANDAN

BY KARL BODMER

Bernard De Voto said of this illustration: "If we were to be limited to a single picture for imaginative insight into the life of the Plains Indians, this one would serve better than any other ever made." Prince Maximilian described the dance: ". . . they wear the skin of the upper part of the head, the mane of the buffalo, with its horns, on their heads; but two select individuals, the bravest of all, who thenceforward never dare to fly from the enemy, wear a perfect imitation of the buffalo's head, with the horns, which they set on their heads, and in which there are holes left for the eyes, which are surrounded by an iron or tin ring . . . they have a woman, who during the dance, goes round with a dish of water, to refresh the dancers, but she must give this water only to the bravest, who wear the whole buffalo's head . . . The men have a piece of red cloth fastened behind, and a figure representing a buffalo's tail; they also carry arms in their hands. The men with the buffalo heads always keep in the dance at the outside of the group, imitate all the motions and voice of this animal, as it timidly and cautiously retreats, looking around in all directions. . . ." Bodmer painted the buffalo dance later, for he was not able to sketch it as it happened, if indeed he actually saw the Mandans perform it.

NO-WAY-KE-SUG-GA, AN OTTO

BY GEORGE BIRD KING

No-way-ke-sug-ga was an Oto, and his name means "He who strikes two at once." He was painted by King in 1837. The Oto were a small tribe of not much importance, and they had to spend most of their energies defending themselves from the larger neighboring tribes.

Arickarees

I obtained their system of relationship through Pierre Garrow [Garreau][116] a half-breed Arickaree and half French, with some assistance from Mr. Girard,[117] Factor of the Company at Fort Berthold, and another Frenchman, who also talked Sioux, which Garrow also talked as well as French. I sat up until 1 A.M. to make a sure thing of it, as I knew the interpreter would be wanted in the daytime. It is not as complete as I could have wished, but it is respectably done. I shall make some further inquiries on my way down. Girard took a blank and said he would go over it. Garrow is their sole interpreter and not an Arickaree or a Mandan, speaks English. Garrow is a solid and intelligent looking man. The Arickaree women are inferior to the Mandan and Minnetare women.

Gros Ventres of the Prairie

These are distinct in language from the G[ros] V[entre] of the Missouri. Their language is said to be the same as the Arapahoe and F. De Smet thinks them allied to the Snakes and Comanches.[118] The Minnetare on the other hand are said to be kindred with the Crows. There is a woman on board with a Frenchman for a husband, who is a Gros Ventre of the Prairie. He cannot speak her language nor she his, and yet she is his Indian wife, and now alone with him several hundred miles from her country. She talks Blackfoot which he does not know. I have arranged with Mr. and Mrs. Culbertson to interpret for me, and am this afternoon to try for their system of relationship. There are also two Crow Indians on board, but not a soul who can talk their language. The language of signs is said to be a definite and somewhat complete language of itself, so much so that a man and wife can make it answer. F. De Smet told me he had known a good many instances of the same kind in the mountains.

Buffalo Swimming the River

We saw three small bands of buffalo today swimming the river about ⅓ of a mile ahead of us. Only their heads appeared above the water and they kept very close together, so much so as to make it look rather inconvenient [?]. We have also seen the white wolf swim the river. Today I took out my gun. We shall now probably see buffalo in the river daily. We saw small bands last evening and this morning on the prairie feeding. At the old Arickaree deserted village by Fort Clark we saw quite a large band of buffalo coming over a hill towards the river. It is probably the first time a band has been seen from the site of the village for 40 years. They do not come within a number of miles of the settlements, but it would seem that they had found out that the village was deserted, and had ventured near it. We see wild geese quite frequently, but in small flocks of half a dozen. The day is rainy and cool. I put on my overcoat on deck this morning.

Indurated Clay Banks

Above Fort Berthold for 50 miles the bluffs are quite picturesque. They appear to be of indurated clay and they rise terrace upon terrace, and in abrupt and isolated peaks and pyramids. They are nude, irregularly stratified, and deeply cut with water marks. The effect in places is very fine. I cannot describe it. There are great banks and mounds of clay, one rising behind the other, with cones, pyramids, truncated cones and long embankments in all forms and combinations, with their faces at an angle of 70° or 80°, worn into fantastic forms. They form a group sometimes extending up and down the river two miles and back in successive terraces for half a mile, grassed at their bases.

Below Fort Berthold about 20 miles, on the south west side of the river I noticed one of these naked clay hills which interested me a good deal from the water marks in the clay, now indurated, which looked as if the work of man, but for the abundant evidence to the contrary. I thought it might explain the Runic inscriptions on the island off the coast of Maine, plaster casts of which were presented at Albany at the meeting of the Association in 1856. (See *Transactions*) Albany Meeting, 1856.[119]

[Morgan has a sketch of the banks here.]

There were distinct lines of stratification as shown above and on one of the faces there were deep lines sunk in the clay which appeared in the distance as represented above. If I remember aright the characters above include all of those represented on the island rock in Maine with the exception of ⟨and⟩, both of which are represented in the X. If this indurated clay ever hardens into rock by atmospheric influence, or geological cause still in operation, the rock inscription above mentioned, which is conjectured to be Runic [words torn out] fully accounted for.

Schedule of Gros Ventres of the Prairie

This morning by the aid of Alexander Culbertson and wife, the latter is a full blood Blackfoot of the Blood Nation, I obtained the system of relationship of the Gros Ventres of the Prairie,[120] through the G[ros] V[entre] woman on board before referred to, who cannot talk to her husband except by signs. She talks Blackfoot, however, and thus I obtained it. It is one of the best made. The Gros Ventres of the Prairie are Algonkins clearly, and if the Arapahoes speak the same language they are the same. The G. V. formerly resided on the north side of the Missouri on the Moreau River. This woman and Peter Askew's wife were saved from death by Culbertson. They were both wives of one man and were ill treated for which they deserted the nation.

Saturday, June 7, 1862

This afternoon we stopped at an encampment of the Assiniboines on the north side of the river about 65 miles above the Great Bend between Forts Berthold and Union, and not far above the mouth of White Earth River, say 20 miles. Here the bluffs were close to the river and rising about 80 feet high. (Catlin called them the Vermilion Bluffs.) They were chiefly of clay with rock formation here and there in eccentric positions. Below the bluff which in places were nearly perpendicular, and on the slope near their foot were several different kinds of rock, such as characterize the river for the last 150 miles below, with the exception of lignite which appears in seams here and there, and which reappeared on the west or south side two or three miles above in the largest and blackest seam I have yet seen. It was two feet thick, and about 50 yards long. At the first place named I obtained some fine specimens for Prof. [Henry A.] Ward, such as the sand rock, brown, white, and grey; red rock nearly brick color which appears to have been thus colored by heat by the combustion of lignite; petrified wood, a large quantity, which was scattered along the lower slope, and among the fallen masses under the bluff; nodules of dark brown stone. I think they will please him, and also Dr. Dewey.[121]

We have just passed through a beautiful range of bluffs on the north side of the river, the finest we have seen. Great pyramids, cones, cliffs, and peaks, abrupt and irregularly elevated masses of earth, naked on the river side, where the sides have fallen, thus forming the bluffs, and in other places thus formed by denudation. They relieve the monotony of the prairie, and suggest very forcibly the beginnings of mountain scenery.

The Assiniboines numbered about 200, and had a good number of horses. They were better dressed as a whole than any we had seen before and several had on military coats. One was a regular Indian dandy in full Indian costume with red blanket, fringed gun cover, worked leggings, fringed moccasins, hunting pouch hanging on his back, his face painted, and feathers in his hair. His black hair was plaited like that of the Minnetare, and spotted with white earth. His garments were all new and clean and in the distance he made a splendid and dashing appearance as he stood under the bluff, or with that in the background. The Arickarees were about to erect near this place their annual Medicine Lodge, of which I will give some account as I descend the river.

Monday Morning, June 9, 1862[122]

We are now about twenty miles from Fort Union and the mouth of the Yellowstone. The river still maintains the character of a great river, ranging from ⅓ to ¾ of a mile in average width. Yesterday we went through some places where it was about ¼ of a mile wide. The Yellowstone is as large as the Missouri above the junction. We expect however to go with this boat to the mouth of Milk River, some 150 or 200 miles above Fort Union. From that place the *Key West* goes on to Fort Benton at the foot of the mountains. It will take then 12 to 15 days to make the 500 miles from Milk River to the Fort, in consequence of the strength of the current and the rapids which occur frequently. They are obliged to [?] the boat over the rapids, that is take out a cable and secure it to the bank ahead and draw up the boat with the capstan. They are also hindered by sand bars.

Yesterday Mr. Chouteau saw a grizzly bear in the brush where we stopped to get wood.

Saturday I shot at an elk twice in the river from the deck of the boat; both balls passed over, the first just above the tip of the ear. We saw only the head and a small part of the neck. Twenty shots were fired without hitting. She was swimming the river followed by a calf, and afforded a fair shot. We have not a first rate marksman on the boat. On Friday last we got in the midst of a large band of buffalo, crossing the river. I shot at two and missed them. We secured but one yearling bull and one calf, which was done by going down with a yawl and getting quite near them. We also saw the same day an immense band of several thousand buffalo.

Since writing the above we have passed through a band of buffalo crossing the river and killed 8 or ten bulls, four of which are now on the boat. I put a ball into one and missed three others. Every buffalo killed required several shots.

I also saw two beaver, swimming near the bank, one of which was at first sitting on his lodge just above the water. This one was shot just as he went into the water and sank.

I have also this morning obtained a Mandan vocabulary from Joseph Kipp.[123] His mother is a Mandan and his father an American. They are the only two persons living who talk Mandan and English. The Mandans now number but 200 and are incorporated with the Minnetares, or G.[ros] V.[entres] and live in the same village at Fort Berthold as one people. I also obtained from Joseph the Mandan system of relationship imperfectly. He does not understand it fully. It has Dakota terms, but differs from the latter. The Mandans and G. V. have no tribes or clans: they have tribes [Morgan's insertion] neither have the Assiniboines. Saturday I commenced a Crow schedule through Dakota or Assiniboin interpreters and had a hard time. We resumed this morning and they got tired out and backed out. A Minnetare who talked Crow and Assiniboin, and two Crow young men, and Mr. Culbertson who talks Assiniboin made up the working party. It is easy to see how difficult it must be to work it out right in such a way. But we got far enough to see that the Crow and Minnetares were originally one people, and that their systems are about the same. I shall make a new one with Meldrum, the Crow interpreter at the Fort. He is to go with us to Milk River, and return on the boat.

Above Fort Union, June 9, 1862
We reached Fort Union this noon at one o'clock. It is an old-fashioned Fort, belonging to the Am. Fur Company with two small square towers of stone or adobe and stone at opposite angles, containing loop holes, with a strong wooden picket about 12 feet high enclosing perhaps 2 or three acres. The bastions or towers forming the two angles. Inside is the house of the chief factor, a long one story ware house and store on one side, house for the families of the traders on the other, and several small buildings. Inside the pickets it is roomy and quite respectable. The house is on the back side of the enclosure and a story and a

half of frame. The general appearance is rude. It is finely situated on a low bluff about three miles above the mouth of the Yellowstone River on the north bank. The Government has no fort above Fort Randall. All the others this side the mountains belong to the Fur Company.

Yellowstone River

I have had a longing for some years to see this river and now I have seen it. Its mouth is from one half to three fourths of a mile wide and its banks look pleasant. It is quite as large as the Missouri and some consider it the main river. Above its mouth the Missouri becomes a moderate but still a noble river, as large as the Hudson. It is deeper than the Yellowstone, and passes a larger volume of water, which makes the Missouri the main branch or river. To my surprise the river continues quite as well timbered between Berthold and Union as between the latter and Randall, and if anything a little better. The trees are as large and the forest as dense, but from this point to Fort Benton, 750 miles by river, it is much less, so I am told.

Robert Meldrum[124]

This well-known trader of the American Fur Company got on board at Fort Union with his wife, a Crow woman, to go up to Milk River 250 miles above. It was understood that he was to come on board, and I was to look to him for the Crow. I have already had one full talk with him and obtained some valuable information which will follow below. He is a Scotchman, 57 years old and has been 36 years in the country. He is a perfect master of the Crow language. He says he can talk it now better than the English, and likes it better. That he can think better and work better in it than in

any other. That the gutturals one comes to like when once mastered. He was identified with the Crows for many years and became a chief among them. He sustains the reputation of an honest man and enjoys the full confidence of the Company. He is sociable and full of intelligence, particularly in Indian affairs. There is no man in the country who knows the Indian and his character and ways better than he.

Ab-sär′-o-ka, or Crow Tribes

The meaning of their national name is lost. It does not mean either a crow or raven. They make the sign of the Crow as their national sign. That is, they place a thumb at each ear and move the hands up and down like the wings of a bird, and hence the name. They are divided into tribes, 13.[125]

Crow Tribes [Clans]

1. A′-che-pa-be′-cha   Rich Prairie Dog
2. E-sach′-ka-beek   Bad Leggings
3. Ho-kä-rut-cha   Pole Cat or Skunk
4. Ash-bot-cha′-ä   Treacherous Lodges
5. Co′-sä-bot′-see   Butcher without Killing
6. Ah-shin′-nä-de′-ä   Lost Lodges
7. Ese-kip-kä′-buk   Bad Honors
8. Ash-hä′-chick   Moving Lodges
9. Ship-tet′-sa   Bear Paw Mountain
10. Ash-käm′-na   Blackfoot Lodges
11. Boo-a-du′-cha   Fish Catchers
12. O-hot-du′-sha   Antelope Eaters
13. Per′-e-cha-be-ruh-pä-ka   Raven

The Bear's Paw Mountain tribe [clan] was named after the Bear's Paw Mountain,[126] which was their original home country, now possessed by the Blackfeet. They say while they occupied the Blackfoot country, the Snakes occupied theirs and the Comanches that of the Snakes.

The Blackfoot tribes were originally of the Blackfoot Nation, but they lived with the Crows until they became Crows and hence the name.

A Man Cannot Marry in His Own Tribe [Clan]

This law is still strictly preserved. All the members of the tribe are blood kindred and cannot intermarry. It brings disgrace and censure upon anyone who should break the law.

Crow Dances

1. Bä-shu′ -sha	Tobacco Dance	Men & Women
2. I-tchu′ -na	Scalp ”	” ” ”
3. Ar-a-ho′ -a-cha	Society ”	Men Alone
4. Bis′ -ka-za-mä′ -ha	Full Dog ”	” ”
5. Imp-cha-dish′ -sha	Medicine Pipe ”	” ”
6. E-hu-ka	Fox Dance	” ”
7. Bis-ka-ä′ -ta	Big Dog ”	” ”
8. Mä′ -na-he′ -sha	No Song ”	” ”
9. Ese-tu-she-pe′ -ä	Muddy Hand Dance	” ”
10. E-she-pe-ä	Black Mouth ”	” ”

Children Are of the Tribe of the Mother

This is still the law of descent among the Crows. It is an interesting fact because it is followed out by all of its logical consequences. The son does not succeed his father as chief. It descends in the tribe and is bestowed in reward of merit. The chief who succeeds must be of the tribe of which he becomes chief. Neither does a brother, or sister's son, succeed. None can become chiefs unless he has first distinguished himself in war. If he has struck the enemy, he has become honorable. If he leads a party, and the party is successful, he wins an honor, although he does not personally strike the enemy. The conjunction of the two honors entitles him to wear hair on his arm. This is the scalp hair. He hangs it in the fringe of his deer or elk skin shirt, and also in the fringe of his leggings. He then becomes a chief, *ipso facto* Meldrum says. They have a great number of chiefs, but only one head chief of each tribe. He says it is a matter of frequent dispute which is the head chief. It thus appears that the office of chief is hereditary in the tribe, but in no family or branch of it. Merit is the source of office.

Descent of Property

Property given to a person goes back to the tribe from which it came. Property made, or stolen horses, if they belong to the mother, goes to her children. If to the father it does not go to his children but to his relatives in his own tribe. If he gives property to his children in their life time in the presence of witnesses, they keep it. If a man gives horse to any person and dies, unless the person goes into mourning for him, cuts off a finger joint, or does some other recognized mourning act, the property must be surrendered to the tribe of the deceased, or they may go and take it. Here then is the tribal organization pure and simple at the base of the Rocky Mountains.

The opportunities for prosecuting my inquiries on our Steam Boat at the present moment are quite remarkable. Of natives there is one Mandan who talks English. One Minnetare, or Gros Ventre of the Missouri who talks Sioux and Crow, a fine looking man and a chief. Several Assiniboins, with several who talk English and Sioux. Two women who are Gros Ventres of the Prairie, one the wife of Andrew Dawson, chief factor of Fort Benton. They both talk Blackfoot and there are several Blackfoot interpreters, as Culbertson, Clark, and Dawson. Several Crow women and two Crow young men with Meldrum, who talks Crow, and one Blackfoot, Mrs. Culbertson. All these I have seen and talked with and with some of them a good deal. In all these respects my trip has been fortunate and successful.

Young Beaver

I saw at Fort Union a tame beaver about six weeks old. Meldrum took it three weeks ago and carried it to the Fort where the Indian women took turns in nursing it at their breast until it began to bite occasionally when they gave it up. I saw an Indian woman milk from her breast into a saucer, but did not then know what it was for. Soon after I heard a cry like that of a baby and supposed it was her nursing child. It lasted for some time. The similarity was complete except that the cry was not as full toned. I then ascertained that it was a beaver and went to see it. While it was lapping or sucking the milk from the saucer, the baby was pulling its tail and the beaver was making this cry. It is now on the boat with us, Meldrum having given it to Fanny.[127] They are fine pets, cleanly and harmless, and become very tame and affectionate. I must get one.

[Five pages on the beaver and a note on specimens for Ward have been omitted.]

Wednesday, June 11, 120 miles
above Fort Union

This morning we shot two antelope and brought them on the boat. They have no horns at this season and are shedding their hair. In some places the skin is bare and the hair comes off in handfuls. They are a fine looking animal and much larger than I expected. They are nearly as large as the common deer, white bellies and white around and below the tail which is flat and short.

Had another long talk with Meldrum this morning on several subjects. Obtained the Minnetare tribes [clans] and law of descent, also the Crow method of bestowing and changing names, and also in the changes in language, which are given below.

Minnetare Tribes [Clans], Gros Ventres of Missouri[128]

1. Mit′ -che-ro-ka   Knife Tribe
2. Min-ne-pä′ -ta   Water   ”
3. Seech′ -ka-be-ruh-pä′ -ka Prairie chicken
4. E-tish-sho′ -ka   People of the Hills
5. Ah-mah′ -ha-nä′ -me-ta   Meaning lost —
6. E-ku′ -pä-be-ka   Low Hat, or Bonnet
7. Bä-ho-hä′ -ta   Dirt Lodges

All the individuals of the tribe are consanguine. No man or woman can marry a person in his own tribe and the children are of the tribe of the mother. They carry out the law of female line succession as to chief and property, the same as the Crow. These facts were obtained by Meldrum from the Minnetare chief on board, who talks Crow and with whom and the two Crow young men I made the first attempt at a Crow schedule.

Mandan Tribes [Clans]

The Mandans he says are divided into tribes and have descent in the female line, the same as the Minnetares, but he could

A Mandan village, by George Catlin. Morgan, like others who traveled up the Missouri River, was interested in obtaining information about the Mandan Indians. These Indians were all but extinct from the ravages of smallpox when Morgan passed their abandoned villages.

not talk Mandan.[129] None of the Minnetares talk Mandan, but the latter talk the former.

Crows Change Their Names and Manner of Christening

A few days after a child is born, usually about six, there is a family council of the relatives on the father's side who give the name, instead of the mother's tribal relatives. The person who is to give the name places roots of some kind upon coals of fire and as the smoke ascends, the child is placed in his hands by the mother. He then holds him in the smoke and at the same time announces the name which he gives the child. He raises him up gently in the rising smoke towards heaven and invokes the Great Spirit to give him many days with success in war, in horse stealing, and a happy life. This is the substance of the ceremony.

When he wins his first honor, by striking the enemy or stealing a horse, on his return his relatives on the father's side who are out of the tribe come to his lodge and dance around it in his honor and then change his name, by taking away his boy's name and giving him that of a man. This is generally repeated once in subsequent life. Meldrum says there are few Crows who have become elderly men who have not their third name.

After a person dies his name is never mentioned in the presence of his immediate relatives out of delicacy for their feelings. It would revive their grief.

Mourning for Relatives

The Crows are sincere mourners, like the Minnetare, if the suffering which they inflict upon themselves may be taken as evidence. Last July the only son of Meldrum, a man 30 years of age, was killed by lightning. He was highly esteemed by the Crows and this Spring the only son of the latter died. When the Crows came to see him soon afterwards, they began to express their pity for his calamities in the usual manner, by sticking their knives in their heads, cutting their arms, and crying the while most piteously. He begged them to desist. He told them this would not restore his son or his grandson to life. That he knew they grieved with him, and he did not like to see them butcher themselves in this way on his account. But they would not listen to his remonstrances, and performed the usual ceremony.

Crow Son-in-law and Mother-in-law

The son-in-law never speaks to the mother-in-law, never passes between her and the fire, never enters the lodge where he knows her to be. Custom allows no intercourse. She has a right to send to him for gifts of this or that article from time to time, such as a kettle or a horse, and it is expected that he will give it. This is the Creek custom, also Sheyenne.

Polygamy and Wife's Sisters

Some men have five or six wives. If a man marries the oldest sister, he is entitled to all the others if he wishes them. If he does not take or declines them they may be married to another. Meldrum took his present wife a prisoner from the Blackfeet when a child and gave her to his then wife's mother. She was adopted by her and thus became his wife's sister. After his wife died, he took her and was entitled to her. The Crows buy their wives, but not always. These marriages are the most respectable and the most enduring.[130] In other cases they frequently put them away. Meldrum's wife is a solid and a bright, smart, and fine looking Indian woman.

Crows Do Not Kill Women and Children

The Crows spare and adopt the women and children. They regard it as disgraceful to kill a woman or a child. But the Sioux do both. Thus children are often sought by their parents and attempts made to buy them. Sometimes they are successful, but not often. The child is a servant until it learns the language of its captors and then it is treated as a brother and becomes by aid of him one of the Nation [Tribe], and will not usually leave it. I have heard of a number of affecting instances of children meeting and finding their father or their mother after 20 years and beg usually to return. F. De Smet told me of a Blackfoot boy taken by the Nez Perces when a child. Twenty years afterwards at a peace council the father who was then a Blackfoot chief saw his son for the first time. He was told it was his son, but he believed him dead and would not believe it. After a moment he bethought himself of an accident by which the child had burned his shoulder. He said at once if he is my son, he must have a scar on the shoulder. He looked and found it. His joy was great and his feeling deep. He wanted him to return. He gave him a horse, he offered him a herd of horses, and told him he could make him his successor as a Blackfoot chief. The boy behaved well. He said he must return with his relatives and with his mother who raised him. That he loved his mother and she depended upon him and it

A Crow Indian, Very Sweet Man (Bi-eets-ee-cure), painted by George Catlin in 1848. A good example of Catlin's frequently stiff portraiture, this painting tells us much more about the costume, jewelry, and manner in which the hair was decorated than it does about the man.

would not be right to desert her. That his young companions were dear to him and he could not leave them. The father offered to take his adopted mother to his lodge and adopt her. But the young man still declined. He said he would return with his people and think of it and advise with his friends and then decide. The final result F. De Smet never heard.

They will always ransom their children with horses and with all they have.

Degree of Rapidity in Changing Dialects[131]

We took up this subject again. He had not thought of it in the meantime. He said the Minnetare and Crow had not widened much since he knew them 36 years ago. He did not [know] however the former very much. He cannot understand many of their words, but can catch the meaning of the most of them. He says the first change is in the loss of a syllable and sometimes of half of the word. This would of course shift the accent and might vary the pronunciation of the remaining syllables. Then new words are constantly being added and especially since they knew the whites. The old words such as corn, beans, squashes stand well, but the new ones are made for the occasion and are significant, e.g.,

Corn   Ho′-ha-she   Meaning lost
Beans   Ah-mä′-sa   ″   ″
Squashes Ho-ko′-ma   ″   ″
Coffee   Min′-ne-she-pit′-ta Black water
Sugar   Bät-see-koo′-ä Sweet Lee-koo-a
                                              Sweet
Tea   Mä-nä′-pa Leaves of Bush
Rice   Be-sha′-che-cha′ Looks like
                      maggots. Know lately.
Watch   Ah-nä′-sha Follows the Sun.
             Meldrum[132] gave this name
The first name of coffee was Min-ne-she-pit-ta-e-de-o: What you make black water out of. Now they say black water.

Send Book [Systems] *to Following Persons*

Rev. Henry W. Reed. Mount Vernon, Linn Co., Iowa
Rev. Peter John De Smet. St. Louis, Missouri
Alexander Culbertson. Peoria, Illinois
Andrew Dawson, Fort Benton, c/o Charles Chouteau, Jr., St. L. Brown, St. Louis, Missouri
J. T. K. Hayward [possibly a fellow passenger]. Supt., Hannibal and St. Jo. R.R., Hannibal, Mo.
H. B. Branch. Gen. Ind. Supt., St. Joseph, Missouri
Write John G. Shea,[133] New York for Penobscot, Jesuit Father
Send one to Robert Meldrum, Fort Union, c/o C. Chouteau, Jr., St. Louis.

PART VI

Crow Burial Customs

Mr. Meldrum estimates the Crows at 350 lodges with an average of 9 in a lodge, and one quarter more of women than of men.

They bury on scaffolds, in trees, and in some instances in the ground. The former is the usual way. The body is first dressed in its ordinary apparel. Around this is wrapped a buffalo robe, which is tied. Over this is placed an outside wrapper of lodge skin, which is buffalo skin tanned without the hair, which they use to make their tents with. It is then secured upon the scaffold, and allowed to remain for one or two years at the end of which time the bones only remain, and are free from offensive smell. Their principal burial place is at the foot of the mountains. To this place they expect sooner or later to remove the bones of their kindred. They remove or take them from the scaffold, tie them up in a bundle first in scarlet cloth, if they have any, and around this a lodge skin, and then carry them on horseback for hundreds of miles to the mountains, where they place them in clefts of the rocks, or in crevices, where they will be sheltered from the rain and snow. They leave tobacco and meat beside the bones and renew the offering whenever they visit the place. They do the same on the scaffold. Meldrum's son who was killed by lightning last July was buried upon a scaffold and this summer his bones are to be carried by his relatives to the common bur-

ial place at the foot of the Rocky Mountains, a distance of 400 miles. He offers no objection as it would give offense. They usually make the scaffold and put the body in trees.

They also bury in the ground. The arms are placed by the side of the body, the knees flexed somewhat and the body, Meldrum says, is placed in the grave on its back dressed and covered as in the former case. Around it they arrange a covering of timber over which they spread the lodge skin and then cover it with earth. In such cases they often remove the bones in due time to the mountains, but dislike this mode of burial for the reason that the bones continue to smell offensively when they have lain in the ground which is not the case in scaffold burial. If it is a woman they bury with her a bowl or dish.

Mourning Customs of Crows

They often commence crying while the person is dying and even cut off a finger before the person dies, that is, the mother or a brother or sister will do it. After the death the mourning is continued for a year and sometimes for three years. Meldrum says a mother never ceases mourning for her child, addressing it by name and that children never cease mourning for their mother. There is no funeral ceremony. The mourning is made at different times as they feel so disposed. The relatives of the tribe paint and dress the body and place it on the scaffold which Meldrum says is always placed in trees to conceal it from their enemies, who would throw it down. Whenever they visit the place they address the body as if it could hear them. This is repeated for years. They think the spirit can assist them. They cut their heads in mourning, and let the blood run down their face and dry upon it. They cease washing their faces for months.

They gash their arms with knives, cut off the joint of a finger, cut off their hair. These things are repeated, but not with so much severity as at first. They think the soul remains near the body for some years, perhaps always, and that when they move the bones to the mountains the spirit accompanies it. If a man is killed in war the relatives mourn for him in the same manner, but after they have obtained revenge upon the enemy, they cease to mourn for him. The men do all the work of burying on scaffolds. When the body is buried in the ground the women dig the grave and the men bury. There is no ceremony.

Son-in-law and Mother-in-law

The son-in-law and mother-in-law often live in the same lodge in which case the place of the son-in-law is to the right of the lodge entrance and hers to the left. The mother-in-law cooks the meat for him and not his wife, but she never hands it to him, but to her daughter for him. If they are alone in the lodge, they will converse. If a third person comes in they will not. When they live in different lodges if the mother goes to her daughter's lodge and finds no one there but her son-in-law, she does not enter, but he goes at once for his wife. If he goes to her lodge and finds her alone, then the mother goes for the daughter. The Assiniboins have the same practice, Meldrum says.

Religious Beliefs of Crows

The Crows recognize a Great Spirit, to whom their reverence is chiefly directed. The word means "Who made it," or our Maker. They offer prayers or make invocations to the Great Spirit for aid. The sun they reverence as the father of light and heat. They throw smoke to him, and meat, and are careful not to offer him any indignity such as voiding excrement with back towards the sun. They also reverence the clouds, the rivers, and the earth. They sometimes make an image of the animal of which they dream most, and invoke that. This is the personal manitou of the Chippewas. But the Great Spirit is the chief object of their worship.

Sleeping Nude and Bathing

The Crows strip at night with the exception of the breech cloth and roll up in a blanket or robe. If married man and wife sleep under the same robe, the woman does not undress except to take off the moccasins and leggings. In the morning throughout the year, except in the severest weather, the man as soon as he rises goes to the water to bathe. He walks in usually and first washes his face, then wets his head, then, with his hands throws it upon his shoulders and back and over his whole body, after which he puts on his robe and goes back to the lodge to dry himself before the fire. He wipes himself with a lodge skin in front while his wife with another wipes his back. He is then soon dressed. In winter this is the way. They do plunge in. The women bathe frequently but not as often as the men. The women dry the men's moccasins when they are taken off wet and put them down near the door of the lodge.

Mother's Brother, or Uncle

[Morgan has discovered, and here describes, a feature of many kinship systems known as the *avunculate*.]

The Crows have no term for Uncle. He is an elder brother to his nephew who is his younger brother. He is more in authority than the father. When any act is to be done for the nephew which with us would de-

volve upon the father, the uncle does it. He is of the same tribe [clan] as the nephew and niece. The Crows now choose wives and buy wives. If they ask a girl to become their wife [she] will refer him to her mother's brother, who, with her own elder brother, has the disposal of her, and the same if she is bought. It is in strictness the right of the elder brother to sell his sister. The Uncle through life stands by his nephews and nieces as a sort of father. This would seem to spring from the tribal [clan] tie. He is the senior relative usually in the tribe to the person. See another reference to this topic *supra*. The brother is always anxious to do well for his sister in her marriage and is quick to resent her ill treatment after marriage. In their domestic relations Meldrum says the Crows are our superiors. They are kind, respectful, obliging, sociable, and generous, and live together in harmony. But the men are allowed to beat their wives, and the women do not dislike polygamy.

Fort Charles, Wednesday, June 16, 1862

We are now at Meldrum's post, which is called Fort Charles and is about 75 miles below the mouth of Milk River. It is raining and cold. We have a fire in the stove. Yesterday it was quite hot. Meldrum is to go on with us to Milk River. I sat up last night until 12 to talk with him. He is the most intelligent man in Indian affairs I have met on the river.

Communism of Food[134]

Among the Blackfeet the usual rule prevails of sharing with each other while there is anything in the camp. But they have special rules. If a man kills a buffalo any one who comes up may help himself, but if alone he may take half. If two, they may take a third each. If many, they take the whole and it is no cause of complaint. In every case, however, they must leave the robe and the tongue for the hunter who killed the buffalo. These have a market value to sell, and are not therefore perishable. The rule therefore is founded in reason. If however a hunter loads the meat and returns to his lodge, they must ask it of him and he may give it or refuse and give no offense. If they want but a few pounds he gives it usually. When the meat is delivered to the wife it is at her disposal. He has nothing further to do with it. The women then are not as free as the men. They look out for the wants of their immediate family first. Clark once sent out his brother-in-law to hunt for him. He killed five cows, but brought back no meat. His simple answer was, others took it. It was of course right, and no cause of finding fault. Clark says the Indian is a perfect gentleman in his lodge. He is quite enthusiastic on this point.

Crow Declension of Nouns

They have nothing which may be called a declension. They can express the force of the prepositions *for* and *with* by involving the pronoun in the inflection, but not as well as the Iroquois. [Morgan lists a few terms here, such as "my pipe," "his pipe," etc.]

Medicine Lodge

Several of the nations of the Upper Missouri set up an annual Medicine Lodge. This is done by the Minnetares, the Assiniboins, Gros Ventres of the Prairie, the Crows and the Blackfeet. Culbertson has attended the Blackfoot Medicine Lodge, and he has just given me the following particulars. It is usually set up in June. Anyone can announce his intention to do it and then his relatives come forward with gifts and offerings to the Great Spirit. The people assemble at the place agreed upon and the first thing done is to erect an immense lodge, large enough to hold 200 or 300 people. He says they are much larger than the Arickaree dirt houses, which are 40 ft. in diameter. A large cottonwood tree 20 or more feet high is cut, and set up as the centre pole and other long poles are set around it in a great circle. This is the frame. The spaces between are covered with brush, with the leaves on, so as to make a leaf house, fully enclosed. The offerings are then hung up on the centre pole. They consist of kettles, blankets, guns, coats, and other valuables except horses and robes. And these offerings are left hanging in the lodge when the ceremonies are over and the camps break up. The ceremony lasts four days usually within the lodge. The chiefs and head men sit in the centre around the pole, where the fire is kept burning. The medicine men usually about six sit upon one side. The people who go in and out as they please occupy the remainder of the space but preserve perfect order and decorum. The medicine men are nude except the breech-cloth, their bodies and faces are blacked with a mixture of grease and coal, and their part of the performance is to dance and fast for four days and nights, except they smoke, and at the end of the time and often before they are perfectly exhausted. During the performance anyone is allowed to come in or get up and make a speech telling his exploits on condition that he makes a present to some one, whomever he may choose. He makes known his intention by a rap or a whoop, when the medicine men cease the dance, and all are still, while he relates his principal exploit of striking the enemy or of horse stealing, both of which are alike honorable. When he is done and has made his present the dance goes on to the music of the bone whistle and the drum, until again interrupted by another brave. This is the order of business during the four days the lodge ceremonies last. At the first one Mr. C[ulbertson] attended, he received as presents from those who related their deeds of bravery three horses and as many robes as he could pack upon them. He was not allowed to make any present in return. Such is not the rule in this case.

There must be other ceremonies which he did not notice or mention showing in what way the unseen powers are invoked.

Meldrum says the Medicine Lodges are set up for revenge to invoke the aid of the Great Spirit against their enemies in war. Among the Crows the bulls horns are then drawn around the lodge inside, and it is continued until the skin tears out or the person is about to fall by exhaustion, when his relatives cut the strings, which they have a right to do. It is on this occasion also that the sticks fastened in the skin of the breast are tied to the centre pole of the lodge, and the person sitting back upon it walks around the pole crying until the skin tears out in the course of five or ten minutes, or is cut by his relatives for the same reason as in the other case that he can bear it no longer. This is not penance in any sense. Neither has it any relation to past sins, but to obtain a future good. It is to obtain the favor of the good spirits for success against their enemies during the year. The fortitude of the Indian in submitting to such acute personal suffering is quite remarkable.

Milk River, Friday, June 13, 1862

We have just passed the mouth of this river. It is 250 miles above Fort Union and 500 below Fort Benton, and the commencement of the Blackfoot country on the north side of the Missouri. It is about 50 yards wide, and now full. The water is a little lighter than the Missouri, which still retains its yellowish muddy color. When the river is low the color of Milk River is whitish, from the white earth through which it passes in places, and hence the name.

We are now within 260 miles of Fort Benton by land. How much further up this boat will go is not determined, but it is expected that it will go to the Muscle Shell River, which is a long way above this. How far I have not heard.

This morning I obtained from Meldrum the geographical names of the Crow country in the Crow language. I have also ob-

tained from him a Crow vocabulary. Their system of relationship agrees in one remarkable feature with the Choctaw and Creek. My father's sister's son is my father and I am his son. That they were immediately derived from each other I think is tolerably certain from this fact alone,[135] and if it is sustained by a comparison of vocabularies it will be a remarkable confirmation of the stability and utility of a system of consanguinity in minute ethnology. The Crow language is a fine one, and fairly developed although the guttural *h* is of frequent occurrence. Its pronouns and declensions are not well developed, and it is not a high specimen of the Indian language like the Ojibwa or Iroquois.

Whirlpool, or Eddy

This morning at a sharp bend in the river we were detained by a remarkable whirlpool which we had some difficulty in pass-

ing without being drawn in. It was shown by a large amount of flood wood which was moving around in a circle. [Morgan has a sketch of the river, a whirlpool, and a steamboat here.]

The river at the eddy was about half a mile wide or near that, and the diameter of the whirl was more than half the width of the river. The current moved in the direction of the arrows, and was a mass of flood wood. The appearance of the wood as it coursed around in a great circle was quite remarkable. F. De Smet pronounced it the most remarkable sight he had ever seen on the river.

Pomme Blanche[136]

I have two large specimens of the white apple, a tuber which is found abundantly on the Missouri. It is a root which forms deep in the soil, covered with a thick rind. The meat is white and is good to eat raw or dry

Left: Blackfeet Indians hunting buffalo at Three Buttes, by John Mix Stanley. The artist visited the Blackfeet while with the Northern Railroad Survey party in 1853. He reported, "... I was treated with the greatest kindness and hospitality, my property guarded with vigilance ..." The drawing was first published as plate XXVII in volume 12 of RAILROAD REPORTS.

or boiled in soup. The Indians are very fond of it. It is pleasant to the taste, but like the chestnut is rather hard to digest.

Routine of Indian Life

Heard Meldrum just now explain it as he found it when he lived with the Crows as one of them, which he did for seven years. He married a woman of the Crows, and his family consisted of his father-in-law and mother-in-law, his wife, and himself. This made the household. In the morning before daylight it was his duty to get up and loosen the horses, take them out on the prairie to good grass, and stay with them until it was fairly light and they were properly feeding. He then returned to the lodge and went to the river or water to bathe as before explained. He then returned to the lodge and sat down until his mother-in-law had cooked his breakfast, which was her duty and not his wife's. The mother-in-law

waked him if he overslept for the Crows are early risers. She removed the ashes from the fire and made a new one and hung on the kettle. This would be done before he returned. After breakfast an hour was spent in smoking and talking and visiting. After that he went again to the horses, saw that they had water and took them to a new pasture ground, where he would remain with them for a time. Towards midday or sometime after a light meal would be prepared for him by his mother-in-law, after which another smoke and more visiting, after which he would go out for the horses, remaining with them until evening, when he would bring them to the lodge. After which it was the duty of the women to secure them for the night. The breakfast was the principal and the only regular meal of the day in point of time.

He was bound to keep his father-in-law and his mother-in-law in meat, and his father-in-law was bound to clothe him, to keep him in guns or bows and ammunition according as he was able. He was also bound to keep him in tobacco. The wife had an easy time while her mother lived. If he went out to hunt and returned with meat his father-in-law took care of the horses in his absence and for the day after his return. If he killed buffalo, anyone could butcher it and take it away, if one, $\frac{1}{3}$; if 2, $\frac{2}{3}$; if three, all but tongue and robe. He might not as a good Indian butcher his own meat if others went to it, but he could go and cut when others had killed. When a young man gets meat, he gives it to his mother and sisters, and thus it is well distributed. He has known one buffalo cut up on the field into 500 pieces for as many persons. A bull will weigh 1300 pounds undressed, and yield 90 pounds of marrow. If a man violated the customs in relating to sharing meat, he

would be despised and shunned. The wife accompanies her husband on the hunt.

Swearing by the Sun—the Father of Light

It sometimes occurs that an Indian to purge himself from some charge is required to take a solemn oath. They have three oaths. They swear by the gun, by the knife, and by the pipe, of which the former is the most solemn, and the one which they most fear to take. It is done in the presence of the people, and to exculpate from a serious charge. The form and manner of the oath are as follows. Taking a gun in his hand, and pointing the barrel towards the sun, he says "Father of Light, if what I have now stated is not true, may I perish. May this be the end of me." He then draws the gun barrel along through his lips and against the tongue for a foot in length. It is certainly quite a commanding mode of asseverating the truth. They believe if they take the oath falsely it will bring a curse and a punishment upon them and their children after them.

Swearing by the Knife

They raise the knife in the right hand and point towards heaven saying "I have stated the truth." They then draw it between the lips and are required to touch the tongue to the blade. Those who swear falsely in this way attempt to avoid touching the tongue, which appears to be necessary to complete the oath.

Swearing by the Pipe

They affirm the truth of an assertion by saying the words through the pipe. This is the lowest form, but a false oath in this way destroys a man's reputation for veracity and he is afterwards known as a liar. Last winter at a game of ball-guessing it was

This drawing of **Milk River** near its junction with the Missouri was also made by **John Mix Stanley.** Morgan was obviously very impressed by the wild, spectacular landscape through which the Missouri flows in this area of Montana. The drawing was first published as plate **XVIII** in volume 12 of **RAILROAD REPORTS.**[137]

guessed to be in a certain man's hand, where it really was, but in the movement of hands he passed it into his other hand, and it was seen by others before it was covered. He asserted it was in that hand at the time of the guess and affirmed the truth of it by saying it through the pipe. His companions knew the oath was false. The next day in running the buffalo his horse fell and broke his leg. Of course the Crows believe it was a punishment for his false oath. This from Meldrum.

Monday, June 16, 1862, below Muscle Shell River

It has rained more or less for the last four days, which has made the weather cool, and fires necessary morning and evening.[137] The season is backward this year. The river continues to rise and this is increased by the rain rise. It is now I understand pretty much determined to take this boat to Fort Benton, which has never yet been done by a large boat. The rise occurs at the right time and the river is much fuller than usual.

Yesterday and day before we passed through the Bad Lands of the Missouri. The scenery is the most stupendous I have yet seen. I think it must have continued for about 80 miles. The whole face of the country is thrown up into irregular masses in every form which can be conceived. From the river and from the peaks, one of which I ascended yesterday, it has the appearance in miniature of mountains rising beyond mountains in every direction. Great peaks and ranges with jagged outline and deep valleys alternate. The hills are clay with scarred faces, most of them dingy, some whitish, without grass, and mostly barren. Some of them have scattered clumps here and there and wild sage bushes in the valleys and on the lower slopes. They would not improperly be called Black Hills. They look utterly desolate and yet grand from the great and picturesque outline. They assume the form of immense walls, with buttresses and flanking towers, domes, and almost anything you may choose to imagine. They rise the highest of them from three to four hundred feet from the river within the distance of half a mile, and one and two miles from it. This country is very difficult to traverse for man or beast, except the big horn sheep who delights in such a home. We saw his tracks down a cliff of dark clay with some rock forming a bluff which rose out of the water and over a hundred feet high almost a sheer perpendicular. The angle of the face must have been at least from 75° to 80. His tracks in one or two places went directly up the cliff, in other places along the shoulder, where a stone two inches in diameter would not rest. [Morgan has sketch of mountain sheep tracks on the bluff here.] These tracks were perfectly distinct, side and side and but a few inches apart. We have seen none as yet. Last evening we saw a drove of about 70 elk in a bottom as the boat tied up for the night.

Bad Lands[138]

The Bad Lands above referred to commence about 30 miles above the mouth of Milk River, and the most of them are passed when you reach the point where the Little Rocky Mountains are seen, which we have passed this morning. They extend northward to and across Milk River, and southward to and across the Yellowstone, and no doubt extend southward to the Black Hills and to the Bad Lands south of them. We expect to reach the Muscle Shell River today, and we are still in country of the same general description, although not so abrupt and broken. This broken character of the country extends all the way to the mountains with dividing ridges over which travel is possible. To drive a wagon through the Bad Lands would, I think, be impossible. To take a horse through, unless you were familiar with the best passes, would be a terrible undertaking. The character of this belt of land and its forbidding and sterile appearance have an important bearing upon the migrations of the Indian family. The country will be more particularly described going down. Fort Benton which we shall reach in 4 or five days is at the foot of the mountains and but 195 miles from the Bitter Root valley on the opposite side of the chain.

Muscle Shell River, Monday, 2 P.M. June 16

We have just passed the mouth of this small stream, and in about an hour will come in sight of the Little Rocky Mountains, a detached group of mountains lying about 40 miles north of the river. I thought we had passed the place this morning but was mistaken. The tracks of the mountain sheep on the sides of the almost perpendicular bluffs are still abundant. We are often quite near them. In some places the banks are of clay and fine brown sand, looking quite dark, and the tracks stand out with singular distinctness in straight lines, the steps alternating about four or five inches apart [Morgan sketches the lines of tracks], sometimes parallel with the water, others perpendicular, others curving.

Beaver Tree Cutting

Yesterday about 20 miles below the Muscle Shell I obtained the stump of a fine cottonwood which measured 3 ft. 11 inches in circumference and is 15 inches in diameter. It is some larger than the first. While stoping for wood one of the passengers caught a young beaver in a scoop net while swimming in the river. He is about a month old and now on board. Fanny Culbertson also has one given to her at Fort Union, so that we can see their performances daily. The latter one is tame. We also have an eagle in a cage with his wing only injured and a young bull buffalo calf which we caught some distance below. An hour ago I shot at an elk in the river with just the head out. My first ball went over her head, the second barrel I fired at the same instant Campbell[139] did, or a second first, and the elk dropped her head dead. Campbell claimed the killing. I did not see his ball or mine strike. Neither did the bystanders. I think we both hit, but I may not. Culbertson gave the shot to me. F. De Smet to Campbell. A wolf was shot at the same time under the bank. He was after the elk. I shot from the stern of the boat and we did not stop to get it. I wanted very much to know how many balls her head would show, and the size which would have settled the question.

Opposite Little Rocky Mountains,
June 17, 1862

The range on the maps of this name on the north side of the river is now nearly opposite us. Yesterday afternoon I went to the top of the hills after specimens for Ward and saw this range above us to the north west. It was about 40 miles off and some ten miles above.

Meldrum's wife I have mentioned before. He took her at the age of seven years from the Blackfeet and she is now 26. Her sister was also taken. She was 14 and remembered her mother's and father's name. The last one is now dead. Neither of them have seen their mother since. This mother is now at Fort Benton, and her daughter expects to see her for the first time in 19 years. Meldrum told me she was much pleased with the idea. It will be an affecting spectacle particularly on the mother's part. The Indian woman, whatever else she may be, is a tender mother. It will be to her a great happiness to see her lost child.

Specimens

Just above Emmet's Island on the west side in Bad Lands I found high up a brown ammonite, the best yet, and with it two specimens of the sandstone rock which crops out in fugitive masses. We are yet below Judith River but near it, 150 miles from Fort Benton. We have just passed some remarkable bluffs rising 500 feet and assuming fantastic forms, looking like masonry, mostly brown clay, with heavy masses of brownstone cropping out here and there and dipping in different directions, and some naked peaks of rock. It cannot be described. We have just got a black tail deer and shot 2 buffalo cows in the river before dinner and took them on board. We also blazed away at a wolf crossing the river without killing and saw antelope and wild geese. Later in the day at Snake Point, south side, 140 miles below Fort Benton, I found 3 fine specimens of petrified wood and F. De Smet two shells, and another person one or two.

Prairie Dog Village

Yesterday F. De Smet called my attention to one of the villages. It was on a light grass bottom, without trees, and the row of huts which resembled ant hills, was about ten rods back from the bank. We did not see any out. There were 30 or 40 burrows.

Above Little R[ocky] M[ountains]
Wednesday Morning, June 18, 1862

The scenery on the river continues to be very fine, approaching the grand. All day yesterday and today we are shut in by great walls of clay seamed here and there with rock. The river is less than a quarter of a mile wide, and the walls are less than half a mile, the cutting against one wall or the other usually the south one. As the river winds constantly, we have three walls, in fact four, one on each side of us and one front and rear. In looking back we cannot see the river for more than half a mile and the same ahead. These clay banks assume many fantastic architectural forms, and out of them an order of architecture might be studied. The abutments in a series, one below another, are arranged to give solidity to the clay fabric, sometimes rounded in a half circle. Sometimes a pillar capped with stone with niches, panels, mantles over fire places, battlements, fountains, pinnacles, cones, round towers, and so on.

Mountain Sheep or Big Horn

Several of these were seen this morning climbing the hills and one yesterday. I have not as yet seen one. They are said to be numerous in the Bad Lands which extend along the river for at least five hundred miles to Fort Benton.

Wednesday, June 19,[140] 1862

Cordelling Boat

Yesterday we came about 25 miles, passing over three rapids over which the boat was cordelled. Two ropes were sent ashore and fifty men took one and thirty the other and drew the boat through. At night we reached one harder than the others, and one of the ropes broke and we fell back and tied up for the night. In the morning they took out an anchor and secured it above the rapid and then used the capstan which is worked by steam and we thus went through it before we were up. We are now about 100 miles from the Fort.

Prairie Dog Villages

Yesterday we passed another of these villages. I saw the dogs sitting on the little mounds into which their hole enters. They are of a reddish brown color and a little larger than a squirrel. At night we tied up by one and I went out to see the holes. A little mound is thrown up made by the excavation and the hole descends into the centre of it. It looks like a little crater. The hole, which is about five inches in diameter, turns under and they say their holes are connected under ground. They select a bottom where the grass is light with no trees, where grasshoppers and ants are likely to be abundant. Some of the passengers saw them and heard them bark or chirup as they approached the hole.

I should have stated before that this boat [the *Spread Eagle*] intended to go as far as the water would allow and the small boat [the *Key West*] was brought along to make the rest of the trip. It usually goes to Milk River. The present year the June rise exceeds all former ones known to the oldest residents, which means for 40 years and the large boat [the *Spread Eagle*] has decided to go on to Fort Benton.[141] It has never been done before. The *Emilie* also has gone on. We expect to be there by Saturday. Yesterday near the rapids F. De Smet procured seeds of the white onion [?] for me.

Mandan Tribes [Clans][142]

1. Ho′ -ra-ta′ -nu-mäke	Wolf Tribe
2. Mä-to′ -wo-mäke	Bear ″
3. See-poosh′ -kä	Prairie chicken
4. Tä-ma′ -tsu-ka	Good Knife
5. Me′ -te-ä′ -ke	High Village
6. E′ -stä-pa′	Tattooed
7. Ki-tä′ -ne-mäke	Eagle (Brown and yellow)

A man cannot marry a woman of his own tribe and the children are of the tribe of the mother. From Joseph Kipp, and the Minetare chief. Joseph Kipp's mother is of the See-poosh′ -kä tribe, and he is of the same.

White Earth Walls or Stone Wall Bluffs

We are now passing the most remarkable bluffs on the river. A whitish clay, indurated, and bearing the appearance of rock, rises up upon a foundation of brownish earth in perpendicular cliffs from 100 to 200 feet with deep recesses, and looking like mined walls of immense buildings with pinnacles, columns capped with stone— niches, battlements, on the grandest scale. Lewis and Clark named them, I am told, the white walls. They stand up like round castle keeps[143] adjoining long walls, the base line of which is extremely sinuous.

On the tops we see almost all forms, the effect of water, statues, urns, vases, steam boats, for there is one called the steam boat standing by itself. At first they were confined to the north side. Now they appear on both. The earth is of a whitish color, not a rock, but a clay or a friable sandstone. It cannot be described, that is, the grand and stupendous forms which it assumes. It is the castellated formation which repeats itself in the West in so many forms. [Morgan has a sketch of these walls and cliffs here.]

Tariff of American Fur Company, 1833–59

1 Buffalo Robe	=Standard of Value
1 Cup Sugar	=1 Robe
1 Lb. Tobacco	=1 ”
1 Cup Coffee	=1 ”
1 Gun	=10 ”
2½ Pound Blanket	=3 ”
1 Saddle	=6 ”
1 Bridle	=1 ”
2 Knives	=1 ”
25 loads ammunition	=1 Robe
¼ yard Scarlet cloth	=1 ”
1½ Calico	=1 ”
3 Pd. Blanket	=4 ”
1 Gallon Kettle	=1 ”
2 ” ”	=2 ”
3 ” ”	=3 ”
10 ” ”	=10 ”

This from Mr. Alexander Culbertson, who executed the exchange. After 1859 there was an advance. They now give 3 cups of sugar and one of coffee for a robe. The nominal price is 4 dollars—sugar and coffee at a dollar the pound, and calico at a dollar the yard. But it must be remarked that the goods were carried up in keel boats by the cordel process for years on the Upper Mississippi, and by traces [?] I suppose to Fort Pierre and perhaps to Fort Union.

Last evening at 6 o'clock we passed the mouth of Judith River, a small stream which comes in from the south. We also saw in the north the Bear's Paw Mountain. It looked grandly as it rose out of the plain about 40 miles off. The main part is a regular dome about 3000 feet high, F. De Smet estimates it, with a spur jutting out to the north west [Morgan has a sketch here]. It receives this name from the configuration of the spur.

We are now about 70 miles from Fort Benton and 35 by land. We may reach there late tomorrow if the next rapid does not detain us long. For the last 200 miles there has been but little wood. We have used dead and fallen pieces chiefly until yesterday when we had some cord wood cut on an island by the Company for the boat.

PART VII

[We have omitted comparative vocabularies of Mandan, Gros Ventres of the Prairie, and Crow—names of body parts, common names such as sun, bow, fire, etc.—about eight pages in all.]

It will be seen that the Crow and Minnetare vocables are quite unlike, the greater part of them, a few are identical, and others are partially similar. Meldrum says that the Minnetare words have lost syllables. He says he can follow the language with great difficulty and make out some part of it through the Crow, and that the Minnetare can understand the Crow better than the latter the former, and that the Minnetare can adopt the Crow idiom form or dialectical difference easier than the Crow can the Minnetare. When he meets one, he gets them to talk poor Crow rather than attempt himself to talk poor Minnetare.

[Again Morgan has many pages of comparative vocabularies of Crow and Mandan, of Blackfoot, Dakota, and Crow geographical names, Crow numerals, etc.]

Thursday, June 19, 1862, White Wall Bluffs

We stopped an hour ago to take on wood and I went back under the white earth cliffs for specimens for Ward. I brought back one specimen of the white earth rock which is a friable sandstone of a greyish white, one of gneiss, one of brown sand stone. These are the three kinds which appear so grandly now on both sides of the river, and have for some fifteen miles. Nine tenths or more is the white earth. The gneiss shoots [?] up in spires, pinnacles, and always in irregular and vertical masses. The brown stone appears to run in beds two or three feet thick, horizontal, and sometimes two of them fifty feet apart, and above them the summit layer of white earth rock. I think in some places I have seen it above the white rock. F. De Smet brought me a fine specimen of gneiss, and also the large round ball which will weigh ten pounds. I got a small one in another place, and saw others. They were split into disks and segments.

The scenery continues to increase in interest as we ascend. With a little aid from the imagination you can see everything in the nature of man's work. Just below on the north is a cathedral of gneiss standing above upon a high base, with a low tower in front. Just below a sand slide is good copy of a walled city of great extent of which you see two sides looking down the river, with towers, domes, buttresses, battlements, and other appointments of the same kind. We have just passed on the south side a cathedral wall of immense extent, through one of which walls is a hole near the top which at the distance of two miles and at an elevation of from 400 to 500 feet from the river appears to be two feet in diameter. It must be ten or 12 feet, and looks like an oval window. Along the tops of these walls are vases, urns, sentinels, spires, turrets, balls, and capped balls.[144] Everyone on the boat is enthusiastic. F. De Smet says he has seen nothing more grand west of the mountains. We must now be about 60 to 70 miles from Fort Benton.

The first steamer came up in 1831 to Fort Pierre and in 1832 to Fort Union, since which time the Fur Co. has sent up a steamer annually, and for a few years a small one to Fort Benton.[145]

[Three pages of notes on the scenery have been omitted.]

Friday Morning, June 20, 1862

We are now wooding at a place twenty-five miles below Fort Benton and expect to be there by noon. The *Emilie* went down yesterday,[146] and I must carry my own letter home. Our boat will start on her down trip, and I think we shall make it to St. Joseph in ten days, which would bring us there the 30th of June. The river is higher now by 5 to six feet than ever known before, and it makes an immense difference on the question of sand bars on which so much time is lost. The full current also helps the boat and we shall run 250 miles per day from 3 A.M. to 10 P.M.

It is a delightful morning, with a bright sky and a cool air. There was a fire in the saloon this morning. It is about like a June day in Rochester in the fore part of June, but this is not an ordinary season here. It is late and cooler than usual. We have had no mosquitoes thus far in our rooms. They are around by day and are thick at midday on the bottoms, but the cool evenings keep them down. This has been an indescribable comfort. We have had no bed bugs either, greatly to my relief. The Missouri River boats are famous for this nuisance, as I know by experience in 1859 and 1860, but I understand that roaches destroy them, and there are a few of these on the boat. We see them and hear them occasionally. I have been told that they introduce them on the boats as a preventive, with how much of truth I know not.[147]

The passengers are overhauling their baggage and getting ready for the landing. There are upwards of sixty of them and they are an intelligent class of men, much above the ordinary run of adventurers, and they are full of hope. There is a party from St. Louis, David Risley, Mr. Smith, Mr. Lowthan, Nére Vallé, Mr. De Lane,[148] and one or two others who are secessionists and have left St. Louis to get away from the troubles incident to the rebellion. They are business men except De Lane, who is a young man in pursuit of health and pleasure. I should have enjoyed this expedition beyond all expression but for the one anxiety about my daughter Mary, and the unknown result of her sickness. At Sioux City I shall know the worst or the best and I begin to dread the heading downward of the boat. I know I must pass through a great excitement. May the slight hope on which I have rested prove real, and I shall again be one of the happiest of men.

Saturday, June 21, 1862, Fort Benton

We reached the Fort yesterday afternoon at 3 o'clock. We were detained about 3 hours at a rapid a mile below the Fort where a frightful accident occurred, resulting in the drowning of four men before our eyes, and the bare escape of three others. After an hour's work it was found impossible to get the boat over by steam. The mate, Jacob Saunders, took six men and the yawl and went up stream and secured the cordel rope to a tree, and then came down to the boat which steamed out into the current to meet it. The boat came down letting out rope and found the line exhausted a few feet ahead of the steam boat. Another rope was thrown and fastened to it, when the men held the yawl by the rope which was not yet secured on the steam boat. In attempting to let the yawl back to the boat in the rapid and powerful current she was thrown across the bow and capsized. Four of the men, including the mate, went into the river, three held to the rope, of whom two we got on board. The third was caught by the hand, but the man could not hold him without being drawn overboard, and he let him go. He was probably killed by the wheel which was not stopped, as he did not rise again. I saw three of the other four above water as they passed swiftly by within a few feet of me, and the fourth just the hair of his head which for a few moments was above the surface, and then went under. Saunders, who is a powerful man, kept up bravely, shouting as he went by "Lower the small boat, be quick." His brother was in it a moment, and another man, and they shot down the current after them. They continued in sight for a quarter of a mile, alternately sinking and rising, when finally the mate alone remained. He had gone under and risen two

TENS-QUA-TA-WA, THE SHAWNEE PROPHET

BY JAMES OTTO LEWIS

Painted at Detroit, this is "the open door," the Shawnee Prophet, brother of Tecumseh.
Tens-qua-ta-wa created a religious furor among the tribes of the Old Northwest in 1806
by announcing he had received a vision from the Master of Life. In the simplest terms he
preached a renunciation of White ideas and civilization and a return to the old ways of the
Indian. His influence over the tribes was lost at the battle of Tippecanoe in 1811. He later
removed to Kansas where he was interviewed and painted by Catlin in 1832.

Left: "Fort Benton — head of steam navigation on the Missouri River," by Gustav Sohon. The artist was also a member of the railroad survey party, but it is presumed he drew this view of Fort Benton between 1860-62. It first appeared in the report of Lt. John Mullan, published in 1863.

or three times. When the boat reached him and put out an oar, he went under again with the oar in his hand, but came up with it, was caught, and raised into the boat exhausted. They turned him on his face and made for the shore. At the end of ten minutes he was brought on board and became conscious. Today he is out, but scarcely able to stand. He looks like a tired man, entirely used up. He says he dove to escape death from the wheel, and was under so long that he was in such want of air, that he had to put his hand over his mouth, as he could not help but open it. He was an expert swimmer, but did not try to swim, as all he wished to do was to keep above water. Nothwithstanding all his efforts, the eddies in the stream were constantly drawing him under and took him under two or three times in spite of his exertions. The yawl and the bodies of the four other men went down the river and disappeared.[149]

About an hour before on coming in sight of the Fort, the passengers had held a meet-

Above: A view of Fort Benton from an early stereo photograph. The fort, built in 1846, was named for Senator Thomas H. Benton (although it was first called Fort Clay), and was the most important trading center in Montana.

ing, passed resolutions of thanks to the officers and men and congratulating each other on the successful termination of the expedition, and the pleasure it had afforded, and concluding with the use of a basket of champagne.

It was a sorrowful accident and cast a gloom over the company. I hope I may never witness another such a scene.

At the next attempt the steam boat went up the rapid by crowding steam which made us apprehensive of another accident which might involve us all. But we went through safe.

The Fort gave us the usual reception by firing a cannon several times, but we took no interest in it.

Fort Benton[150] like Fort Union is a quadrangle about 200 to 250 feet square with bastions at two of the alternate angles. Inside are the house of the chief trader, Andrew Dawson, the ware houses, stores, tenements, and cattle yard. It is built of large adobe brick made of mud and straw, with the walls of the buildings about 3 to four feet thick. About 70 men, women, and children live in the Fort. There are about 20 Blackfeet tents pitched around on the three sides of the tent [fort]. All of these, with the passengers, make quite a crowd. Yesterday evening and today they are unloading. It was expected that we would start today on our return, but I now understand it will not be until tomorrow. Of course I am impatient to return.

Last evening I went up on the highest bluff to see if I could see any of the peaks of the Rocky Mountains at or near the foot of which great chain we now are. On the south west the Belt Mountains rise up grandly out of the plains. To the north east the Bear's Paw Mountains appeared, each range rising about 3000 feet. The Rocky Moun-

tain peaks are not in sight. You do not see them until quite near as the eastern declivity is gentle. At the Falls of the Missouri which are but 25 miles west of this place two of the peaks are distinctly visible. I feared to leave the boat or I would have rode there expressly to see them, but I am satisfied to have had it in my power, by an afternoon ride, to see with my own eyes this one of the great land marks of the physical world.

It is hot today and the mosquitoes are abundant, but it was cool last night and will be again tonight.

Twilight—Its Lateness

Last night at ½ past 9 I could see the time on the dial plate of my watch. By the boat time it was ¼ to 10. On a white face I have no doubt the time can be read at half past ten.

Tame Buffalo Cow

There is a tame full grown buffalo cow in a small herd of domestic cattle pasturing near by. She is fat. Shows the buffalo complete and perfectly tame.

Sunset

Last evening I went up on the bluff back of the Fort, which rises from 250 to 300 feet, to witness a sunset behind the Rocky Mountains, although themselves invisible. It was a grand spectacle. The horizon in its complete circle was the dead level of the prairie except the Bear's Paw, and the Belt Mountain above mentioned and a slight swell in the west. As the last rays were fading away, I thought of home, my wife, and children, and especially my darling Mary. Was she in the spirit land, or among the living?

Monday, June 23, 1862, Homeward Bound

We left Fort Benton yesterday at 3½ P.M. and ran down 100 miles, passing before evening entirely through the White Walls and enjoying once more this grand scene under the most favorable circumstances. The second visit does not weaken but rather increases the admiration and wonder excited. The steam boat, the cathedral, the ruined castle, the spires and pinnacles look grand in their grotesqueness.

Grizzly Bears

Last evening we saw two large bears of this kind on opposite sides of the river. They are brown, nearly black, and very large. They run with a gallop. I shot at one of them at 200 yards and shot over him.

Mountain Sheep

We also saw three different bands of the bighorn sheep about a dozen in a band. They are something of the color of the antelope, but a little heavier. Most of them were females. They ran along the cliffs at a furious rate and it was a beautiful sight. These bluffs are full of them and their tracks are seen abundantly. Above Fort Benton, and opposite, they are all over the bank. I am glad to have seen this singular animal, and did not know before that he was found away from the mountains this side.

On the down current our boat runs about 18 miles per hour. At this rate we can make St. Joseph in ten or eleven days. But at this season the boat is often obliged to lay by for wind storms which blow the boat ashore. We have also less men to cut wood. We shall at all events make a quick trip.

It is cool this morning. An overcoat would not be uncomfortable. The men have just been shooting at buffalo at 300 yards. We saw them yesterday and antelope, but none in the river as yet.

Left: The confluence of the Yellowstone and Missouri rivers, by Karl Bodmer. This graphic view of the fantastically shaped bluffs along the Missouri River on the Montana-North Dakota boundary once again demonstrates the artistic ability of Karl Bodmer.

PART VIII

Medicine Lodge of Crows
Meldrum

[This is an account of the Sun Dance, a ceremony performed by most of the Plains tribes. Morgan is apparently recording as Meldrum dictated.]

The medicine lodge is usually set up by a person who has lost a near relative, that is, some such person starts the work and it then is made a national [tribal] affair in which the whole nation assists and participates. It is not annual. I have known three made in a year, and three and four years without any. They will do it at any season, but if in summer it is covered with brush, if in winter with buffalo skins.

In the first instance a medicine lodge is announced by some person as about to be set up. The first thing done is to collect buffalo tongue and choice pieces of meat. This is continued for 8 or 10 days and they are for feasting the people. The day and place are announced in advance. They always arrive and encamp on the ground in the evening which ends the week of the first day. Next morning the first thing is to go and select the poles for the lodge. When this is done there is one certain tree which is taken out for the first. This tree must be cut by a virtuous woman, not a virgin. The man that makes the medicine lodge selects and calls out the woman. She says "If there is any person in the nation [tribe] who says I am not fit to cut this tree as a chaste woman let them come forward and say it." If no one says nay she cuts the tree. In some cases the woman is accused and set aside.

Chastity is the qualification for cutting the tree. As soon as the tree is cut, the top branches are removed and the tree is taken off into the prairie. They then call out for the bravest man in the nation [tribe], and after a committee of ten or twelve persons have decided who is the bravest person they compliment him by giving to him this tree, which is usually 40 feet long and is made the centre pole of the lodge. It is his property although it remains standing with the lodge. After this 9 other poles are cut, trimmed and carried out on to the prairie and laid side and side. They are cut by anybody. These are assigned as honors to nine other persons who have distinguished themselves for bravery. This is one of their modes of bestowing honors. After this 26 other poles are cut for the lodge, 36 being used in all. No more, no less. The 26 are not assigned. The poles are then hauled to the ground selected around which the tents are already pitched. Four poles of the nine and the centre pole are then tied with raw hide and are then raised up. As soon as they are raised a dried scalp is tied to the centre pole about 6 feet from the ground. The remaining 31 poles are then raised up and put in their places. If in the summer, the branches are cut and covered over the whole, tied on with dress cords so as to make it water proof. If in winter the lodge skins for a covering are prepared in advance. The poles are all 40 feet long, so that the diameter of the lodge would be from 30 feet to 40 feet.

As soon as it is covered they clean the grass from the inside of the tent and then cut two cedar trees about 4 inches in diameter and 8 or 10 feet long. These are planted in the west end of the lodge side and side, 8 or ten feet apart, a few feet from the edge. After they are planted, three rows

of white sand, the whitest they can get, are placed from the trees inward towards the centre pole. These rows are 8 feet long and a foot high, and about three feet apart. Between these rows the man who makes the medicine lodge dances during the ensuing ceremonies. This sand must be drawn by a person, a man who has never had carnal connection with his blood relatives on the father's side. They never, never infringe on the mother's side, and it is a disgrace to do it on the father's. The person selected by the man who makes the lodge says before the people "If I am not fit to carry the sand, take me away." There is usually no failure here.

The door of the lodge always opens to the East. Inside the lodge about 6 feet from the door a tripod and sometimes, two and three are put up to hang the kettles on to boil the tongues and meat, with three fires, if as many tripods. On each side of the cedar trees there is a hole dug in the ground about a foot deep and 8 inches in diameter, 2 in all. Behind these trees, the principal mourners come forward and sit down, men and women, and particularly the father or mother who has lost the child. These persons first bathe and rub white clay mixed with water so as to make a paste on the bodies, and also spot the hair with it. The men are nude except the breech-cloth (Bod-a-in′-cha-sä′-cha, Hide our forward side), and a lodge skin used as a robe. The women are nude except a skirt of skin tied around the waist, and extending to the knee, and a lodge skin robe, feet are bare. No vermilion on their faces. Mourners are not allowed to use vermilion. From the time they enter the lodge they neither eat nor drink during the time they remain in the lodge. Some can stand it but for a day, others two and three,

Left: This photograph is believed to be of a Sioux Sun Dance held on the Pine Ridge Reservation on July 29, 1883. The Nebraska State Historical Society has a series of photographs of this 1883 Sun Dance, but the photographer has not been identified.

Below: Sun Dance making chiefs, an artist's conception of the self-torture phase of the Sun Dance. This drawing shows both methods of self-torture used in the Sun Dance: the thongs through the chest, and the thongs through the back, weighted by buffalo skulls.

and some five days before exhaustion compels them to leave. They are allowed to smoke. There are no ceremonies inside the lodge the second day. This finishes the inside for that day.

Outside the lodge on the second day a second set of mourners, consisting of those who have lost their connection by the public enemies, and those inside as the same, take up the skin of the shoulder blades and run a knife through it always in two places, and run a cord under the skin about 12 feet long, one from each cut. These strings are attached to the dried skull of a bull buffalo, and these are dragged around the lodge. As they go, crying, they say "Ah-ha, our father, or E-sä′-kä-boa′-ta," "What formed

us" or the Great Spirit, "Make us fortunate" (us the nation) "Deliver us from diseases" "Furnish us with game, I am a man. I wish to be a man. Make us fortunate in raising colts or horses. Make the women fortunate in child birth. Raise up our children to become men and women. Deliver us from great cold weather. Deliver to us our enemies. My children have nothing to carry them (means give us horses)." I have seen at one time as many as 50 or 60 drawing skulls around the medicine lodge at one time on the second day. There is none after that. They drag them until the skin wears out and breaks loose. Sometimes it lasts five or six hours before this is done. I have often seen them fall down with exhaustion. They leave them there until they get up themselves. Their friends then take the cord out of the skin. They never ask to be cut loose, and they never do it themselves. Those who have fallen down often pretend they have seen the Great Spirit. It is common for their friends to go up and ask them if they have seen the Great Spirit or have had any manifestation of him. If they say not they remain. If they say they have, they are then cut loose and taken away. Sometimes they say "I have seen the Great Father and he has made me glad." This is all that is said at the time, the particulars are not sought.

The second day in the morning the man who made the medicine lodge, and if two, the two dress in their own lodge with a skirt of skin from the waist to the knee and otherwise nude, take a doll or image of a man fully formed about eight inches long, which is an old relic which they say they got from Mexico centuries ago. There are eight of these in the nation, all of which came from the same place they say, and which are kept for these occasions and

loaned to the person or persons who make the lodge. If two, two are used. They are sent in by them and tied on to each tree. This must face the East. They belong to the nation [tribe]. In the evening of the second day as soon as they come out of their lodge they commence dancing and dance the whole way to the medicine lodge which they enter, and then put their arm around the cedar tree and kiss the tree. They dance up to the tree the first thing they do. The medicine lodge before this was open to anyone who desired to enter. Inside they do their dancing between the rows of sand. They have down taken from the tail or root of the tail of the eagle tied on each little finger, and a bone taken out of the wing of the eagle made into a whistle. This is attached around the neck. They raise this to their mouth from the neck and blow it. The singers come in after them, mostly men, who sit in front of the cedars and outside of the rows of sand in a semicircle, while the inside mourners are behind the trees. If women singers join, they sit behind the men. The singers have the drum only, which is a circle, a skin stretched over a hoop like a tambourine. It is beat with one stick. There are about 12 of these, one to about every singer.

After this the names of distinction, not those who took the honors of the 9 poles, but were recognized as braves and had perhaps taken them on former occasions, come in with their wives and mothers, and seat themselves between the sand rows and the lodge poles. Their wives bring in the arms, such as guns, lances, bows and arrows, and axes taken by them in war. At the same time the one or two who set up the lodge commence the first dance, and dance for seven or 8 minutes. At the close of this dance one of the braves says "Attention. I have come

to tell you what I have done." This he goes on to do, giving a brief account of the principal events of his life. At such a time and in such a party I struck my enemy, and took their arms. He then raises up the weapon referred to. (The scalps taken belong to the captain of the war party.) If he did not take the weapon fairly, some one disputes his claim. Then he is not allowed to lay it down. That ends it, and it is thrown away. If it is not disputed he lays it down. It is then his honor and it can never afterwards be disputed. Then the dance goes on again as before. At the end of the dance another does the same, and this continues until all have spoken. (Something like the speeches in the Iroquois war dance.)

Before the dance commences a fire is made in the two holes by the side of the cedar trees and is fed with dried juniper twigs and leaves which emit a pleasant odor or smoke. One person is assigned to each fire and keeps it going through the whole time the ceremonies of the lodge continues. It fills the lodge with its fragrance. The mourners and the nation [tribe] in the meanwhile are calling on the Great Spirit and other spirits for benefits, and it is probable that their idea is that their prayers ascend to the powers above with the smoke.

After a brave has finished speaking and before a new dance is started any one of the mourners or any other person can by a rap call attention and the musicians by a roll of their drums repeat it. Then this person gets up and, raising up both hands and says, looking up, "Father of all things, that formed the earth and all that is in it, we as a nation, bow down and do this for you. Have pity upon us. Make us fortunate. We have suffered as a nation from our enemies. Now we wish revenge. Not that it will bring the dead to life. The people who have killed our

fathers, our mothers, our wives and children, deliver them into our hands." This is a general form usual to such occasions, and the same ideas are repeated in different ways by different persons. Up to this time no one is admitted to the lodge, or rather enters except the braves to tell their exploits, the mourners, the dancers, the musicians, and the keepers of the fire. But the people outside hear all that is going on.

As soon as the dance commences the pot or pots containing the tongues and meat are already cooking. As soon as the first man has finished his narrative of his exploits, a tongue is removed from the pot by a woman appointed to supervise the feast and is presented to him. He takes it off the stick and gives it to some woman who he desires to compliment or win as a wife. It is given to an unmarried woman. It is an honor to a woman to receive a tongue from the medicine lodge. It usually has reference to marriage, but she is not obliged nor her friends to accept. It is a mere overture. Such compliments please the fancy of the girl, and is often mentioned by them as an honor ever afterwards.

Each one who states his exploits and is not questioned receives a tongue and it is disposed of in this way. These ceremonies continue until about midnight and thus this part of the ceremony is ended.

On the same day after the dance is over and as the last thing done, two buffalo robes never used are brought in to the lodges. One of them is laid down and upon it the dancer or dancers if there be two, lays down upon it, and is covered with the other. The mourners remain in the lodge and thus ends the second day.

Third Day

The first thing in the morning is to raise up the dancers. This is done by one of the oldest chiefs. He has a bowl with white clay and water in it. The old man rubs him over with white clay. At this time the musicians come in. As soon as the clay dries on his body the dancer commences the dance and the same ceremonies are gone through with which marked the second day within the lodge. Shortly after the dance commences, those young men who wish to become great warriors come into the lodge and strings are inserted in each breast by cutting with a knife as in the former case. Sometimes a stick or piece of wood is put through the cut and the cord tied to each end of it on each side. The two cords are then attached to the centre pole and they then commence leaning back so as to draw on the skin. They then commence a howl or cry, which lasts near an hour, during which they circled around the pole a short way and back with their face turned upward. All this time they dance and the narrative of personal exploits is going on. All the bystanders, friends, and relatives at the time cry and howl with them, making it an awful scene to witness. I [Meldrum] have seen 20 thus tied to the centre pole at one time. Oftener more than less, and of those outside hundreds of them, for it seems nearly all participate. During their crying, those on the string call upon the Great Spirit the same as those who draw the horns. The people outside as they cry name the names of the dead in war for whom they are mourning. They ask the dead to look at them and do something for them to make them fortunate, that they can intercede with the Great Father to make them fortunate in peace and war. This is continued for about an hour by

which time the string in some cases pulls out the skin when the person thus liberated retires, but in some cases it holds for four or five hours. In the meantime the dance continues.

After these are disposed of and in case any of them fall from faintness, the string is cut by the relatives on the father's side. Then new persons come in. They are usually young men in all cases who undergo this self torture under 20 years of age. These come in naked except the breech cloth with whips in their hands and lash their legs and body. All the time crying and saying "My mother has got nothing to ride (no horse). My sisters are poor. (Me, myself) I wish to become a man, i.e., a chief. Make me fortunate." This continues about an hour or less. None of these people eat or drink until the end of the medicine lodge. Those who have been tied to the pole and have fallen exhausted often say to those who inquire that they have seen the Great Spirit and are pleased with what they saw, but not telling what it was. They are then free to go home. It is an end of the ceremony with them. Others remained five, six and even seven days until they were nearly skeletons and were then sent away without receiving any recitation as they call it from the Spirit World.

Others go out in the hills during the third day in sight of the medicine lodge and remain there without eating or drinking during the time of the medicine lodge and sometimes longer, very often cutting off their fingers at the first joint, one or more of them. These are saved in a willow bowl, and are left in the lodge tied to the centre pole. I have never seen less than 40 fingers left at a medicine.[151] They cut them off with a knife and as they do say "I give this to the sun. I expect that this will not be

lost. I and my people will have not lost it entire." They expect payment of some kind from the Great Spirit.

Fourth Day

The dance continues, the fast continues, but no bulls horns are drawn after the second day, and none are tied to the pole after the third; but the dances and the speeches continue until about the fifth day when they go out of the lodge, the one who set up the lodge taking the lead. I have known it continued for seven days and never less than three. The last number is considered a poor one (lodge). The lodge is left entire, except the scalp and image and cooking utensils which are removed. The lodge skins are left if it is winter. I never knew one to die from fatigue on these occasions, but I have known many of them to so far injure their constitutions as never to recover from it. Some of them are taken up nearly dead.

The medicine lodge, Meldrum says, is set up for revenge. There is no return of thanks for past favors, but only a supplication and self torment to obtain the favor of the Great Spirit in their future enterprises against their enemies. The old people dread the medicine lodge, the young like it. The ceremony is not addressed to the bad spirit. They say there is such a spirit but they seldom mention him. The lodge is to invoke the Great Spirit alone. The sun they call the Father of light, Sä-sa-ruh'-sha. Ah-hä-sha, the sun. The sun is not invoked. The sun is not worshipped by the Crows. It is common in smoking to send smoke towards the sun. When lighting a pipe a Crow will lift the end of the stem and point it toward the sun and say "Smoke." They then bring it down to the ground and say smoke, then toward the place where they think the moon

Crow Indians, by Karl Bodmer. Bodmer managed to portray several Crow costumes in this illustration.

is and say the same and then towards the morning star, saying the same. They call the morning star E-ka-deh′-ha. E-ka—an egg, deh′-ha, bright. They get up in the morning and look at it and I have known them to cry facing it, saying "Have pity upon me. Make me fortunate. Make me healthy. Preserve my family." They say they are ashamed to look at the sun. It is too bright. When they address a prayer to the sun they say "Father of Light, we are weak, you are powerful. You know what we want better than we do ourselves. Do what is right. Be good to us." Medicine Lodge, Is-kis′-sha= Worship; Great Medicine, Mam-bali[?]-päk= [blank]

Ceremonies for the Benefit of the Nation [*Tribe*]

Ahk-bä-shu′-su. It is bought. There is a class of persons among the Crows who are called by this name. They buy the privilege of serving in this capacity from the old people who have served before them with goods and horses. Hence the name. They are about equal in their position to the Iroquois "Keepers of the Faith." The purchase is of the medicine bag which contains each different article, e.g., the weasel, the skin of it. The medicine bag is made of elk skin. Bä-da-ish′-sha, name for medicine bag. A pheasant's skin, head, feet, and tail on. A

belt of otter skin, which he wears around his waist. Tobacco seed, the native plant. This is the bag of the Minnetare chief. It contains some smaller articles.

The Crows and Minnetares have religious ceremonies regularly at the new and full moon throughout the year. The medicine men are looked to to secure favorable weather, the health of the people, good crops, the growth of the grass, the safe birth of children. In a word, the chief necessities of the people. They perform their religious ceremonies for the people free of charge.

New Moon Ceremonies

At the new moon there is a general meeting of the medicine men called by those who have provided the corn, sugar, and coffee, bread, meat, and any kind of fruit or berries which they gather themselves, and collect for a feast on this occasion. As soon as they come together they commence singing. They make a bed of coals, and then burn pine leaves, or any herb which they may have or sweet grass, and thus raise a species of incense. They hold each of them their medicine bag in the smoke. They then sing, sitting in a ring. The person who gives the feast gives the Im-poh′-ha or raw hide rattle filled with gravel to the person sitting at the right from the inside of the lodge as they speak, but on the left as you enter the lodge door. The ceremony is at the house of the persons who give the feast. Usually three families unite and turn their tents into one so as to accommodate 60 or 70 persons. The feast is prepared in advance.

They meet at early evening usually. They then sing their medicine song. Very often they all join in the song but the song is led by the one who holds the rattle. When this is done he hands the rattle to the next and he leads a second song in which all join, and so on around. Each is sort of prayer asking for a particular favor. He [the Minnetare chief] is now singing the first song he learned, the Minnetare chief—Dah-pee-to-a-push, Nose of the Bear or face. Black Fish, Boo-a-she-pish-ish. His real name. He has given the other away although is still called by it—who went up with us to Fort Benton and is now returning. Meldrum thus translated the words. "The buffalo are coming. We will feed and feast. We wish to be fortunate and we expect it." This is one song. It is a regular song, the words being in a sort of monotone. He has just sung the second. It takes one or two minutes with the accompaniments. 2nd song. "I want the robes, the skins of the game animals, the meat of the game animals. Bring them to me. Let us enjoy ourselves." 3rd song. "Spring from the earth, food for our children. Give us good health. Let us grow up, and become ripe." 4th song. "If the clouds come good, our tobacco will grow. We will be happy." Each of the preceding he has sung. Meldrum gave me the meaning. He says all of these are their devotions to the Great Spirit to make them live long and happy, etc. Their medicine bags they can sell and it carries with it a special and absolute property in the several songs which belong to the bag, or the single song as the case may be. These songs and bags are of great value in their estimation and it is not uncommon to give a horse for a bag and even for one song a bag. No one has a right to sing the songs of a bag not his own, although he may perhaps assist the proprietor. I saw a

Blackfoot medicine bag at Fort Benton which I was told the present owner gave two horses for. The medicine men receive no fees for their ceremonies. They have a full feast out of it and that appears to be the only profit. They believe the Great Father blesses their ceremonies by granting the good sought. Hence some of them assert they can make it rain. Others that they can bring the buffalo, and they may believe it in the same manner that Christians believe their prayers are sometimes specially answered. The medicine of the Indian is a misnomer. It means a religious ceremony or an act of worship. Nothing more, nothing less, accompanied when performed for sick persons with such forms as to show the extent of the superstition which penetrates their faith and worship. The Crows are regular in the observance of the new and old moon ceremonies throughout the year and when we remember the severity of the self-inflicted torments which they undergo, it is no mean evidence of the deep religious fervor implanted in their hearts and of the natural fortitude of their natures.

These several songs are named after the different objects in the several bags. Thus the Minnetare chief has the song of the weasel, the song of the pheasant. All of the bags contain the seed of tobacco. These ceremonies are addressed to the Great Author of all things. [Numbers 1, 2, and 3 do not appear. Whether Morgan copied from previous notes and omitted them or whether they were left out for some other reason we do not know.] 4. Song of the weasel. It is the song of the weasel, but relates to the horse into which he changes himself. We wish a drove of weasels transmuted into horses. The words are repeated and the syllables contain this meaning. With it is an imitation of the cry of the weasel. 5.

Song of the pheasant. "My child, I do this for you. I give this to you." The principal part of this song is an imitation of the strutting of the pheasant, his manner of carrying his head, and some other peculiarities. 6. Song of the elk, about a minute long. It is supposed that the elk in their whistling are courting, and in singing the song of the elk they are doing the same thing. The elk invokes the Great Spirit in their place. The words are "Bring them to me. Bring them to me. Bring them to me." This is asking of the Great Spirit matrimonial favors. The song of the elk for this reason brings a large price. 7. Song of the Bear. In this song they imitate the motion of the bear in walking and running as they sing. This song relates to war. They do not invoke the aid of the Great Spirit but ask the bear to do it for them. The words are "Make my heart as powerful as your own. Lead me to conquer." They think the bear has influence with the G[reat] S[pirit]. When out on a war party they will add words to this by means of which through the bear they invoke the G. S. 8. Everything in existence belongs to some person or animal or thing. Therefore they address the G. S. through these animals or the gun or the bow. 9. Song of the White Man. They think the white man has great influence with Great Spirit, and this song is often used. Anything which comes from the white man is a symbol of him and as such goes in the bag. He is now singing it, tapping the table as he sings to mark time. It is longer than most of them, about a minute and a half. The words or purport of the syllables is, Yellow Eyes, look at me and look for me. Let me see. They call the white man "yellow eyes." This is strictly their name for the French. They call the Americans "Long Knives." 10. Song of the Gun. "What we charge upon.

Eat them for us." The song contains it but he afterwards repeats in words to Meldrum what words the symbols contain. The symbol of the gun is not represented in the bag. They fear the gun. Each one is sold separately.

Minnetare Language

Song of the Gun   Oo-wä-za-ue-zä-ho-ka
  "   "   " White Man   Mä-she-e′ -de-sheh
  "   "   " Weasel   Oo′ -se-sa-e′ -de-sheh
  "   "   " Bear   Dähk′ -pit-za-e-de-sheh
  "   "   " Elk   Bä-ro′ -ka-e-de-sheh
  "   "   " Pheasant   Sesch′ -ka-e′ -de-sheh
  "   "   " Bald Eagle   E′ -pä-tuck-e

They have no rain song but they invoke the Great Spirit for rain through birds. Particularly the bald eagle, who, they think, has special influence with the Great Spirit in giving rain. They think thunder is a bird, that the lightning is the flash of the eye and therefore they ask for rain through the song of different birds. The man who has the eagle song in his bag often secures a present to sing it for rain. If it rains in 24 hours or in a reasonable time, he keeps it. Otherwise they take it back under the belief that his medicine or ceremony is bad or without virtue. Song of the bald eagle. E′ -pä-tuck-e. Both ends white. "We want what is real. We want what is real. Don't deceive us." Song for women in child birth. He did not want to give it. He is afraid we will take his medicine away by putting it on paper. He says he has given us a good deal.

Planting Festival. Crows

The hunting season commences ten days before the planting. They want the buffalo marrow bones and the tongues for this festival so they make a hunt to get them. This is the largest feast in the year. On their arrival on the ground where they intend to plant they first collect wood or sticks of the size of the finger and lay it on the old garden beds and the whole is burnt over. They then dig it up with hoes, formerly with hoes made of elk horns. After the ground is made ready for the seed, in the morning just after sun rise, they go and plant the seeds (never in the evening) corn, beans, squashes, and tobacco. More of the last than all of the others. This ground is staked off to keep each family's lot separate. After the crop is put in and they move away, they next make four short encampments, that is, go for a short distance each day. They are not there again until [word undecipherable; looks a bit like "conscience"] brings them there, or until the crop is half grown. Tobacco needs no cultivation.

The first evening before the seeds are planted, a feast is made and given to those who gather the wood, burn the ground, and dig it up. No one partakes but those who do the work. The next day, before the seeds are planted, which are steeped in water 4 days, they go through four different dances. 1. E-de-su′. Beginning Dance. Men and Women. 2. Seet′ -ka-e′ -de-su. Prairie chicken Dance. 3. Oh′ -ha, Antelope Dance. 4. Dah-peet-za′ -e′ -de-su. Bear Dance. The seeds are then laid down with the hand and covered with the earth and pressed down with the hand. They dance then to the Bear, the chicken, and the Antelope. There is some connection of these animals with the crop. The dance is a form of worship to the Great Spirit.

When the tobacco blossoms and the seed leaf [tassel?] of the corn appears, they dance and sing again. So also when the corn silks they do the same. When they gather the corn they do it again. They boil the corn, and eat it as hominy. They also parch it when ripe, pound it into flour, mix grease with it and use it on war parties and for lunches at home. It is eaten dry. Beans are eaten in the camp. They are not fond of beans. They won't eat them green. The squash they dry and carry with them.

Tuesday, June 24, 1862
Above Milk River

We started with 22 boat hands and about 30 mountaineers, all of whom worked in wooding. We now have 18 boat hands, having lost four by the casualty before referred to, and three or four mountaineers going down who assist in getting wood. We stop twice a day and it takes from an hour and a half to two hours to take in a supply. The boat needs 25 cords per day. When in motion we move at a wonderful rate, in some places 18 and even 20 miles per hour, a fair railroad speed. In others 12 to 15 per hour. As we start at daylight, 3½ A.M. and run until the close of twilight, 9½ P.M., the daily progress is between 200 and 300 miles. If we escape hindrances on sand bars, it will be a quick trip down. We shall be at Fort Union about noon tomorrow. The Minnetare chief is a most amiable, intelligent, and agreeable man. He is a splendid sign talker and is much at it. His motions are graceful, easy, and expressive. He goes up from Fort Berthold to Fort Benton and back every year with the Fur Co. boat and is a great favorite. I get him and Meldrum at the table three or four times a day and work at particular subjects. He will not sit more than half an hour at a time, but is quite willing to repeat. He is like all Indians in this respect. When they work they do it with all their might.

Meldrum's Quiver and Bow Sheath, Bä-da-is′ -sa-ish-sha′ — "it holds our bow and arrow."

The Old Bear (Mah-to-he-ha), a distinguished Mandan brave, by George Catlin. The Old Bear is represented here as a medicine man; his medicine pipes are in his hands, and he is ready to make a final visit to his patient to cure him with his particular brand of magic.

He gave me yesterday his quiver. He said it was one of the finest in the Crow country. It is of Otter skin and looks well. As a relic of Meldrum's Indian life it is quite a memento. I am to purchase this morning a Par Flesh[152] as they call it, a raw hide bag, used in pairs to pack on horses, and carry anything they choose to put in it. It is trunk, carpet bag, hunting bag, etc.

Shield

I saw yesterday a Crow arrow proof shield, but could not purchase it. They are made of a circle of raw hide about two feet in diameter, made by means of an outside cover of big horn, or elk skin, tanned white to assure a convex form next the body and a flat face outside, so as to make them about four inches thick in the centre. Whether there is anything between the skins I know not, but I think from the weight there must be several thicknesses of raw hide. They do not use them much now as they are no protection against [musket] balls. They have connected medicine performances with these shields and thus they attach to them a fictitious value. I saw also sacs of white raw hide in the shape of a quiver for the Indian head dress, satchels, and saddle bags for horses made in the best manner of white raw hide, with heavy fringes of the same in long strings. Meldrum's Fort, Fort Charles, about 100 miles above Fort Union was broken up yesterday. That is the property was removed, and the families of the traders living in the Fort were brought on board to be carried to Fort Union. It is the intention to build a new post for Meldrum at the mouth of the Muscle Shell. This removal of effects brought these articles to light. But as they know not the value of money, and I have no goods to trade except a few trinkets which I brought along to present to those who give me information, I cannot obtain them.

Big Horn Sheep. Lower Missouri

The Big Horn is not confined to the mountains, neither does he take to the prairie. The high bluffs of the river give him a favorite home. Meldrum says they are full of them. They are now abundant from Fort Benton to about 70 miles above Milk River where the Bad Lands terminate, and they used to range the bluffs as low down as the Cannon Ball river. Seven years ago he shot two on Heart River, which is above the Cannon Ball.

Robert Meldrum

He was born in Scotland, Dumfriesshire, in 1804. Came to Canada in 1812 with his father and mother. In 1816 moved to Kentucky with his father and mother. His father was naturalized in Boston where he first went from Canada. He was a man of property. This naturalized Robert. In Shelbyville, Ky., he went to school a year and a half. They then emigrated to Illinois in 1824. In 1825 Robert went to the Indian country. His health failed and he went in company with Genl. Ashley[153] to hunt and trap in the Rocky Mountains. There he remained five years, part of the time with Fish Jackson[154] and Sublette,[155] who were fur traders. He was with the Snakes and Bannaks and Crows. He took his first wife with the Snakes in 1826. He went into the service of the Am. Fur Co. in 1827 and has remained in it ever since. He was established on the Yellowstone at Fort Van Buren 3 years. In 1830 he moved to Fort Cass on the Yellowstone at the mouth of the Rose Bud. He then went to Fort Union at the mouth of the Yellowstone where he remained and at Fort Charles above until the present time. He has been a chief trader for the last 13 years.

The Crows adopted him in 1827 and that year he put away his Snake wife and took one from the Crows. He became a Crow chief in 1830 and he is now a Crow chief. He has been in their fights against the Blackfeet and Sioux. He has killed five Blackfeet and took the scalps with his own hands, and three Sioux, doing the same. Their shots and killings they do not count, but the scalps. He has had 112 [sic] wives and now has but one proper wife. Of these ten or twelve are now living. He has had 12 children, only four are now living and ten grand children now living. Has taken four guns out of the hands of enemies, one bow, two lances, one battle axe. He struck first four times. Had three horses killed under him in one fight in one day. At other times two others. Never was wounded. The Indians say his medicine is great. He has no body while in action. He once on an excursion stole 19 horses. He was alone in this. At another time 5 at Laramie Fork, all from the Sioux. Four times from the Blackfeet, 4, 2, 1, 5, = 12 in all. Twice from the Assiniboins. 2 first and one last. Once five from the Snakes. He has lost from 400 to 600 horses the same way taken from enemies. During the seven years from 33 to 1840 he lived with the Crows altogether. His business was to buy beaver skins, red fox skins, otter. During this time the fights occurred. He never set up a medicine lodge, but has narrated his exploits in them. He took the fourth tent pole once. He is now in independent pecuniary circumstances. He knew Beckwith[156] well. Says he was a humbug. The whole narrative was humbug. He was a white man from Virginia and his mother a negress. He was therefore a mulatto. He had Crow wives but was not a chief. He was adopted into a good family. His wife was not the daughter of a chief, a pretty woman, but of low stock. His influence was but little except while he was interpreter for the company. He never distinguished himself in fights. Meldrum was with him in three fights. He was not a coward, but was awkward. James P. Beckwith said he killed the enemy, but Meldrum thinks he never did.

Fort Union, Wednesday, June 25, 1862

We reached the Fort at 12 o'clock M. having made the sum of 750 miles in 2 days and 20 hours. It was like railroad travel, particularly in the rapid part of the river. It was estimated by some of the passengers that we made 25 miles per hour in some places. I think it was near it. I have never ridden at such a rate on a steam boat. We could compare it with railroad speed by the passing of objects on the bank. It was a grand ride, particularly through the 35 or 40 miles of the White Walls, and not much behind through the 450 miles of the Bad Lands. The current of the river is estimated by Captain Bailey at 12 miles per hour at the points where we used the cordel, and if the lower Missouri is five and six miles at high water, above the Yellowstone it will average from seven to eight. The current is much swifter. Between the Forts the timber is confined to the bottoms as it is below, but the bottoms are much narrower, and the bluffs nearer together. The river will average above the Yellowstone from $\frac{1}{4}$ to $\frac{3}{8}$ of a mile in width. In some places it widens out half a mile or more and in others it is about twice the length of the *Spread Eagle* which is 225 feet long. Below Fort Union we shall not make such tremendous progress, as the current is not so strong and there are no rapids. At 5 P.M. a great storm of wind and rain came on with thunder and lightning. The *Key West* broke loose and went down stream and stopped on a sand bar. Our boat was at once secured with extra cables and rode it out. It was a regular gale and we took to the Fort for safety. It was well for us that we were moved at the time it came on. A band of about 100 Cree were encamped near the Fort and upon invitation they came forward Indian fashion, marching in a crowd, singing and firing guns at irregular intervals. They were received by the mountaineers at the fort with a similar salute. They came with robes to trade and we soon had them on board. They looked rather squalid, but behaved well. Their dogs were all in harness drawing fills loaded with camp traps [the travois].

PART IX

Spread Eagle,
Thursday, June 26, 1862

We left Fort Union this forenoon about 11 o'clock and expect to be at Fort Berthold sometime tomorrow. The distance is estimated at about 300 miles. We now have but a few passengers. Mr. I. H. Smith [unidentified], one of the St. Louis gold hunters,[157] changed his mind and is now returning. Mr. Charles Chouteau, Jr.[158] is also with the boat. Mr. Riter,[159] chief trader at Fort Union is now going below to return in the fall. He is from Philadelphia and has been nine years in the country and has an Indian child, and a bright looking boy, to whom he is much attached. I like him very much for his frank and pleasant manners. He is a man of more character and refinement, I think, than any of the traders, not excepting Mr. Dawson, who occupies the position of General Agent of the Company.

Buffalo

We saw a large number of buffalo today and found them in the river at two or three places. We shot several and wounded them badly and got two on board, a bull and a cow, which gives a supply of beef. We also took two calves which are now in the pen to be domesticated. This a separate operation. The small boat is lowered when a calf is wanted and four oarsmen soon overtake the cow and calf and lasso the latter and take it on board. Since tea the last one was taken. There was a cow, a calf, and a year old bull in the river crossing where it was near half a mile wide. The small boat put out, caught the calf, took it on board and then the year old, but as they could not take this on board it drowned after they took it. I have now seen and shot at buffalo until I am tired and satisfied. I am sure I put a ball in both of these now on the boat, but as a dozen shots are fired at each no one claims the game. We shall have good hunting down to Fort Pierre, which is from 700 to 800 miles below Fort Union.

Young Animals on Board

There are now two young tame beaver, one young antelope already tame and following the children around the boat, quite a beautiful animal. Three or four young buffalo, a young elk, an eagle. We had also a tame wolf for sometime but I think he went off at Fort Benton, and also a pair of owls. The Big Horn and the grizzly bear are the only animals we have not had on board. It is from the horns of the former that the famous horn bows are made.

Bow and Arrow

This is a truly formidable weapon as used by the Indian. They always carry it even when they have a gun. When the arrow enters the body of a man it is difficult to extract. It will often penetrate a bone and bend in it such a way that it cannot be removed with forceps. I saw a man at Fort Union shot by a Sioux who still had the arrow in his body and his case was considered hopeless although he was shot two or three months ago.

Yesterday we got a buffalo in the river. He was killed and when taken on board an arrow was found back of the foreshoulder in the vital part, buried in his body within 3 inches of the feather. I saw it pulled out and the boy who shot it from the bow of the boat. He was about twelve years old. At Fort Charles a bull buffalo passed on a run with his tongue out within 20 rods of the boat. A boy 12 years old mounted a horse, and without the least fear rode up to his side within ten feet of him and planted an arrow in his side. His horse then fell in crossing a slew, in which the buffalo came near miring, but he was killed a few yards from this place. The buffalo is a timid animal except when wounded, when he sometimes, but not always, turns and charges. The cow, they say, never charges. At this place in the evening quite a number crossed the river and I had several shots. I also went down the river to watch them coming over. Here I heard the loud breathing or rumbling of buffalo. In the full herd they say it sounds like thunder. I believe it, for the noise of the low or blowing of a dozen was tremendous.

Fort Berthold, Friday, June 27, 1862

We arrived at 9 A.M. at this post and remained until 3 P.M., when we left, and are now wooding five miles below. In the meantime we had had another thunder storm, attended with hail, which was equally if not more severe in wind than the other. Two large hawsers held the boat, with the aid of the full power of steam to keep the head of the boat to the back. The anchor sunk to the eye yielded at the commencement. The hail stones were some of them as large as walnuts. The rain came down very copiously, and the thunder was frequent and heavy. The dirt house in the village stood it well.

Barbarous Rites of the Minnetares

Yesterday the annual ceremonies of this people closed, it being the fourth day. They were held in the Medicine Ring in the centre of the village, before referred. It is a large open space in the midst of the houses about 150 feet in diameter, which with the adjoining housetops accommodates the entire population. The ceremonies of yesterday were described to me minutely by a young man who witnessed them, as he has on former occasions, having been in the Indian country from a child. Among other things two fresh killed bulls' heads were tied together and two young men with two cuts each in the back through which a stick was inserted and around this a slip in loose were tied to the heads each by two strings, and they thus dragged them a distance of two miles and a half outside the village. But the worst act was a piece of self torture by another young man who was tied in the same way to a pole in a scaffold, and drew on sometimes with his entire weight, swinging from side [to side], and at others pulling and straining on it to break himself loose by tearing out the skin and muscle. He was thus tied for four hours without being able to free himself, until he fell or rather hung exhausted and apparently dead. He was then cut loose. A boy 12 years old then had the strings inserted in the same manner, and after two or three jumps to free himself, and much pain, he was released by his relatives giving a horse as an offering for his release, and they then cut him down. They could not bear to witness his sufferings. There are two ways of doing this. If in haste, the person who intends to ransom him with a horse takes a stick about six inches long and throws it in towards the center of the ring. It is at once understood and he at once cuts him down. Otherwise he leads the horse in first, and then does it. The first one who picks up the stick or lays hands on the horse becomes its owner.

Another young man yesterday was tied to a pole with strings inserted in his breast below the nipple and remained in it several hours until he fell exhausted, and without tearing out the skin. He was then cut loose. All this is done with cries to Great Spirit for good fortune and personal favors.

The young man said a raw bull's head would weigh 100 pounds. He once saw an Arickaree at Fort Clark draw a bull's head cut off near the shoulder which he estimated would weigh with the neck 200, from the place where he was killed to the village, a distance of two miles, and around the vil-

lage after he reached it. He had also seen one man draw seven dry bulls' skulls at one time. The government ought to prohibit these cruel usages, as well as the cutting off of the fingers among the Crows. Out of a dozen or two Crow women at Fort Charles not over one in three had a perfect left hand. Some had taken off one, some two joints of the little finger. Some, one and some two of the second finger. Always of the left hand. I did not see any mutilated hands among the Minnetares. I did not observe until it was too late, although I saw the whole nation as well as the Mandans at

their village, in their houses, and on the bluff, and on the boat.

Yesterday also they had a comic entertainment for the diversion of the people. About 40 persons dressed up in peculiar costumes and personated, in their dress and actions, the ways of the animals they represented. There were the buffalos, the bears, the antelopes, and the snakes. The latter crawled on their bellies and were striped crosswise, black, yellow, clay color, white, and red. The antelope with horns first appeared on the house tops and then came down into the ring, walking on hands

Left: Although George Catlin painted this picture of the Sun Dance, he did not actually observe the ceremony. He arrived a few days after the Sioux had danced near the mouth of the Teton River in Montana. The painting is relatively accurate, although the Sioux Sun Dance was always held under cover of one kind or another.

and feet. The bears walked the same, but sometimes stood up like the bear. The buffalo wore horns and walked on all fours. There was one person who personated either a clown or the Evil Spirit. He wore a mask, was painted black, with white rings, and red spots in middle. On his back was painted the new moon. He wore a beaver skin bonnet, and showed in front the male organ in wood of large size, with buffalo hair pendant. All in the ring yielded him precedence. The bears were but three. These ceremonies were continued for some time for the amusement of the people. The bears had paws containing corn which the antelope tried to get, etc. There were three musicians who sang meanwhile and marked time upon the drums. Within the circle of pickets was the war post and stone.

Sun Dance of Dakotas

He had often seen this performance. It is called Ne-wä′-gwa-wa-che′-pe. They fast and dance for four days. On one of these is practiced the insertion of strings in the breast and pulling back from the pole to which they are tied until it tears out. This is the only ceremony which they have analogous to the Minnetare usage.

Minnetare Mourning

They wear usually the breech cloth and blanket. I saw bare backs, arms, and chests in great number. Some of them were terribly scarred. In addition to the parallel cuts, which indicate string work, there were long

scars on the arm parallel. The cicatrix [sketch] was four, five, 6, and even 7 inches long and from ⅜ to ½ an inch wide. These scars are very common. I saw two scarred across the breast like this [sketch]. One of them had seven parallel scars, the longest 6 or 7 inches and as wide as in the former case, and the three semi-circles or segments of circles, concentric, the longest one being four or five inches. These were large and powerful men, particularly full about the chest. Bear's Nose, the Minnetare chief, Nä-kue-she-ä′-pish, Bear's Nose, has three parallel scars on right arm 6 inches beginning above elbow and three below nearly as long.

Minnetare and Mandan Burial Customs

I went out today to the scaffolds. They are not as numerous as they look in the distance, perhaps there are about 50 or 60

standing, from which I infer, as well as from actual graves which I saw here and there that they bury in the ground. There were skulls lying here and there on the ground where the scaffolds had fallen, and the other bones with them. On several of the scaffolds, the skulls were visible, and in one case the skeleton of the right hand projected beyond the blanket. I notice this more particularly as the mode of burial was apparent. A garnished [?] buffalo robe was under the body and still firm. A pillow was under the head. The head was turned a little on one side towards the East. The arms down partly, the hand pointing a little outward. Just below the chin was a large pipe of red stone, belted on the rim and

A Dakota village, by Seth Eastman, from THE AMERICAN ABORIGINAL PORTFOLIO. Eastman painted this village about 1845, and described the dwellings as "summer houses" made from the bark of the elm tree. The scaffolding was used to dry skins and corn.

stem with lead and having a long flat stem, the whole of which was visible. The feather in decay still projected over the bleached skull and a bundle of clothing was tied on the scaffold at his feet.

I noticed two cases of coffins on scaffolds which were a great improvement upon the other. They were simply boxes obtained at the Fort and too short for the body of a man, unless unjointed, which some Indians do. Some of the bodies were covered with scarlet cloth. The scaffolds were of four posts about six feet above ground and some of them six inches in diameter and firmly constructed. The cross pieces were in the natural forms and the slabs of wood were secured with rawhide strings.

Minnetare Village as Seen Coming Down

[Morgan has a sketch of village and river here.]

Between each of these houses others appear. I counted the number of these houses through from the Fort to the river and made the number ten, and seven through the other way. There are about 80 houses in all including a few log houses. The round houses are all alike and not less than 40 feet in diameter with hard clean floors and water tight roofs and sides. I mentioned before I think the poles which constitute the frame of the house are covered first with matting made of willows, then dry hay or grass, then earth. Around the outside just below the first joint in the roof is set a row of poles entirely around resting on crutches to stay the earth against washing by rain. Its prac-

tical use is evident on inspection [sketch]. I examined today with some care one of the best of these houses again and it was certainly a grand piece of work for Indian hands. The four centre posts were massive. All the main poles and rafters were of straight round timber without bark and the regularity and symmetry of the polygon was worthy of praise. The opening for the smoke was square and a square timber was framed in against the end of the poles. The floor was hard and clean. The fire place circular, in the centre, and excavated about six inches. I wish I had full drawings of the interior as well as the exterior.

Brush Fence

I noticed a simple but effective fence around their garden beds outside of the pickets. A row of brush wood was set up close and sunk in the ground after which willow poles outside and in were placed horizontally, and tied together with rawhide strings. It

was six feet high, and a perfect protection against cattle. It was also as cheap a fence as could be made and would probably last four or five years.

Saturday, June 28, 1862

We passed the old Arickaree village last evening about sun down and tied up several miles below for the night. During the night we had another thunder storm with wind nearly as severe as the one in the morning. The mosquitoes also for the first time on the trip were really troublesome. They sang around my bars and kept me awake for some time but did not break through. This morning by way of contrast, a fire was built in the forward cabin.

Sunset at Arickaree Village

[Sketch of sunset] The principal cloud was fan shaped of a bluish color, thin, but impenetrable to the rays of the sun. The outer edge was tipped with silver and crimson.

The Fourth of July Dance at the Crow Agency in 1894. Here the Crows are dancing to celebrate a holiday whose real significance they could scarcely grasp. The tribe was still in transition from its wild and free life; the dances were not yet staged entirely for the tourist.

Its gorgeous character was produced by the two great openings 1 and 2 in the center, looking like two great islands, or windows. There were small fleecy clouds of a crimson hue within the opening, but the edges or border of these openings were illuminated with a rich deep golden color of yellow and crimson light. Two pillars of light came through as shot up as represented by three and four. They were whitish yellow and gold, and the whole taken together was gorgeous in the extreme. I have never seen a sunset where the golden colors were so rich, so profuse, and so brilliant. I thought of Dr. Dewey who would have been in raptures over it. It is the only one I have noticed which particularly arrested my attention, and I think it altogether the finest I ever witnessed.

Bä-da-e′-sha. Catch-all. The name of Crow satchel got of Meldrum.

Original Country of the Crows

I have before referred to this. Their oldest traditions carry them to the Three Forks of the Missouri above the Falls, and they have no knowledge of any anterior migration, or when or where they separated from the Minnetares. They first obtained the horse from the Comanchees of Texas. Old people of the Crow Nation told Meldrum when he first went among them that they saw the first horses ever brought into their country. This would make it about 100 years ago that they first obtained the horse. The Assiniboins had but a few when Meldrum first knew them.[160] The Crows lost some of their horses the first winter for want of food. This induced them to make war on the Snakes to get possession of the Yellowstone country where they could winter horses, and they succeeded in expelling them, and have since occupied that coun-

try. Of their Creek affiliation the evidence in their system of consanguinity is strong, and of the two alternatives it is the more probable that they remained in or near the home country while the Creek family migrated either down the Missouri to the Gulf or along the mountain chain to the Arkansas, and then eastward to the Mississippi valley, which appears the more probable, and that the Minnetares at a later day went down the river Missouri.

Timber Forts

Along the Upper Missouri from the mouth of the Yellowstone these Forts occur very frequently. They are large enough to accommodate a war party of 20 persons. They are made of drift wood, and are on the bottoms near the river. They are usually hexagonal, sometimes pentagons. I have examined and measured them. [Has ground plan, top and side view sketched.] The logs are piled up drawing inwards about six feet high and the top covered except an opening for smoke. At night they close up the opening after going in. They are thus safe against a night attack. We saw them by the dozen, scattered along the river for 750 miles. The most together was three at a bend 150 miles below Fort Benton. The opening for smoke and light is about five feet square.

Timber on Upper Missouri

There is but little timber from Milk River to Fort Benton. It is confined to the bottoms which are narrow, as the bluffs come near together. But there is enough all along for fuel for any number of Indians. The difficulty of the country is the absence of fish and the precariousness of game. The game is abundant, but the buffalo migrate and the elk and antelope are shy, and to move camp

and follow them without horses must be next to impossible, and a permanent Indian village would scare away the game on the prairie for 50 miles around. The timber is confined to the bottoms as low down as Fort Pierre certain, and I think as low as Omaha, but as you descend the tributaries increase, all of which are wooded, but the main difficulty about game is not permanently removed.

Fort Pierre, Monday, June 30, 1862

We reached this place at sundown yesterday, and just before reaching the bank to tie [?] were struck by a squall, and drove on a bar, and for some time were in a dangerous position. We got off in time, and went up the river a mile and tied up for the night. This is the third heavy blow since we started. There was danger each time of the smoke stacks, and the cabin deck blowing off, and it made the passengers uneasy. But we escaped each time and were thankful when it was over.

Some reference is made to the troubles among the Dakotas about receiving the annuities.[161] Some of the bands refused to come in and threatened those who did to shoot them if they accepted the goods. Of those who came in the Metakozhees and [blank] refused to take theirs, and they were given [to] or taken by the Uncpapas. The next morning Bear's Rib, the head chief of the Uncpapas was shot by a Metakozhee and one from the [blank] band, and general fight would have occurred if the latter bands had not at once taken refuge in the Fort.[162] I visited the grave of Bear's Rib this morning. He was buried by the chief trader at the post, a picket placed around the grave, and the American flag planted over it on a flag staff. Bear's Rib was a true friend of peace and of the whites.

I heard him speak with others at the Council, but cannot recall his appearance.

It seems that the unsettled condition of the Dakotas is in part owing to representations from Red River that the English intended to attack the Americans and drive them from the country. The Dakotas are entirely ignorant of the numbers and strength of the whites, and refuse to believe all that is told them on the subject. The large delegation sent to Washington in 1858 whom I went with from Suspension Bridge to Detroit[163] told them of what they saw and the Dakotas set them down as liars. They really believe that they are able to cope with the government. They, in common with the Assiniboins, Minnetares, Crows and Blackfeet, hate the whites and say they would clear their country of them to a man if the white man had not become necessary to them. They want his guns, powder, and ball, coffee, blankets, and camp furniture, which have now become indispensible, and they therefore submit to his presence among them.

After we left, one of the bands who received annuities went to a little post called the Moro, above here, and back from the river and robbed it of its provisions and 400 packs of robes=4000, worth about $12,000, giving the three men in charge warning to leave, if they would save their lives, and firing upon and wounding one of them as he ran. It is said they are now on their way to Fort Berthold to resell them to the Company. Of course the Co. are without remedy, and if they get them finally for sugar and coffee at a dollar the pound will not lose greatly.

Dakota Burial Scaffolds

Back of the Fort are several scaffolds. Some of them with two, three, and one with four bodies upon it. All but one or two are in boxes, covered with red cloth. The bodies are parallel with the river which here runs north and south and the one not boxed has his head to the north. It is wrapped in a lodge skin, with a pillow under the head and covered with a blanket tied with raw hide strings. The boxes are also tied in the same way to the scaffold.

We are now five days run from St. Joseph, if no detention occurs, and expect to reach there Friday night or Saturday morning. I hope it will be Friday, that I may reach Chicago Sunday.

[Morgan devotes about 500 words here to a description, with sketch, of Pueblo houses, given him by a fellow passenger, and some comments upon architecture of Central America.]

Above Fort Randall, Tuesday, July 1, 1862

We are making very good progress and expect to reach Fort Randall about 3 P.M. If we do, we shall get quite near Yankton tonight. We have seen no game for the last two days, and expect to find none below this. All our thoughts now are upon home and each one is marking the progress of the boat. With me the circumstances are peculiar. We are about two days from Sioux City and when I reach there I shall know the fate of my daughter Mary. With all my anxiety to reach home, I dread this place.

[A few pages, with sketches, about the beaver on the Missouri have been omitted.]

Below Yankton, Wednesday, July 2, 1862

We reached Fort Randall at 7 P.M. having stopped 3 to 4 hours to take on a large quantity of wood. At Randall we received the first news from the seat of war since May 20 and several heard from their families. There is a post office at this Fort, and a semi-weekly mail. It is the last one on the river going up. I supposed Sioux City was the last and I expect to hear from my family there which we shall reach tonight. We came on to Yankton last night. We are now running splendidly on the seasoned wood which makes a great difference. Before this we have had to cut down standing dead trees. It looks fair now that we shall reach St. Joe Friday evening, which will enable me to get away Saturday morning and reach Chicago Sunday morning. The weather this morning is cool and the air delicious. It is a beautiful summer day. The abundant rains have covered the prairies with a rich carpeting of grass and nature smiles upon us, on every side. I am perfectly well and have been on the entire trip, with the exception of some trouble in digestion at the outset. I weighed yesterday 159½ pounds, which is below my usual summer weight which is 165. I think I have lost the difference on the trip, although my appetite was never better. The climate from Fort Pierre up is very dry and stimulating. It keeps a person hungry. It must be a grand atmosphere for the dyspeptic. Mr. Riter, Chief Trader at Fort Union, went into the country nine years ago a confirmed dyspeptic. He is now large, fat, and cured. He said it took three years in his case to effect a permanent cure, and he finds when he goes below a tendency to a return of the difficulty. He thinks in time the climate would raise anyone out of it.

I must finish this journal today. I am endeavoring and have been for some days to prepare my mind for the intelligence which awaits me at Sioux City. But I am not prepared for the worst. Hope is still alive, and without it, I could not have performed the labors of this last 40 or 50 days. The hope however is slight.

I must add a word about the officers of the boat. It is extremely well manned, and the spirit among the officers and men is excellent.[164] Capt. Robert Bailey I have found to be a very intelligent, agreeable, and cultivated man. He has read extensively, is a good thinker, and a pleasant companion. The pilot Frank Constance I have not become acquainted with. The Mate, Jacob Snider, is a most valuable man, and fills his place, which is one of great responsibility for the safety of the boat with indefatigable perseverance. He is the one who so narrowly escaped death near Fort Benton from drowning. His quick eye saved the boat in the two gales above referred to by promptly putting out additional hawsers. The engineer is evidently a superior man, the clerk, Mr. Isaacs, is the spirit of amiability and accommodation. Sam Johnson, the bar keeper, is an original genius with special gifts in the comic line. And not least is Postlewaite, the steward and musician. He is the head of the well-known Postlewaite band of St. Louis, and a very superior performer as well as composer. He and three others have given us most excellent music. The *Spread Eagle* is a fine traveller. We are making from 250 to 300 miles per day, running 3½ A.M. to 9 P.M. Mr. Charles P. Chouteau, the managing director of the Am. Fur Co. has the general charge of the boat, and the business. I have not become much acquainted with him, after several conversations. He is a perfectly polite man, quiet, but attentive to business, very discreet, and popular with officers and men; or rather I should say commands their entire respect. He has been up with the boat for the last ten years and adjusts all the business of the Company at the posts. He appears to be well qualified for the task. The trip which in fact is a great expedition has been remarkably successful. The high stage of the

Indians traveling, by Seth Eastman, was painted about 1845. It shows the family on the move. The horses, with passengers and travois, and the women do all the work, while the proud brave disdains such menial labor and rides his horse in haughty silence.

water is the reason. We have also been free from the mosquitoes which some years are very troublesome. And no accident has as yet occurred except the one before referred to. The boat carries down and *Key West* about 50,000 robes, worth $150,000.

[A page or so of descriptions, with sketches, of the Bad Lands and the White Walls has been omitted.]

Tribes [Clans] of Blood Blackfeet

I forget whether I transcribed the names of these tribes and therefore I do it here.[165]

1. Ki′-na — Blood Tribe
2. Mä-me-o′-ya — Fish Eaters
3. Ah′-pe-ki — Skunk
4. A-ne′-po — An animal, extinct
5. Po-no-kin′ — Elk

Blood Language. Mis-tek′, Mountain. Mis-tek-sque, Rocky Hill.

A man can marry a woman of his own tribe. This could not have been the ancient law, and I doubt whether it is now, unless the tribal organization is decaying.

It is common for a man to call his brother's son Nis-kan′, younger brother, but stepson is the proper term.

Arickarees have tribes, but I could not ascertain them.

Minetare Strap Swinging

Mr. Riter, chief trader of the Co. at Fort Berthold [Fort Union] the last winter. He has seen the ceremonies of drawing the horns, and hanging by the back. He saw these performed the day before we arrived. Poles were set up in the medicine ring or church yard with a cross pole about 7 feet above the ground. The person after the sticks were inserted under the cut, and the strings secured, was lifted up and the strings tied to the pole. He was then left hanging with his feet clear of the ground, but quite near, actually dangling in the air. In a short time by the stretching of the cord, and of the skin of the back his feet came to the ground. He remained thus hanging for 4 hours and when removed, as the skin did not tear out, he was apparently dead. He has seen three thus hanging to one pole. The Mandans now reduced to 17 lodges, and the Arickarees now practice the same ceremonies.

Below Sioux City, July 3, 1862

It seems fitting that I should add one word concerning the awful intelligence which awaited me at Sioux City. My daughter Mary died on the 15th day of May, the day after the telegram was sent to me. She was 7 years of age. My youngest and only remaining daughter, Helen, sickened, and after a partial recovery, she too died two weeks later. Two out of three of my children are taken. Our family is destroyed. The intelligence has simply petrified me. I have not shed a tear. It is too profound for tears. Thus ends my last expedition. I go home to my stricken and mourning wife, a miserable and destroyed man.

July 7, 1862. I reached St. Joe July 4. Chicago, Sunday morning, July 6, and Rochester Monday evening, July 7, 1862.

Notes

Chapter I

1. Notes by Herbert M. Lloyd to Morgan's *The League of the Ho-de-no-sau-nee, or Iroquois* (New York: Dodd, Mead and Co., 1904), II, 155.
2. Lewis H. Morgan, *The League of the Ho-de-no-sau-nee, or Iroquois*, p. 33; see also Herbert M. Lloyd's notes in the same work, pp. 156, 200–201.
3. Arthur C. Parker, *The Life of General Ely S. Parker,* Publications of the Buffalo Historical Society, XXIII (1919): 82. See also Morgan's brief mention of his adoption in *Ancient Society* (New York, 1877), p. 81, n. 1.
4. "Laws of Descent of the Iroquois," *Proceedings of the Eleventh Meeting of the American Association for the Advancement of Science, August 1857* (Cambridge, Mass., 1858), Part II, p. 142.
5. From an entry made by Morgan in a journal on October 19, 1859. In it he traced the course of events which culminated in the publication of *Systems.* See "How Morgan Came to Write *Systems of Consanguinity and Affinity,*" Leslie A. White, ed., *Papers of the Michigan Academy of Science, Arts, and Letters,* XLII (1957): p. 262.
6. "Laws of Descent of the Iroquois," p. 142.
7. Morgan's abilities as observer and reporter frequently stand out sharply in his journals of his European tour in 1870–71; see *Extracts from the European Travel Journal of Lewis Henry Morgan,* edited by Leslie A. White (Rochester Historical Society Publications, XVI [1937]: 221–390).

Others, too, have commented upon the abilities of Morgan as a field worker: see the tribute paid him by Professor Robert H. Lowie in "Lewis H. Morgan in Historical Perspective," in *Essays in Anthropology Presented to A. L. Kroeber* (Berkeley, Calif.: University of California Press, 1936), pp. 169–70. The late Clark Wissler regarded Morgan as "a pioneer, if not the initiator, of field study in cultural phenomena" (*An Introduction to Social Anthropology,* New York, 1929, p. 340).
8. See the 2nd, 3rd, 4th, and 5th reports of the Regents of the University to the State Senate, or Assembly, Albany, 1849 to 1852.
9. Parker, *The Life of General Ely S. Parker.* A biographic sketch of Ely Parker may be found in the Lloyd edition of *The League,* II, pp. 180–82.
10. "Sketch of Lewis H. Morgan," *Popular Science Monthly,* XVIII (1880): 115.
11. *Early Civilization* (New York, 1922), p. 418.
12. The house, which is pictured in *Rochester Historical Society, Publication Fund Series,* II (1923), opposite p. 1, was razed in 1954.
13. "How Morgan Came to Write *Systems,*" p. 262.
14. *Ibid.,* pp. 262–63.
15. *Ibid.,* p. 263.
16. See note 4 above.
17. "Journal of a Trip to Marquette, Michigan, 1858" (unpublished).
18. Morgan has a rather full account of this investigation in one of his journals (unpublished). He refers to it also in *Systems of Consanguinity and Affinity,* pp. 3, 287.
19. "How Morgan Came to Write *Systems,*" p. 263.
20. At this point I am not sure whether or not Morgan ever made the acquaintance of Lafitau's *Moeurs,* although it may have been brought to his attention in the discussions of kinship evoked by the publication of *Systems.* It was Edward Burnett Tylor (1832–1917), the distinguished English anthropologist, who first brought Lafitau's discussion of Iroquoian kinship to the attention of anthropologists generally—at least so far as I know—in his notable essay, "On a Method of Investigating the Development of Institutions . . ." in the *Journal of the Anthropological Institute,* 18 (1888): 245–69.

21. J. H. McIlvaine, D.D., "The Life and Work of Lewis H. Morgan, LL.D.," in *Rochester Historical Society, Publication Fund Series*, II (1923): 49–50.

22. "How Morgan Came to Write *Systems*," p. 260.

23. "Laws and Descent of the Iroquois," p. 132.

24. *Ibid.*, p. 142.

25. See his *The American Race* (New York, 1891), p. 32.

26. See the various papers, published under that general heading, in *American Anthropologist*, 14 (1912): 1–59.

27. "How Morgan Came to Write *Systems*," p. 263.

28. Stephen Return Riggs (1812–83), an American missionary among the Dakota-Sioux. The work referred to here is *Grammar and Dictionary of the Dakota Language*, published as Vol. IV of the *Smithsonian Contributions to Knowledge* in 1852. Riggs assisted Morgan in the collection of data on kinship as we shall see later; see also reference to him in *Systems*, p. 283.

29. "How Morgan Came to Write *Systems*," p. 263.

30. "System of Consanguinity of the Red Race and Its Relations to Ethnology," read at the 13th meeting of the American Association for the Advancement of Science in August, 1859; it was listed by title, but not published in the proceedings. We quote from the very manuscript that Morgan read at the meeting; we are assured of this by a postscript to the paper signed by Morgan.

31. *Ibid.*

32. *Ibid.*

33. "Laws of Descent of the Iroquois," pp. 144–45.

34. See *Systems*, p. 290. "Of all the Indian nations," Morgan wrote to Spencer F. Baird of the Smithsonian Institution on May 7, 1860, "the one whose system of relationship I most desire is the Eskimo. Dr. [Samuel G.] Morton and others after him have placed him in the Polar Family and deny his connection with our North American Indians." When he finally obtained the Eskimo system he found it was very different from that of most North American tribes; in fact it was hardly a classificatory system at all except on the second ascending and second descending generations. Evidence from the Eskimo proved not to be in close accord with Morgan's theories.

35. See note 25 above.

36. Joshua Hall McIlvaine, D.D. (1815–97), was pastor of the First Presbyterian Church in Rochester for many years and a close friend of Morgan. He was professor of belles lettres at Princeton University from 1860 to 1870. He founded the Evelyn College for Women in Princeton in 1887, of which he was president until his death. It was to McIlvaine that Morgan dedicated *Ancient Society*.

37. J. H. McIlvaine, D.D., "The Life and Works of Lewis H. Morgan; an address at his funeral," in *Rochester Historical Society, Publication Fund Series*, II (1923): 50–51.

38. "How Morgan Came to Write *Systems*," p. 266. In *Ancient Society*, years later, he laid the Seneca-Iroquois and the Tamil systems side by side (pp. 447–52) to demonstrate that they were "substantially identical through upwards of two hundred relationships . . ." (p. 436).

39. "How Morgan Came to Write *Systems*," p. 267.

40. *Ibid.*

41. Joseph Henry (1797–1878), distinguished American physicist and Professor of "Natural Philosophy" at Princeton University, 1832–46, was a prime mover in the organization of the National Academy of Science of which he was the second president; helped to organize the American Association for the Advancement of Science; was chosen the first secretary of the Smithsonian Institution in 1846 and served in this capacity until his death.

42. "How Morgan Came to Write *Systems*"; see also *Systems*, pp. ix, 5.

43. The "Circular" was published in *Smithsonian Miscellaneous Collections*, II (1862): 34.

44. We have not found this expression in the correspondence between Morgan and Joseph Henry, Secretary of the Institution. It may of course have been arranged in personal conversation since the two men saw each other occasionally. In any case, the statement made here is a necessary and valid inference from known facts.

45. Joseph Henry's account of the fire appears in the annual report of the Board of Regents of the Smithsonian Institution for the year 1865 (Washington, 1866), pp. 14 ff.

46. Spencer Fullerton Baird (1823–88), an American ornithologist, went to the Smithsonian Institution in 1850 as assistant to Joseph Henry and succeeded him as secretary upon the latter's death.

47. The Club was organized on the evening of July 13, 1854, at Morgan's home. "He was evidently the prime mover of this new venture." Morgan was chosen secretary. Between 1854 and 1880, Morgan read 32 papers before the Club, many of which were published. See W. C. Morey, "Reminiscences of 'The Pundit Club,'" in *Rochester Historical Society, Publication Fund Series*, II (1923): 99–126, and also Lloyd's notes to *The League*, pp. 178–79.

48. The delays and frustrations attendant upon publication are illuminated briefly in "The Correspondence Between Lewis Henry Morgan and Joseph Henry," by Leslie A. White, in *The University of Rochester Library Bulletin*, XII (1957): No. 2, pp. 17–22.

49. Morgan offers his own appraisal in his *European Travel Journal*, pp. 370–71.

50. Haddon, *History of Anthropology* (New York, 1910), p. 165. R. H. Lowie, *The History of Ethnological Theory* (New York, 1937), pp. 63, 66. A. R. Radcliffe-Brown, "The Study of Kinship Systems," *Journal*

of the Royal Anthropological Institute, 71 (1941): 1.

51. R. H. Lowie, *The History of Ethnological Theory*, p. 62.

52. George P. Murdock, *Social Structure* (New York: Macmillan, 1949), p. 91.

53. *Kinship and Social Organization* (London, 1914), pp. 4-5.

54. R. H. Lowie, "Lewis H. Morgan in Historical Perspective," p. 176.

55. *University of Washington Publications in Anthropology*, Vol. I (1925): No. 2.

56. *Op. cit.*, p. 91.

57. *Op. cit.*, p. 7.

58. Marx planned to write a book on Morgan's researches and theories, but did not live to do so. His co-worker, Friedrich Engels, undertook to do this in Marx's stead, however, in *The Origin of the Family, Private Property and the State*, published in 1884. Marx's notes on Morgan have since been published, in Russian translation, by the Marx-Engels-Lenin Institute, under the editorship of M. B. Mitina, Archives of Marx and Engels, Vol. 9 (Moscow, 1941).

59. *Ancient Society*, p. 552.

60. A contemporary sketch of Morgan's life was written by his friend, Major J. W. Powell, Chief of the Bureau of American Ethnology, in 1880 (*Popular Science Monthly*, 18 [1880]: 114-21). An address delivered at Morgan's funeral by his friend, the Rev. J. H. McIlvaine, some personal reminiscences, and other memorials on Morgan were published by the Rochester Historical Society in their *Publication Fund Series*, Vol. II, in 1923. Charles H. Hart read a "Memorial of Lewis H. Morgan of Rochester" before the Numismatic Antiquarian Society of Philadelphia on May 4, 1882 (published in their *Proceedings*). The *Proceedings of the American Academy of Arts and Sciences*, XVII (1882): 429-36, contained a memorial of "Lewis Henry Morgan, LL.D.," written, no doubt, by one who knew him; Stern attributes it to F. W. Putnam. A small

biography, *Lewis Henry Morgan: Social Evolutionist*, by Bernhard J. Stern, appeared in 1931 (University of Chicago Press); it is marked by numerous errors and distortions, however. An appraisal of Morgan's work by Professor Robert H. Lowie may be found in "Lewis H. Morgan in Historical Perspective," in *Essays in Anthropology Presented to A. L. Kroeber* (Berkeley, Calif.: University of California, 1936), pp. 169-81. Three of my essays dealing with Morgan may be mentioned: Introduction to *Pioneers in American Anthropology: the Bandelier-Morgan Letters, 1873-1883*, Leslie A. White, ed. (2 vols.; Albuquerque: University of New Mexico Press, 1940), pp. 1-108; "Morgan's Attitude Toward Religion and Science," in *American Anthropologist*, 46 (1944): 218-30; and "Lewis Henry Morgan: Pioneer in the Theory of Social Evolution," in *An Introduction to the History of Sociology*, Harry Elmer Barnes, ed. (Chicago: University of Chicago Press, 1948), pp. 138-54.

Chapter II

1. *Kansas, a Guide to the Sunflower State*, Federal Writers' Project (New York: Viking, 1939), p. 78.

2. For a brief but interesting and instructive account of McCoy and Indian emigration, see "Rev. Isaac McCoy," *Kansas Historical Collections*, 2 (1881): 271-75.

3. Quoted by Addison E. Sheldon, *Nebraska, Old and New* (Lincoln, Neb.: University Publishing Company, 1937), p. 105.

4. Quoted in *Kansas*, by the Federal Writers' Project, p. 45.

5. Edward E. Hale, *Kansas and Nebraska* (New York, 1854), p. 227.

6. *Report of the Commissioner of Indian Affairs for 1859*, p. 149.

7. *Ibid.*, p. 15.

8. *Ibid.*, p. 152.

9. *Ibid.*; italics his.

10. *Ibid.*, p. 17.

11. *Ibid.*

12. *Ibid.*, pp. 16-17.

13. *Ibid.*, pp. 5, 15, 143.

14. *Ibid.*, p. 15.

15. *Ibid.*, p. 16.

16. *Ibid.*, p. 17.

17. *Ibid.*, p. 143.

18. *Ibid.*, p. 16.

19. *Report of the Commissioner of Indian Affairs for 1860*, p. 6.

20. *Ibid.*

21. *Report of the Commissioner of Indian Affairs for 1859*, p. 3.

22. *Report of the Commissioner of Indian Affairs for 1860*, p. 111.

23. *Report of the Commissioner of Indian Affairs for 1859*, p. 3; see also the account of the massacre by the Superintendent of Indian Affairs of Utah Territory, pp. 369-72.

24. W. L. Bartles, "Massacre of Confederates by Osage Indians in 1863," *Kansas Historical Collections*, 8 (1904): 62-66.

25. Ray Allen Billington, *Westward Expansion* (New York: Macmillan, 1949), pp. 655-57.

26. *Ibid.*, p. 658.

27. *Ibid.*, p. 663; see also Hill P. Wilson, "Black Kettle's Last Raid," *Kansas Historical Collections*, 8 (1904): 110-17.

28. Billington, *op. cit.*, p. 602.

29. See the personal recollections of this convention by Benjamin F. Simpson, in *Transactions of the Kansas State Historical Society, 1881*, II, 236-47.

30. See *Transactions of the Kansas State Historical Society, 1902*, VII, 536-52, for contemporary accounts of this tour.

31. *Kansas*, by the Federal Writers' Project, p. 53.

32. *Ibid.*, p. 53.

Chapter III

1. Robert H. Lowie, "Lewis H. Morgan in Historical Perspective," in *Essays in Anthropology Presented to A. L. Kroeber* (Berkeley, Calif.: University of California Press, 1936), p. 169.

Chapter IV

1. The population of St. Louis in 1860 was 160,773. The city extended 6½ miles along the river front, and westward three to four miles (Thomas M. Marshall, "St. Louis," in *Encyclopaedia Britannica*, 14th ed., 1929, Vol. 19, p. 845).

2. This was the Pacific Railroad Company, the parent of the Missouri Pacific. It was organized in 1850; construction began a year later. The line reached Jefferson City in 1855, but did not reach Kansas City until 1866 (*ibid.*).

3. The *John D. Perry*, built in 1857 at a cost of $50,000, was destroyed by fire in 1869. She was 220 feet long; beam, 33 feet; capacity, more than 500 tons. "She was one of the best boats ever built for the Missouri River, and one of the most successful" (Phil E. Chappell, "Missouri River Steamboats," *Transactions of the Kansas Historical Society, 1905–06*, IX, 304–5).

4. Its population in 1860 was 4,417, according to the *Encyclopaedia Britannica*.

5. Pueblo Indians of New Mexico today speak of the early Spanish colonists and their descendants of today as Castillians, or Kastira, as they pronounce it.

6. This may have been her first trip up the Kansas River. The Kansas City *Journal* of May 24, 1859, announced that "the steamer *Colona* . . . arrived at our levee yesterday. She is a staunch little side-wheeler . . . and makes the third regular packet now running on that [i.e., the Kansas] river." The issue of June 11 described her as "one of the safest and best boats on the river" (Albert R. Greene, "The Kansas River—Its Navigation," in *Transactions of the Kansas State Historical Society, 1905–06*, IX, 349–50).

7. But on her return trip she made the run from Lawrence to Kansas City in four hours and forty-five minutes, "the best time that was ever made by a boat between these two points" (*ibid.*).

8. As early as 1850, settlers near Pittsburg, Kansas, were exploiting this resource for their own use (*Kansas, a Guide to the Sunflower State*, by the Federal Writers' Project, New York: Viking, 1939, p. 513).

9. On May 21, 1856, Sheriff Jones entered Lawrence with an armed force, burned the Free State Hotel, destroyed the offices of the newspapers, the *Herald of Freedom* and the *Kansas Free State*, robbed stores, etc. (Noble L. Prentis, *A History of Kansas*, Topeka, Kan.: 1904, pp. 62–63; and *Kansas*, Federal Writers' Project, pp. 121–23).

10. Morgan had great difficulty and little success with the Pueblo Indians for years.

11. By treaty in 1854, the Shawnees surrendered 1,600,000 acres of land to the government and received "one-eighth of it back for distribution among the tribe . . . Voluntary allotment in severalty was a prominent feature of the treaty, and the division of the diminished reserve was to be made upon the basis of 200 acres for every individual . . . In the winter of 1856–57, Lot Coffman, a surveyor, was appointed by the federal government to take a census of the Shawnees and to distribute the land in accordance therewith" (Anna Heloise Abel, "Indian Reservations in Kansas and the Extinguishment of Their Title," in *Transactions of the Kansas Historical Society, 1903–04*, VIII, 93).

12. See *ibid.*, pp. 88–90.

13. At this time Morgan used the term *tribe* to designate what we now call (and Morgan later called) a *clan*.

14. It was probably the American egret, *Casmerodius albus*, although this species does not have any black on the head.

15. The shrewdness of Morgan's foresight is indicated by the following: In 1926, Kansas had "10,147,000 acres of wheat, producing 150,084,000 bushels, valued at $178,599,000. This was more than twice that of any other state . . . Wheat is by far the most important agricultural product . . ." ("Kansas," *Encyclopaedia Britannica*, 14th ed., 1929, Vol. 13, p. 259).

16. Their proper name was Kansa (see "Kansa," in *Handbook of American Indians*, Part I, Washington, D. C.: Bureau of American Ethnology, 1907). Major Long rendered it Konzas in 1819 (*An Account of an Expedition from Pittsburgh to the Rocky Mountains . . . under the command of Maj. S. H. Long . . . by Edwin James*, Vol. I, Chap. VI, London, 1823). Morgan spells it Kaw´-za´ in *Systems of Consanguinity*, p. 285, and in *Ancient Society*, p. 156, and states that this is the name by which these Indians call themselves. Kaw is no doubt a contraction of this. See also the interesting, but perhaps not very scholarly, article "Kaw and Kansas: a monograph on the name of the State," by Robert Hay, in *Transactions of the Kansas State Historical Society*, IX (1906): 521–26.

17. Population in 1860: 759 (*Encyclopaedia Britannica*).

18. This was the Pottawatamie Baptist Manual Labor School under the superintendency of John Jackson. In 1859 it had 70 Indian boys and 40 girls in attendance (Jackson's report to the agent for the Potawatomis, in *Report of the Commissioner of Indian Affairs for 1859*, p. 150).

19. We could not be sure whether this word was *thills* or *fills*. It could have been either. The Oxford English Dictionary defines fill

20. In *Systems*, p. 285, Morgan acknowledges the assistance of Joseph James (Gi′-he-ga-zhin′-ga, "Little Chief"), a half-blood Kaw, as interpreter, in obtaining the Kaw kinship system from a Kaw chief.

21. Morgan wrote his journal in parts; when one was finished it was mailed to Mrs. Morgan. At the conclusion of the trip all parts were bound in a volume along with other manuscripts.

22. Morgan had never been abroad at this time. He toured England and the Continent in 1870–71; see *Extracts from the European Travel Journal of Lewis Henry Morgan*, Leslie A. White, ed. (Rochester Historical Society Publications, XVI [1937]: 219–389).

23. "All Indians are immoderate riders," says Morgan, in a footnote in *Systems* (pp. 224–25), commenting upon Indian horsemanship, prairie trails, etc.

24. See the report of the Reverend John Schultz, Superintendent of the Manual Labor School, St. Mary's Pottawatamie Mission, to the government agent of the Potawatomis, in *Report of the Commissioner of Indian Affairs for 1859*, pp. 150–51.

25. See Supt. Jackson's report of the activities of the School for 1859 submitted to the government agent of the Potawatomis. The boys were instructed in farming, the girls in housework; all were taught the three R's. There were four male teachers and "five females to take charge of the girls . . ." Ninety acres of land were under cultivation, "all in corn and potatoes" (*Report of the Commissioner of Indian Affairs for 1859*, p. 150).

26. Mr. and Mrs. Gerard Arink were close friends of the Morgans in Rochester. They were buried in the plot in front of the Morgan vault in Mt. Hope Cemetery in Rochester.

27. As a young man Morgan made a talk on "Temperance" at Tuppers Corners, in 1842; the manuscript of this address is in the Morgan archives, University of Rochester. He was not a teetotaler, however; he took wine with his meals when he and his wife and son were in Italy in 1870 (*Extracts from the European Travel Journal of Lewis Henry Morgan*, pp. 278, 282).

28. New York state passed a law in 1845 that prohibited or restricted the sale of liquor. The sale of liquor to Indians in Kansas was prohibited in 1860. The State Temperance Society held its first meeting a year later. In 1881 a state prohibition law was passed (*Kansas*, Federal Writers' Project, p. 58).

29. Almost all Indian agents and virtually all missionaries of this period speak of the devastating effect of whiskey upon the Indians. "Fire water" was, no doubt, an apt name for the kind of liquor sold by Indian traders. One Indian agent speaks of it as "strychnine whiskey"—the precise meaning of which is not clear (see report of the agent of the Sac and Fox Agency in *Report of the Commissioner of Indian Affairs for 1859*, p. 153).

30. According to Lewis and Clark, the Kansas lived in two villages on the Kansas River. In 1825 they ceded to the United States their lands in northern Kansas and in southeastern Nebraska and relinquished all claims to lands in Missouri, but retained a large tract in Kansas. In 1846 they ceded 2,000,000 acres of land to the United States, and a new reservation was established for them at Council Grove where they remained until 1873, when they were removed to Indian Territory.

31. Neblazhetama ('blue river village,' from *nablezan*, the Kansa name for Mississippi River, and *tamman*, 'village'), an ancient Kansa village on the west bank of the Mississippi, a few miles above the mouth of the Missouri River. The article "Neblazhetama" in *Handbook of American Indians* cites Morgan's article "Indian Migrations" in *North American Review*, 110 (1870): 45, as author-

ity for this name and identification.

32. The government agent of the Kansas Agency in 1859 reported that there was no farm, school, or blacksmith on the reservation at that time, and urged their establishment. The Indians fared well by hunting during the summer, but suffered much want during the winter. Their annuity was, he said, a "mere pittance," and they were driven by hunger to theft and depredations (*Report of the Commissioner of Indian Affairs for 1859*, pp. 155–56).

33. The Kansa, or Kaws, were one of five tribes comprising the Dhegiha group of the Siouan language family. The other tribes were the Omaha, Osage, Ponca, and Quapaw. There were six other groups of languages within the Siouan family besides the Dhegiha.

34. See Rev. Joab Spencer, "The Kaw Indians: Their Customs, Manners, and Folk-Lore" (*Transactions of the Kansas State Historical Society*, X (1908): 373–82). Rev. Spencer lived among the Kaws from 1865 to 1868. See also the informative article, "History of the Kansa or Kaw Indians," by George P. Moorehouse (*ibid.*, pp. 327–68).

35. J. O. Dorsey lists sixteen gentes, or clans, of the Kansa, comprising seven phratries. One is named "Deer"; the Racoon is called a subgens (*Siouan Sociology*, Washington, D.C.: Bureau of American Ethnology, Fifteenth Annual Report, 1897, pp. 230–32; see also *Systems*, p. 176 ff. and *Ancient Society*, p. 156).

36. Morgan did obtain some data, however. In *Systems* (p. 287), Morgan acknowledges the assistance of Buraseau, "an educated Potawattomie," but adds "I was not able to perfect this schedule from want of time."

37. Previously Morgan had stated that Buraseau went to Madison University. The recorder of Hamilton College reports that there is no evidence that Buraseau attended that institution.

38. We find no record of any book published by

this Buraseau; it is highly probable that it was never published.

39. In *Ancient Society* (p. 167), Morgan lists fifteen gentes for the Potawatomi.

40. "The Kaws are among the wildest of the American aborigines, but are an intelligent and interesting people," Morgan, *Ancient Society*, p. 156.

41. "According to the traditions of all three tribes, the Potawatomi, Chippewa, and Ottawa were originally one people . . ." ("Pot-awatomi," in *Handbook of American Indians*).

42. The *Handbook of American Indians* gives "*Potawatomiñk* . . . people of the place of the fire." It further states, "The Pottawatomie are called the 'Nation of Fire' in the *Jesuit Relations*."

43. Not French but English, as he states later.

44. Pronounced O-tä′-wä (*Systems*, p. 202).

45. The government agent in 1859 reported that "their missionary, Rev. E. Willard, is doing much good among them, and is well received . . . A number of them are converted Christians, and members of the Baptist denomination" (*Report of the Commissioner of Indian Affairs for 1859*, p. 154).

46. The government agent reported that on July 7, 1859, "J. T. Jones, Esq., an adopted Ottawa," had requested him "to attend a council of the tribe, called for the purpose of devising ways and means to have a permanent school fund." The council proposed to sell some of their land for this purpose (*ibid.*).

47. "A large portion of the Ottawas have good fields under cultivation . . . They are industrious . . ." (*ibid.*).

48. See Morgan's article "Factory System for Indian Reservations" (*The Nation*, 23 [1876]: 58–59) for a later statement of his views on this subject.

49. He was a half-breed Potawatomi, according to the Federal Writers' Project book, *Kansas*, p. 266, and his name was John Tecumseh Jones but was commonly known as Tauy Jones. In *Systems*, p. 287, Morgan cites "John T. Jones, an educated Potawattomie . . . [who] speaks the Otawa fluently," as the interpreter who assisted him in procuring the Ottawa kinship system.

50. Jones was "graduated by the Baptist Education Society, from which grew Colgate University, N. Y." (*Kansas*, Federal Writers' Project, p. 266).

51. "In 1845, he married Jane Kelly, a white missionary. He was subsequently adopted into the Ottawa tribe, largely, it is said, because of the affection the Indians held for his wife" (*ibid.*, p. 267).

52. The Ottawa Baptist Mission, founded by the Rev. Jotham Meeker, became a headquarters of the Free State party. Jones had become closely associated with Meeker in missionary work; both were staunch abolitionists. "John Brown, a warm friend of Jones, told the Massachusetts Legislature" of the destruction of Jones' house and hotel "by the ruffians . . ." (*ibid.*).

53. Morgan came to believe, as a consequence of his investigations, that "American Indian tribes were universally organized into gentes [i.e., clans] at the epoch of European discovery, the few exceptions found not being sufficient to disturb the general rule" (*Ancient Society*, p. 185). If he could not find clan organization in a tribe he was inclined to think it had been "lost." See discussion of this point in the present writer's introduction to *Pioneers in American Anthropology: The Bandelier-Morgan Letters, 1873–1883* (2 vols.; Albuquerque: University of New Mexico Press, 1940), I, 22–23, 27–30.

54. In *Systems*, p. 203, Morgan remarks that "a similar order . . . existed among the Iroquois; the Mohawks, Onondagas, and Senecas were collectively styled 'Fathers,' and the Cayugas, Oneidas, and Tuscaroras 'Sons.' "

55. Two groups of Sauk and Foxes were settled on reservations in Kansas: the Missouri group in the northeast corner of Kansas in 1837; the Mississippi group on the Marais des Cygnes in 1845. It is the latter group that Morgan refers to here.

56. Abel says they numbered "less than a thousand souls" when they came to Kansas in 1845 (Anna Heloise Abel, "Indian Reservations in Kansas and the Extinguishment of Their Title," in *Transactions of the Kansas State Historical Society, 1903–04*, Vol. VIII). The Indian agent in his report for 1859 stated that their number was 1,237 (*Report of the Commissioner of Indian Affairs for 1859*, p. 152).

57. The Indian agent in 1859 said that the population was decreasing "considerably," due "mainly to dissipation" (*ibid.*).

58. Morgan acknowledges Mills' assistance in *Systems*, p. 287.

59. Morgan spelled this name "Paoli" in *Systems* (p. 288) also. Originally the town was called Peoria Village, named for Baptiste Peoria (see below), but the name was changed to Paoli, or Paola; the *r* was changed to *l* as it often is when Japanese speak English (*Transactions of the Kansas State Historical Society, 1901–02*, VII, 443, 482).

Lykins County was named for David Lykins, superintendent in 1855 of the Wea Mission for the Weas, Piankeshaws, Peorias, and Kaskaskias. The name was changed to Miami in the early 1860's (*Transactions of the Kansas State Historical Society*, VIII, 451, 453).

60. He was indeed. Born about 1800 near Kaskaskia, Illinois, he later moved to Kansas. He is said to have learned several Indian languages—"Shawnee, Delaware and Pottawatomie, besides the several Confederated Tribes, and also English and French" (Cutler). He served as interpreter for many years in eastern Kansas. His name appears frequently in the annals of this region and is invariably spoken of in terms of highest praise. The Indian agent of the Weas, Peorias, Miamis, etc., in 1855, wrote of him: "The character of this man for honesty,

truth, and the great influence he wields over the Indians, together with his expanded knowledge of their affairs, seemed to make it necessary that I should have him near me [Beach, the agent, had located his agency at Peoria's home] . . . Much of the credit for sobriety and industry, and the consequent advancement in the paths of civilization . . . is due to Batties [*sic*] Peoria . . . I do think, that if he was taken from amongst the Indians here by death or otherwise, they would be like bees without their legitimate head; they would scatter and decline and die . . . They look to him as children to an affectionate father" (*Report of the Commissioner of Indian Affairs for 1855*, pp. 107, 110–11). Seth Clover, Indian agent for the Peoria, Piankeshaw, Kaskaskia, and Wea tribes in 1859, spoke of Baptiste Peoria as the leading man among the confederated tribes: ". . . a man of rare ability, much attached to the Indians in this agency, and, as their managing agent in the transaction of business, is of incalculable advantage to the tribes" (*Report of the Commissioner of Indian Affairs for 1859*, p. 158).

In *Systems* (p. 288) Morgan acknowledges the assistance of Battise Peoria in obtaining the kinship nomenclature of the Peorias.

He went to Indian Territory with the removal of the confederated tribes and died there in 1874 (*Collections of the Kansas State Historical Society, 1911–12*, XII, 339, n. 4, an excerpt from Cutler's *History of Kansas*, p. 876).

61. The Indian agent in 1859 noted that Peoria was "extensively engaged in the mercantile business, farms largely, buys and sells stock, and does not hesitate to engage in any legitimate traffic, and seems to conduct his business affairs generally with that ability necessary to insure success" (*Report of the Commissioner of Indian Affairs for 1859*, p. 158).

62. Seth Clover, agent of the Osage River Agency in 1859, mentions Luther Paschal as one of the prominent Indians under his supervision (*Report of the Commissioner of Indian Affairs for 1859*, p. 158).

63. Morgan acknowledges the assistance of Luther Paschal, "a half-blood Kaskaskia," for the Kaskaskia nomenclature (*Systems*, p. 288).

64. This view was held for many decades after Morgan's first trip to the Plains. Thus in 1907 Clark Wissler wrote that "the peopling of the Plains proper was a recent phenomenon due in part to the introduction of the horse . . ." ("Diffusion of Culture in the Plains of North America," *Proceedings* of the Fifteenth International Congress of Americanists, pp. 45–46, Quebec, 1907). And as recently as 1939 A. L. Kroeber held much the same view. Plains culture, he said, "has been one of the well-developed and characterized cultures of North America only since the taking over of the horse from Europeans . . . previously there was no important Plains culture, the chief phases in the area being marginal to richer cultures outside" (*Cultural and Natural Areas of Native North America*, Berkeley: University of California Publications in American Archaeology and Ethnology, 38 [1939]: 76).

This view was a reasonable one, in the opinion of a recent student of Plains culture history, William Mulloy, so long as archeological testimony was lacking. In the first place it appears that many of the "typical Plains tribes" entered the Plains area relatively recently. Secondly, the area was not well suited to agriculture. And, finally, "bison-hunting without horses appeared difficult" (William Mulloy, "The Northern Plains," in *Archeology of Eastern United States*, James B. Griffin, ed., Chicago: University of Chicago Press, 1952, p. 124). Archeological excavation has, however, demonstrated a rather considerable occupation of the Plains area prior to the coming of the white man and the introduction of the horse. In some regions the use of bison traps suggests "that at times they were able to take this animal in large numbers" (Mulloy, *op. cit.*, p. 137). Some sedentary tribes, living in earth lodges and practicing agriculture, inhabited the eastern part of the Plains area in prehistoric times.

Wissler, in the paper cited above, reasons that "it is difficult to see how the central group [of Plains tribes] . . . could have followed their roving life without this animal [the horse]" (pp. 44–45). But we have, in the chronicles of the Coronado expedition, 1540–42, a description of "a roving tribe," before the introduction of the horse, living in the grassy plains "level as the sea . . . [where] there was such a multitude of cows [bison] that they are numberless . . . these Indians are not settled in one place, since they travel wherever the cows move, to support themselves" (George Parker Winship, *The Coronado Expedition, 1540–1542*, Washington, D. C.: Bureau of American Ethnology, Fourteenth Annual Report, 1896, Part I, p. 570). "The . . . sustenance of these Indians comes entirely from the cows . . ." They ate their flesh, drank their blood, used their skins to make tents, their sinew for thread, their bones for awls, and their dung for fuel. "These people have dogs . . . and they load . . . [them] like beasts of burden, and make saddles for them like our pack saddles . . . and when they move . . . these dogs carry their houses, and they have the sticks of their houses dragging along tied on to the pack-saddles [i.e., the travois] . . ." (*op. cit.*, pp. 570–71).

Today's available evidence, ethnographic as well as archeologic, thus makes it clear that the Plains were not nearly as difficult of human occupation before the introduction of the horse as has long been supposed.

65. In a footnote in *Systems*, pp. 206–7, Morgan expresses his conception of the Indian's "nature" as contrasted with that of the white man. He also presents some ideas on race mixture somewhat different from those set forth here.

66. One of the very first questionnaires sent out by Morgan, in December 1858, was addressed to Friend Simon D. Harvey. It was returned promptly with the Shawnee system completely worked out. In 1860, Harvey accompanied Morgan to reservations in southern Kansas. Morgan had great respect and high regard for Harvey (see footnote in *Systems*, pp. 217–18).

67. In accordance with a treaty with the United States in 1854, the Shawnees "surrendered their immense reserve of 1,600,000 acres and received one-eighth of it back again for distribution among the tribe . . . upon the basis of 200 acres for every individual . . ." (Abel, *op. cit.*, p. 93).

68. Morgan seems to be confusing Tecumseh (1768–1813), the celebrated Shawnee chief, and Elskwatawa, or Tenskwatawa (1768–1837), the famous Shawnee prophet and Tecumseh's twin brother.

    Tecumseh was a vigorous opponent of the westward migration of the white man. He fought with the British in the War of 1812, falling mortally wounded in a battle with Harrison's troops near Chatham, Ontario. He has been called "the most extraordinary Indian character in United States history."

    His brother, Tenskwatawa, after returning from "the spirit world" began to preach a new religion which was leveled against the encroaching white man. He exerted a profound influence among many tribes. He, too, sided with the British in the War of 1812, living in Canada on a British pension for some years after the war. He eventually rejoined his people in the States, went finally to Kansas where he died in 1837. The celebrated artist, George Catlin, painted his portrait in 1832. See the biographic sketches of these men in *Handbook of American Indians*, F. W. Hodge, ed., Part 2.

69. *History of the Shawnee Indians from the Year 1681 to 1854, Inclusive*, by Henry Harvey, a member of the Religious Society of Friends (Cincinnati, 1855).

70. The Chouteaus were both numerous and prominent, as traders, in the Missouri River country for many decades. Towns, counties, and crossings were named for them. For a time they had a virtual monopoly of trade with the Osage Indians, and one of them at least, namely Colonel A. P. Chouteau, had children by an Osage woman (Grant Foreman, *The Last Trek of the Indians*, Chicago: University of Chicago Press, 1946, p. 53). The captain of the *Spread Eagle*, the steamboat in which Morgan ascended the Missouri River in 1862, was Charles P. Chouteau.

71. Graham Rogers was a foreman at the Methodist Manual Training School among the Shawnee near Chouteau's Trading Post in 1837. (See the address by E. F. Heisler at the dedication of a monument to mark the site of the first Methodist Mission to the Shawnee Indians in Kansas, in *Collections of the Kansas State Historical Society, 1915–18*, XIV, 194.)

72. According to Nancy Chouteau, her father, John Francis, was a hereditary chief of the Shawnee. "After his death the office of chief became elective" (Joab Spencer, "The Shawnee Indians: Their Customs, Traditions and Folk-Lore," *Transactions of the Kansas State Historical Society, 1907–08*, X, 392, n. 7).

73. Nancy Chouteau was born in Wapakoneta, Ohio, in 1831, daughter of John Francis, a hereditary chief of the Shawnees. She attended a Quaker school but later joined the Methodist church. When she married Cyprian Chouteau she joined his, the Roman Catholic, church. In 1906 she was living with her daughter in Kansas City, Missouri (*ibid.*). Morgan acknowledges the aid of Mrs. Chouteau and Mrs. Rogers, "educated Shawnee half-bood women," in *Systems*, (p. 288).

74. Prior to 1859, if not at that time also, Cyprian Chouteau had a trading-house on the north side of the Kaw River, some seven miles west of Westport and near the Shawnee Manual Labor School. It was here that Fremont fitted out his party for his 1842 expedition (Wm. A. Bernard, "Westport and the Santa Fe Trade," *Transactions of the Kansas State Historical Society, 1905–06*, pp. 559, 573).

75. This was undoubtedly Charles Bluejacket, the grandson of the famous Shawnee war chief, Bluejacket, who fought General Anthony Wayne in 1794 and who signed the treaty of Ft. Industry, Ohio, in 1805. Charles Bluejacket was born in Michigan in 1816, but was taken to Ohio by his parents when he was a small boy. In 1832 he migrated with his parents to the Shawnee reservation in Kansas.

    He was converted to Christianity, joined the Methodist church, served the Rev. Joab Spencer as interpreter for several years, and in 1859 he was licensed to preach; he served as a minister until his death. Bluejacket was a progressive and prosperous Indian of mixed blood. He was married three times and had twenty-three children. He moved to Indian Territory in 1871 and died there, at the town of Bluejacket, in 1897 (Rev. J. J. Lutz, "The Methodist Missions among the Indian Tribes in Kansas," *Transactions of the Kansas State Historical Society, 1905–06*, IX, 182–84; see also *Transactions . . . 1903–04*, VIII, 253–55, 267 and *Collections of the Kansas State Historical Society, 1911–12*, XII, 154).

76. When Dr. C. F. Voegelin was doing field work among the Shawnee in 1933 and 1934, he found that "mention of a female deity was forever on the lips of informants from all three bands of Shawnee in Oklahoma. She was commonly called Our Grandmother (kohkomheena) . . ." (see Dr. Voegelin's interesting article, "The Shawnee Female Deity," *Yale University Publications in Anthropology*, No. 10, 1936, pp. 3–21).

77. See Morgan, *The League of the Iroquois* (Rochester, N. Y., 1851), Book II, Ch. 2.

78. This is the so-called sweat lodge, widely used by Indians of North America for religious, medical, and even social purposes (see "Sweating and Sweat-houses," by H. W. Henshaw, in *Handbook of American Indians*, F. W. Hodge, ed., Part 2).

79. See Anna Heloise Abel, "Indian Reservations in Kansas and the Extinguishment of Their Title," *Transactions of the Kansas State Historical Society, 1903–04*, VIII, 93–94.

80. Tooly or Tooley or Tula was a Shawnee of mixed blood, Christianized (Methodist), who operated a ferry at Bluejacket's crossing on the Wakarusa River (*Transactions of the Kansas State Historical Society, 1905–06*, IX, 184, 331–32; also see the *Transactions* of 1901–02, VII, 495–96).

81. In *Systems* (p. 289) Morgan acknowledges the assistance of William Adams, "a young Delaware, educated at Delaware Mission in Kansas," in obtaining the kinship system of the Delawares.

82. Morgan was much interested in the method of bestowing names upon individuals in Indian society. Upon his return from this trip he read a paper, "Indian Mode of Bestowing Names," at the 13th meeting of the American Association for the Advancement of Science in Springfield, Massachusetts, in August; it was published in the *Proceedings*, pp. 340–43. It seems probable that he suspected that he might find here a distinctive characteristic of Indian culture—as he apparently regarded the custom of sleeping nude and wearing the breechcloth, frequently mentioned in *Systems*—that could be used for purposes of historical reconstruction.

83. Charles Johnny Cake (or Journeycake, as he signed his name, as a representative of the Delawares, to agreements with the United States in 1854) was a chief and prominent leader of the Delawares in Kansas. He was baptized in 1833, and later became "the most noted Baptist preacher" among the Delawares. Charles' brother, Isaac Journeycake, was quite prominent, also. One of Charles Journeycake's daughters, Nannie, married the eldest son of Mr. Pratt, Lucius, in the spring of 1860: "the bride was dressed in white muslin, with veil and orange blossoms, and looked very pretty" (Clara Gowing, "Life Among the Delaware Indians," *Collections of the Kansas State Historical Society, 1911–12*, XII, 186–87; *Home Mission Monthly*, Vol. 14, 1892).

In *Report on Indians Taxed and Indians Not Taxed in the United States* (Washington, D. C., 1894) there are three pictures dealing with Journeycake: (1) a portrait of him alone, 1890 and (2) a photograph of his residence, 1890 (both following p. 296), and (3) photograph of Journeycake with a delegation of Indians in Washington in 1867 (following p. 298).

84. There were many Ketchums among the Indians, not only among the Delawares, from 1830 to 1880 or later. "Captain" Ketchum is listed as a signatory of agreements with white organizations in 1832, 1843, and 1844 (*Transactions of the Kansas State Historical Society*, IX, 204; *Collections of the Kansas State Historical Society*, Vol. 16, pp. 755, 761). John Ketchum, Que-sha-to-wha, along with Charles Journeycake and other Delawares signed an agreement with Commissioner George W. Mannypenney in 1854, ceding lands. A James Ketchum was a member of the delegation of Delawares—which included Charles Journeycake and Agent Pratt, also—that went to Washington in 1867; he appears in the group picture mentioned in the previous footnote. In April, 1860, Mr. Pratt and a teacher at the mission drove out "to see chief Ketchum, who was sick." The teacher has left us a vivid picture of Ketchum's residence (Clara Gowing, *op. cit.*, p. 188).

85. From Algonquian Mingwe, "stealthy, treacherous." Used also by whites during the late colonial period to designate a detached band of Iroquois who settled in Pennsylvania (James Mooney, "Mingo," in *Handbook of the American Indians*, F. W. Hodge, ed.).

86. The school was begun in 1833; the first baptism occurred four years later. The school was moved out of low bottom lands in 1848 to its 1859 location (Rev. S. F. Smith, "Brief History of Missions in Kansas and Missouri," in *Home Mission Monthly*, Aug. 1879; Clara Gowing, *op. cit.*, p. 183, n. 3).

87. John Gill Pratt was born in Hingham, Mass., in 1814. He graduated from Andover Seminary in 1836 and was licensed to preach. In 1837 he married and immediately set out for Kansas. He served at the Shawnee Baptist Mission, where he printed religious material for Indians, and helped to publish a newspaper, the *Shawanoe Sun*. He worked with the Stockbridge Indians from 1844 to 1848, when he took charge of the Delaware Baptist Mission. Mr. and Mrs. Pratt had seven children. Mr. Pratt died in 1900; Mrs. Pratt, a short time later (Gowing, *op. cit.*, pp. 183–84, n. 4).

88. Elizabeth S. Morse, born 1814, was "sent out from Boston in 1842 by the American Baptist Mission Union" to teach school among the Cherokees. She went to the Delaware Mission School about 1848, where she taught until the Delawares were removed to Indian Territory in 1867, when she went to live with friends. She died in 1899 (Gowing, *op. cit.*, p. 183, n. 2).

89. In October, 1859, Miss Clara Gowing arrived at the Delaware Mission School. She was born in Massachusetts, had been president of the W.C.T.U. in Reading, Massachusetts, had taught in colored schools in Virginia, etc. She has left us a very interesting account of her five years at the Delaware Mission, in her article, previously cited, pp. 183–93.

90. In *Systems* (p. 289) Morgan acknowledges the aid of "Lemuel R. Ketchum (Wool-le-

kun-num, 'Light of the Sun'), a Delaware."

91. The following data on the religion of the Delaware are taken from Part Five of the Journal.

92. The Stockbridge Indians were originally the Housatonic, a tribe of the Mahican confederacy, living in Massachusetts. About 1735 they came to be called Stockbridge after one of their principal villages. After the American Revolution the Stockbridge Indians were removed to New York where they lived with the Oneidas. In 1833, together with the Oneidas and the Munsees, they were removed to Green Bay, Wisconsin. Here they became merged with the Munsees. Some years later they were again removed, this time to Kansas Territory where they were settled near Leavenworth. In 1856, however, all but a few of the Stockbridges were returned to Wisconsin.

93. *Totem* is derived from the Algonquian *ototeman*, "his brother-sister kin"; the Potawatomi were Algonquian-speaking (J. N. B. Hewitt, "Totem," in *Handbook of American Indians*, F. W. Hodge, ed.).

94. This was, without doubt, William Walker. He was born in Wayne County, Michigan, in 1800. He belonged to the Big Turtle clan (his mother's) of the Wyandot tribe. He was educated at a Methodist school in Worthington, Ohio, and is said to have "read and spoken" Greek, Latin, and French, besides speaking Wyandot, Delaware, Shawnee, Miami and Potawatomi. He went to Kansas with the Wyandots in 1843. Ten years later the Wyandots "met in their council house at Wyandot, organized Kansas-Nebraska into a Provisional Territory and elected a delegate to Congress" (who, however, was not seated). William Walker became Provisional Governor. He died in 1872. (A special publication of the Nebraska Historical Society, *The Provisional Government of Nebraska Territory and the Journals of William Walker*, edited by William E. Connelley, Lincoln, 1899, is

devoted to Walker, his family, and this period.)

In *Systems* (p. 283), Morgan acknowledged the assistance of Matthew R. [William's brother] and William Walker, "educated half-blood Wyandots," in obtaining the Wyandot system.

95. Outigamies were the Foxes (*Handbook of American Indians*, F. W. Hodge, ed., p. 1113).

96. Sioux is an abbreviation of Nadowessioux, a French corruption of Nadowe-is-iw, the Chippewa name for the Dakotas; it means "snake," "adder," and by metaphor, "enemy" ("Siouan Family," in *Handbook of American Indians*, F. W. Hodge, ed.).

97. Joseph Williams, born in Pennsylvania in 1801, served as associate justice in Iowa Territory and state. In 1857 he was appointed associate justice of Kansas Territory by President Buchanan; he served until 1861. He made his home in Ft. Scott; died in 1870. For an account of some of Williams' activities in Kansas in the fall of 1859 and 1860, see *Collections of the Kansas State Historical Society, 1915–18*, XIV, 205–6, 230; *Transactions of the Kansas State Historical Society, 1901–02*, VII, 402.

98. This is probably one of the earliest accounts of the Winnebago Medicine Dance, performed by a secret society in summer only. Its purpose is to prolong life and to cultivate certain nonmartial virtues. The Winnebago Medicine Dance is closely related to the Algonquian Midéwiwin, to the Dakota "Mystery Dance," and to the Omaha "Pebble Ceremony." See "The Ritual and Significance of the Winnebago Medicine Dance," *Journal of American Folk-Lore*, XXIV (1911): 149–208, and *The Winnebago Tribe* (Bureau of American Ethnology, 37th Annual Report, 1923), both by Dr. Paul Radin; see also "Winnebago," in *Handbook of American Indians*, edited by Hodge.

99. Jonathan Carver, *Travels Through the Interior Parts of North America in the Years

1766, 1767 and 1768* (London, 1778).

100. Leavenworth was founded in 1854. Although it suffered great destruction by fire in 1858, the population in 1861 was 8,000. It was the largest city in Kansas until 1880.

101. There was a Major Sibley at Ft. Leavenworth in the fall of 1855; we have not identified Charlotte Saxon (E. T. Carr, "Reminiscences Concerning Fort Leavenworth in 1855–56," *Collections of the Kansas State Historical Society, 1911–12*, XII, 377).

102. The *Twilight*, Captain J. Shaw, was "one of the finest and most popular [steamboats] . . . on the [Missouri] river in 1858" (Phil E. Chappell, "A History of the Missouri River," *Transactions of the Kansas State Historical Society, 1905–06*, IX, 287, 293).

103. In *Ancient Society* (New York, 1877) Morgan lists all of these clans (or gentes) with the exception of Dog and Buffalo as being clans of the Comanche, stating that he had obtained this information in 1859 from "Mathew Walker, a Wyandotte half-blood . . . [who] had lived among the Comanches . . ." (p. 177).

104. Population in 1860: 1,883.

105. Probably Jesse Olney (1798–1872), *A Practical System of Modern Geography: or a View of the Present State of the World* (Hartford, Conn.: D. F. Robinson and Co., 1828–29). Olney wrote other textbooks also: on arithmetic, history, a reader, etc.

106. Omaha was laid out in 1854, immediately after the opening of Nebraska Territory, although the site had been previously occupied by fur traders, and by Mormons (1846–48). Omaha was chartered as a city in 1867.

107. Some 12,000 Mormons established a great camp at "Winter Quarters" (called Florence after 1854) between 1846 and 1848. A picture of the migrants with their handcarts may be found in Addison E. Sheldon, *Nebraska, Old and New* (Lincoln, Neb.: University Publishing Company, 1937), p. 168. Florence was annexed to Omaha in 1917.

108. In *Ancient Society*, Morgan lists all of these clans, together with their native names, with the exception of Beaver as clans, or gentes, of the Otoes and Missouris which have "coalesced into one" (p. 156). William Hamilton's notes listed Beaver clan for both Otoe and Iowa.

109. In *Systems* (p. 285), Morgan states that he obtained a list of Otoe kinship terms from "an Otoe woman, the wife of M. Dupee, a French trapper, Dupee acting as interpreter." Charles Rulo's assistance is also acknowledged (p. 283).

110. There have doubtless been many prominent Indians named White Cloud. The famous Iowa chief by this name of whom Morgan speaks should not be confused with the famous Chippewa chief, Wabanaquot ("White Cloud"), born about 1830, or with half Sauk, half Winnebago, medicineman, Wabokieshiek ("The Light" or "White Cloud"), born about 1794. In *Systems* (p. 285), Morgan describes Robert D. White Cloud as "a man of fine natural abilities," and acknowledges his assistance with the Iowa schedule.

111. In *Ancient Society*, Morgan lists the following, with the exception of Beaver, as gentes of the Iowas (p. 156).

112. The Reverend William Hamilton was a Presbyterian missionary who had served at the Iowa and Sac Mission on Wolf River and who acquired much information on the Iowa tribe. Morgan visited him at Bellvue in 1860; see the Journal entry for June 6, 1860.

113. The *Peerless*, like the *Twilight*, was one of the fine boats on the Missouri River in the late fifties. She was commanded by Captain Bissel.

114. This is, without doubt, the Wakonda. Though difficult to define, it is an important religious concept of such tribes as the Omaha, Ponca, Osage, Kansa, Oto, Iowa, and Missouri. (See Alice C. Fletcher, "Wakonda," in *Handbook of American Indians*, F. W. Hodge, ed.)

115. This is not too far from the mark: see Fletcher's exposition, *op. cit.*

Chapter V

1. This was probably Thomas Frothingham, a Rochester attorney who had graduated from Union College in 1835 and was admitted to the bar in 1849.

2. The *Black Hawk* was a lower-river side-wheeler, built in 1860, sunk near Weston, Mo., in 1862 (Phil E. Chappell, "A History of the Missouri River," *Transactions of the Kansas State Historical Society, 1905-06*, IX, 299).

3. There was a great drought in Kansas in 1860. There was much suffering among the recently arrived white settlers, and many desperate appeals for help were sent to the east during this year. (See George W. Glick, "The Drought of 1860," *Transactions of the Kansas State Historical Society, 1905-06*, IX, 480-85.)

4. Simon D. Harvey, of the Society of Friends, in charge of the Shawnee Mission. It will be recalled that Morgan visited this mission in 1859, but Friend Harvey was not there at that time.

5. This was probably James Stanley and his wife Rachel, who are listed as being at the Mission in 1860 by R. W. Kelsey in *Friends and the Indians, 1655-1917* (Philadelphia, 1917, note, p. 144). There were, however, other Stanleys engaged in the missionary work of the Society of Friends in Kansas during this period. (See "Friends' Establishment in Kansas Territory," *Transactions of the Kansas State Historical Society, 1903-04*, VIII, 250-71.)

6. The older Keokuk (c. 1780-1848) was a renowned leader of the Sauk tribe. His mother is said to have been half French. He was not a chief by birth, but through ability, eloquence and scheming he became the chief of the Sauk. "It is said that the announcement of his elevation to supreme power was made in open council, and that it so aroused the anger and contempt of Black Hawk [the chief who led the Sauk in the "Black Hawk War"; Keokuk did not co-operate with Black Hawk in this venture] that he whipped off his clout and slapped Keokuk across the face with it. The act of creating Keokuk chief of the Sauk has always been regarded with ridicule by both the Sauk and the Foxes, for the reason that he was not of the ruling clan" (William Jones, himself a member of the Fox tribe, in "Keokuk," *Handbook of American Indians*, F. W. Hodge, ed., Washington, D. C., 1907).

After the death of Keokuk in Kansas in 1848, the chieftainship "with its unsavory associations, went to his son, Moses Keokuk (Wunagisa, 'he leaps up quickly from his lair') ... Moses Keokuk was acknowledged the purest speaker of the Sauk dialect. The Sauk were never tired of his eloquence ... Late in life he embraced Christianity and was baptized a Baptist; ... his death [at the Sauk and Fox agency in Oklahoma, in August, 1903] was regarded by the Sauk as a tribal calamity" (Jones, *loc. cit.*). See also Charles R. Green's interesting *Early Days in Kansas in Keokuk's Time on the Kansas Reservation* (Olathe, Kansas, 1912).

George Catlin painted portraits of both Keokuks, father and son (*The North American Indians*, Edinburgh, 1926, Vol. II); photographs of both men appear in Green's *Early Days*.

7. Clark Wissler classifies (after J. W. Powell) Sauk and Fox with the Eastern-Central division of the Algonquian language family along with the Shawnee, Kickapoo, Menominee, and others (*The American Indian*,

2nd ed.; New York: Oxford University Press, 1922, p. 403).

8. This is a characteristic of the Omaha type of kinship system. (See Sol Tax, "Some Problems of Social Organization," in *The Social Anthropology of North American Tribes*, Fred Eggan, ed., Chicago: University of Chicago Press, 1937, pp. 4–5.)

9. We cannot be sure of this name but it looks like Clover. Seth Clover was the Indian agent of the Osage River Agency, with headquarters at Paola, in 1860. This reservation contained Weas, Peorias, Piankeshaws, Kaskaskias and Miamis in that year (see *Report of the Commissioner of Indian Affairs for 1860*, pp. 114–15).

10. Allen Ward was made supervisor of Paola township in May, 1858 (*Transactions of the Kansas State Historical Society, 1889–96*, v, 492).

11. J. N. B. Hewitt gives "Osákiwug, 'people of the outlet,' or, possibly, 'people of the yellow earth,' in contradistinction from Muskwakiwuk, 'Red Earth People,' a name of the Foxes" ("Sauk," in *Handbook of American Indians*, F. W. Hodge, ed.).

12. Morgan acknowledges the aid of Antoine and Louis Gookie, "educated Menomines," in securing the Menominee schedule, in *Systems* (p. 288). Antoine Gokey is listed as interpreter at the Sac and Fox agency in 1853; his name appears among those participating in a "treaty or council" with the Commissioner of Indian Affairs at the Sac and Fox agency in 1859. Lewis Gokey is listed as "assistant smith" at the Sac and Fox agency for 1859–61, and "interpreter and physician" at the agency, 1863–65 (*Collections of the Kansas State Historical Society, 1923–25*, XVI, 731, 734–35, 738, 765).

13. Morgan lists these clans in *Ancient Society*, p. 170. Tax says the Fox "tribe was divided into a number of presumably [*sic*] patrilineal clans . . ." ("The Social Organization of the Fox Indians," in *The Social Anthropology of North American Tribes*, Fred Eggan, ed., p. 244; see also pp. 262 ff.).

14. In *Systems* (p. 289), Morgan says that he obtained the Munsee system in June, 1860, from Mrs. Haome Samuel (Mi-je-na-oke, "Plain Looking"), a Munsee woman who spoke English fluently.

15. Wissler assigns these tribes, plus the Omaha and Ponca, to the Dhegiha division—one of seven divisions—of the Siouan language family (*op. cit.*, p. 410). It must be remembered that Powell's classification of North American Indian languages was not worked out until many years after Morgan's trips to Kansas.

16. In *Systems* (p. 287), Morgan says that William Turner acted as interpreter for "Clear Sky . . . an Ojibwa chief, and his daughter, the wife of William Turner," in obtaining the Ojibwa schedule.

17. In *Systems* (p. 288), Morgan reports that he obtained the Sawk and Fox system from Moh-wha'-tä, "Yelping Wolf," a Sawk woman, and Antoine Gookie (Mok-kut-up-pe, "Big-set"), a Menominee, but the government interpreter for the Sawks and Foxes.

18. In *Systems* (p. 288), Morgan lists the Peoria and Kaskaskia systems as having been obtained in 1859, and we have already noted them. The Piankeshaw and Weaw systems were obtained in June, 1860, the former from Frank Vallé, "Red Sun," a half-blood Piankeshaw, the latter from John Mitchell, "Hard Knot," a half-blood Weaw. No doubt Morgan rechecked his 1859 data on his second trip.

19. Samuel M. Cornatzer was appointed census taker for Shawnee township in 1858 (George W. Martin, "Early Days in Kansas," *Transactions of the Kansas State Historical Society, 1905–06*, IX, 30, n. 9).

20. A Shawnee boy, named Levi Flint, age 17, entered the Shawnee Methodist Manual Labor School in November, 1842. His studies included Latin, English, grammar, arithmetic, philosophy, penmanship, declamation, etc. (Rev. J. J. Lutz, "The Methodist Missions Among the Indian Tribes in Kansas," *Transactions of the Kansas State Historical Society, 1905–06*, IX, 187).

21. See *ibid.*

22. Dr. Samuel G. Morton (1799–1851), the great pioneer in physical anthropology in the United States, believed that the American Indian constituted a distinct race, unrelated to any other. The Eskimos, he said, were a subdivision of the Polar race. They had come over from Asia in "small and straggling parties," whereas the American Indians were, presumably, indigenous in the New World. (See Morton's *Crania Americana*, Philadelphia, 1839, pp. 52, 63, 264.)

23. See Morgan's tribute to Harvey in *Systems* (pp. 217–18).

24. We have found no reference to this steamer.

25. This steamer, whose master was Joseph La Barge, was built in 1859. She was a sidewheeler, 225 feet long, 32-foot beam, with a hold 6 feet deep, and could carry 500 tons; she "was one of the most famous on the river" (Chappell, *op. cit.*, p. 301). She figures prominently in an episode on Morgan's trip up the Missouri River in 1862, as we shall see later.

26. Both belong to the Dhegiha division of the Siouan language family (Clark Wissler, *The American Indian*, 2nd ed.; New York: Oxford University Press, 1922, p. 410).

27. According to J. Owen Dorsey, the Omaha had ten gentes, five in each moiety (*Siouan Sociology*, Washington: Bureau of American Ethnology, Fifteenth Annual Report, 1897, pp. 226–27). The Catada (Morgan's la-ta-da) gens was divided into four subgentes, of which Bear and Turtle in Morgan's list are two. Thus Morgan recorded the names of the ten gentes and of two of four subgentes.

28. Morgan had previously found this term and concept among the Iowas.

29. Moody Martin, "Long Wing," was "an intelligent young Omaha" who assisted Morgan in obtaining the Omaha schedule and other data (*Systems*, p. 284).

30. Morgan acknowledges the assistance of Henry Fontenelle in *Systems*, p. 284. Fontenelle was a member of a rather numerous family of Omahas who were descended from a marriage between Lucien Fontenelle, a Frenchman from New Orleans, and an Omaha woman. See Mrs. A. L. Thompson, "Interesting Historical Notes Pertaining to the Fontenelle Family . . .," *Transactions and Reports of the Nebraska State Historical Society*, I (1885): 90–93. He was described as a "reliable, intelligent, educated half-blood" Omaha by the editor of the *Transactions and Reports of the Nebraska State Historical Society* who requested him to write a "History of the Omaha Indians," published in I, 76–85.

31. Rev. Charles Sturges, Presbyterian, at the Omaha Mission, Blackbird Hills, Nebraska Territory (*Systems*, p. 284).

32. Fontenelle was quite right on every point: Pawnee and Arikara are dialects of the Caddoan language family; Omaha and Dakota are members of the Siouan family of languages.

33. Hamilton was born in Pennsylvania in 1811. In 1837 he was ordained and sent to Nebraska Territory by the Presbyterian Board of Missions. He served at the Iowa and Sac Mission on Wolf River and also at the Otoe and Omaha Mission at Bellevue. He acquired considerable information on the Iowa and Omaha tribes; the Reverend J. Owen Dorsey acknowledges receipt of data on these tribes from Hamilton. See various annual reports of the Bureau of American Ethnology: *Omaha Sociology*, Third Annual Report, 1884; *A Study of Siouan Cults*, Eleventh Annual Report, 1894; and *Siouan Sociology*, Fifteenth Annual Report, 1897.

Hamilton and S. M. Irvin established a press, taught themselves the art of printing,

and published a considerable number of books and pamphlets (see James C. Pilling, *Bibliography of the Siouan Languages*, Bureau of American Ethnology, Bulletin 5, 1887, pp. 31-33, for a list of them) of which *An Ioway Grammar*, 1848, is the best known. Douglas C. McMurtrie and Albert H. Allen give a fascinating account of their publishing activities in their little book, *A Forgotten Pioneer Press of Kansas* (Chicago, 1930).

A brief autobiographic sketch of Hamilton may be found in *Transactions and Reports of the Nebraska State Historical Society*, I (1885): 60–73.

34. Morgan met the Reverend Samuel M. Irvin in Nebraska on May 6, 1862; see entry for this date and accompanying footnote on Irvin.

35. *An Ioway Grammar*, by William Hamilton and S. M. Irvin, was published by the Ioway and Sac Mission Press in 1848. Morgan's copy of this work is in the Rush Rhees Library, University of Rochester, at the present time.

36. There is a great deal of information on Allis in "Letters Concerning the Presbyterian Mission in the Pawnee Country, Near Bellevue, Nebr., 1831–1849," *Collections of the Kansas State Historical Society, 1915–1918*, XIV, pp. 570–784: how he went on a summer's hunting trip with a group of Pawnees; how he was fired on by a party of Sioux; his life among the Pawnees as a missionary, teacher, etc. Some sixteen letters from Allis to Rev. David Greene are included in this article. See also Allis' own account of his life in "Forty Years Among the Indians and on the Eastern Borders of Nebraska," *Transactions and Reports of the Nebraska Historical Society*, II (1887): 133–66.

37. We have found no mention of Mills or Glode in *Systems* or elsewhere. Joseph Tesson is described in *Systems*, pp. 284, 288, as a French and quarter-blood Indian (Menominee) who had lived eighteen years among

the Cheyennes, spoke the language fluently, had married among them, reared a family, and become a Cheyenne chief. He assisted Morgan in obtaining the Cheyenne and Ogalalla Dakota schedules.

38. This bird must have been a domestic dove, imported from the east, as there is no native bird of the region that answers this description.

39. Spencer Fullerton Baird (1823–88), an eminent American ornithologist, went to the Smithsonian Institution in 1850 as assistant to Joseph Henry and became secretary of the Institution upon the latter's death in 1878.

40. This was, without doubt, the Swallow-tailed Kite (*Elanoides forficatus*).

41. In *Systems* (p. 284) Morgan says that he obtained the Brulé schedule from a Brulé woman at St. Mary's, Iowa, assisted by George Deschoutte, a half-blood, her husband, as interpreter. He fails to specify the date, however.

42. Morgan did not succeed in obtaining the Pawnee system until his field trip of 1862.

43. S. B. Woolworth was an educator in Albany, N. Y. Morgan had considerable correspondence with him from time to time.

44. Peter Abadie Sarpy, born in St. Louis in 1805. The Sarpy family was prominent in the Missouri River fur trade for many years. Peter Sarpy was in charge of a trading post at Bellevue; he also had a store at St. Mary's. Almost everyone who went up the Missouri met him or knew of him; many travelers mention him in their journals or memoirs: Samuel Allis, "Forty Years Among the Indians . . .," *Transactions and Reports of the Nebraska State Historical Society*, II, 162–63; *Journal of Rudolph F. Kurz*, J. N. B. Hewitt, ed., Washington: Bureau of American Ethnology, Bulletin 115, 1937; S. D. Bangs, "History of Sarpy County," *Transactions and Reports of the Nebraska State Historical Society*, II (1887): 293–306; Charles Larpen-

teur, *Forty Years a Fur Trader* . . ., Elliott Coues, ed. (New York, 1898), II, 299–300.

"Colonel" Sarpy earned that title by some distinction, not as a military man . . ." (Allis, *op. cit.*, p. 162). Sarpy county, on the Missouri River, was named for him.

45. The Rev. Samuel Allis observes that Colonel Sarpy "became addicted to intemperance" (*op. cit.*, p. 162).

46. Among the Morgan archives in the University of Rochester Library there is a manuscript of some thirty pages, "Extracts from the Unpublished Journals of Rev. William Hamilton, a Missionary of the Presbyterian Board for Twenty Years among the Iowas and Sacs of Kansas and the Omahas of Nebraska, now resident in Bellevue." The extracts are from the years 1848–52. They contain considerable ethnographic data. They also report verbatim conversations between Rev. Hamilton and Indians in which the former tries to show the Indians how wrong—not to say ridiculous—their religious beliefs are, and that the religion of the Presbyterians is the only true faith.

47. We have not identified Joseph Sarpy. There was a John B. Sarpy, but he died in 1857.

48. A number of Shoshonean tribes have been called "Snake."

49. James Mooney says "while it is quite probable that the Cheyenne may have had the clan system in ancient times while still a sedentary people, it is almost as certain that it disappeared so long ago as to be no longer even a memory" ("Cheyenne," in *Handbook of American Indians*, F. W. Hodge, ed.).

50. Black Hawk (1767–1838) is said by John R. Swanton to have been "a subordinate chief of the Sauk and Fox Indians . . . born at the Sauk village . . . belonged to the Thunder gens of the Sauk tribe" ("Black Hawk," *Handbook of American Indians*). A renowned warrior, he was much opposed to the encroachment of the white man. He is best known for his leadership in the Black Hawk War of 1832.

51. In *Systems* (p. 288), Morgan reports that he obtained the "Shiyan" system from Joseph Tesson and his family at Rulo Half-breed Reservation, Nebraska Territory, in June 1860.

52. Reverend Cyrus Byington, a missionary for forty years among the Choctaws. In August, 1859, Morgan received the Choctaw system from Byington and his colleague, the Rev. John Edwards (*Systems*, p. 286).

53. In *Ancient Society* (New York, 1877) Morgan reports that when he "visited the eastern Dakotas in 1861, and the western in 1862 . . . [he] could find no satisfactory traces of gentes [i.e., clans] among them" (p. 154). He was inclined to believe that they had lost clan organization as a consequence of an enforced change in mode of life rather than that they had never had clans.

54. In *Systems* (p. 288) Morgan refers to Tesson as a quarter-blood Menominee.

55. Probably Haome Samuels, husband of "Plain Looking," the Munsee woman on the Chippewa reservation from whom he obtained the Munsee system (*Systems*, p. 289).

56. Samuel N. Latta, U. S. agent of the upper Missouri, had the following to say on this point: "This old American Fur Company (so-called) is the most corrupt institution ever tolerated in our country. They have involved the government in their speculations and schemes; they have enslaved the Indians, kept them in ignorance; taken from them year after year their pitiful earnings, in robes and furs, without giving them an equivalent; discouraged them in agriculture by telling them that should the white man find that their country would produce they would come in and take their lands from them. They break up and destroy every opposition to their trade that ventures into their country, and then make up their losses by extorting from the Indians" (*Report of the Commissioner of Indian Affairs for 1862*, pp. 340–41).

57. This was, in all probability, Alfred J. Vaughan (1801–71). He was agent of the Osage agency in 1845, subagent for the Iowas, Sacs and Foxes, 1848–49, agent for the upper Missouri Indians, 1852-57, and agent for the Blackfeet until 1861. He had an Indian wife. Father De Smet baptized one of Vaughan's daughters on board the *Yellowstone* in 1864. He was commonly called "Major," as were all Indian agents; perhaps a major became a colonel when he became advanced in years (see *Contributions to the Montana Historical Society*, X, 272–73; Larpenteur, *op. cit.*, II, 417; and the reports of the Commissioner of Indian Affairs for 1853–61).

58. Near Rulo, Nebraska.

59. The Blackfoot schedules, both Piegan and Blood, used by Morgan in *Systems* (p. 289) were obtained on subsequent trips.

60. See Captain W. P. Clark's *Indian Sign Language* (Philadelphia, 1885); Col. Garrick Mallery's *Sign Language among North American Indians* (Washington: Bureau of American Ethnology, First Annual Report, 1881). See also Morgan's footnote in *Systems*, p. 227.

61. Morgan expatiates upon this theme in a long footnote in *Systems* (pp. 206–7). A pure-blood Indian has very little "animal passion," he says; in the half-breed it is "sensibly augmented," and in a three-quarters-blood "it becomes excessive, and tends to indiscriminate licentiousness." The passion of love, says Morgan, was virtually unknown among Indian tribes. He ascribes these differences in attitude and behavior to fundamental differences in physiological processes.

We should remember, in this connection, that no less a scientist than Dr. Samuel G. Morton of the University of Pennsylvania in his *Crania Americana* (Philadelphia, 1839) characterized the Iroquois as "proud, audacious, and vindictive . . . cautious and cunning . . . not much affected by the passion of love . . ." (p. 191). Indian men in general were "habitually cold" in their manner to the gentler sex, stern to their children (p. 80). The Indian, according to Morton, is naturally indolent (p. 77), has a "demoniac love of slaughter which delights in the shriek of the wounded and the groan of the dying. Revenge is his ruling passion . , ." (p. 79). On the whole (p. 81), the Indian was "decidedly inferior" in "intellectual faculties" to the Caucasian and Mongolian races (p. 81).

Morton died in 1851. Morgan's views of nine years later seem rather moderate by comparison.

62. See R. H. Lowie's discussion of "wife purchase" in aboriginal North America in *Primitive Society* (New York, 1920), pp. 21–22.

63. Morgan has high praise for American missionaries in *Systems*: "There is no class of men upon the earth, whether considered as scholars, as philanthropists, or as gentlemen, who have earned for themselves a more distinguished reputation." More encomiums follow (pp. viii–ix).

64. As we noted in Chapter III, everyone wanted to do something for the Indians' good. But the almost inevitable consequence of this altruism was to transfer lands held by the Indians to the white man.

65. This is the steamer that Morgan boarded on June 4, 1860, at St. Joseph for the trip up the river.

66. Pedro de Castañeda, one of the chroniclers of the Coronado Expedition, more than once observes that groups of bulls only are encountered (George P. Winship, *The Coronado Expedition*, Washington: Bureau of American Ethnology, Fourteenth Annual Report, 1896, Part I, pp. 508, 543).

67. It is a significant and an impressive fact that this device of primitive culture was not superseded by modern technology until the latter part of the nineteenth century—less than a century ago.

68. The *Hendrick Hudson* was put into service on the Hudson River in 1845. Its tonnage was 1,179, the first steamboat on that river to exceed 1,000 tons. The *New World* also was a Hudson River boat which began service in 1848. She was the largest steamboat of her day: 1,418 tons, 371 feet long. Her paddle wheels were 46 feet in diameter and 12 feet wide; her engine had a 76-inch cylinder and a 15-foot stroke; her speed, 20 m.p.h. (Fred E. Dayton, *Steamboat Days*, New York: Tudor, 1925, pp. 56, 58).

69. Built in 1854–55 by John Augustus Roebling (1806–69), a German-born engineer. This was the first bridge over the Niagara. Roebling and his son, Washington Augustus Roebling, built a number of great suspension bridges, the most notable of which was the Brooklyn Bridge ("Roebling" and "Suspension Bridges" in *The Columbia Encyclopedia*, 2nd ed.; New York: Columbia University Press, 1950).

Chapter VI

1. Undoubtedly to attend to his business interests; see Chap. I.

2. St. Paul was a village of but 32 houses in 1849 when it was designated as the capital of the newly organized territory. It was incorporated as a city in 1854.

3. See below, notes 58 and 62, for Tate and Bird; we cannot identify Rune, or Rerne.

4. Probably Rev. Alonzo Barnard (1817–1905). He and other missionaries, under the leadership of Rev. F. Ayer, were sent by the Presbyterian Missionary Society of Oberlin, Ohio, to northern Minnesota in 1842 or 1843. Barnard worked at Red Lake, Cass Lake, and at Little Winnipeg; he established

a school and a mission for the Indians. See in the *Collections of the Minnesota Historical Society* Rev. Stephen R. Riggs' article, "Protestant Missions in the Northwest," VI (1894): 156–58; D. A. J. Baker, "Early Schools in Minnesota," I, 82; Rev. C. Hobart, "Religious Movements in Minnesota," I, 86; Minnesota Biographies, XIV (1912).

5. We have not been able to identify him further. He may have meant Mr. Coldwell, editor of the Nor'Wester at Fort Garry; see below, p. 218, note 66.

6. Joseph James Hargrave, F.R.G.S., published a book, *Red River*, in Montreal in 1871. In it he recounts many incidents of his journey to Fort Garry in company with Morgan which we shall cite from time to time. He describes Morgan as "Mr. Lewis H. Morgan, a legal gentleman from Rochester, in the State of New York . . . making a tour to Red River Settlement on a scientific mission . . ." (p. 42).

7. Morgan faced this question again in 1862 on the upper Missouri (see p. 145).

8. Elisha Kent Kane (1820–57), received the M.D. degree from the University of Pennsylvania; served as surgeon on arctic expeditions; wrote *Arctic Explorations* (Philadelphia, 1856) and other works on this subject.

9. Morgan and Hargrave shared a double bed in a "solitary house" at Kandotta, says Hargrave. Morgan "passed the evening working up his correspondence, using the broad side of his valise for a writing desk" (*op. cit.*, p. 45).

10. "Of the large party which had travelled to St. Cloud," writes Hargrave, "only three continued their journey westward, Mr. Morgan, Mrs. Cook, and myself. Mrs. Cook was a lady who, having passed the earlier part of her life in London, had several years before 1861 quitted England, and, along with her husband and family, settled down on a farm at a place called Alexandria, about 170 miles west from St. Paul" (p. 45).

11. Probably Charles T. Stearns (1807–98), who lived in St. Cloud; Stearns country was named for him; he served in the territorial legislature. See William B. Mitchell, "St. Cloud in the Territorial Period," *Collections of the Minnesota Historical Society*, XII (1908): 642; also Minnesota Biographies, *ibid.*, XIV (1912).

12. "The party coming from Georgetown had heard rumors of Indian disturbances, and were anxious to make all haste in the direction of St. Paul . . ." (Hargrave, p. 46). In August of the following year there was a rather widespread uprising of Sioux who laid waste a number of settlements and killed their inhabitants, not far from the route traversed by Morgan and his companions (see "History of the Indian War," Report of Lt. Gov. Donnelly, in *Report of the Commissioner of Indian Affairs for 1862*, pp. 203–12).

13. Hargrave (pp. 48–50) has a fuller account of their night at Fort Abercrombie.

14. In *Systems* (p. 284), Morgan acknowledges the aid of Louis Roubillard, a half-breed Yanktonais, interpreter at Ft. Abercrombie, in obtaining the Yanktonais kinship system.

    Hargrave reports: "After dusk we retired within doors and spent the evening together in a public room, the majority of the company smoking, sipping their whisky and water, and watching the progress made by Morgan who, book and pen in hand, was closely questioning a couple of Indian half-breeds whom the Colonel had procured for his satisfaction" (p. 49).

15. J. C. and H. C. Burbank & Co., "a St. Paul firm under whose auspices the whole transport business on the line is carried on" (Hargrave, p. 51).

16. Hargrave says that "Mr. Morgan was much chagrined at this intelligence . . . and he seriously thought of giving up the project of going further, and returning by the first stage to St. Paul. I felt, however, so disinclined to part with such a pleasant travelling companion as he that I exerted all my powers of persuasion to induce him to finish his trip, and I succeeded" (p. 52).

17. The names in this list correspond with those given in the article "Dakota," in *Handbook of American Indians*, F. W. Hodge, ed. (Part I; Washington, D. C.: Bureau of American Ethnology, 1907).

18. Stephen Return Riggs, a missionary long resident among the Sioux.

19. According to James Mooney, Cheyenne is from the Sioux name Sha-hi´-yena or Shai-ena, "people of alien speech" ("Cheyenne" in *Handbook of American Indians*, F. W. Hodge, ed.).

20. George W. Northrup (1837–64), born in New York state, went to St. Paul in 1852, became a well known Indian trader, hunter, and guide; he was killed in battle during the Civil War; see Minnesota Biographies, *Collections of the Minnesota Historical Society*, Vol. XIV (1912).

21. Many works on the Hudson Bay area have pictures of dog trains; for example, Douglas MacKay, *The Honourable Company* (rev. ed.; New York: Bobbs-Merrill, 1949), plates at pp. 94 and 199.

22. In *Systems* (p. 286), Morgan records that he obtained the kinship system of the Cree of the Woods at Georgetown in July, 1861, from a half-blood Cree woman from Pembina Mountain. In *Systems*, however, he equates Cree of the Woods with Na-he-a-wuk, whereas in the present journal entry this is the name of the Swampy Cree.

23. In *Ancient Society* Morgan says "like the Dakota . . . [the Cree] have lost the gentile organization which presumptively once existed among them" (p. 167).

24. According to W. R. Gerard, in *Handbook of American Indians*, F. W. Hodge, ed., Pembina is a corruption of Cree nipiminan, "watered berry"; it is commonly applied to the high-bush cranberry, *Viburnum opulus*.

25. "Georgetown was a mere village, consisting of a few dwelling houses and stores erected by or for the Hudson's Bay Company . . ." (Hargrave, p. 51).

26. Alexander H. Murray, a Chief Trader of the Company. According to Hargrave, Murray was not in Georgetown when he and Morgan arrived on July 12, but arrived by boat from Red River Settlement about the 17th. It turned out that Murray had met Hargrave in Scotland in 1857. It happened, also, that the man who had filled out the Gaelic schedule for Morgan, the Reverend Duncan McNab (see *Systems*, p. 77), was a relative of Murray (Hargrave, pp. 53–56).

27. We omit much of this record here. In *Systems*, Morgan devotes most of pp. 237–38 to information obtained from Murray.

28. Morgan questioned his informants closely on matters of topography. He was especially interested in the location and extent of prairie because of its bearing upon Indian settlement and migration.

29. Acknowledged in *Systems*, p. 286.

30. In *Systems*, p. 207, Morgan says she was a quarter-blood Cree.

31. Morgan got his Cree names and their English equivalents confused, as we have already seen.

32. According to *Systems* (p. 287), his Lowlands Cree schedule was filled out at Fort Garry.

33. Hargrave frequently speaks of the great swarms of mosquitoes, but the relationship between them and malaria was not known at that time.

34. This may have been Coldwell, the editor of the Nor'Wester; see below, p. 218, note 66.

35. J. C. Burbank of Burbank & Co., the transportation company previously mentioned. Mr. Burbank was a very prominent businessman in St. Paul; he is frequently mentioned in the *Collections of the Minnesota Historical Society*; see Gen. Judson W. Bishop, "History of the St. Paul and Sioux City Railroad, 1864–1881" (of which Burbank was a director), X, 400–401; see also Henry S. Fairchild, "Sketches of the Early History of Real Estate in St. Paul," X, 428, 434–35.

36. Material in this paragraph was used in *Systems*, p. 277.

37. Much of the following data on the Kutchin was later used in *Systems*, pp. 237–38.

38. The material in the following paragraph was used in *Systems*, p. 238.

39. This statement, used in *Systems*, p. 238, is supplemented in a footnote by an observation Morgan made on his trip up the Missouri River in 1862 (briefly related in his journal).

40. Much of the following paragraph was used in *Systems*, p. 206.

41. Mr. Ohlson was the husband of the half-breed Cree woman from whom Morgan obtained the system of the Cree of the Woods while at Georgetown (*Systems*, p. 286).

42. Acknowledged in *Systems*, p. 287; see also *ibid.*, p. 207.

43. Some of the following examples were used in *Systems*, p. 206.

44. The city of St. Louis has grown up in an area that once contained a considerable number of Indian mounds. In 1819 Thomas Say and T. R. Peale of the scientific expedition under Major S. H. Long surveyed and mapped the mound area (T. R. Peale, "Ancient Mounds at St. Louis, Missouri, in 1819," *Annual Report*, Washington, D. C.: Smithsonian Institution, 1861, pp. 386–91).

45. Morgan believed that the northwest coast of America, because of its great natural abundance of food, played a pre-eminent role in the migrations of Indian tribes after their entry into America and in the subsequent peopling of both North and South America; see *Systems*, pp. 241–43.

46. Hargrave gives us a description of the *Pioneer*: "She was a small vessel propelled by a 'stern wheel' . . . She had been built on the upper waters of the Red River; her machinery . . . had originally belonged to another steamer running on the Mississippi, . . . Her original name was the 'Anson Northrop' [who built one of the first steamboats to navi-

gate the Red River; see Capt. Russell Blakeley, "Opening of the Red River of the North to Commerce and Civilization," in *Collections of the Minnesota Historical Society*, VIII (1898): 48; Morgan has previously referred to Anson Northrup, p. 110]. She was provided with four staterooms, each containing two berths . . . [In addition to these there were] a series of open berths extending along the main saloon, from which they were separated only by the curtains . . . The steamboat was small and overcrowded, the funnel rose up through the saloon, rendering that chamber extremely warm . . ." Morgan and Hargrave shared one of the four staterooms (pp. 56–57, 60–61).

47. See discussion of Indian migration in Chapter I; also *Systems*, pp. 241–43.

48. This may have been the article on "Indian Migrations," which was not published, however, until 1869 and 1870; see Chapter I.

49. Morgan acknowledges, in *Systems*, p. 287, the aid of Angus McKay, a quarter-blood Cree, in obtaining the system of the Cree of the Lowlands.

50. Manito, or manitou, derived from an Algonquian language, designated "the mysterious and unknown . . . powers of life and of the universe," according to Alice C. Fletcher ("Manito," in *Handbook of American Indians*, F. W. Hodge, ed.).

51. See Hargrave's account of this event (p. 64).

52. Letters were transported overland fortnightly from Fort Abercrombie to Pembina, according to Hargrave (p. 67), which accounts for the fact that letters from Rochester got there before Morgan did.

53. See Hargrave's account of these carts which he calls "Red River carts" (pp. 58–59); see also Gen. James H. Baker, "History of Transportation in Minnesota," *Collections of the Minnesota Historical Society*, IX, 20–21, for description of these carts and their use.

54. W. R. Gerard, in his article "Pemmican" in *Handbook of American Indians*, says that the word is from Cree *pimikan*, "manufactured grease."

55. This is most interesting. A number of northern Plains tribes had members of a warriors' society serve as police prior to and during a communal buffalo hunt to see that the orders of the hunt chief were carried out (see R. H. Lowie, *Primitive Society*, New York, 1920, pp. 385–86). Did the Indians borrow this trait from the whites, or was it the other way around?

56. "We made our way to the Governor's residence," says Hargrave, "where Mr. Morgan produced his letters, and stated his mission" (p. 186).

57. "On returning to Bachelor's Hall, Morgan, who had only one day in which to get through his business in order to return to the United States with the steamboat, got very restless, and after filling his pipe, quitted us precipitately. I regret to say he did not return and I never saw him again" (Hargrave, p. 187).

58. There were several families of Taits in Red River Settlement; Hargrave has much to say about John Tait (pp. 267–68, 350).

59. This was James Bird, a half-breed Cree (*Systems*, p. 289).

60. James Bird "was known in British territory as 'Jim Jack' " (Anne McDonnell's notes to "The Fort Benton Journal, 1854–1856 and the Fort Sarpy Journal, 1855–1856" in *Contributions to the Historical Society of Montana*, X [1940]: 260).

61. In a footnote in *Systems*, pp. 206–7, Morgan states that "the Hudson's Bay Company, at an early day, induced Orkney men to emigrate to their territory" to serve as traders and trappers. "These adventurers took the Cree women, first as companions, and afterwards, under religious influences, as wives . . ." Morgan speculates about the consequences of this rather large-scale mixing of races and cultures, which he characterizes as "an exceedingly interesting experiment."

62. James Bird was quite a character. He was the son of James Bird (b. *ca.* 1778 in England), who entered the service of the Hudson's Bay Company at York Factory in 1788 and later

was Chief Factor at Red River. His mother was a Cree woman. James, Jr. was taken prisoner in 1816 when the Northwest Company attacked Selkirk (i.e., Red River) Settlement. Later he was in the service of the American Fur Company on the upper Missouri. Maximilian met him at Fort Mackenzie in August, 1833; he describes him as "a treacherous, very dangerous man, who had great influence among the Blackfeet. He had been formerly in the service of the American Fur Company, had then gone over to the Hudson's Bay Company, and cheated both . . . spoke the language of the Blackfeet perfectly, and lived constantly among them" (*Travels in North America*, Vol. 23, p. 135, of *Early Western Travels*, Reuben Gold Thwaites, ed., Cleveland, O., 1906).

Bird served as Father De Smet's guide on one occasion, but deserted him in the hope that he would perish in the desert (*Life, Letters and Travels of Father De Smet*, edited by H. M. Chittenden and A. T. Richardson, New York, 1905, II, 526–27).

Bird had been captured by the Blackfoot and remained among them for some time, eventually becoming an influential chief. Antoine Godin, who was a trader of the American Fur Company at Fort Hall, together with a Flathead chief murdered a Blackfoot chief at Pierre's Hole in revenge for the death of Godin's father. Later, in 1834 or 1835, a party of Blackfeet, led by James Bird, appeared on the opposite side of the river from Fort Hall. Bird requested Godin to come across the river and buy furs. "Godin complied, not suspecting treachery. He sat down to smoke . . . when Bird signalled to some Indians, who shot him in the back. While he was yet alive, Bird tore his scalp off and cut the letters "N.J.W.," Wyeth's [Wyeth was in charge of Fort Hall] initials, on his forehead" (Hiram M. Chittenden, *The American Fur Trade of the Far West*, New York, 1935, II, 655).

Bird returned to the Blackfoot reservation

in extreme old age. He died in 1892 at the age of 107 years. See Anne McDonnell, *op. cit.*, pp. 256–60; Douglas MacKay, *The Honourable Company*, pp. 160, 169.

63. In *Systems*, Morgan records that he obtained the Piegan Blackfoot system "from the wife and daughter of James Bird, Piegan Blackfoot women, and James Bird, a half-blood Cree, as interpreter" (p. 289).

64. He obtained the system from Iron Woman, an Assiniboin woman, with James Bird as interpreter (*Systems*, p. 284). In the summer of 1862, he obtained another Assiniboin schedule on the upper Missouri (*ibid*)

65. In *Systems* Morgan states that he obtained an Okinaken (Okinagan) schedule from Mrs. Ross, "an Okinaken woman from Washington Territory, and her daughter" (p. 290).

66. Mr. Coldwell was the editor of the Nor'Wester, a paper in Red River Settlement that came out fortnightly. A James Ross was associated with Coldwell in this enterprise; he is said to have been "a distinguished scholar at the Red River college of St. John" (Hargrave, p. 146). Hargrave does not say whether James Ross's wife was an Okinaken or not.

67. In *Systems* Morgan merely says that he obtained the Red Knife system from "two half-blood women of that nation" at "the Convent of St. Boniface, Red River Settlement" (p. 289). This tribe is listed as the Tatsanottine in *Handbook of American Indians*, F. W. Hodge, ed. The name, which Morgan spells Tal-sote′-e-na, means, according to the anonymous author of the *Handbook*'s article, " 'people of the scum water,' scum being a figurative expression for copper" (II, 698). Morgan translates it "Red Knife," i.e. "copper." Tin′ -ne is the Athapascan word for "people."

68. The other Athapascan schedule must have been from the Hare Indians, who call themselves, according to Morgan, Ta-na′ -tin-ne (they are listed as Kawchodinne in Hodge's *Handbook*). In *Systems* Morgan says he obtained this system in 1861 at Red River Set-

tlement "from Angeline Irvin, a half-blood native resident at Fort Good Hope, and James Bird, interpreter" (p. 289).

69. Built in 1821, named for Nicholas Garry, Deputy Governor of the Hudson's Bay Company.

70. In 1811 Thomas Douglas, Fifth Earl of Selkirk (1771–1820), acquired from the Hudson's Bay Company, in which he had a large investment, possibly amounting to control, a large tract of land at the confluence of the Red and Assiniboine rivers, upon which he settled immigrants from the Scottish Highlands in 1812. The rival to Hudson's Bay Company was the North West Fur Company of Montreal. In 1816 this rivalry erupted into bloody conflict in which Governor Semple of the Hudson's Bay Company and 20 of his 27 attendants were killed. The two companies were merged in 1821 (see Douglas MacKay's chapter about Selkirk, "A Gentleman Unafraid," in *The Honourable Company*).

71. The engineer's chain is 100 ft. long; Gunter's, or surveyor's chain, 66 ft.

72. "The most serious calamity which has yet befallen the Catholic missions in the [Red River] country was the burning of the old cathedral of St. Boniface . . . on 14th Dec., 1860 . . ." (Hargrave, p. 138).

73. "In the convent at St. Boniface there are now educated forty young ladies, of whom twenty-one are boarders, while in the same establishment there is an orphanage . . . of forty girls . . ." (Hargrave, p. 139).

74. Alexandre Antonin Taché (1823–94), a priest in the Order of Oblats, became Bishop of Arath in 1851, went to Red River Settlement in 1854 (Hargrave, pp. 130, 132, 134–36). He published a book *Vingt Années de Missions* [1845–65] *dans le Nord-Ouest de l'Amerique* (Montreal, 1888). See Donatien Frémont, *Mgr. Taché et la Naissance de Manitoba* (Winnipeg, 1930).

75. The Right Reverend David Anderson, from Exeter College, Oxford; consecrated first Bishop of Rupert's Land in 1849, the year of

his arrival in Red River Settlement (Hargrave, pp. 111, 190–91). Some account of his work, and that of his church, particularly with reference to prohibition of sale of liquor to Indians, is given by MacKay (*op. cit.*, pp. 228, 269).

76. Reverend James Hunter became Archdeacon of Cumberland in 1853; he came to Rupert's Land in 1844, and returned to England in 1865 (Hargrave, p. 112).

   Hargrave has two excellent chapters (ix and x) on ecclesiastical organizations, Protestant and Catholic, in the Red River country.

77. We do not find Captain Smith mentioned in Hargrave's narrative, but he does observe that "on the day of our arrival at Fort Garry, being the last Sunday of the residence of the Company of Royal Canadian Rifles . . . previous to their return to Canada . . ." (p. 187).

78. Hargrave has a fine account of the people and mode of life in Red River Settlement in various chapters of his book.

79. "When in Hudson's Bay Territory in 1861," says Morgan, "I was unable to procure either the Sussee system of relationship, or a vocabulary of their language. It seems to be generally understood that they belong to the Athapascan stock" (*Systems*, pp. 232–33). Both belong to the Northern group of Athapascan languages, according to the Wissler-Powell classification (Clark Wissler, *The American Indian*).

80. James Bird was also called "Jemmy Jock" (McDonnell, *op. cit.*, pp. 258–60).

81. Morgan equates Mountaineers with Red Knife. "Mountain Indians" included the Chipewyan and several other Athapascan groups (*Handbook of American Indians*, F. W. Hodge, ed., ii, 1094).

82. Robert Kennicott (1835–66), naturalist and explorer; one of the founders of the Chicago Academy of Science; spent some time in the Red River country, and from 1859 to 1862 in northwestern Canada; during the winters of 1858–59 and 1862–63 he worked on collec-

tions and field notes at the Smithsonian Institution (Frank C. Baker in *Dictionary of American Biography*, 1937). In 1860, Kennicott sent Morgan the kinship nomenclature of the Slave Lake Indians; in 1863, he obtained partial data on the Utahs from a delegation in Washington, D. C., which he sent to Morgan (*Systems*, pp. 232, 252, 289–90).

   In August, 1863, Kennicott reached Fort Garry on his way from the Mackenzie River country to Washington. Due to the Sioux uprising in Minnesota, then in progress, Kennicott "was detained for a considerable time at Fort Garry," says Hargrave, "and we saw much of him" (pp. 245–46).

83. The matter discussed here is so complicated and involved that the reader is merely referred to *Systems* for the comprehensive statement of Morgan's theories, and to p. 235 of that work for his appraisal of Athapascan systems in particular.

84. "Lower Fort Garry is built of limestone, quarried from the rock existing not far from where it stands. The Roman Catholic cathedral and the Bishop's residence are really fine stone buildings . . ." (Hargrave, p. 180).

85. Henry A. Ward; see index for other references.

86. See Morgan's previous entry on August 3. Hargrave describes Pembina as "a small, isolated settlement of Americans and half-breeds chiefly connected with the fur trade." On the American side of the boundary there were a customs house and a post office; on the British side, a Hudson's Bay trading post (Hargrave, p. 67).

87. Henry McKenney came to Red River Settlement from Canada to establish a business, which included the Royal Hotel (Hargrave, p. 200 and *passim*).

88. This may have been Frank L. Hunt (1825–1903), who wrote a pamphlet, "Britain's One Utopia," History and Science Society of Manitoba, *Transactions*, No. 61, 1902.

89. On the trip down the river passengers shot ducks and prairie chickens from the *Pioneer*'s

barge, but, says Hargrave, "the captain resolutely turned a deaf ear to all proposals about slackening speed for any feathered game" (p. 64).

90. In *Systems*, p. 287, Morgan lists all of the following schedules as having been obtained on the 1861 trip except the Ojibwa of Red Lake. However, he already had five Ojibwa schedules before he set out on his trip in 1861.

91. The Oxford English Dictionary says that "moschito" is an obsolete form of "mosquito." Hargrave speaks repeatedly of swarms of large and aggressive mosquitoes.

92. This is undoubtedly a facetious allusion to the so-called "degradation theory" of the day. A theological explanation of primitive cultures was that they were the result of degradation that followed the Fall of Man. We say facetious because Morgan explicitly repudiated the "Mosaic cosmogony" (*Ancient Society*, p. 8). E. B. Tylor specifically opposes the degradation theory in *Primitive Culture* (London, 1871), Chapter Two.

Chapter VII

1. Audubon says that Catlin's pictures misrepresent or distort facts, and that his descriptions are "trashy stuff" (*Audubon and His Journals*, ii, 108; see also pp. 10, 27, 47).

2. Rudolph Kurz' *Journal* (Washington, D. C.: Bureau of American Ethnology, 1937), pp. 130, 162, and *passim*.

3. See Smithsonian *Annual Report*, 1885, Pt. ii, pp. 368–83. Almost 1,000 pages of this huge volume are devoted to The George Catlin Indian Gallery in the U. S. National Museum, with memoir and statistics by Thomas Donaldson. This memoir contains an account of Catlin's life, itinerary of his travels,

catalog of his paintings, criticisms and appreciation of his work, etc.

4. A large side-wheeler; she was burned by the Confederates in the battle of Glasgow, Mo., Oct. 16, 1864 (Phil E. Chappell, "A History of the Missouri River," *Transactions of the Kansas State Historical Society, 1905–06*, IX, 312).

5. Morgan had been aboard the *Emilie* twice in 1860, going both up and down river on her.

6. Reverend Henry W. Reed went up the river on the *Spread Eagle* in the summer of 1862 to assume his duties as agent for the Blackfeet. His account of this trip appears in *Report of the Commissioner of Indian Affairs for 1862*, pp. 322–25. He is mentioned several times by Charles Larpenteur (*Forty Years a Fur Trader on the Upper Missouri, 1833–1872*, 2 vols.; New York, 1898, II, 348, 349, 351, 380), and by H. M. Chittenden (*History of Early Steamboat Navigation on the Missouri River*, New York, 1903, II, 300, 314, 316, 397).

7. On his field trips of 1859 and 1860.

8. The Narraganset and Pequot were Algonquian-speaking tribes of Rhode Island and Connecticut, respectively.

9. Paola; Morgan always spelled it with an *i*.

10. Morgan visited the Allis home in June, 1860, but Mr. Allis was not there at the time (see Journal of 1860).

11. Alice C. Fletcher renders the native names of the bands: Chaui, Kitkehaki, Pitahauerat or Tapage, and Skidi (article "Pawnee," in *Handbook of American Indians*, F. W. Hodge, ed., Washington, 1910). Clark Wissler (after Powell) places all four bands in the Pawnee type of the Caddoan language family (*The American Indian*, 2nd ed.; New York, 1922, p. 405).

12. In *Ancient Society* (pp. 164–65), Morgan says it is doubtful if the Pawnees had gentes (clans), but cites Allis' belief that they did. Apparently they did not, for Alice C. Fletcher discusses their social organization without mentioning clans (Fletcher, *op. cit.*, II, 215).

13. Benjamin F. Lushbaugh, Indian agent, prepared the report for the Pawnee Agency, Nebraska Territory, for 1862 (*Report of the Commissioner of Indian Affairs for 1862*, pp. 266–68).

14. Reverend Samuel M. Irvin, sent to Kansas by the Presbyterian Board of Missions in 1837, served at the Iowa and Sac Mission for many years. He collaborated with William Hamilton on two works: *An Ioway Grammar* (Ioway and Sac Mission, Kansas, 1848) and "Iowa and Sac Tribes," in *Information Respecting the History, Condition, and Prospects of the Indian Tribes of the United States*, H. R. Schoolcraft, ed. (Philadelphia, 1853), III, 259–77. See Pryor Plank, "The Iowa, Sac and Fox Indian Mission and Its Missionaries, Samuel M. Irvin and Wife" (*Transactions of the Kansas State Historical Society, 1907–08*, X, 312–25).

15. We have not been able further to identify these persons.

16. Indian agent John A. Burbank reported that the Iowas "have been unusually industrious, and are making rapid strides towards civilization . . . [they are] anxious to live like the whites" (*Report of the Commissioner of Indian Affairs for 1862*, pp. 277–78).

17. He assisted Morgan in 1859 in obtaining the Iowa kinship system.

18. Agent Burbank reported in 1862: "The school cannot be called a success. In the spring the parents keep the children at home to help put in the crop, and the children are not disposed to attend . . ." (*Report of the Commissioner of Indian Affairs for 1862*, p. 278).

19. Daniel Vanderslice was agent of the Great Nemaha agency for the Iowas, Sacs, and Foxes of the Missouri for several years prior to 1860.

20. A General Bayless came to Kansas in 1856 and settled in Highland, apparently (*Transactions of the Kansas State Historical Society, 1907–08*, X, 242).

21. In 1860, W. P. Badger was agent for the Kickapoos.

22. C. B. Keith was Kickapoo agent in 1862.

23. Alfred J. Vaughan, usually referred to as "Colonel" or "Major," was a well-known figure on the upper Missouri for many years. He was born in 1801, entered the Indian service in 1842, was subagent for the Iowas Sacs, and Foxes in 1848–49, agent for the upper Missouri Indians 1852–57, then agent for the Blackfeet. Vaughan had an Indian wife; both were passengers on the steamboat *Shreveport* up the Missouri in the summer of 1862. Larpenteur describes Vaughan (*op. cit.*, II, 417); Father De Smet baptized a daughter of Vaughan on the *Yellowstone* in July, 1864 (Anne McDonnell's notes to "The Fort Benton Journal, 1854–1856 and The Fort Sarpy Journal, 1855–1856," in *Contributions to the Historical Society of Montana*, X [1940]: 272–73).

24. H. B. Branch, sometimes addressed as "Colonel," was a superintendent with offices in St. Louis. The agents on reservations in Kansas and Nebraska territories reported to him annually, while he reported for the region to the Commissioner of Indian Affairs.

25. Unidentified.

26. Samuel Buel Woolworth graduated from Hamilton College in 1822. He was principal of Cortland Academy in Homer, N. Y., and of Albany State Normal School from 1852–56; secretary of the Board of Regents for the State of New York from 1855 to 1880, the year of his death. Morgan had considerable correspondence with him during the 1870's.

27. Hewitt was a judge in the 3rd Puget Sound District about 1860–61. He held a judgeship in Washington for eight years. He is described (in H. H. Bancroft, *History of Washington, Idaho and Montana*, San Francisco, 1890, p. 279) as "honest but not scholarly." He once served as a captain of a company of volunteers, and as such visited the scene of the White River massacre (Edmond S. Meany,

History of the State of Washington, New York: Macmillan, 1909, p. 184).

28. The *Spread Eagle*, Charles P. Chouteau, master, was one of "the finest and most popular" steamboats on the Missouri River in her time. Built in 1857, she was owned by the American Fur Company and made regular trips up the river from 1859 through 1862. She was sunk at Bates' woodyard, above Washington, Mo., in 1863 (Chappell, *op. cit.*, pp. 283, 293, 311).

29. They reached Fort Benton on June 20.

30. Benjamin F. Lushbaugh was the agent for the Pawnee in 1862. He has some account of his farming activities in his report for that year. A special farmer, Chas. H. Whaley, assumed his duties on the reserve on July 1, 1862 (*Report of the Commissioner of Indian Affairs for 1862*, pp. 266–68).

31. Father Pierre-Jean De Smet, S.J. (1801–73) was indeed well known, not to say famous. He was born in Belgium in 1801 and came to the United States in 1821. In 1838 he was sent, with another priest, to found a mission among the Potawatomis, near Council Bluffs, Iowa. For the next thirty years or so he became a familiar figure in the upper Missouri River region, known to countless residents and travellers, Indians and whites alike. He made several trips to Europe, and once sailed around Cape Horn to Oregon. Towns have been named for him in Idaho, Montana, and South Dakota; a contemporary steamboat bore his name. He has some account of his trip up the Missouri on the *Spread Eagle* in 1862: "The respectable and worthy captain, Mr. Charles P. Chouteau, had had a little chapel prepared on board—I had the great consolation of offering the holy sacrifice of the mass every day . . ." (extract from a letter by De Smet in *Life, Letters, and Travels of Father Pierre-Jean De Smet, S.J.*, Hiram M. Chittenden and Alfred T. Richardson, eds., 4 vols.; New York, 1905, II, 783–88).

32. He did not do so, however, but returned on the *Spread Eagle*. On September 5, 1862, he addressed a letter to "Hon. Mr. Mix, Acting Superintendent of Indian Affairs, Washington, D. C.," telling of these plans and, apparently, his reason for changing them: unrest and hostility toward the whites among the Indian tribes, especially the Sioux (*Report of the Commissioner of Indian Affairs for 1862*, p. 358).

33. Wilcox, in his diary of the trip, says there were 75 persons aboard the *Spread Eagle* of whom one-half were passengers.

34. One of these was James Henry Morley, whose diary has already been referred to.

35. The *Key West* is listed by Chappell as an "upper Missouri river steamboat" in 1860–62 (*op. cit.*, p. 315). It was common practice for two steamboats to ascend the river together, one large, the other small. By the time the larger boat had ascended the river as far as she could go she would have discharged most of her cargo. The balance of cargo and passengers were then transferred to the smaller boat for the rest of the journey up the river.

36. Alexander Culbertson (1809–79). A very prominent person in the upper Missouri River region for many years. Born in Pennsylvania, he first went up the Missouri in 1833, the year in which Prince Maximilian visited Fort Union and Fort McKenzie. By 1840 he had been put in charge of Fort McKenzie, and eight years later he took charge of all the forts of the upper Missouri outfit on the upper Missouri and Yellowstone rivers. He acquired great wealth, and established himself on an estate at Peoria, Illinois, where his fortune was rapidly dissipated. He died at the home of his daughter Julia in Nebraska in 1879.

Culbertson's "knowledge of the Indians and the western country was considered superior to anyone of that time," says Anne McDonnell (*op. cit.*, p. 241). Although accounts of him are numerous, probably the best brief sketch is hers. Other accounts may be found in Maximilian's journal, Father De Smet's *Life and Travels*, Audubon's journals, the journal of Rudolph Kurz, Larpenteur's journal, the journal of Thaddeus Culbertson, Alexander's half brother, etc.

37. Mrs. Culbertson was Natawista Iksana or Medicine Snake Woman, the daughter of Menestokos, a Blood Blackfoot chief. She married Alexander Culbertson when a young girl about 1840. "This marriage was of immense value to Culbertson in his business dealings with this tribe . . ." (McDonnell, *op. cit.*, p. 243). Five children were born to this union. Rudolph Kurz, an artist, described her as "one of the most beautiful Indian women . . . an excellent model for a Venus, ideal woman of a primitive race" (*op. cit.*, p. 224). Audubon speaks of her with admiration. And, of course, both Larpenteur and Father De Smet knew her. Best sketch of her is by McDonnell (*op. cit.*, pp. 243–46).

38. McDonnell has much information on what became of Culbertson's wealth and also his children (*op. cit.*, pp. 240–46). Probably many of his descendants are living in the West today.

39. This was Malcolm Clark (1817–69); passenger Wilcox mentions him by full name. Like almost all other "Majors" and "Colonels," his title was honorific. He was born in Indiana and went up the Missouri River to engage in the fur trade about 1840. He had at least two Indian wives; he "was married in June, 1862 [shortly after Morgan met Clark] by Father De Smet to 'his young wife' at Fort Benton." Clark has been described as "a noted frontier character of good family connections . . . and possessed of a bold and desperate character, which brought to his name the stigma of more than one crime" (Hiram M. Chittenden, *History of Early Steamboat Navigation on the Missouri River . . .*, New York, 1903, I, 233). His best known act in this respect was the killing of Owen McKenzie—in cold blood, according to tradition. Clark was killed by a Piegan Indian in 1869. Accounts of him may be found in Lar-

penteur's journal, in the *Life and Travels of Father De Smet*, Lt. James H. Bradley's journal, "Affairs at Fort Benton, 1831 to 1869" (*Contributions to the Historical Society of Montana*, III [1900]), etc. There is a sketch of him by his daughter, Helen P. Clark, in *Contributions to the Historical Society of Montana*, II (1896) : 255-68. See also McDonnell, *op. cit.*, p. 263.

40. H. B. Branch was Superintendent of Indian Affairs, Central Agency, with offices in St. Joseph, Mo., in 1861-62.

41. Benjamin Gratz Brown (1826-85), born at Lexington, Ky., graduated from Yale University in 1847, went to Missouri in 1849, was active in formation of Republican party in 1860, was elected to the Senate in 1863, and became governor of Missouri in 1870 (*Dictionary of American Biography*, 1937).

42. Andrew Dawson (1817-71), born in Scotland, entered the fur trade on the upper Missouri in the 1840's, served at Fort Benton, Fort Clark, and Fort Benton successively. He had three wives: the first was a daughter of Pierre Garreau, the second was a Brulé Sioux, the third a Gros Ventre. In 1862 Dawson succeeded Alexander Culbertson as top man in Pierre Chouteau, Jr. and Company. He acquired a considerable fortune and then returned to his old home in Scotland, where he died (James Dawson, "Biographic Sketch of Major Andrew Dawson, 1817-71," in *Contributions to the Historical Society of Montana*, VII [1910]: 61-72; McDonnell, *op. cit.*, p. 266; James B. Bradley's journal; Father De Smet's *Life and Travels*, etc.).

43. "Factory" meant "trading post," and "factor" a "trader," in the eighteenth and early nineteenth centuries.

44. Wilcox and Morley, expecially the former, mention by name in their journals passengers on the *Spread Eagle* for this trip, but neither one mentions Morgan, by name or otherwise.

45. This information does not agree with that given by Chittenden and Richardson, *Life,*

Letters and Travels, p. 9, who say that Father De Smet's father was born in 1738, that he had two wives, the first of whom bore him six children; the second, nine, of whom Pierre-Jean was the fifth, born in 1801.

46. Morgan credits De Smet with this nomenclature in *Systems* (pp. 74, 77).

47. In view of Morgan's severe criticism of the Roman Catholic Church (see, e.g., *Extracts from the European Travel Journal of Lewis Henry Morgan*, Leslie A. White, ed., Rochester Historical Society Publications, XVI [1937]: 298, 347-49), it is interesting to note the cordial relations between Morgan and this Jesuit priest. Obviously, Morgan distinguished between an institution and a creed on the one hand, and a fellow human being on the other.

After this summer's trip Father De Smet wrote Morgan a most friendly and cordial letter from "Washington City, Sept. 10, 1862." He had a "firm intention of paying you a visit in Rochester and of returning to you, personally, my high regards of respect, esteem and gratitude." He thanked him profusely for "the part you have taken in obtaining for me" a set of the Documents Relative to the Colonial History of the State of New York from John Van Schaick Lansing Pruyn, Chancellor of the University of the State of New York. We do not know whether Father De Smet visited Morgan in Rochester or not.

48. The Morgans had three children: Lemuel, b. 1853; Mary, b. 1855; and Helen, b. 1860.

49. George H. Ely, a friend and one-time client of Morgan's in Rochester; brother of Samuel P. and John F., "the leading millers of Rochester," and Heman B. Ely of Connecticut (Algernon S. Crapsey, "Lewis Henry Morgan, Scientist, Philosopher, Humanist," *Rochester Historical Society, Publication Fund Series*, II [1923]: 12).

50. This was probably Dr. Edward Mott Moore (1814-1902), a prominent physician and public citizen of Rochester. He taught at the

University of Buffalo for many years. He was a member of the Pundit Club for 41 years. He became the first president of the New York State Board of Health; served as president of the board of trustees, University of Rochester; was first president of the Rochester park commission. There is a statue of him in Genesee Valley Park, Rochester.

51. Sioux City was incorporated in 1857 with a population of 400.

52. These letters have apparently not been preserved; at least, they are not in the Morgan archives at the University of Rochester.

53. Father De Smet called Blackbird Hill "the most remarkable butte along that portion of the Missouri" River (Chittenden, *Life and Travels of Father De Smet*, IV, 1384). George Catlin painted a picture of Blackbird Hill (*North American Indians*, Edinburgh, 1926, Vol. II, Pl. 79). Reuben Gold Thwaites states, in a note in John Bradbury's journal, that Blackbird Hill "was for many years a well-known landmark upon the river, but is now scarcely noticeable" (Bradbury's travels, Vol. v of *Early Western Travels*, p. 86).

54. This story, in various versions, is told and retold by many travelers: by Lewis and Clark, *Expedition of Lewis and Clark*, Elliott Coues, ed. (New York, 1893), p. 71; by the chronicler of Major S. H. Long's expedition in 1819, *Account of an Expedition . . .*, compiled by Edwin James (London, 1823), I, 204-7; by Maximilian, *Travels . . .*, Reuben Gold Thwaites, ed., in *Early Western Travels*, XXII, 277; mentioned by Audubon, *Audubon and His Journals*, by Maria R. Audubon, I, 485-86; by Kurz, *op. cit.*, p. 179; by Washington Irving in *Astoria* (Philadelphia, 1836), Chap. XVI; and by others. Father De Smet has recounted it himself in *Life, Letters and Travels*, I, 187-88.

The legend as told by the half-breed Omaha, Henry Fontenelle, who had assisted Morgan in 1860, differs substantially from the versions cited above. Blackbird, according to Fontenelle, "held supreme command over his people. His words were law and obeyed as such ... his memory is held sacred by the Omahas ... [he had] a good and gentle disposition and [was] loved by his subjects"; he died of smallpox (Henry Fontenelle, "History of Omaha Indians," *Transactions and Reports of the Nebraska Historical Society*, I [1885]: 76–85).

George Catlin says that he cannot believe that Blackbird was guilty of wholesale poisoning by arsenic; he pictures him as a "noble chieftain," and a good and just man; he died of smallpox and was buried astride his favorite white horse who was alive at the time of interment (Catlin, *op. cit.*, pp. 6–8). Catlin removed Blackbird's skull from his grave; in 1885 it was in the U. S. National Museum ("The George Catlin Indian Gallery," *Annual Report* of the Smithsonian Institution for 1885, Pt. II, p. 263).

55. *A Selish or Flat-head Grammar*, by G. Mengarini (New York, 1861).

56. Chittenden and Richardson make no mention of this in their account of Father De Smet's family (*Life, Letters and Travels*, I, 9); this was probably gossip among the *Spread Eagle*'s passengers.

57. More gossip; perhaps an attempt to cast De Smet into an American "success story" pattern. De Smet attended the Seminary of Malines until his twenty-first year when, inspired by a missionary, he and five of his fellow students decided to volunteer for foreign service (Chittenden and Richardson, *op. cit.*, I, 10–11).

58. Rudolph Kurz says that "Indian dogs differ very slightly from wolves, howl like them, do not bark, and not infrequently mate with them" (*Journal*, p. 239).

59. This date is probably wrong. The next journal entry is dated Thursday, May 22, and that date fell on Thursday in 1862.

60. Henry Augustus Ward (1834–1906), American naturalist; taught Natural Sciences at the University of Rochester; founded Ward's Natural Science Establishment in Rochester.

61. In *Systems* (p. 284), Morgan states that he obtained the Ponca system of relationship at the Niobrara River in May, 1862, from Wa-de-hah-ge, a Ponca warrior, with Catharine Woodges, a Yankton girl, serving as interpreter.

62. Morgan lists these clans (gentes) in *Ancient Society*, p. 155.

63. In *Systems* (p. 284), Morgan gives "Pun-kä′, signification not obtained," as the term by which they designated themselves. We do not know the significance of Oateamin.

64. A. H. Redfield was agent for the Yankton Sioux in 1859. His long and interesting report for that year, his first annual report, is in *Report of the Commissioner of Indian Affairs for 1859*, pp. 121–28.

65. Walter A. Burleigh was agent for the Yankton Sioux in 1862 (see report of W. Jayne, Governor and Superintendent of Indian Affairs to the Commissioner of Indian Affairs in *Report of the Commissioner of Indian Affairs for 1862*, pp. 321–22).

66. Established in 1856 by General William S. Harney, named for Surgeon B. Randall, U.S.A. Morley states in his journal that there were 300 soldiers at Fort Randall in May 1862.

67. Morgan distinguished three stages of cultural development: savagery, barbarism, and civilization. The middle status of barbarism began, in the Old World, with the domestication of animals (*Ancient Society*, 1877, p. 11).

68. Scaffold and tree burial were practiced by the Chippewa, Sioux, Mandan, Blackfoot, Gros Ventre, Arapahoe, and other Indian tribes.

69. Fort Pierre, built by the American Fur Company in 1831–32, was named for Pierre Chouteau, Jr. It was occupied until 1855 when the company sold the post to the United States government for military use: General Harney and 1200 troops wintered there in 1855–56. In 1857 the government abandoned Fort Pierre for Fort Randall, and

the old post was dismantled and abandoned. A second Fort Pierre was built in 1859 about two miles up the river from the first post. It was abandoned in 1863 during the Sioux uprising. Maximilian has one of the earliest and best descriptions of Fort Pierre (*Journal*, Vol. 22, p. 317 ff.).

70. It was Tuesday. Morgan has already noted that they were only 9 miles below the Fort on Tuesday, the 27th. The 27th of May was a Tuesday, and agent Latta reports that they reached Ft. Pierre on the 27th (*Report of the Commissioner of Indian Affairs for 1862*, p. 336).

71. The Uncpapa, or Hunkpapa, a division of the Teton Sioux.

72. This word is indistinct; agent Latta has Minnicongies [Miniconjou], a division of the Teton Sioux (*op. cit.*, p. 336).

73. In October, 1861, an American naval vessel intercepted at sea the British mail steamer, *Trent*, and took off two Confederate commissioners accredited to France: James M. Mason and John Slidell. They were taken to Boston and imprisoned, but released upon the demand—and threat of war—of Britain and allowed to proceed to Europe.

Father De Smet, in a letter to "Hon. Mr. Mix, Acting Superintendent of Indian Affairs," dated "Washington City, September 5, 1862," reported that considerable "excitement took place when the news reached the upper country [i.e., in the vicinity of Forts Berthold and Union] of the difficulties created between the two countries [the United States and Great Britain] by the arrest of Slidell and Mason." American traders told Father De Smet that the English traders in Canada were trying to turn the Indians of the northern plains against the Americans; they "were promised that they would be provided in due time with all that was necessary to expel the Americans from their Indian country." Father De Smet adds: "I give the above statement on mere hearsay, without proof to substantiate the assertion" (*Report of the Commissioner of Indian Affairs for 1862*, p. 358).

74. Samuel N. Latta, agent of the upper Missouri. He was on the *Spread Eagle*, having boarded her in St. Louis with goods to be distributed by him to Indians at various points on the upper Missouri. In his report to the Commissioner of Indian Affairs of August 27, 1862, he gives his account of the affair at Fort Pierre, which, naturally, differs considerably from Morgan's understanding of it (*Report of the Commissioner of Indian Affairs for 1862*, pp. 336–37).

75. Morley, in his journal, observes that the agent "had some difficulty satisfying the Indians at Fort Pierre." Wilcox states in his diary that at one point some of the Indians actually fired on the *Spread Eagle*, and demanded ammunition.

76. This is Latta's version, also.

77. Charles P. Chouteau, b. 1819, son of Pierre Chouteau, Jr., an official of the American Fur Company.

78. According to Latta the Indians were both courteous and reasonable.

79. Trouble was widely prevalent in the upper Missouri country in 1863. Agents Latta and Reed, joined by La Barge, Harkness and Co., reported that troops would be necessary to maintain peace. Edwin M. Stanton, Secretary of War, ordered a regiment of cavalry to be dispatched to the region (*Report of the Commissioner of Indian Affairs for 1863*, pp. 160–66).

80. Latta makes no mention of the interpreter in his report.

81. Dogs were commonly eaten in the northern plains, and not infrequently regarded as a delicacy. Rudolph F. Kurz tells of "roasted dog as a choice dish" offered to guests in an Arikara village in the summer of 1851 (*Journal*, J. N. B. Hewitt, ed., Washington: Bureau of American Ethnology, Bulletin 115, 1937, p. 72). Francis Parkman entertained his Indian hosts in an Oglala village

with a dog feast (*The Oregon Trail*, 6th ed.; Boston, 1877, pp. 195 ff.). See also Larpenteur, *op. cit.*, I, 206–7; Thaddeus A. Culbertson's *Journal*, p. 55.

82. Shafts.

83. This was, of course, the travois, characteristic of Plains culture, adapted to the horse as well as the dog.

84. On the map published in 1863 by F. V. Hayden, in "Ethnology and Philology of the Indian Tribes of the Missouri Valley" (*Transactions of the American Philosophical Society*, Vol. XII, n.s., 1863), the Minnetarees, "or the Gros Ventre as they are called by the traders," are shown south of the Missouri River between Fort Union and Fort Berthold. It was a Siouan-speaking tribe that once lived with the Mandans (Hayden, p. 420). The name Gros Ventre was applied also to a detached band of the Arapaho (Algonquian-speaking), located on Hayden's map just south of Fort Benton.

85. In *The American Beaver and His Works*, Morgan identifies this as the "bull boat," widely used by Indian tribes of the upper Missouri River region (n. 1, p. 205). It is illustrated, too, in Plate XXIII of that work.

86. In *Systems* (p. 285), Morgan cites Smith as the interpreter who assisted him in obtaining the Minnetaree system from these two warriors.

87. In *Systems*, Morgan states that he obtained the Blood Blackfoot system from Mrs. Culbertson, assisted by her husband, Alexander (p. 289). The Algonquian-speaking Blackfoot were divided into three groups: Piegan, Blood, and Northern Blackfoot.

88. Morgan obtained the Uncpapa and Blood Dakota systems at Fort Pierre in May 1862, the former from an Uncpapa chief, the latter from a Blackfoot Dakota warrior; G. La Beauchamp served as interpreter for both (*Systems*, p. 284). The Blackfoot and Uncpapa (Hunkpapa) were two of seven subdivisions of the Teton Dakota; the Teton was one of a number of Dakotan tribes.

89. Walter A. Burleigh, agent of the Yankton Sioux agency in 1862.

90. William Jayne, Governor and Superintendent of Indian Affairs, Yankton, Dakota Territory, gives a rather glowing account of this farm, which he visited, in his report to the Commissioner of Indian Affairs, 1862. Burleigh, he says, had succeeded in persuading the restless, warlike, nomadic Indians to settle down and till the soil: "they seem to appreciate the advantages of labor . . . The crops are excellent, and never before have the Yanctons had such a prospect of abundance . . ." (pp. 321–22). Jayne also observed that some "unprincipled [white] men had tried to prejudice . . . [the Indians] against the agent by false and malicious stories," but that the Indians "found out that the agent is their true friend, and that he has labored faithfully for their advancement and welfare . . . Mr. Burleigh is a man of . . . character . . . and that he will not allow . . . the Indians to be fleeced out of their money and goods received from the government" (*Report of the Commissioner of Indian Affairs for 1862*, p. 322).

91. Alfred J. Vaughan, A. H. Redfield's predecessor as agent for the upper Missouri Indians.

92. Clark Wissler has a picture of a shoulder-blade hoe, in use by the Hidatsa, in *The American Indian* (2nd ed.; New York, 1922), p. 22.

93. "As pumice is often floating down the Missouri, I made frequent inquiries of the hunters if any volcano existed on the river or its branches . . ." John Bradbury, "Journal" in *Early Western Travels*, Reuben Gold Thwaites, ed., V, 165.

94. Kinnikinnick, from an Algonquian (Cree or Chippewa) word meaning "what is mixed." Quite a variety of plant materials was mixed with tobacco in various regions: sumac leaves, red willow, dogwood, bearberry, etc. (Alice C. Fletcher, "Kinnikinnick," in

Handbook of American Indians, F. W. Hodge, ed.).

95. In *Ancient Society* (p. 159), Morgan lists seven gentes (clans) for this tribe.

96. The Minnetarees were an offshoot of the Hidatsa who spoke the same dialect of the Siouan language as spoken by the Crow.

97. Unidentified; undoubtedly a trader and a fellow passenger on the *Spread Eagle*.

98. In his journal entry of June 1, Morley states that the passengers of the *Spread Eagle* were organized into four hunting parties, to take turns hunting when the boat stopped to wood.

99. Wilcox says that one of the passengers, Johnson, and two Indians aboard the *Spread Eagle* cut across the great bend of the Missouri one night. Johnson became separated from the Indians who returned the next day to the boat without him. The steamer blew its whistle and rang its bell while wooding in the hope of reaching Johnson. He finally appeared, exhausted, very frightened, half-dressed—he had swum a channel of the river—and quite sick.

100. Four steamboats reached Fort Benton in the summer of 1862: the *Spread Eagle* and the *Key West* of the Chouteau Trading Company, and the *Shreveport* and the *Emilie* of the opposition company, La Barge and Harkness.

101. Fort Clark, named for William Clark of the Lewis and Clark expedition, was built in 1831 by James Kipp for the American Fur Company.

102. Fort Berthold was built in the fall of 1845, named for Bartholomew Berthold of Pierre Chouteau, Jr. & Co.

103. Agent Latta states that they reached Fort Berthold on June 5 (*Report of the Commissioner of Indian Affairs for 1862*, p. 338); Morley says they arrived on the 4th.

104. Agent Latta states that "the Mandans and the Gros Ventres live together at this place, in a village built principally of dirt lodges, with now and then a log cabin . . . after the western style . . ." (*Report of the Commissioner of Indian Affairs for 1862*, p. 338).

105. Samuel N. Latta, who delivered goods worth $2,148.82 to the Indians at this place.

106. Unidentified; probably a fellow passenger.

107. It should be kept in mind that these are not the Gros Ventre, or Atsina, related to the Arapaho.

108. They were often called simply Rees; agent Latta so refers to them in his *Report* for 1862 (p. 338).

109. Agent Latta gives a brief account of the abandonment of the one village and the founding of the new one (*Report* for 1862, p. 338).

110. "They received their goods, $1,496.54 in value, and seemed to be well satisfied" (*ibid.*).

111. Agent Latta, in his report to the Commissioner of Indian Affairs for 1862, recommended that the department expend $1000 to break the prairie for farming, and $600 to hire a farmer to "conduct the farm and instruct the Indians" (p. 339).

112. Unidentified.

113. We have learned nothing else about this youth.

114. This must have been June 6, which fell on a Friday; moreover, the event described in the next sentence took place on June 6, according to both James Harkness of the firm of La Barge, Harkness and Company (Harkness' diary of the trip of the *Emilie* up the Missouri River in 1862, *Contributions to the Historical Society of Montana*, II [1896]: 347), and to passenger Wilcox.

115. It is difficult to understand Morgan's laconic report of this incident which was much more serious than appears from his statement. According to Harkness, the *Emilie* and the *Spread Eagle* were "having a race, (probably) the first ever run on the upper Missouri. She passed us and then we passed her, when she ran into us, breaking our guards and doing some other damage. There was a good deal of angry talk" (*op. cit.*, p. 347). Morgan's fellow passenger A.

H. Wilcox wrote in his diary for June 6: ". . . an exciting race with the *Emilie* . . . [she] ran across our path upon which our pilot ran into the *Emilie*, breaking some of her guards. La Barge pointed his gun at Capt. Bailey. *Spread Eagle* passengers pointed guns at La Barge who then put his gun down; the two steamboats separated and the *Emilie* went on ahead."

The collision and its aftermath are described by Hiram M. Chittenden as follows: As the *Emilie* was about to get ahead of the *Spread Eagle*, "the pilot of the *Spread Eagle* with quick eye realized that he had been outmanoeuvered, and seeing no other way to prevent the *Emilie*'s passage, determined on wrecking her. He accordingly left the main channel and made for the chute that the *Emilie* was entering. He steamed alongside of her for a moment, but found that he was losing ground. The boats were scarcely fifty feet apart, when the pilot of the *Spread Eagle*, seeing that he could not make it, deliberately put his rudder to port, and plunged the bow of the boat into the *Emilie* immediately opposite her boilers. Several of the guards were broken and the danger of wreck was imminent. La Barge was in the pilot-house at the time and was not looking for such a move, for he did not believe that even the American Fur Company would play so desperate a game when human life was at stake. He instantly called out to Bailey, the pilot of the *Spread Eagle*, to stop his engines and drop his boat back or he would put a bullet through him. The passengers likewise became thoroughly aroused, and some of them got their arms and threatened to use them if the *Spread Eagle* did not withdraw. These threats were effective; the *Spread Eagle* fell to the rear and was seen no more on the voyage" (cited in Chittenden, *The History of Early Steamboat Navigation on the Missouri River*, II, 289–90). When the *Spread Eagle* "returned to St. Louis charges were preferred against

Bailey . . . He was brought to trial . . . and his license was cancelled" (*ibid.*, p. 291). Through the intercession of Captain La Barge, however, Bailey's license was later restored to him.

Even if Morgan had been taking a nap when the collision occurred one would think that he would have learned of the incident later from fellow passengers. Perhaps he did, but neglected to make another entry in his journal about it.

Morley's diary, which lets few incidents go unnoticed, makes no mention whatever of the race.

116. Morgan acknowledges, in *Systems* (p. 286), the assistance of "Pierre Garrow, a half-blood Arikaree." Dr. Washington Matthews, too, thought he was a half-breed: "When you see his portrait," he wrote, "I think you will recognize Gallic features in it, though he was as dark as any Indian" (Letter to Elliott Coues, in Larpenteur's journal, *Forty Years a Fur Trader*, I, 125–26). Henry A. Boller asserts, however, that Pierre's mother, an Arikara, married the "Mr. Garrow" of the Lewis and Clark journals, who had settled among the Arikara *ca.* 1785, after her husband died but while she was carrying Pierre. "Mr. Garrow" adopted Pierre and gave him his name (*Among the Indians*, Philadelphia, 1868, p. 182). Pierre was a "noted interpreter" for many years although his command of English is said to have been "not good" (Dr. Matthews). One of his daughters married Andrew Dawson. Pierre Garreau is mentioned by Larpenteur, Kurz, Chittenden, and others.

117. Frederic F. Girard, b. 1829 in St. Louis of French parents; he served as clerk and trader in several posts of the Pierre Chouteau, Jr. and Company (McDonnell, *op. cit.*, p. 290).

118. The Gros Ventre and the Arapaho spoke the same dialect of Algonquian; the Comanche spoke a Shoshonean language. A number of Shoshonean groups, but especially those of Oregon, were called "Snake."

119. "Supposed Runic Inscriptions," by Dr. A. C. Hamlin, *Proceedings of the American Association for the Advancement of Science*, 10th meeting, August 1856, Part II, pp. 214–16.

120. In *Systems* (p. 288), Morgan states that he obtained the kinship system of the Ah-ah-ne-lin, "the vulgar name . . . is Gros Ventres of the Prairie," from a Blackfoot-speaking Ahahnelin woman, Mrs. Culbertson interpreting, on the Missouri River in June 1862.

121. Probably Chester Dewey, D.D., of the University of Rochester, to whom Morgan acknowledges his indebtedness in the preface of *Systems* (p. ix). But it may have been Charles Ayrault Dewey, M.D., Morgan's physician, and, with Morgan, one of the founders of the Pundit Club (see *The Rochester Historical Society, Publication Fund Series*, II, 1923).

122. Agent Latta states that they arrived at Fort Union on June 8 (*Report* of 1862, p. 339). June 9th, 1862, was a Monday.

123. Joseph Kipp, b. 1849, son of James Kipp and Earth Woman, a Mandan. James Kipp was a prominent and well-known trader on the upper Missouri for many years. He was born in Canada in 1788 and came to the upper Missouri in 1822 as agent for the Columbia Fur Company; later he joined the American Fur Company. He was Catlin's interpreter in the Mandan village. Maximilian met him at Fort Clark in 1833 and Audubon met him at Fort Union in 1843. Kurz worked for Kipp at Fort Berthold in 1851. He is mentioned also by Larpenteur, Father De Smet, Lt. Bradley, and others.

Kipp lived long among the Mandans and is said to have been the first white man to master their language. He "had several Indian families as well as a white wife and children . . . in Missouri" (McDonnell, *op. cit.*, p. 270). He died in 1880.

In *Systems*, Morgan says that he "had no difficulty in obtaining a vocabulary" from "a half-blood Mandan, Joseph Kipp, son of the well-known interpreter James Kipp," but "found it impossible to obtain their system of relationship complete" (p. 184).

124. Robert Meldrum was born in Scotland in 1802 according to Lt. James H. Bradley ("Affairs at Fort Benton from 1831 to 1869," *Contributions to the Historical Society of Montana*, III, 254–55). Anne McDonnell says that he was born in Shelby County, Kentucky, in 1806 (*op. cit.*, p. 284). But Morgan reports, on the basis of many conversations with him, that he was born in Scotland in 1804. He went out west at an early age. He lived with the Crow Indians for twenty-five or thirty years, married a Crow woman, was adopted into the tribe, adopted their dress and customs, learned their language fluently, and became a chief. He was in the service of the American Fur Company for many years. Many people, such as Edwin Denig and Father De Smet, knew him (*Life and Travels*, III, 1063; IV, 1310, 1484, 1495). It was Father De Smet who performed the marriage ceremony when Meldrum took a Blackfoot wife in 1864. See, in addition to the above references, Thaddeus A. Culbertson's *Journal*, pp. 12, 116, 134. Morgan gives considerable information about him in a footnote in *Systems*, pp. 186–87.

125. Morgan "discovered the matrilineal exogamous clan organization of the Crow," says Lowie, "an observation once doubted but wholly confirmed by later research" (Robert H. Lowie, "Lewis H. Morgan in Historical Perspective," in *Essays in Anthropology Presented to A. L. Kroeber* [Berkeley: University of California Press, 1936], p. 169). In *Ancient Society*, Morgan tells us that the names of the Crow clans "are more suggestive of bands than of gentes [clans]" and "for a time . . . [he] was inclined to discredit them. But the existence of organization into gentes was clearly established by their

rules of descent, and marital usages, and by their laws of inheritance with respect to property" (p. 159). Morgan lists the Crow clan names in *Ancient Society* and gives Robert Meldrum credit for helping him obtain data on the Crow.

126. "This beautiful mountain range rises out of the plains about fifty miles east of the Falls of the Missouri, and stretches from near the Missouri to Milk River. Its highest peaks are about twenty-five hundred feet high. Although quite near the foot of the Rocky Mountains, it is entirely detached, and forms a conspicuous and striking object in the landscape of the prairie" (*Systems*, n. 2, p. 185).

127. Undoubtedly Fannie Culbertson, b. *ca.* 1850 (McDonnell, *op. cit.*, p. 244).

128. Morgan lists these clans in *Ancient Society*, p. 159.

129. About a week later Morgan ascertained and recorded names of Mandan clans.

130. Among the Crow, says Robert H. Lowie, marriages by mutual consent, apart from purchase, "were not to be compared with marriages by purchase, which ranked as more honorable and are said to have had far greater likelihood of permanence" (*Primitive Society*, New York, 1920, pp. 24–25).

131. Morgan's investigations in kinship were undertaken, as we have seen in Chapter I, in order to reconstruct racial history and to prove that the Indian came from Asia. He was eager, also, to establish "some criterion . . . for determining the degree of rapidity or slowness with which dialects of unwritten languages depart from each other" (*Systems*, p. 186). He incorporates much of the data here recorded in a footnote in *Systems* (pp. 186–87).

132. I.e., Meldrum coined and introduced this word (see *Systems*, n. 1, p. 186). Morgan lists these Crow words in *Systems* (p. 186), omitting rice, but including tobacco, which is not in the above list.

133. John Dawson Gilmary Shea (1824–92), a very prolific American writer and historian; Richard J. Purcell has termed him "the greatest American Catholic historical writer" (*Dictionary of American Biography*, 1937, Vol. 17, p. 51). He specialized in the history of Catholics and their missions in America.

134. Communism in living, and especially with respect to food, was a fundamental characteristic of primitive society, according to Morgan (*Ancient Society*, pp. 446, 453; *Houses and House-Life of the American Aborigines*, Chap. III).

135. It will be recalled that Morgan believed that if two peoples had like kinship systems the systems, and consequently the peoples, were related.

136. This was the white, or prairie, apple, *Psoralea esculenta*. Audubon described it and its use (*Journals*, I, 505–6); see also Melvin R. Gilmore, "Some Native Nebraska Plants with Their Uses by the Dakota" (*Collections of the Nebraska State Historical Society*, XVII [1913]: 365–66).

137. Harkness, too, reports in his diary that it rained hard every day, June 12 to 15 inclusive, and that they had to have a fire for warmth. The weather cleared, however, on the 16th (James Harkness' *Diary*, pp. 348–49).

138. These are not to be confused with the Mauvaises Terres of Thaddeus Culbertson's *Journal*, which are the Bad Lands of southwestern South Dakota today.

139. This may have been Thomas Campbell (1830–82), an employee of the American Fur Company for many years.

140. It was either Thursday or June 18th.

141. In his journal entry for June 16, passenger Morley states that freight was transferred on that day from the *Key West* to the *Spread Eagle*.

142. Morgan lists these clans [gentes] in *Ancient Society* (p. 158), except that there he has Flathead instead of Tattoed.

143. Maximilian and his companions named these formations "The White Castles" (II, 54, in *Early Western Travels*, Vol. 23). Bodmer's sketch of them appears on Pl. 70 in Vol. 25.

144. If it be thought that Morgan let his imagination—and his vocabulary—run wild, one may recall that Maximilian saw "gates or windows of knights' castles" in these formations (II, 28). He also remarks that certain formations, "when seen from a distance so perfectly resembled buildings raised by art that we were deceived by them, till we were assured of our error" (II, 54).

145. The *Yellowstone* was the first boat to reach Fort Union, in 1832. In 1859, the *Spread Eagle* ascended the Missouri on her first voyage. She got as far as Fort Union where her freight for Fort Benton was transferred to the *Chippewa*. With John La Barge, brother of Joseph, as captain, the *Chippewa* got as far as Brulé bottom, about fifteen miles below Fort Benton (Chittenden, *History of Early Steamboat Navigation on the Missouri River*, I, 218–19; see also Alfred J. Vaughan's account of this trip. We have already met Vaughan as agent of the Blackfeet Agency in 1859; *Report of the Commissioner of Indian Affairs for 1859*, pp. 115–16).

146. The *Emilie*, Captain Joseph La Barge, left St. Joseph on May 18, after the *Spread Eagle*, but overtook her and reached Fort Benton on June 17. She began her return trip on the 19th (James Harkness' *Journal*, pp. 343, 350; Chittenden, *History of Early Steamboat Navigation on the Missouri River*, II, 288).

147. Here as usual, Morgan distinguishes sharply between hearsay and ascertained fact. This characteristic stands out in his *European Travel Journal* also.

148. Of these we have been able to identify Néree Vallé only. He was the son of François B. Vallé (1785–1851) and Catherine Beauvais. Néree married Aglae Chouteau, daughter of Henry Chouteau (Mary Louise Dalton,

"Notes on the Genealogy of the Vallé Family," *Missouri Historical Society Collections*, Vol. II, No. 7, p. 70).

149. Both Wilcox and Morley describe this accident in their journals; the former has an especially vivid account. James Harkness has a laconic report of the tragedy: "The *Spread Eagle* came into view early; she had four men drowned while getting over the rapids, and it was late in the day before she made port" (*op. cit.*, p. 350). Chittenden comments: "She lost four men on one of the rapids by the grossest carelessness" (*op. cit.*, II, 290–91).

150. Fort Benton was built by Alexander Culbertson in 1846 who named it for Senator Thomas H. Benton of Missouri.

151. Morgan cites this in a footnote in *Ancient Society* (p. 160).

152. Parfleche, "a word of doubtful origin," says James Mooney, "but . . . appears in French narratives as early as 1700, and is probably from some old French root, possibly from *parer*, 'to parry,' *flêche* 'arrow,' in reference originally to the shield . . . of rawhide" ("Parflêche," with illustration, in *Handbook of American Indians*, F. W. Hodge, ed.).

153. General William Henry Ashley (1778–1838), "one of the most enterprising and successful of St. Louis fur traders," according to Coues. Larpenteur says that Ashley "was in the habit of hiring as many as 100 men every spring" in the early 1830's (*op. cit.*, I, 6–7). He was a general of the Missouri state militia. See sketch of his life in Chittenden, *The American Fur Trade*, I, 247–51.

154. This was probably David Jackson, one "of the more prominent of the 'enterprising young men' whom Ashley took with him to the mountains" (Chittenden, *The American Fur Trade*, I, 261). He was much associated with Sublette. Chittenden says that Jackson Hole, Wyoming, may have been named for him (*ibid.*, p. 289).

155. William L. Sublette (1799–1845), "one of

the most distinguished and successful of the fur traders . . ." (*ibid.*, I, 254). He, too, worked for Ashley.

156. He was "plain Jim Beckwith" until his autobiography (*The Life and Adventures of James P. Beckwourth*, T. D. Bonner, ed., New York, 1856; republished by Alfred A. Knopf, 1931) was published, after which he was James P. Beckwourth. Chittenden says that "there is probably not a single statement in . . . [his book] that is correct as given." He went to the mountains with Ashley, acquired influence with the Crows, and worked for the American Fur Company (Chittenden, *The American Fur Trade*, II, 679–81).

157. Gold was found sporadically in western Montana in the late 1850's. "In the winter of 1861–62 . . . sluicing in a systematic way on Gold Creek . . . was the beginning of the gold industry in Montana. Although nothing particularly remarkable was found . . . reports soon got abroad that the findings were very rich. The greater part of the emigration from the East in 1862 was bound for the Idaho mines, but did not get beyond . . . points in western Montana" (Chittenden, *History of Early Steamboat Navigation*, II, 268).

158. Charles Pierre Chouteau (b. 1819), the master of the *Spread Eagle*, had a son Pierre (b. 1849). This may be the person Morgan is referring to here.

159. Frederick G. Riter, agent in charge of the American Fur Company's post at Fort Union, according to agent A. H. Redfield in his report for 1857 (*Report of the Commissioner of Indian Affairs for 1857*, p. 422). He was apparently relieved by a Mr. Hodgkiss in the summer of 1862, for agent Latta says in his report for that year "at Fort Union on the 4th of July . . . Mr. Hodgkiss, who had just come in charge of this post . . ." (*Report of the Commissioner of Indian Affairs for 1862*, p. 341; see also Larpenteur, *Forty Years a Fur Trader*, II, 352, who says that

Hodgkiss was in charge at Fort Union in 1863).

160. According to Clark Wissler "Horses were numerous among the Blackfoot as early as 1751, and they were used by the Assiniboine about the same date. They had not been acquired by the Mandan in 1738 . . . They are first definitely mentioned for the Teton Dakota in 1742 . . ." ("The Influence of the Horse in the Development of Plains Culture," *American Anthropologist*, 16 [1914]:5).

161. In 1854, agent Alfred J. Vaughan reported that "all the bands of Sioux have already received their presents [their annuities in goods] with great appearance of friendship except the Minnecowzues, Blackfeet [a small division of the Teton Sioux] and the Honepapas [Uncpapas]" (*Report of the Commissioner of Indian Affairs for 1854*, p. 87). Later, he held a council with the chiefs of these groups and they told him that they "would not receive any presents from the government . . . that they preferred the liberty to take scalps and commit whatever depredations they pleased, in preference to goods from their Great Father. They talked very hostile . . ." (*ibid.*, p. 89).

162. Agent Samuel N. Latta gives an account of this incident in his report for 1862. Bear's Rib, he says, was a "chief of the Sioux nation appointed by General Harney." He said "in a most touching manner that for eleven years he had been the friend of the white man and the government; that for years he had relied upon promises made by General Harney and former agents to send him assistance, yet none had come; that if he received those presents . . . he not only endangered his own life but the lives of all present; yet he loved his Great Father and would this once more receive for his people the goods present, but closed by requesting me to bring no more unless they could have assistance. A few days after the delivery, and after I had left, that portion of the Sans-

Arc band opposed to any intercourse with the government came in from the prairies, assaulted and killed, within the gates of Fort Pierre, this true man, the best friend the white man had in the Sioux nation" (*Report of the Commissioner of Indian Affairs for 1862*, pp. 336–37).

163. See Chapter 1, p. 5.

164. These comments are interesting in light of the fact that Pilot Bailey had his license revoked for ramming the *Emilie* and for the loss of four men of the crew through "the grossest carelessness."

165. He did not list them earlier. This list of clans was published in *Ancient Society* (p. 171).

Stone walls on the upper Missouri, by Karl Bodmer. Bodmer has captured the eery but fantastic beauty of the time-sculptured walls of the upper river. Many travelers remarked on the resemblance of certain formations to castles, spires, and similar works of man.

Index

Acknowledgments for the Illustrations

(*listed by page*)

BILLINGTON, RAY A., *Westward Expansion,* Macmillan, 1949: 24

BODMER, KARL, *Kupfer Zu Prinz Maximilians von Wied Reise durch Nord America,* Coblentz, 1843: facing 20, facing 53, facing 69, facing 85, facing 100, facing 101, facing 164

BUREAU OF AMERICAN ETHNOLOGY, Smithsonian Institution: 45, 83, 100, 103 top, 114

CATLIN, GEORGE, *North American Indian Portfolio,* London, 1844: facing 53, facing 84

DENVER PUBLIC LIBRARY WESTERN COLLECTION: 103 bottom, 154

GARRETSON, M. S., *The American Bison,* © New York Zoological Society 1938: 70

HISTORICAL SOCIETY OF MONTANA: 72, 133 bottom, 144, 153 bottom, 181 top, 181 bottom, 185, 196

ILLINOIS STATE HISTORICAL LIBRARY: 4, 16, 17, 25 upper left, 73, 95, 98, 104, 105, 107 bottom, 110, 125, 150, 164, 182, 188, 195, 199, 229

KANSAS STATE HISTORICAL SOCIETY: 15, 18 top, 18 bottom, 19 left, 19 upper right, 19 lower right, 20, 26, 28, 29, 31 upper left, 31 lower right, 34, 38, 41, 48, 49, 52, 53, 62, 71, 76 upper left, 76 lower left, 84, 94

LEWIS, JAMES O., *The Aboriginal Portfolio,* Philadelphia, 1835-36: facing 36, facing 37, 59, facing 148, facing 181

LIBRARY, HUDSON'S BAY COMPANY: 118

McKENNEY, THOMAS L., and HALL, JAMES, *The Indian Tribes of North America,* 3 volumes, Philadelphia, 1834-44: facing 68, facing 116, facing 165

MINNESOTA HISTORICAL SOCIETY: 7, 107 top, 122

MORGAN, LEWIS H., *The American Beaver and His Works,* Philadelphia, 1868: 151

NEBRASKA STATE HISTORICAL SOCIETY: 14, 37, 44, 65 top, 65 bottom, 87, 89, 92, 134, 136, 141 lower right, 153 top, 155, 156, 158, 160, 184

SMITHSONIAN INSTITUTION: 67, 76 right, 79 top, 79 center, 79 bottom, 127, 133 upper right, 145, 169, 170, 191, 194

STANLEY, JOHN M., *Railroad Reports,* Vol. 12, Washington, 1860: 163, 174, 176

UNIVERSITY OF ROCHESTER LIBRARY: 2, 23 top, 23 center, 23 bottom

WHITE, LESLIE A.: 75, 106, 132

The decorative material which appears on pages 10, 57, and 128 was taken from plates in Bodmer's Kupfer Zu Prinz Maximilians von Wied Reise durch Nord America.